The Brain Is the Screen

The Brain Is the Screen

Deleuze and the Philosophy of Cinema

Gregory Flaxman, Editor

University of Minnesota Press
Minneapolis
London

Copyright 2000 by the Regents of the University of Minnesota

"The Brain Is the Screen: An Interview with Gilles Deleuze," copyright Éditions de Minuit, 1986.

All rights reserved. No part of this publication may be reproduced, stored in a retrieval system, or transmitted, in any form or by any means, electronic, mechanical, photocopying, recording, or otherwise, without the prior written permission of the publisher.

Published by the University of Minnesota Press
111 Third Avenue South, Suite 290
Minneapolis, MN 55401-2520
http://www.upress.umn.edu

Library of Congress Cataloging-in-Publication Data

The brain is the screen : Deleuze and the philosophy of cinema / Gregory Flaxman, editor.
p. cm.
Includes bibliographical references and index.
ISBN 0-8166-3446-7 (HC : alk. paper)—ISBN 0-8166-3447-5 (PB : alk. paper)
1. Motion pictures—Philosophy. 2. Deleuze, Gilles—Views on motion pictures.
I. Flaxman, Gregory.
PN1995.B714 2000
791.43′01—dc21

99-053120

Printed in the United States of America on acid-free paper

The University of Minnesota is an equal-opportunity educator and employer.

11 10 09 08 07 06 05 04 03 02 01 10 9 8 7 6 5 4 3 2

The system was breaking down. The one who had wandered alone past so many happenings and events began to feel, backing up along the primal vein that led to his center, the beginning of a hiccup that would, if left to gather, explode the center to the extremities of life, the suburbs through which one makes one's way to where the country is.

—John Ashbery, "The System"

Contents

Acknowledgments / ix

Introduction / 1
GREGORY FLAXMAN

APPROACHING IMAGES

1. Of Images and Worlds: Toward a Geology of the Cinema / 61
JEAN-CLET MARTIN

2. Cinema Year Zero / 87
GREGORY FLAXMAN

3. Escape from the Image: Deleuze's Image-Ontology / 109
MARTIN SCHWAB

4. The Eye of Montage: Dziga Vertov and Bergsonian Materialism / 141
FRANÇOIS ZOURABICHVILI

MAPPING IMAGES

5. The Film History of Thought / 153
ANDRÁS BÁLINT KOVÁCS

6. Into the Breach: Between *The Movement-Image* and *The Time-Image* / 171
ANGELO RESTIVO

7. Signs of the Time: Deleuze, Peirce, and the Documentary Image / 193
LAURA U. MARKS

8. The Roots of the Nomadic: Gilles Deleuze and the Cinema of West Africa / 215
DUDLEY ANDREW

THINKING IMAGES

9. Cinema and the Outside / 253
GREGG LAMBERT

10. Midday, Midnight: The Emergence of Cine-Thinking / 293
ÉRIC ALLIEZ

11. The Film Event: From Interval to Interstice / 303
TOM CONLEY

12. The Imagination of Immanence: An Ethics of Cinema / 327
PETER CANNING

AFTER-IMAGE

13. The Brain Is the Screen: An Interview with Gilles Deleuze / 365

Contributors / 375

Index / 377

Acknowledgments

There is almost no way to describe how humbling I have found the experience of putting this book together. Initially, perhaps even necessarily, I undertook the project the way any child accepts a dare—arrogantly and naively. It is to Leo Charney that I am obliged for first opening my eyes to the sobering reality of what this project would entail. As he predicted, I have had to rely on a great many people for a great many reasons. These debts are staggering, but, in retrospect, this is the modest cost of confirming the truly cooperative spirit from which the collection has emerged.

At the earliest stages, I received critical advice and encouragement from John Mowitt, Ellen Messer-Davidow, and Jochen Schulte-Sasse. At the University of Iowa, where I first began bringing the essays together, Dudley Andrew, Lauren Rabinovitz, and Rick Altman were particularly encouraging, and I will always be grateful that they allowed me the leeway to explore, among other things, Deleuze's philosophy. This exploration was a group effort, one that I carried out with my colleagues and subjected on my students. Among a great many, I wish to thank Alison Latendresse, who provided invaluable editorial help, Chris Keathley, Jay Beck, Marie Therese Guirgis, Melanie Nash, Martti Lahti, Clark Farmer, as well as the undergraduate film theory class I taught in the spring of 1997. I also profited from conversations with Gregg Lambert, Peter Canning, Tom Conley, Timothy Murray, and from reader's reports by Daniel Smith and Timothy Murphy.

At the University of Pennsylvania, where the book was completed, I have received a great deal of support from Liliane Weissberg, Rita Barnard, and Jean-Michel Rabaté, among other faculty.

I also want to extend my gratitude to a number of my colleagues and friends, including Martha Schoolman, Caitlin Wood, Mathew Hart, Suzanne Verderber, Joanne Dubil, Carol Schrage, Irina Patkanian, Chris Edwards, Erin Nelson, and Jen Bilik, whose good will and fellowship have made my own task so much easier. For questions of translation I must acknowledge a great debt to Steven Miller, and I would also like to thank Marie-Chantal Kalissa, Laura Spagnoli, Natalia Vayner, Jennifer Wild, and Jennifer Wolf. Generous support for the index was provided by the Graduate College at the University of Pennsylvania.

Additionally, I wish to thank my editors at the University of Minnesota Press, William Murphy and Pieter Martin, both of whom pursued this project with exceptional enthusiasm.

Finally, I wish to thank my parents for their enduring support.

Introduction

Gregory Flaxman

THE SYSTEM

In *The Movement-Image*, the first of his two volumes on cinema and philosophy, Gilles Deleuze launches toward a moment of remarkable visibility: "The essence of a thing never appears at the outset, but in the middle, in the course of its development, when its strength is assured."[1] Beyond the context of cinematographic evolution, Deleuze's claim seems to encompass its own writing, reflecting (or pre-flecting) an intuition about the fate of his books. "When a thing is considered in terms of its beginning," Deleuze once wrote with Félix Guattari, "a thing is always poorly judged."[2] But what does it mean to embark with the certainty that one's words are destined for misunderstanding, controversy, and even reproach? Beginning must be undertaken in spite of what awaits, and so inevitably it resonates with a sense of audacity; to lift Nietzsche's phrase, Deleuze makes his "entry into society"—the society of cinema—"with a duel,"[3] and more than anything this explains why discussion of the two volumes is so long overdue.

The Movement-Image and *The Time-Image* were first published in 1983 and 1985, respectively, with English translations appearing shortly thereafter, in 1986 and 1989. Initially, the response was both enthusiastic and perplexed, though the former was far more characteristic of the reception in France, where readers had been effectively prepared for the cinema books. Unlike other French luminaries such as Foucault, Lacan, or even Barthes, Deleuze was widely regarded as "vraiment cinéphile,"[4] an avid filmgoer whose cinema books were the fruit of long-standing reflection.[5] Moreover, the books themselves emerged within, or from, an intellectual climate that had begun to veer away from structuralist and psychoanalytic models that still dominated discourse in England and the United States;[6] Deleuze's *pensée-cinéma* was prefigured by philosophically minded critics such as Serge Daney, Pascal Bonitzer, and Jean-Louis Schefer, all of whom Deleuze invokes at points in the cinema books.[7] In every sense of the word, then, the appearance of the cinema books had been *anticipated*, and, as D. N. Rodowick reports, *The Time-Image* "was rumored to have sold out its first printing on its first day in bookstores."[8]

In Anglo-American circles, by contrast, interest in the two volumes was tempered by skepticism, not only about the source (a philosopher) but also about the sweep (roughly six hundred pages). Deleuze's arguments were rehearsed, but few substantive investigations or applications of the cinematographic philosophy followed. Because the cinema books are positioned in an immense oeuvre, part of "une vie philosophique,"[9] they discourage reflection in toto, and so Deleuze's cinematographic philosophy was adapted piecemeal, usually based on intersections with prevailing trends in film theory. Soon enough, the books were relegated to intermittent allusions and fugitive references, the initial intrigue having given way to the subtle labor of evasion. Perhaps, finally, the audacity of "the cinema books" hit home:[10] for while complaints about the cinema books range across a spectrum of smaller concerns, the real sticking point remains the spectrum itself, the grandiose, even gaudy scope of the two volumes. Like Borges's great map of the world, Deleuze's cinematographic philosophy aspires to cover so much ground as to be a world unto itself. Populated at turns by Bergson and Wenders, Kant and Murnau, Hitchcock and Peirce, Leibniz and Renoir, Nietzsche and Welles, Whitehead and Vertov, this is alien terrain, unfamiliar as traditional philosophy or film theory.

Ironically, this sense of confusion is often identified with the state of the cinema books themselves.[11] The English translations are notorious for botched film titles, fumbled footnotes, and even an occasionally distorted plotline, all of which have made it easier to reduce Deleuze's ambitious experiment to eccentricity, as if the cinema books represented a kind of Spruce Goose—bizarre and unwieldy. But what these deprecations acknowledge, however tacitly, is the degree to which the cinema books resist easy assimilation, for Deleuze's two volumes are, in their own way, astonishing. Whatever their intricacies and digressions, *The Movement-Image* and *The Time-Image* fundamentally contend that, beyond all other arts, the cinema opens the possibility for deterritorializing the cogito, the rigid "image of thought" that in one form or another has dominated Western philosophy. The cinema provokes us to see, to feel, to sense, and finally to think *differently*, and while this induces Deleuze to write his two volumes, those volumes in turn compel us to return to the cinema, to see its images in the light of our own captivity to the rituals of representation, the philosophical-narrative program we have been running. Ultimately, the cinema books should be read precisely because of their ambition, because they constitute, to twist a phrase of Foucault's, an "introduction to non-fascist thinking."[12]

From the time of his earliest works, Deleuze placed himself among thinkers who strayed outside the main—Platonic, Hegelian, phenomenological—thoroughfares of Western philosophy. Like the concept of "minor literature" that he and Guattari developed in their book *Kafka* (1975), Deleuze pursued the "becoming-minor" of philosophy: "Is there a hope for philosophy, which for a long time has been an official, referential genre?"[13] Deleuze's "hope" consists in deregulating thought in such a way as to unleash it from the referential rudiments of traditional philosophy (i.e., contrariety, similitude, identity, analogy), that is, to deterritorialize the cogito.[14] But if this is the case, why turn to art and why, especially, turn to the cinema? In *Difference and Repetition* (1968) Deleuze announced that "[t]he search for a new means of philosophical expression ... must be pursued today in relation to the renewal of certain other arts, such as the theatre or the cinema."[15] Although art and philosophy are materially different enterprises, the arts can be used to effect a new philosophical style because, Deleuze claims, they are comparable and even compatible. Directors, painters, architects, musicians, and philosophers are all essentially "thinkers."[16] The difference is that artists, unlike philosophers, do not create concepts; rather, they create "percepts" and "affects," which are particular to a given medium but which philosophy can engage conceptually.

This engagement, into which philosophy enters with science as well as art, is defined as constructivism; in other words, philosophy for Deleuze is the process of constructing, creating, and inventing concepts. Constructivism should not be understood as a process of hermeneutics or even metaphysics, both of which presume, albeit often negatively, the presence of an "always already," an ideal or truth that remains to be rediscovered. Even truth is "solely the creation of thought,"[17] but it is a creation so powerful as to overtake creation because it founds a vast moral system that hijacks thinking, governing its processes, circumscribing its provinces, determining its objects. The history of philosophy has been dominated by various guises of the True, which regulate thought according to this metaphysical program or "official genre" that Deleuze, like Nietzsche before him, seeks to lay bare as a "system of judgment." In this "revaluation of values," Deleuze looks to art and, above all, to the cinema to mobilize the "powers of the false" so as to supersede the representational categories that have been invented, procured, and ultimately naturalized for the purpose of judgment. While the arts create percepts and affects, Deleuze explains, each art does so according to its own "blocks": for instance, painting invents blocks of lines and colors. The cinema, by contrast, invents blocks of movement and time, hence its significance for Deleuze: philosophy engages cinematographic images because *"time has always put the notion of truth into crisis."*[18]

Critics have often situated the cinema in the history of arts (as, for instance, the "Seventh Art"), but Deleuze situates the cinema in the long and vexed relationship between philosophy and time. The ancients generally subordinated time not only to eternal Ideas (Plato) but, concomitantly, to space (Xeno), a predilection that classical philosophy revisited by claiming that "we see all things in God" (Malebranche), that is, by reducing time to the divine space in which it can be measured or, more precisely, made measurable. Time was reduced to *Cardo*, the cardinal points or hinges on which it was seen to turn, but, as Deleuze argues, the appearance of Kant's *Critique of Pure Reason* marked a tremendous philosophical reversal. Whereas space was previously the ground against which all change was gauged as succession, Kant defines time as the a priori form of intuition: time is the "form of everything that changes or moves,"[19] and so time no longer extends but encompasses succession, duration, and simultaneity as its *modes*. "With Kant," Deleuze writes, "time ceases to be originary or derived, to become the pure form of interiority, which hollows us out, which splits us, at the price of a vertigo, an oscillation that constitutes time: the synthesis of time changes direction by constituting it as an insurmountable abstraction."[20] Deleuze describes this vertiginous unhinging of time from space with Hamlet's phrase, "The time is out of joint," and it is to this "formula" that he returns in the cinema books.

According to Deleuze, the trajectory of the cinema recapitulates that of philosophy and its gradual discovery of, and immersion in, time. *The Movement-Image* begins by adumbrating an evolution of forms, from Griffith's mature experiments with montage to prewar

French and German cinemas, all of which treat time as the movement in or the traversal of space. What predominates among movement-images is the degree to which these images and the links between them are rational; in classical Hollywood cinema, for instance, situations readily provoke actions that generate new situations, providing the constituents of the basic trajectory of narrative that Aristotle first noted.[21] The "régime" of the movement-image bespeaks a process of regulation that Deleuze ascribes to a "sensory-motor schema," a neural network that "affectively" contains the image-flux: the images procured are recognizable, capable of being linked to other images along a methodical, and ultimately normative, chain. The sensory-motor schema is the mechanism of our relation to the world of images, the result of which is narrative, but this narrative must be understood as having been underwritten by a moral exigency, the promise to make good, common sense. Historically or even epistemically speaking, with the sensory-motor schema we entrusted ourselves to the system of Truth, the guarantor of which was the enduring assurance that ours was "best of all possible worlds" (Leibniz), guided by God or *Geist* toward an enlightened future. Ostensibly, wars, anonymous violence, even epic savagery would be redeemed later as part of the program, but how does one continue to believe when faced with the inconceivable twentieth century, our modern "theater of cruelty" (Artaud)? For Deleuze, this old order of things is irremediably deregulated by World War II and its collateral destruction of "illusions"; not only is "this world" far from the best possible one, but its abominations seem to have been perpetuated by precisely the very sensory-motor schema that was supposed to have produced a happy ending. Scientific enlightenment reveals itself as a destructive-aggressive drive, the thrust of civilization discloses its hygienic racism, communal consensus exposes its grounding contempt and xenophobia . . .

In the tracts of postwar destruction and reconstruction there is no longer any good, any *justifiable*, reason for the rational linkage of images, and so the cinema undergoes remarkable mutation. What happens? Emancipated from the coordinates of action, images cease to make sense, devolving instead into the bizarre and the banal; once cohered by movements, the unity of space splinters into so many disparate fragments. These "any-spaces-whatever" (*espaces quelconque*)—irrational, disconnected, aberrant, schizophrenic spaces—no longer obey laws of traditional, commonsensical causality. At every turn, the hope for resolution is frustrated; in Antonioni's

L'avventura, for instance, the disappearance of the young woman at the beginning triggers a sense of suspense to which no action is equal, and so characters are left to search without any hope of success, to wander, to wait. For Deleuze, a self-proclaimed philosopher of "patience," the indeterminacy of images induces a new cinematic "pedagogy." Beyond the reflexive scheme of action and re-action that, almost to the point of a dialectic, predominated in classical cinema of the movement-image, postwar European cinema discovers a cinema of inaction, waiting, and exhaustion (*épuisement*); the image does not extend to new spaces but "intends," involuting into the mind, opening up a whole new sense of mental duration (*durée*), an involution into psychic states. In other words, *The Time-Image* tracks a cinematic lapse from active extension into the intensity of the brain, memory, thought; the cinema discovers "subjective images, memories of childhood, sound and visual dreams or fantasies, where the character does not act without seeing himself acting."[22] In Resnais's *Muriel,* for instance, characters are so haunted by the traumatic branchings of memory that even the prospect of action, of the future, is saturated by the past. Images are suffused by thought, and so the cinema itself begins to suffer from self-consciousness, begins to come into consciousness of its own production of clichés. Gradually, the confidence of old-style montage cedes to an interrogation of the medium whereby the cinema confesses its own "internal conspiracy," namely, its immanent relation to industrial capital; in Wenders's *The State of Things,* for instance, the action of the cinema itself freezes when a production budget is drained, the spectacle of the filmed film surrendering to an inexorable hiatus. By developing new images, the modern cinema thus establishes a new logic among images, that is, a new kind of montage. No longer linked by the sensory-motor schema, the relation between images becomes noncommensurable: between one image and another a gap opens, an "interstice" in which thought experiences its own duration. Whereas the logic of the sensory-motor schema had relegated the image to an indirect presentation of time, a movement-image, this new logic ushers in the direct presentation of time, a time-image. A little bit of time "rises up to the surface of the screen."[23] As Deleuze sums it up, "when the cinema goes through its 'Kantian' revolution, that's to say when it stops subordinating time to motion, when it makes motion depend on time (with false moves manifesting temporal relations), the cinematic image becomes a time-image, an autotemporalization of the image."[24]

But if the cinema thus redoubles the course of modern philosophy and its discovery of time, in so doing it also lends itself to the practice of philosophy: the cinema creates images and signs, the conceptualization of which revitalizes thought. For Deleuze, image and thought merge on what he calls the "plane of immanence," a transcendental, preindividual, and even prephilosophical field of infinite variation. The plane of immanence is a virtual plane, which is not to say that it is "unreal" or "imaginary" or even something like a field of "possibility"; by "virtual," Deleuze means that the plane is composed of incorporealities (events, singularities) that are not the "conditions of possibility"[25] but the genetic conditions in which possibilities are created. The plane, as such, is the "milieu" of thought, of concepts, but within the concept there is already a relation to the image, just as within each image there is a relation to the concept.[26] On the one hand, then, all thinking "with" the cinema takes place on this plane, because it is here that images give rise to conceptualization, concepts as such being defined by their "intensive features"[27] rather than any pretense to unity. As Jean-Luc Nancy writes, "the word 'concept' means this for Deleuze—making cinematic."[28] On the other hand, the cinema opens up a "better" plane of immanence, in the sense that Deleuze says Spinoza formulated the "best" plane of immanence, the "one that does not hand itself over to the transcendent."[29] In other words, the cinema augurs a "path" to a plane that, superseding the limits of normal perception, deterritorializes the classical coordinates of philosophy. To reverse Nancy's formula, "the cinema means this for Deleuze—making concepts."

In this regard, however, the prospect of Deleuze is doubly problematic for film studies. Not only does Deleuze inevitably dismantle the discourses that traditionally nourished film studies, discourses such as phenomenology and structuralism, but more generally, and perhaps more importantly, his books buck the current trend in film studies toward theoretical indifference. In recent years, film theory has more or less gone underground; the tenets of semiotics, psychoanalysis, and (Althusserian) Marxism are still called upon, but without the same conviction, as if they constituted the rituals of a faith in which we no longer quite believe. In their stead, historicism, spectator studies, cultural studies, and cognitivism have come to dominate the field. The result is a peculiar, and peculiarly fashionable, absence of debate—about what film is, about its difference from other arts, about its effect on thought, about the way its images can be distinguished—in which a set of traditional assumptions quietly cement themselves. Without the old analogies to Plato's cave, Freudian dream-work, or linguistic models, which at least made clear that certain fundamental questions were at stake, the cinema is understood (tacitly but perhaps more firmly than ever before) as a system of re-presentation, one that calls upon the inherent conventions of the human mind (e.g., schemata, deep structures, rules of signification) first to create and then to make sense of images. Such an understanding of cinema appeals to the conventional division of subject and object, spectator and image, that is, the very "strata"—"the organism, significance and interpretation, and subjectification and subjection"—that Deleuze and Guattari condemn in *A Thousand Plateaus* (1980) as our human prison.[30]

To read the cinema books, then, is to find many of the organizing principles of film studies eradicated, for while Deleuze borrows a great number of the discipline's historical commonplaces, the coordinates within which those commonplaces made common sense have been left behind. Gone are the familiar conceits about a basic sense of cinematographic structure, about the cinema's momentous transition from silent films to talkies, and its telling elaboration in classical Hollywood narrative; instead, Deleuze writes of the cinema's signaletic material (*matière signalétique*), its transition from movement-images to time-images, and its realization in postwar Europe. For both film studies and philosophy, finally, the cinema books constitute a duel, an affront, a defiant and "untimely meditation" (Nietzsche). As Deleuze and Guattari once wrote, all truly original thought "determine[s] its moment, its occasion and circumstances, its landscapes and personae, its conditions and unknowns."[31] The moment for a cinematographic philosophy was no less boldly selected, though not to appeal to an audience; instead, Deleuze chose a moment in order to enter a given milieu, to affect the inclination of its forces, tendencies, and even habits—"acting counter to our time, and therefore acting on our time and, let us hope, for the benefit of time to come."[32]

Rosa Luxemburg once said something to the effect that a revolution is by necessity launched prematurely, but it also seems that revolution, or any such "untimely" thought, only reaches its moment of maturity when things are most desperate. The past catches up with the future when the future lapses into dismal inertia. So we find the cinema books (or maybe they find us) as the twentieth century winds down and its frenzy of images winds up, our audiovisual culture having reduced us all to the feeling that we are unwilling repositories of and accomplices in a plan to populate the world with mindless images. Today, technology and capitalism conspire as never before to proliferate such clichés; accelerating, they overrun our homes, workplaces, supermarket checkout lines, and airports, hunting us down in our most private moments. One need look no further for perverse signs of our "visual turn"[33] than the headlong flight of a black Mercedes into a Parisian underpass—the paparazzi strewn, literally, in the wake—to grasp the way that, even as we scorn images, our scorn is turned into an image, merging into a endless découpage that is recycled from one medium to the next. To this sick state of affairs Deleuze himself lent the phrase the "[c]ivilization of the image,"[34] for the process of making images civilized, of reducing them to clichés, is tantamount to civilization—or, rather, civilization is tantamount to the labor of producing a "concerted organisation" of clichés and, thence, "*misery*."[35] How can we understand, evaluate, and finally value images when the entire culture seems to have gone visual? Are there differences among images or has their propagation flattened out all distinctions? Is there still a reason left to esteem cinematographic images apart from those we see on television or in tabloids? Finally, is there really any use in theorizing the cinema at all?

Pressed by such questions, Deleuze readily admits that "[t]he usefulness of theoretical books on the cinema has been called into question (especially today, because the times are not right)"; but he counters that film theory, like philosophy, must be transformed, that it must leave behind all the antiquated notions of what theory is. "For many people, philosophy is something which is not 'made', but is pre-existent, ready-made in a prefabricated sky," he explains. "However, philosophical theory is itself a practice, just as much as its object."[36] The assertion sounds surprisingly like the rhetoric of cognitivism and its "posttheoretical" appeal, but while cognitivists like David Bordwell and Noëll Carroll denounce "grand theories," they continue to proceed on the basis of their own schematic, and universal, assumptions.[37] In this respect, Deleuze is much more the avatar of the end of grand theories: for him, the specificity of cinematographic images invariably eludes the rigid determinations of any overarching schematism. The result is a philosophy whose rigor is always local, reflecting the emergence of rules immanent to each given "zone of indetermination." The concepts that theory develops "must relate specifically to cinema,"[38] Deleuze writes, and so the cinema itself is thereby made the mode for understanding the world, our world. Cinema inspires—in the very sense of breathing life, providing fresh air—philosophy. As Deleuze announces at the end of *The Time-Image*, "there is always a time, midday-midnight, when we must no longer ask ourselves, 'What is cinema?' but 'What is philosophy?'"[39]

In *What Is Philosophy?* (1991), the last book Deleuze ever wrote, he and Guattari dismiss the "idle chatter" about the death of philosophy. "Today it is said that systems are bankrupt," they write, "but it is only the concept of the system that has changed."[40] In the past, Deleuze has cited examples of this new system in science and logic,[41] and we might further specify cosmology, which attests to the development of "poised systems"[42]—not systems that graft order on to chaos but systems that ride the delicate crest between chaos and order. In this respect, Deleuze's cinematographic philosophy is as much about the creation of an open system as it is itself a system, and this understanding invariably conditions the collection before you. On one level, the contributors often question and criticize the cinema books, but this is only the most obvious example of a broader strategy. However much they elucidate Deleuze's cinema books, the essays in this collection tend to move beyond exegesis: if Deleuze is right and the power of cinema does lie in the capacity to exile us from familiar conceptual terrain, then the system is tantamount to its own formation, a becoming-system, a "process" (Whitehead) that we undertake each time we return to the cinema.

How is it possible, then, to organize such a collection? In part the answer lies in Deleuze's own work, which, despite its extraordinary size and range of subject matter, constantly betrays patterns, the philosopher having returned on so many occasions to the same concepts, spinning them each time a little differently. Likewise, the reader of this collection will find that the same problems and ideas invariably recur from one essay to the next, though often framed or phrased differently; in other words, although one cannot (and should not) hope to produce a "unified field theory" of Deleuze's cinematographic philosophy, this collection unfolds along those tendencies, those vectors of thought, that distinguish the cinema books. Whence the three main sections that make up this collection: the first section, "Approaching Images," dwells on Deleuze's extended considerations of images and philosophy, and especially the way the cinema consummates this "intercession"; the second section, "Mapping Images," reflects on Deleuze's notion of cinematographic development, not only the broad transition from movement-images to time-images but also how this transition suggests a new sense and system of history; finally, "Thinking Images," the third section, extends properly cinematographic questions into the domain of thought and life, where profound and pragmatic concerns come together in an exuberant new aesthetic. Indeed, one can imagine that these three sections roughly reflect the philosophical areas to which Deleuze devoted himself: ontology, epistemology, and ethics. The remainder of the introduction constitutes an attempt to contextualize the essays in the collection within these broad areas and, hopefully, to provide the reader with a more rounded sense of Deleuze's "philosophy of cinema." The book's final section, or "After-Image," has been set aside for Deleuze himself, for as we embark upon the cinema books it seems only appropriate that we grant their author the last word.

APPROACHING IMAGES

Deleuze's extensive writings on literature, painting, and especially cinema gravitate toward "thought from the outside" (Blanchot), a kind of thought that reaches beyond the chains of common sense. The problem is that the world is increasingly composed of clichés that condition a whole network of conceptual reflexes. The world has become a bad film, Deleuze says, that we inhabit and that inhabits us as a "habitus," a mode of regularity and "control" (Burroughs). In philosophical terms, this means we operate in accordance with fixed Ideas that, like clichés, consign us to the accord of a particularity with a faculty that thus produces consensus between the faculties—literally, common sense. If the plane of immanence is, as Deleuze says, "the image thought gives itself of what it means to think, to make use of thought, to find one's bearings in thought,"[43] a kind of shifting "desert" on which concepts are the "intensive ordinates of movement,"[44] then common sense amounts to a coordination of concepts that aspires to transcendence, totalization, and the pretense of organicity. Referring to classical philosophy, Deleuze terms this image of thought "dogmatic." Rather than submitting to receptivity ("passive synthesis"), the dogmatic image is conceived in advance of empirical vicissitudes and thereby projects itself into the future as an anticipative matrix that turns any encounter into one of recognition. "Thought is thereby filled with no more than an image of itself, one in which it recognises itself more than it recognises things: this is a finger, this is a table, Good morning Theaetetus."[45]

To this regimen Deleuze's entire philosophy constitutes a singular response: *one must think without an image*. But how do we distinguish between the dogmatic image of thought and the images to which Deleuze devotes so much time in the cinema books and elsewhere? To begin with, Deleuze's exhortation refers to an overarching image of thought that seals us off from chance and improvisation, the essence of thinking. The relation between this overarching image and images in general is crucial because images can just as easily reinforce as pry open the structures (Cogito, Ego, Apperceptive Unity, Self) that constrain us within any given habitus. In other words, the difficulty here lies in grasping what Deleuze means by an image that is related to thought but that is not strictly tantamount to, or subsumable to, an image of thought. On the one hand, Deleuze clearly aligns the artistic image with the specific capacity to dislodge (deterritorialize) the image of thought, thereby narrowing the definition in order to designate a certain affective and even effective possibility; on the other hand, this seemingly limited context actually extends Deleuze's understanding of the image beyond familiar definitions because the image is no longer restricted to what we "see." For instance, Deleuze finds in Samuel Beckett's works moments when discursive "hiatuses, holes, or tears ... widen in such a way as to receive something from the outside or from elsewhere"; the "something seen or heard" that seeps through this hole, Deleuze says, "is called Image."[46] As such, the artistic image is neither a representation of an object nor even a visual impression, the first of which connotes mere recognition and the second a limited sensory bandwidth. Rather, the image is a collection of sensations—a "sensible aggregate," or what Deleuze will ultimately call a "sign"[47]—that we cannot simply re-cognize and that we encounter, as such, at the very limit of the sensible. Sensations possess the capacity to derange the everyday, to short-circuit the mechanism of common sense, and thus to catalyze a different kind of thinking; indeed, sensations are encountered at a threshold we might call the "thinkable."

In contrast to representation, which subsumes (re-presents) a particularity under a transcendental idea or category as common sense, thinking for Deleuze begins with a "disorder of the senses" (Rimbaud). Although Deleuze cites Nietzsche as the philosopher who initiated, or risked, a new means of philosophical expression with respect to art, the specific promise of this "disorder" he traces to Kant's *Critique of Judgment*. Unlike Kant's earlier critiques, those of pure reason and practical reason, where a certain faculty mastered the others in order to assure a rigorous regularity, the third *Critique* suggests the possibility of deregulation.[48] In the "Analytic of the Sublime," Kant explained that certain experiences—whether colossal or terrifying, for both are ultimately confrontations with chaos—launch the imagination to its efficacious limits. Trying to comprehend these experiences, the imagination recoils, and out of this withdrawal there emerges a dehiscence between "what can be imagined and what can be thought, between imagination and reason."[49] Kant compares this agitation to a "vibration" between faculties, and this is precisely what Deleuze means by sensation; as he writes in *Difference and Repetition,* "Something in the world forces us to think."[50] Sensation always initially betokens a kind of violence: insofar as the dogmatic image of thought solidifies itself in its own inertia (habits, rituals, conventions), sensation is like the setting off of a trip wire, the communication of a kind of synaptic frenzy through the faculties.

Needless to say, sensations can be produced in any number of ways, procured under any variety of circumstances, as Kant himself established. But, whereas Kant saw art as an instance of sensation and by no means the most important one, Deleuze is specifically invested in artistic sensation. As early as *Proust and Signs* (1964), he explained that a "work of art not only interprets and not only emits signs to be interpreted; it produces them, and by determinable procedures."[51] A work of art is a "machine" constructed for the very purpose of producing sensations, and therein lies its privileged relationship to constructivism. Released from the prison of referentiality by sensation, thought turns to sensation to discover a model for its own construction of concepts. Sensations do not refer to anything outside themselves, they are autopoetic, "purposiveness without purpose" (Kant), and this is why philosophy engages art: like the production of sensation, which refers only to itself, the construction of a philosophical concept is self-referential, a creation not based on adequation but on "taste."[52] The concept is the performance—the "contour" or "fragmentary whole"[53]—of thought insofar as it is moved by sensations and intensities. While the concept has no referent outside of itself or, more properly, no referent that is not the result of its own positing, the concept is the expression of sensations because sensations mobilize the differential forces that make thinking possible. The process of considering art or, in this case, of "approaching images" is always linked to the genetic forces of thinking itself, to the question of ontology, and nowhere is this more in evidence than in the cinema books. As Deleuze writes in *The Movement-Image,* "Camera-consciousness raises itself to a determination which is no longer formal or material, but genetic and differential."[54]

In "Of Images and Worlds: Toward a Geology of the Cinema," the essay that opens this collection and that traces the various tendrils of Deleuze's thinking that lead to his *pensée-cinéma,* Jean-Clet Martin describes how sensations erode the architecture of conventional thought. Sensations burrow through the determinative and dogmatic structures of thought, but in so doing they reveal that structure as such: in terms deployed by Deleuze and Guattari, sensation reveals our "molar" existence as a dimension, formation, or perspective within a "molecular" universe (in Spinozan terms, the expressed within the process of expressing).[55] In the same way that Deleuze looks to Francis Bacon in *Logique de la sensation* (1981), Martin looks to van Gogh to suggest that sensations traverse the membrane separating *Innenvelt* and *Umvelt,* breaking it down until we are left with an in-between (as Deleuze once explained, "the painter is *already* in the canvas").[56] Deleuze's resulting methodology, which Martin sums up as "never begin with terms that are exterior to one another," testifies to a kind of monism or, more specifically, a "natural philosophy." The basis of natural philosophy is that all things—brains, bodies, subjects, objects—are composed of the same material, their ostensible differences the result of individuation, modes, haecceities, or functions of that material or matter. Deleuze's own natural philosophy is originally inspired by Schelling (*Naturphilosophie*), guided at so many turns by Spinoza ("nature naturing itself"), but ultimately finds its substantial basis in Bergson, whose understanding of images constitutes the point of departure for the cinema books.[57]

Deleuze's engagement with Bergson is one of the most extensive of his career, in large part because in Bergson's thought "there is something that cannot be assimilated" by traditional philosophy.[58] Deleuze has returned to this "something" on several occasions, but the cinema books provoke a unique reconsideration of Bergson, one in which his ontology or "material universe"[59] comes to the fore. In particular, Deleuze returns to the remarkable first chapter of Bergson's *Matter and Memory* (1896); collapsing the distinction between subject and object, cutting through the deadlock between realism and idealism, the book begins with an implicit question: what happens when we open our eyes, say, in the morning, when we get up? "Here I am in the presence of images," Bergson answers, "in the vaguest sense of the word, images perceived when my senses are open to them, unperceived when they are closed. All these images act and react upon one another in all their elementary parts according to constant laws which I call the laws of nature."[60] In other words, to open our eyes is not to find static objects qua representations but a dizzy swirl of moving images; indeed, the image is by definition a moving image insofar as it does not "resemble an object that it would represent." As Deleuze explains it, "The movement-image is the object; the thing itself caught in movement as continuous function. The movement-image is the modulation of the object itself."[61]

For Deleuze, the cinematographic image is, or begins as, such a movement-image, and so the conceptualization of its sensation begets, by definition, an investigation into the universe in its molecular aspect, that is, as an "aggregate" of such images.[62] This investigation can be understood from two perspectives. On the one hand, if the cinema provokes ontological consideration, it does so as a cosmology; *The Movement-Image* amounts to a "story of the universe"—a story the cinema induces but also one in which, on the other hand, the cinema itself plays the crucial role because its images allow us to go "back up the path" along which the human world of molar perception develops and thus to glimpse the molecular universe about which Bergson writes. The confusion here is not so much that of a vicious circle as it is that of a feedback loop between sensation (the cinema) and Bergson's aggregate of images on which Deleuze confers a kind of "degree zero" status. At its birth, the universe is only images, a molecular chaos of gaseous light: there is no center, no left or right, no high or low on the plane—there are only images, and each image is a "road by which we pass, in every direction, the modifications propagated throughout the immensity of the universe."[63] In this agglomeration, images are matter and matter is movement; there is no centered perception because the eye is diffused in the deliriums of light, just as the painter's eye was "in" the canvas, spread along its membranous textures. This nonhuman and prephilosophical milieu, in which image = matter = movement = perception, Deleuze defines as the "plane of immanence," bearing in mind that it is treated here within the broad sweep of a cosmology. In other words, the plane of immanence undergoes a "cooling down" in the same sense that scientists speak of the universe as having undergone this process, the initial chaos eventually giving way to a gradual organization, the emergence of strong and weak forces (what scientists consider nuclear forces), electromagnetism and gravity—that is, the basic constituents of our world.

But what of life? What distinguishes life, or, as Deleuze and Bergson say, the brain, from the universe? If the universe is composed of image-matter, then, as Deleuze explains in *Bergsonism* (1966), "There cannot be a difference in kind, but only a difference in degree" between matter and its perception.[64] This difference in degree is not spatial so much as it is temporal or "interval," for life is simply a moment's delay or cut (*écart*) introduced into the image-flux: from the earliest protozoa, which constitute barely any interval, the course of evolution introduces ever-larger synaptic gaps, images in which the flood of the world is captured. The human brain constitutes the largest of these gaps, like a kind of photographic plate on which convolutions of light are momentarily "prehended." The question of prehension is borrowed from Whitehead and developed in concert with Leibniz, most notably in *The Fold* (1988), and it lies at the heart of this very different notion of thought.[65] For Deleuze, the "brain is a screen" that emerges in the world of images, and although this formula will prove crucial in the cinema books, it is not specific to the cinema. In essence, the screen constitutes the development of the plane of immanence: "the brain is a screen" in the sense that it is a filter that extracts itself from chaos. This screen is a form of relation, of interchange, of mutual synthesis between the brain and the universe; as Deleuze explains, "if the world is in the subject, the subject is no less *for the world*."[66]

In *The Movement-Image*, however, this baroque architecture is transposed into a broader trajectory of human evolution and, by extension, cinematographic evolution, according to which we try to graft order on to chaos rather than sharing in its dynamism. To begin with, the brain's extraction tends toward a kind of subtraction, for what is living tends to perceive what interests it and to disregard the rest; in fact, for Deleuze the definition of subjectivity, and its unfavorable connotation, derive principally from this subtraction. By subtracting or "framing" the image, the subject already undertakes an "analytic" preparatory to action: in the interval, the delay, elements are selected and thus made ready for action (or, more properly, re-action); the delay allows the brain to "select their elements, to organise them, or to integrate them into a new movement."[67] Deleuze often refers to Spinoza's remarkable claim that "we do not yet know what a body can do," and it is precisely in this context that we can understand this sense of unexplored potential, for the brain and body have been reduced to a neuro-network deflecting images from perceptions into actions, a regulated system of feedback that

Bergson calls the "sensory-motor schema." In this schematism, in other words, images are recognized (as perception) and, in the interval (or affection), they are transformed (as action). Such are the rudiments of a dogmatic image of thought, one that Deleuze especially identifies with classical Hollywood cinema. But this leaves us with a question: can one conceive of another possibility and, if so, what would this mean? For some time film studies has attempted to excavate a "cinema before cinema," a prehistory of the cinema that looks to technological precursors.[68] For Deleuze, however, the prehistory—or "geology," to use Martin's phrase—of the cinema lies in philosophy, above all in Bergson's *Matter and Memory*: when the cinema ceases to imitate normal human perception it discovers what Bergson already saw, "the universe as cinema in itself, a metacinema."[69]

In order to grasp this thesis, however, we must gradually work through its constituents, especially the prima facie problem with this argument. Indeed, this is the problem that opens *The Movement-Image*, for, while Deleuze begins with Bergson's theses on movement to explain the extraordinary nature of cinematographic images, Bergson's own appraisal of the cinema in *Creative Evolution* (1907) might be characterized as underwhelmed. Bergson goes so far as to analogize the technology with the mechanism of our own "normal" perception. As I explain in my own essay in the collection, "Cinema Year Zero," Deleuze dismisses this response by arguing that what Bergson saw was an embryonic cinema, one that had yet to conquer "its own novelty."[70] But, if we reduce Bergson's position to nearsightedness, I argue, we miss the way in which the "turn" from *Matter and Memory* to *Creative Evolution* is indicative of a more general aversion: in effect, *Creative Evolution* aligns itself with the sensory-motor schema and thus situates itself (however uniquely) in a tradition that actually thwarts "self-moving thought."[71] In modern philosophy, the question of putting movement into thought was effectively broached by Hegel, as Deleuze admits, but Hegel did so in a dialectical framework.[72] Hegel's method is indicative of the way philosophy has traditionally insisted on a kind of movement that, according to Deleuze, "refers to intelligible elements, Forms or ideas which are themselves eternal and immobile,"[73] for such Forms are the correlative of the Self that supersedes, the Self that is preserved "in the last instance." Like so many peaks of an EKG graph, these Forms consist in moments that transcend movement and that, in so doing, contrive to represent movement. Deleuze terms this Form the "pose," because, while it is essentially immobile (posing), its synthetic privilege is such as to engage in posturing (posing) as movement.

Movement, however, cannot be attained cardinally, according to the passing of chronological moments, because this reduces time itself to succession in space, à la Xeno. Real movement takes place *between* such spaces, no matter how infinitesimally those spaces are divided, because movement is not the measure of space at all; real movement is an image of time or duration, which Bergson and Deleuze regard as the consciousness of a qualitative change or the "whole of relations." But although Bergson believes as much ideally, in *Creative Evolution* his practical position is that perception withdraws from movement to "take snapshots" of reality that are recomposed, thereafter, like the projection of a film. Deleuze responds by situating Bergson's misdiagnosis in a scientific heritage that "consisted in relating movement not to privileged instants, but to any-instant-whatever."[74] The cinema is the "last descendant" in the line from geometry to physics to calculus, all of which "take time as an independent variable";[75] but, as Deleuze argues, the cinema also goes beyond the conditions under which movement was scientifically considered. While the cinema takes photograms or frames at a regular speed of twenty-four per second, what it produces is not an illusion of movement or a simple succession of frames: what the cinema gives is "immediate movement." There may be privileged instants in the cinema, but these exist within the flow of material sections to which each instant, however spectacular or ordinary, is immanent. In other words, the cinema does not give us a succession of frames but real movement, and this is because cinematographic images are not "strung together" or "corrected" by an intellectual "above"—rather, the process of projection is their stringing together, and this takes place "at the same time as the image appears for the spectator and without conditions."[76]

Now, in one sense Deleuze considers all art to be movement insofar as sensation moves thought; sensation is the *vis elastica* that explains movement.[77] In *Francis Bacon: Logique de la sensation*, Deleuze describes painting as a "sequence or a series" of sensations that play along the nervous system;[78] in *Essays Critical and Clinical* (1993), he describes literature as the movement of becoming, a "passage of Life that traverses both the livable and the lived."[79] In the cinema books, though, Deleuze distinguishes cinematographic movement from these other arts because the latter are essentially "immobile in themselves so that it is the mind that has to 'make' movement." The automatic movement of the cinema propels sensation to a new order of magnitude, thereby realizing the essence of the image,

> *producing a shock to thought, communicating vibrations to the cortex, touching the nervous and cerebral system directly.* Because the cinematographic image itself 'makes' movement, because it makes what the other arts are restricted to demanding (or to saying), it brings together what is essential in the other arts; it inherits it, it is as it were the directions for use of the other images, it converts into potential what was only possibility.[80]

But the potential of the cinema—a kind of image-circuit that Deleuze calls the "spiritual automaton"—remains only a potential unless certain kinds of images are enlisted to propel thinking to its limits, and this is never simple. As an "industrial art," the cinema has "unparalleled economic and industrial consequences," and for this reason the invention of new images and signs is "infinitely easier to prevent."[81] However much *The Movement-Image* augurs the "upsurge of the new thinking image,"[82] this "upsurge" must be seen against the backdrop of what amounts to the development of cinematographic regularity, which gravitates toward the "fortunate inertia of our perception" (Bergson). In other words, the cinema restricts its own potentialities, and in order to understand as much Deleuze recapitulates—and in the process reevaluates—the basic constituents of the cinema, from frame to shot to montage.

For Deleuze, the frame is defined by the way it forms sets (*ensembles*). Just as the brain forms "closed systems," subtracting what it needs from the image, so the cinema frames geometric elements, degrees of light and darkness, in a continuum from rarefaction to saturation. In these terms, Deleuze's theory of the frame is a set theory: the image we see on the screen is necessarily delimited from the rest of the world, not only spatially, in terms of the offscreen, but also and especially temporally, in terms of the "whole of relations," which is "outside" the set but to which each set is open. Whether by a mobile frame or montage, then, shots or movement-images express the qualitative change of sets, which Deleuze calls the "dividual" (by contrast, the time-image will concentrate on mobile frames and montage that exhaust *actual* space, providing an image of *virtual* becoming). Sets divide and multiply, and so the movement-image is an image of changing space or space covered, that is, an indirect image of time. Just as Bergson claimed that perception could be put into contact with the whole of changing relations, so too the qualitative change of the movement-image, the coagulations and dispersions of sets, also faces the "whole of relations." Because relations are always *external* to their terms (in the same sense, for instance, that a concept for Deleuze is not the unity or totality of parts), this "whole" is not a megaset or even the set of all sets—rather, the whole is open, like a thread that weaves through all sets.

"It's very difficult to think about, this relation between time, the whole, and openness," Deleuze confesses, but his point is that the cinema is what "makes it easier for us to do this."[83] Each of Deleuze's cinema books considers this "relation" from a different perspective: whereas movement-images relate only indirectly to the whole, time-images relate to the whole as an "outside" (let us call it both memory and the future) to which thought must open itself, thereby dissolving the artifices of totalization. For this reason, Deleuze says that "[t]he cinema is always as perfect as it can be,"[84] that the movement-image cannot be weighed against the time-image, as if the former were preliminary or had not quite reached the latter's state of perfection. The reason for this is that Deleuze's concern is not with perfection (i.e., a teleological model of the cinema that would be effectively grounded on certain values), but with actualization, in which the image is gauged by the genetic forces that give rise to it. If Deleuze values one kind of cinema over another, this is because he values a cinema that undermines any sense of determinate values. Broadly construed, movement-images are actualized under the conditions of normal perception, and this is what concerns Deleuze—not the lack of perfection but the regularity, the way thought evolves, settling into fixed norms and conventions.

In the next essay in this section, "Escape from the Image: Deleuze's Image-Ontology," Martin Schwab describes this evolution as the formation of a "second régime" in the aggregate of movement-images. Just as Bergson, according to Deleuze, shows how the brain "differenciates" itself from itself, thereby forming an autonomous body or "center of indetermination" in the "acentered universe," so Deleuze himself traces the development of the cinematographic habitus. The cinema is likewise subjected to a centering, first with respect to technical conditions, and later with respect to narrative ones. In early cinema, camera movement and montage were technically impeded, but even when the technical centering of the image was overcome, the cinema manages to center itself by imitating human perception, by providing a point of fluxion control in the image, a grounded or foregrounded node through which the image can be stabilized. As Schwab explains, images are consistently related to a single image qua center; the universe is "incurved" so that we experience the "virtual action" of things on us and, thence, our "possible action" on things.[85] Reading *The Movement-Image*, one is tempted to see this matrix of perception and action (or re-action) as specific to classical narrative cinema and its mechanism of continuity editing, but what Deleuze does is to locate classical cinema (among other cinemas) in the more general regulative matrix of the sensory-motor schema. This dogmatic schema reduces images to a perceptual digestibility that determines an almost instinctive response, in the process governing the excitations of images, reducing them to an "even flow."

The sensory-motor schema insinuates itself in the cinema as a pleasure principle (*Lustprinzip*), a kind of circuit breaker for controlling image-excitations. The schema regulates the images by deflecting them into certain habitual paths; as Schwab explains, perception-images necessitate a brief moment of thought, an affection-image, which in turn feeds into an action-image. In this way we can see how, even before Deleuze ever considered the cinema, he grasped the sensory-motor schema as a "story-telling function,"[86] for it requires images of situations that naturally give rise to action and so to new situations, a narrative trajectory we learn to follow, in cinema and in life, as the norm. "[I]n order not to be rejected,"[87] not to be judged abnormal, the cinema opened up its own "brain" to the sensory-motor schema, but in this Deleuze also glimpses an alternative: why can't the cinema also go back up the "path perception came down"? Deleuze offers Samuel Beckett's *Film* as a primary instance of this a-centering, and Schwab's essay provides an extended explanation of this reading as a means both to grasp and to critique Deleuze's image-ontology. It should be said that the nature of Deleuze's system is such that, although he refers to literally hundreds of films, a select few examples carry a great deal of theoretical weight. *Film*'s exceptional import lies in the way it intends to show how to "extinguish the three varieties" of images (perception, affection, action), which is to say, how to extinguish the centering of the cinema on which these varieties are predicated.[88] Deleuze claims that *Film* attains a full-fledged de-subjectification, no less that it thematizes or remarks upon this process in its diegesis. Indeed, *Film* is as close to an allegory as anything in the cinema books, and as such Schwab rightly takes it to task. If *Film* does not operate to "extinguish the three varieties of images," then how is it possible to talk of a "subjectless cinema," of a preindividual cinema that leaves behind the conditions of the sensory-motor schema? And even if we manage to extinguish the varieties, doesn't this extinguishing of differentiation also imply an erasure of difference altogether?

In order to even consider such crucial questions, it is important to provide a sense of the cinema books as articulating two different means to deregulate or eliminate the subject. These two means refer to different ways of handling the plane of immanence, for while *The Movement-Image* deals explicitly with this "planomenon," *The Time-Image* produces this plane on the body-brain itself, in terms of what Deleuze and Guattari call a "body without organs." The first section of this collection, "Approaching Images," is effectively concerned with *The Movement-Image*, for having analyzed the development of the sensory-motor schema, each of the essays confronts the promise of the cinema as an a-centered perception that would travel "back up the route that natural perception comes down." The last of these essays, François Zourabichvili's "The Eye of Montage: Dziga Vertov and Bergsonian Materialism," addresses this possibility in terms of a *"machine assemblage of movement-images,"* as Deleuze calls it.[89] Zourabichvili explains that, strictly speaking, all films are "machinic assemblages" insofar as they are the products of montage; but Deleuze reserves the term for a certain kind of montage identified with Vertov and experimental cinema. By experimental cinema Deleuze means a cinema that experiments with its own conditions of movement. "All Bergson asks for," Deleuze writes, "are movements and the intervals between movements which serve as units—and it is also exactly what Dziga Vertov asked for, in his materialist conception of the cinema."[90] In Vertov's montage, Zourabichvili claims, Deleuze sees the possibility of a nonhuman eye, that is, a perception unmoored from its normal anchorage, so that it spreads itself into images and, even more important, *between* images.

For Deleuze, the in-differentiation of images gives rise to a kind of thought that exists in the interval—an interval that does not extend into action. Whereas the universe normally incurves around a distinct image, an image that acts, Vertov's découpage derails perception from its stable center, shuttling it along an unpredictable path of movements. In particular, Vertov's montage deploys false continuities so that, as Zourabichvili writes, "[e]ach image thus interacts with other images, instead of organizing itself" subjectively. This operation does not eliminate distinctions between images but, rather, eliminates the distinction between the subject and the image, realizing a radical immanence ("the brain is the screen"); "if the cinema goes beyond perception, it is in this sense that it reaches the *genetic element* of all possible perception, that is, the point which changes, and which makes perception change, the differential of perception itself."[91] Such is the sign of the genesis of perception—a sign that, while it returns us to the "nonhuman" world, must also be seen in the context of cinematographic transformation.

MAPPING IMAGES

Insofar as the cinema produces signs, Deleuze envisions his cinema books as a "logic" of signs: together, *The Movement-Image* and *The Time-Image* constitute a "taxonomy, an attempt at the classification of images and signs."[92] Deleuze is genuinely fond of systems of classification because they are preparatory to the creation of concepts, but the particular system that we discover in the cinema books has little in common with the familiar categories of film studies. "The main genres, the western, crime, period films, comedy, and so on," Deleuze says, "tell us nothing about different types of images or their intrinsic characteristic."[93] However useful these traditional categories, Deleuze discards them in favor of a classificatory system that necessarily arises from cinematographic images themselves, that responds to what is "intrinsic" in images. In part this explains his evisceration of Christian Metz's *"grande syntagmatique"* in *The Time-Image*, for Metz treats the cinema by analogy (cinema is *like* a *langue*, the shot is *like* an utterance).[94] The basis of any such analogy is that system and cinema, thought and image, mind and matter are fundamentally distinct, whereas Deleuze's system of classification insists on precisely the ontological formula we have traced to this point—the identity of image, matter, movement, and perception.

With this in mind Deleuze resolves in the cinema books to draw on Charles Sanders Peirce's "extremely rich classification" of signs in order to supplement Bergson's own varieties of images.[95] Peirce's is a "descriptive science of reality," which is to say that his signs are not recruited from some overarching system or metalanguage; rather, his signs are modes of sensation or sensible aggregates. Although Peirce considers the sign structure as tripartite (the image, the sign that describes the image, and the third image that is its "interpretant"), his logic reflects Bergson's own premise, namely, that mind and matter exist on the same plane and consist in the same material. In terms of the cinema, this means that images consist of a signaletic material (*matière signalétique*), "a plastic mass, an a-signifying and a-syntaxic material"[96] from which signs are composed: the cinema provides a view on what Hjelmslev called "content"—not an utterance but the "utterable," a pre-signifying material.[97] What is intrinsic to the sign is its "genetic and compositional" character; or, inversely, signs give rise to a taxonomy that neither precedes that which is classified, nor approaches it from another kind of system, nor finally totalizes it. As such, Deleuze's system is intended to develop along with the modulations of the cinema itself; although Deleuze speaks of an "essence" of the cinema, suggesting prima facie an ontology that is eternal and fixed, the cinema books affirm that essence to be the "adventure of movement and time."[98] Herein lies the originality, and obscurity, of Deleuze's notion of cinematographic transformation: just as signs arise immanently from blocks of space-time (images), Deleuze's classificatory system is inextricable from a broader sense of cinematographic "becoming."

Having said that, however, the task of understanding Deleuze's notion of cinematographic transformation remains forbidding. The preface to the French edition of *The Movement-Image* begins defiantly: "This study is not a history of the cinema."[99] But, as D. N. Rodowick suggests, here and elsewhere Deleuze means something very specific by *history*.[100] Broadly construed, Deleuze condemns history as an enterprise that stakes out origins and anticipates conclusions, the result of which is a chronological series. This model organizes history as an *organic* process—history as story (*histoire*)—whose naturalization rings with a note of Hegelian inevitability: in other words, history reveals the prototypical movement of Spirit (*Geist*). By contrast, when Deleuze is pressed to define his own sense of cinematographic history he recourses to a model of "natural history," that is, the very kind of history that arises from classificatory systems or taxonomies. The natural history of the cinema is like the classification of animals inasmuch as the various characteristics of an image, like those of an animal, provide the grounds for the typology of a distinct sign[101]; from classification, images and signs emerge in stratigraphic series, sedimented at unpredictable angles and betraying so many peculiar intersections. For Deleuze, classification works "symptomatologically" by selecting certain singularities that bring forth improbable connections and unseen tendencies, but this procedure reveals classification, no less the history to which it gives rise, to be "effective" (Foucault), to be genealogical. Not a quest for origins or a positing of conclusions, classification is a creative process, the production of a map—but a map of what?

The taxonomy Deleuze formulates is a means of classifying images or what we might simply call "light." In *The Movement-Image*, Deleuze explains that the plane of immanence is a plane of light, and so all of the images to which the cinema gives rise are fluctuations of light. Deleuze has often spoken of light in terms that approximate "lighting," as he does in the piece that concludes this collection, but his taxonomy embraces the much larger and more difficult question of the "visible." The notion of the visible (or "seeable") was developed by Foucault, whom Deleuze credits with having formulated a unique neo-Kantianism: in effect, Foucault transposes the design of the first *Critique*—understanding and sensibility, determination and receptivity, above and below—into an audiovisual archive divided between the articulable (statements) and the visible (light).[102] Foucault's work is consistently concerned with the configuration of these domains; modernity, for instance, is largely contemporaneous with a visible that is shaped by statements into various disciplinary guises, the most notorious of which is Bentham's panopticon, a prison that allows one to observe cells like "so many small theatres, in which each actor is alone, perfectly individualized and constantly visible."[103] Above all, then, Foucault describes how the articulable *determines* the visible, and therein lies the key to this revised Kantianism. Kant traditionally defines truth as the adequation of subject and object, but, as Deleuze educes, Foucault's project consists in revealing truth as the determination of the seeable by the sayable, a process that produces their ostensible configuration: ironically, the "light of truth" emerges when light has been contained in any given apparatus (*dispositif*), when the power grid is so overwhelming as to render the resulting representation seemingly adequate.[104]

It is in this regard that we can understand the two senses in which the cinema functions historically for Deleuze. First, the cinema offers a medium in which to grasp the fluctuating relationship of the articulable and visible. Although these zones are traditionally subject to a schematism that links them, the cinema allows Deleuze to focus on the visible (Foucault, by comparison, generally emphasized the articulable). What must be grasped, however, is that this emphasis itself corresponds to new power relations that have begun to leave those of "discipline" behind; the flourishing of our audiovisual culture, especially in the wake of the World War II, corresponds to the emergence of a new *epistēmē*.[105] To map the images and signs of this régime is thus to understand the way forces arrange themselves in our world, and this leads us into the second sense in which cinema functions historically. For Deleuze, the cinema gradually discovers ways to proliferate disjunctions between the visible and the articulable, thereby catalyzing a kind of thought that diverges from strict determination. In *Foucault* (1986), Deleuze writes that

> it is not surprising that the most complete examples of the disjunction between seeing and speaking are to be found in the cinema. In the Straubs, in Syberberg, in Marguerite Duras, the voices emerge, on the one hand, like a story/history [*histoire*] without a place [i.e, without an image], while the visible element, on the other hand, presents an empty place without a story/history [i.e., without a sound image].[106]

These disjunctions disrupt the very continuity of movement-images and, by extension, teleological history: *statements are no longer adequate to determine the visible, to explain our visions*. Deleuze readily admits that new forces of "control" will inevitably put these disjunctions to use, forging vast digital archives, dead spaces that swallow so much vision, but the cinema books hold out hope that this régime can be put to genealogical use—to replace chronology with becoming, to dissolve the structures and habits that govern thought.[107]

The disruption of sayable and seeable bespeaks a historical rupture on either side of which we discover cinematographic régimes—one of which produces a configuration of sayable and seeable according to a determining schematism (sensory-motor schema), and one of which deranges truth conditions. Deleuze is careful to point out that sayable and seeable are never perfectly configured in the first place, truth as such arising from a forced accord, the power of rigid designation to "perform" knowledge in which we can invest belief; as such, truth conditions were bound to fail because the burden they had been given, literally the weight of the world (the assurance of progress, happiness, enlightenment), would come at some point of moral destitution to be reckoned against a world stripped of our good faith, where statements (promises) were no longer sufficient to sway opinion, to make us believe in the "old world." Thus, on either side of this breach—the old world and the new one—a different sign system develops; as Deleuze explains, "one can't say one is 'truer' than the other, because truth as a model or as an Idea is associated with only one [i.e., the first, the older] of the two systems."[108] Deleuze calls the two régimes the "organic" and the "crystalline,"[109] borrowing the distinction from Worringer; as he explains, Worringer "long ago brought out a confrontation in the arts between a 'classic' organic system and an inorganic or crystalline system with no less vitality than the first but a powerful nonorganic, barbarous or gothic life."[110]

But how can we understand these categories vis-à-vis the cinema? In the first essay in this section, "The Film History of Thought," András Bálint Kovács explains that Worringer's categories are in fact psychological, and so we begin to see the outlines of Deleuze's own project. By transposing the organic and the crystalline into quasi-historical categories akin to those devised by Wölfflin or Schiller, Deleuze strives to bring periodization and genetic conditions together. On the one hand, then, the organic and crystalline régime can be aligned with the now conventional distinction between classical and modern cinema; on the other hand, the organic and the crystalline cannot be reduced to, respectively, classical and modern because these régimes refer to the conditions from which forms are made, no less the historical divisions from which forms derive. As Kovács points out, Deleuze's system does not unearth original historical information, nor is it designed to: what is important is the system within which he advances his analyses, for here the accepted notions conditioning history undergo revision. For Kovács, the most significant of these revisions concerns the nature of narrative itself. Modern cinema is often taken to depart from classical narrative insofar as it reflects on itself and the nature of storytelling generally; Deleuze himself superficially echoes this sentiment, but as Kovács points out, closer inspection reveals that the cinema books put forward a more complex and subtle theory of cinematographic transformation. To begin with, the cinematographic image is "a condition, anterior by right to what it conditions";[111] as Deleuze explains elsewhere, "Narrative in the cinema is like the imaginary: it's a very indirect product of motion and time, rather than the other way around."[112] Narration is a "consequence" of images and signs, of their *relations*, and so the broad changes in narrative, from the organic to the crystalline system, extend far beyond a turn toward reflexivity (the cinema, after all, was always a "mixed art," was always reflecting on its place among other arts and its own production) to the most fundamental practice of combining images and creating relations (generally speaking, montage).

What Deleuze calls the organic régime is composed of four different types of montage: (1) the properly organic, which is tantamount to the mode of classical Hollywood cinema; (2) the dialectical, which constitutes Eisenstein's response to the classical; (3) the French, or impressionist, sublime; and (4) the German, or expressionist, sublime. All four modes remain within the sway of the sensory-motor schema, but whereas the first two are based on a principle of action, the latter two produce images and intervals between those images that develop a different relationship to the whole, one that, at moments, already envisions the time-image (as, for instance, in the early Renoir). In a strange sense, then, the first two organic modes are more tenacious, concerned as they are with *economically* channeling affective impulses into a broader narrative drive. Indeed, this is the meaning of Deleuze's more limited sense of narrative, namely, a kind of montage that, having mounted recognizable images or situations, assumes the "normal" functioning of action. In *My Darling Clementine*, for instance, when a "drunk Indian" starts randomly shooting up Dodge City, Wyatt Earp acts to restore order once the action literally incurves around him: Earp is getting a shave when a bullet just misses his head (too close a shave, so to speak), so that his response (disarming the man) is presumed, anticipated, and never in doubt. In this way, the organic model of narrative works on the same principles as those that Deleuze criticizes in the organic model of history (*histoire*): at bottom, both are based on the confidence that history is a coherent progression, one that finally enjoys the reconciliation of an ending, if not an "ending happily ever after." "Cinema always narrates what in the image's movements and times make it narrate," Deleuze writes. "If the motion's governed by a sensory-motor scheme, if it shows a character reacting to a situation, then you get a story."[113]

By contrast, Deleuze says, "suppose a character finds himself in a situation, however ordinary or extraordinary, that's beyond any possible action, or to which he can't react. It's too powerful, or too painful, or too beautiful. The sensory-motor link's broken. He's no longer in a sensory-motor situation but in a purely optical or aural situation."[114] The time-image and the new régime of signs to which it belongs flourish in these situations that preclude action—but where or when do we locate the first hint of these new signs?[115] Angelo Restivo's essay, "Into the Breach: Between *The Movement-Image* and *The Time-Image*," situates this "in-between" as the traumatic point at which we can see the confidence of the action-image disintegrate and the time-image gradually mutate (indeed, if the movement-image "evolves," the time-image "deviates"). Speculating about what caused the rupture, Deleuze mentions "the war and its consequences, the unsteadiness of the 'American Dream' in all its aspects, the new consciousness of minorities, the rise and inflation of images both in the external world and in people's minds, the influence on the cinema of the new modes of narrative with which literature had experimented, the crisis of Hollywood and its old genres."[116] All of these "symptoms" attest to the way action, as a possibility in which to believe, grows increasingly dubious. In this regard, Restivo's essay follows three films—Aldrich's *Kiss Me Deadly* (1955), Antonioni's *Il Grido* (1957), and Hitchcock's *Psycho* (1960)—"each of which falls historically within the chasm" between classical and modern. In each film, Restivo locates a disjunction between sound and image, that is, a point at which the image is derailed by sound (a speech act). The sayable and the seeable no longer accord, and so traditional action misfires. Ideologically speaking, Restivo suggests that these moments of stupefaction are linked to a profound short-circuiting of masculinity. Indeed, as perhaps nowhere else in the cinema books, the failure of the action-image opens up the intriguing, and elusive, question of sexual politics. The lapse of the sensory-motor schema marks a point at which, as we will see, brains and bodies begin to be deterritorialized from rigid identities. Elsewhere Deleuze terms this process "becoming-woman," a kind of "*puisse à la femme*" (Lacan) that is set going when action, which we determine but which also determines us, becomes impossible. These vantages on gender and sexuality are only beginning to be explored, but in the future they will likely play an integral role in any consideration of the cinema books.[117]

From the slackening faith in the action-image to the birth of a new European form or formless form, the coordinates of an epistemic rupture begin to emerge. In this context, the single most important "historical" chapter in the cinema books is the one that concludes *The Movement-Image*. There Deleuze brings together an analysis of Hitchcock with an exegesis of cinematographic signs in order to show how schematic regularity tipped into the "chaosmos" of the crystalline régime. "It was Hitchcock's task," Deleuze explains, "to introduce the mental image into the cinema and to make it the completion of the cinema, the perfection of all other images." Leaning heavily on the work of Rohmer and Chabrol, Deleuze argues that Hitchcock's films suggest a sensibility typical of English analytic philosophy; by "paralyzing his characters" (Jeffries in *Rear Window* remains the greatest example), Hitchcock opens them, and thus the audience, to a "chain of relations which constitutes the mental image, in opposition to the thread of actions, perceptions and affections."[118] Hitchcock thus extends the active principle of thought, or ratiocination, to a point at which the image augurs the "event horizon" of the sensory-motor schema, that is, the point at which the event is not actual in space but affective or virtual in time.

Just as Deleuze relates the Hitchcockian devolution, "a crisis of the traditional image of the cinema,"[119] to Peirce's typology of signs, Laura Marks's essay undertakes the same task with respect to documentary cinema. Like Hitchcock's mental image, Marks argues in "Signs of the Time: Deleuze, Peirce, and the Documentary Image" that recent Lebanese documentaries drive to the very limit of Peirce's initial trajectory/typology of signs. Peirce conceived of signs in terms of firstness, secondness, and thirdness, but, as Marks explains, even before firstness there is a "degree zero" of images, a virtual plane of movement-images (plane of immanence) from which signs take shape. The initial kind of sign to emerge is firstness, an impressionistic and sensible sign that is linked to the affection-image and, especially, to the expressions of the face (faciality). Secondness is the sign to which this affection gives rise, namely, perception, the point at which the affect is distinguished as belonging to a body and a brain. The acts of the body-brain constitute the realm of thirdness, the sign of which, Marks notes, goes beyond action (action was already implied in perception) to mental relations, judgments, and so on. For Deleuze, the ambivalence of thirdness perfectly characterizes Hitchcock: having tried to perfect the action-image and its counterparts, Hitchcock actually effected a "reexamination" of those images, an involution or reflection that finally "unloosened" the sensory-motor schema. Similarly, Marks argues that when documentary begins to examine its own assumptions, especially its notion of reality, it potentially crosses that same threshold into a mental spatium wherein reality itself is derealized.[120]

We might note, in this regard, that *The Time-Image* opens by reevaluating Italian neorealism and, by extension, the very category of reality. Perhaps the most important critical proponent of cinematic realism was André Bazin, who insisted that the facticity of certain cinematic images drew us asymptotically into a relationship to the real (1). For Deleuze, however, this convention maintains perception within stable limits: at most we contrast the real with things "imaginary," but the nature of the distinction reduces thought to the alternation of convention and fancy, each of which stabilizes the other as other. What Deleuze sees in neorealism is, to use a different Bazinian term, an "ambiguity" that confounds the very category of the real. In terms of both narrative and philosophy, realism is essentially based on a distinction between the subject and the world, but in neorealism determinate situations have been replaced by "any-spaces-whatever"—"disused warehouses, waste ground, cities in the course of demolition or reconstruction" (xi). Situations lose their objective assurance, hence the emergence of pure optical and sonic images (opsigns and sonsigns) that have been delinked from the chronological series of the present, cut off from motor extension, from action. Indeed, the characters of modern cinema are no longer those who act, but rather those who see. Modern cinema is populated by a "new race of characters" (xi) who are compelled to witness the world, yet who are entirely unsure of what they witness, lost in the thrall of an "uncertainty principle" (71). In every sense of the word, these characters are "visionaries," and the kind of narratives they provoke diverge from the solidity—which is to say, the conventions, the habits—of the sensory-motor schema. Where classical cinema strove to maintain the world within unequivocal terms, producing a schematic series of images and thereby reducing time itself to that causal succession, the crystalline narrative is characterized by its directionlessness, a kind of meandering that refuses resolution. In this context, Deleuze often invokes the notion of the *bal(l)ade* to characterize modern cinema, for here the film is wedded to a wandering movement in which anything or nothing can happen (as Bazin writes of *The Bicycle Thief*, for example, "A downpour forces the father and son to shelter in a carriageway, so like them we have to forego the chase and wait till the storm is over").[121]

In modern cinema, images cease to conform to tonal rhythms; the most spectacular moments give way to the most banal ones and vice versa, without any sense of rational logic. In the end, the cinema "trips" into an ambiguity so overwhelming that the imaginary and the real become indiscernible[122] (or, as Deleuze says in *The Fold*, "*every perception is hallucinatory*").[123] Broadly construed, the second cinema book supplants the very distinction between real and imaginary, which is ideally suited to the sensory-motor schema, with the distinction between "actual" and "virtual."[124] The notion of the virtual, which is ubiquitous in Deleuze's work, is one of the richest and most difficult aspects of his philosophy. At the most fundamental level, Deleuze affirms that the plane of immanence is a virtual plane, and that the virtual as such should not be taken to mean the possible; the virtual is not imaginary but real in the sense in which it is the reservoir on which thought draws in order to bring about the actual.

In terms of the cinema, the image is actualized from a virtual plane, but it is paradoxically at the point when images become ambiguous—when we cannot tell what is real and what is imagined, what has happened in the past and what is happening in the present—that we begin to see the outlines of how Deleuze understands the virtual aspect of the cinema. Instrumental in this shift is the increasing emphasis on memory in modern cinema, for, although memory existed in classical cinema (say, as flashbacks), the past was always demarcated as such; by contrast, the present in modern cinema seems almost to lapse into the past, or the past to overtake the present.

Now, what is actual is present, but the nature of memory in modern cinema confuses the distinction between actual and virtual, past and present. Images are always surfacing from the past because, as Deleuze quotes Fellini, "We are constructed in memory."[125] Indeed, one can imagine, as Bergson does, that the subject is the point at which images are involuted, such that while we respond in motor movements to images, images are also doubled in memory; the image that gives way to new images in the present is thus reflected and preserved in memory—a vast virtual reservoir of images, the recollection of which produces so many circuits, links between past and present.[126] What this means is that at the most contracted point of these circuits, present and past, actual and virtual converge. Whereas the sensory-motor schema "looked for bigger and bigger circuits which would unite an actual image with recollection-images, dream-images and world-images," the crystalline régime discovers "the smallest circuit that functions as an internal limit for all the others and that puts the actual image beside a kind of immediate, symmetrical, consecutive or even simultaneous double."[127] At the indiscernible point of the crystal, "the image has to be present and past, still present and already past, at once and at the same time.... The past does not follow the present that it is no longer, it coexists with the present it was."[128] From this node, then, time "rises up to the surface of the screen" because the succession of moments/movements engineered by action has given way to presents lapsing back into the past and a past flooding the present.[129]

The régime (not regimen) of these crystal images and signs is elaborated in three general narrative types, which Deleuze calls "description," "narration" (i.e., narration proper), and "story" (*récit*).[130] In descriptions, such as those we find in neorealism, images cease to refer to an object, because reference or representation always takes place in the present (as Deleuze quotes Godard, the present "never exists . . . except in bad films").[131] Taking up this cue, crystalline narration formulates narration that "ceases to be truthful, that is, to claim to be true" (131), which is to say that narration emerges as a power of the false. Finally, the third type, and perhaps the most developed, is the "story" (*récit*); as Deleuze writes, "the story in general concerns the subject-object relationship" (147), that is, the model of adequation and, thus, truth. "The story no longer refers to an ideal of the true which constitutes its veracity, but becomes a 'pseudo-story', a poem, a story which simulates or rather a simulation of a story" (149). To put it another way, the story is based on irrational linkages, a practice of false continuity in which images coagulate and disperse, in which we experience the world as a field of forces. In this respect, each of these three successive modes of modern cinema underscores a critical point at which the organic (or kinetic) régime gives way to the crystalline (or chronic) régime:

1. In contrast to the separation between subject and object that characterizes the organic régime, such that settings and situations seem to exist independently of the camera, the crystalline régime evokes images as "descriptions." In other words, images are tantamount to our descriptions of them, "purely optical and sound situations detached from their motor extension" (126).
2. In contrast to the poles that defined the organic régime, namely, the real and the imaginary, the crystalline régime both confounds this relation and introduces the more genetic opposition on which real and imaginary are based, namely, the actual and the virtual. As Deleuze writes, "the actual is cut off from its motor linkages, or the real from its legal connections, and the virtual, for its part, detaches itself from its actualizations, starts to be valid for itself" (127).
3. In contrast to the Euclidean or hodological spaces of the organic régime, defined as this was by "a field of forces, oppositions and tensions between these forces, resolutions of these tensions according to the distribution of goals, obstacles, means, detours," the crystalline régime develops narration out of anomalies, irregularities, and false continuity. This *fluctuatio animi*, from which the centering of the sensory-motor schema evolved, is rediscovered in new cinematic spaces that Deleuze characterizes as alternately Riemanian, probabilistic, and topological (127–28).

In all of this, one must keep in mind that these coordinates are elaborated with respect to the "soul of the cinema," a kind of ideal (or idealized) cinema in which Deleuze is interested for reasons that we are beginning to clarify.[132] Whereas the "greatest commercial successes" will always follow the "route" of the sensory-motor schema, and whereas blockbusters will always draw on the drive of action-images (perhaps even more resolutely now that the possibility of old-style action, of acting in real life, increasingly seems implausible, or at best a kind of parody), the "soul" will always follow a different path. *The Time-Image* tracks the emergence of new images, signs, and ultimately the development of these new stories, the result of which is a "tendency," a kind of "line of flight" that the cinema follows after the war; as Deleuze says, "[t]he timing is something like: around 1948, Italy; about 1958, France; about 1968, Germany."[133] Given as much, Deleuze makes no pretense to broad historical coverage (so many different offshoots of cinema are left out, and others receive surprisingly minimal treatment). But if we cannot fault Deleuze for the selections that make up this lineage, we can nevertheless wonder what is to become of this lineage. Is it possible to understand the cinema books with respect to the trends of contemporary cinema? If we take the organic and the crystalline to match up with the classical and the modern, can we speak of another phase, the postmodern?[134]

All of the aforementioned essays in this section broach this question, though the first two seem particularly in line with Deleuze's sense, inherited in part from Serge Daney, of a postmodern phase of cinematic "mannerism," such that the proliferation of images threatens to extinguish nature itself.[135] By contrast, in "The Roots of the Nomadic: Gilles Deleuze and the Cinema of West Africa," Dudley Andrew pursues a different path: following Deleuze's own impulse, late in the second cinema book, to look to "minor cinema," Andrew argues that the creative impulse (or "soul") of cinema has shifted to places such as West Africa. Film scholars have traditionally termed this "third cinema," thereby aligning it with the Third World, but Andrew and Deleuze stress the minor as a kind of cinematic dialect developing within a dominant tradition. In *Kafka*, Deleuze and Guattari define minor literature as "that which a minority constructs within a major language," the result of which is that the dominant ceases to secure our belief.[136] Deleuze transposes these terms to the "mass art" of the cinema, arguing that "[t]he death-knell for becoming conscious was precisely the consciousness that there were no people, but always several peoples, an infinity of peoples, who remained to be united, or should not be united, in order for the problem to change."[137] Andrew's essay aims to balance this sense of "a people who are missing" with a vibrant West African cinema, the politics of which, he argues, remains inextricably tied to the idea of a people, a past, and a memory. The tension is perfectly conveyed by the notion of nomadism, of a people whose itinerant ways must, as Deleuze says, be understood as the result of having been *deprived* of their land (habitus or territory): "The land ceases to be land, tending to become simply ground (*sol*) or support."[138] Ultimately, this explains why Deleuze transposes nomadism into a formula for thought: life without ground, cinema without centering, philosophy without *cogitatio universalis* . . .

THINKING IMAGES

What do we mean by "thinking images"? In *The Movement-Image*, Deleuze says that the brain is a very special kind of image, one that opens up an interval in the modulations and variations of the universe. This interval propels what is called thinking, but only insofar as it is preparatory to action: in the interval, a momentary delay, perception is transformed into action, which is to say, a re-action to a given set of images (situation). In the cinema, which initially evolved according to this model, thinking followed the imperative of action and so thinking itself became a reflex. For this reason, Deleuze insists in the cinema books that the brain, our thinking image, "has not even begun to think" (Heidegger).[139] While thought is thrust by the cinema into a circuit of automatic movement, the result of which is a "spiritual automaton," what Benjamin described as a shock to the system,[140] these affections are directed, converted, and ultimately *contained*.

The process of containment begins at the most basic level of spectatorship because what the viewer perceives is "a sensory-motor image in which he takes a greater or lesser part by identification with the characters."[141] Characters are determined within a sensory-motor schema, positioned as points of fluxion control through which predictable chains of action and reaction stream, and so our identification with those characters necessarily implies the impoverishment of the image.[142] We do not perceive the "thing in itself," Deleuze says, because "we do not perceive the thing or the image in its entirety, we always perceive less of it, we perceive only what we are interested in perceiving, or rather what it is in our interest to perceive, by virtue of our economic interests, ideological beliefs, and psychological demands."[143] Of course, the question of ideology has long preoccupied film studies, from broad-based considerations of the cinematic apparatus to criticism of the conventions of editing and narrative. Deleuze seems to tilt toward the latter end of the spectrum, but the resemblance is superficial:[144] not only does Deleuze refuse to discuss the cinema in terms of representation, which remains the conventional point of departure for such ideological analyses, but he regards the very categories of representation as the primary target of the cinematic "war machine." The cinema realizes its potential when it begins to falsify, to engage with "powers of the false" and simulacra in order to reveal those categories as the purveyors of "ideological beliefs." In this sense, Deleuze's cinematographic project proceeds in the same vein in which Nietzsche returned to Kant's transcendental idealism, for that "revaluation of values" was intended to extend the force of critique to the transcendental categories themselves, to discern the hidden morality sustaining the ostensibly impersonal and metaphysical labor of determining judgments.

Whence the transition, in this third section, to an ethical consideration of cinema, the crux of which is an effort to liberate the "image of thought" from its hidden moral foundations: as Godard writes and Deleuze repeats, "pas une image juste, juste une image." The matrix of morality ("une image juste") is the sensory-motor schema, which initially appears to be the simple "nature" of subject and cinema alike—an uncomplicated relation to the world that unhesitatingly triggers action. But the "common sense" of the sensory-motor schema is underwritten (though unsigned) by a whole moral-normal regimen. The very disinterestedness of this metaphysical relay is, as far as Deleuze is concerned, as bogus as political neutrality—not only a contradiction but a cover that allows an "axis" or "dimension" of power to go undetected, passing as transcendental legislation, the way things are.[145] The ostensible impartiality of the sensory-motor schema is nourished by the discovery and prosecution of aberrance, of any kind of thinking otherwise, which the "rational orthodoxy" labels as deviant.[146] Images we cannot recognize, events that elude our understanding, are quickly consigned to error, which in turn sustains the sovereign principle of regulated thought because error "pays homage to the 'truth.'..." This is why Deleuze lingers on "judicial" films, for they provide the most literal instance of the more generalized narrative mechanism of the classical cinema—to develop normal causal connections ("legal connections in space and chronological connections in time")[147] by determining abnormality in the name of higher values, and then to subject abnormality to action as a corrective or reactive force.[148] "Narration always refers to a *system of judgment*," [149] Deleuze writes, but the catch is that the sensory-motor schema is in a position to script its own story, one in which it appears as the unprepossessing protagonist, *cogitatio natura universalis*, whose every encounter is that of innocent observation or honest adequation. Such is the "cunning of power" that we are seduced into this story as if it were our own, and so we submit to, and even support, the circumscription of thought. As Deleuze and Guattari write at the outset of *Anti-Oedipus* (echoing Spinoza and Reich), "Why do men fight *for* their servitude as stubbornly as if it were their salvation?"[150]

Consider in this context Deleuze's brief, even reductive, foray into English Romanticism in the last chapter of *The Movement-Image*. While the Romantics attempted, in Wordsworth's words, to "follow the fluxes and refluxes of the mind when agitated by the great and simple affections of our nature,"[151] Deleuze suggests that the affective encounters are converted, plotted, raised to speculations about an overarching *"organisation of misery"* or "empire of poverty" (take, for instance, "The Old Cumberland Beggar"). "We see, and we more or less experience, a powerful organization of poverty and oppression," Deleuze explains. "And we are precisely not without sensory-motor schema for recognizing such things, for putting up with and approving of them and for behaving ourselves subsequently, taking into account our situation, our capabilities and our tastes."[152] Even at the point when it faces the "the intolerable or the unbearable," the sensory-motor schema contrives common sense by com-prehending the world, as Deleuze claims of postwar American conspiracy cinema. Admittedly, the system in which we find ourselves does suggest an "organization of Power" to which conspiracy generically and cognitively conforms, as Fredric Jameson has argued;[153] but precisely the point at which one presumes this organization in the world, *as* the world, power eludes us, for the organization or conspiracy we "discover" is symptomatic of the resilience of our own sensory-motor schema—a schema that, rather than folding, raises the stakes once more, mounting a paranoid, globalizing explanation, locating the cause for our sick society in whatever deviance certifies the scheme's own normality (the exception proves the rule). Indeed, this is the purpose of the sensory-motor schema—to secure common sense when sense seems most in jeopardy.

How, then, do we get out of this system or invent a better one? Or, as Deleuze wonders, "how can the cinema attack the dark organisation of clichés, when it participates in their fabrication and propagation, as much as magazines or television?"[154] The answer begins with the understanding that a "cliché is a sensory-motor image of the thing,"[155] the reduction of an image to a point of discernibility that Deleuze calls metaphor. Given Deleuze's own descriptive inclination, his penchant for borrowing and inventing new terms, this condemnation of metaphor would seem peculiar. Perhaps the explanation lies in the sense that Deleuze's own images (the crystal, the body without organs, and so on) are expressive-intensive symbols, whereas metaphor-images are tantamount to "evasions"—they "furnish us with something to say when we no longer know what to do: they are specific schemata of an affective nature." When an image grows "too powerful, or too unjust, but sometimes also too beautiful," we grope for metaphor in order to subtract something from the image and thereby subsume it to what we know.[156] This is precisely the process of determining judgment, and as such Deleuze suggests that the shift away from metaphor in modern cinema is effectively a shift to reflective judgment. Of course, the distinction between determining judgment and reflective judgment is lifted from Kant, who formalized it in his third *Critique*. As far as Deleuze is concerned, though, there is a fundamental similarity between these two classes of judgment, for both are based on an "art of invention." The difference is that, in determining judgment, the activity of subsumption or determination is mandated to the schemata wherein the art is "hidden." The schemata are the rules of determination according to which one faculty governs another, but the schemata themselves are shrouded in a "mystery" that conceals the fact that even the rules, no less all conditions of possibility, are created. By contrast, Deleuze writes, "in reflective judgment nothing is given from the standpoint of the active faculties"; in other words, there is no preexistent concept, nor any governance of one faculty by another but, rather, "*a free and indeterminate accord* between all the faculties." As a result, reflective judgment implies the capacity to disclose "a depth that remains hidden" in determining judgment: that which was concealed by determination—the forced accord, the role of power, the contrivance of the schemata—is revealed in reflective judgment.[157]

In refashioning this distinction in the context of the cinema, Deleuze discusses reflection in terms of what he calls "legibility." Images in the classical sense were aligned with the visible or seeable that statements determined (in short, metaphors), but the legible implies a disjunction between determination and visibility that opens the image to a new indeterminacy (new signs).[158] In modern cinema, in other words, images are delinked from any determining schematism, and so what was an enchainment of images becomes a series in which each image is de-framed in relation to the image that follows it, producing a kind of space *between* images wherein thought lingers, oscillates, hallucinates ... Rather than being governed by any category, then, this series moves "in the direction of a category in which it is reflected:"[159] judgment is reflected into the category, derealizing the blanket claim of/to common sense, at which point we see the architecture of power (the thing in itself or what Foucault calls a "diagram") for what it is. For instance, in Rossellini's *Europa '51* (*The Greatest Love*), when the young woman catches sight of workers leaving a factory, Deleuze seizes on her train of thought as the essence of this reflection, for, in the hallucinatory moment, she locates the singularity pattern of another power formation: "I thought I was seeing convicts." The sensory-motor schema has broken, Deleuze explains, unleashing

> the whole image without metaphor, [which] brings out the thing in itself, literally, in its excess of horror or beauty, in its radical or unjustifiable character, because it no longer has to be "justified," for better or worse ... The factory creature gets up, and we can no longer say "Well, people have to work ..." *I thought I was seeing convicts:* the factory is a prison, school is a prison, literally, not metaphorically.[160]

In one sense, *The Time-Image* is largely conditioned by derealization; after all, Deleuze begins the book by dismantling the very category of reality as that which is "represented or reproduced."[161] But the particular evocation of reflective judgment, of an image torn from metaphor, remains perhaps the most elusive aspect of the cinema books—not only does it assume a qualitative change in images and relations but, as such, it assumes the invention of a kind of cinema that, with a few exceptions (Deleuze mentions Rossellini, Resnais, and especially Godard), is exceedingly difficult to nail down. One can go so far as to say that dealing with the second cinema book forces us to imagine, in the spirit of Bazin, a cinema that "has not yet been invented," a cinema of pure potentiality.[162] To understand such a cinema, or the passage to it that Deleuze proposes, one must grasp the strange diptych that the cinema books formulate, for if the brain is a screen, as *The Movement-Image* announces, then *The Time-Image* affirms that the cinema itself is a kind of brain. Drawing on neuroscience, Deleuze describes the brain as "a relatively undifferentiated mass" in which circuits "aren't there to begin with"; for this reason, "[c]reating new circuits in art means creating them in the brain too." The cinema does more than create circuits, though, because, like a brain, it consists in a complexity of images, imbricated and folded into so many lobes, connected by so many more circuits. While the cinema can simply reiterate the facile circuits of the brain, appealing to "arbitrary violence and feeble eroticism,"[163] it can also jump those old grooves, emancipating us from the typical image-rhythms, the calculable flow of images, opening us to a "thought that stands outside subjectivity, setting its limits as though from without, articulating its end, making its dispersion shine forth, taking in only its invisible absence."[164]

In "Cinema and the Outside," the essay that opens this section, Gregg Lambert discusses the promise of cinema, as both art and science, for delivering thought from the circuitry of ideology. Lambert begins by considering Sergei Eisenstein, one of the few directors to whom Deleuze turns in both cinema books. The significance of Eisenstein lies in the cinematographic shock he inaugurates, a "feeling" of thought that augurs a new cinematographic way of thinking. In one sense, then, Eistenstein reveals the shift from classical to modern cinema insofar as he stakes out a kind of "fourth dimension" that is the subject's attempt to think the whole[165] (Eisenstein, Deleuze writes, is a "cinematographic Hegel").[166] Thinking the whole is akin to the dynamism of the sublime, but, as Lambert shows, this confrontation with chaos or "total provocation of the brain" (nooshock) can be mobilized for the project of nationalist or fascist cinema. The sublime effectively gives rise to two impulses, one venturing into destabilization and one "redeeming" it as the prelude to sublation, and it is the latter that, broadly interpreted, inclines toward ideology or propaganda. In effect, the art of the masses turns "thinking the whole" into the "subject as whole," a collective: "the mass-art, the treatment of masses, which should not have been separable from an accession of the masses to the status of true subject, has degenerated into state propaganda and manipulation, into a kind of fascism which brought together Hitler and Hollywood, Hollywood and Hitler."[167]

As Lambert explains, modern cinema in the Deleuzian sense follows the other, destabilizing path, in which the brain experiences the image as a shock wave that cripples its capacity to reconstitute any habitus. The power matrix relents to "a recognition of powerlessness, which does not yet have a bearing *on* cinema, but on the contrary defines the real object-subject of cinema. What cinema advances is not the power of thought but its 'impower' [*impouvoir*], and thought has never had any other problem."[168] For Deleuze, philosophy is always more intimately concerned with problems than with answers because a problem not only coordinates the invention of concepts but, in fact, presses thought to its limit, namely, its exhaustion or "impower."[169] Thought has never had any other problem than the problem of thought itself, which is what remains unthought, unthinkable, and above all outside. This is the kind of cinema for which, contra Eisenstein, Artaud had hoped: "It might be said that Artaud turns round Eisenstein's argument: if it is true that thought depends on a shock which gives birth to it (the nerve, the brain matter), it can only think one thing, *the fact that we are not yet thinking*, the powerlessness to think the whole and to think oneself, thought which is always fossilized, dislocated, collapsed."[170] But what brings about this possibility, what triggers our powerlessness?

For Deleuze, the question begins with the war, in whose wake even Hollywood cinema, the cinema of the "victors," appears somehow untenable. The old genres begin to contort into parodic forms (*Johnny Guitar*), or the distance between what is remembered and our disenchanted present triggers sickening nostalgia (*The Green Berets*), or else the frustration and misery become the basis for paranoia (*The Parallax View*).[171] These are, however, only symptoms of a trauma that European cinema sustains full force: whereas Hollywood still holds tight to the empty husk of an "American Dream" (albeit often negatively, cynically), in Europe the annihilation of the war is the substance of daily experience, a bad dream from which there is no waking up. Especially in the aftermath of the Holocaust, which effectively obliterated any attempt to "make sense," the old-style narrative seems impossible. The system of Truth or sensory-motor schema, which was entrusted with intelligibility even at the cost of illusion, is no longer up to the task: no explanation, no statement, can adequately respond to these images. When Deleuze says that "[t]he most 'healthy' illusions fall,"[172] he means precisely that in the face of these images the eternal and transcendental categories cannot be sustained, and that perhaps the categories themselves are what produced an abomination like Auschwitz and its "healthy" production of corpses.[173]

Like literature, which Deleuze defines as an art of life, the cinema is forced to discover a new kind of health in the nauseating, devastated, death-strewn landscape of the postwar. Deleuze calls this the "powerful, non-organic Life which grips the world,"[174] for it is a force of Life that explodes the organic, teleological premises of faith in any guiding force. In the past, God was entrusted, à la Leibniz, with choosing the best of all possible worlds (*Harmonia Praestabilita*), which effectively meant letting other (not so good) alternatives branch off into the purgatory of nonactualization; in other words, this God sorted through the permutations of all eventualities, all the possible branchings of and in time, selecting the one world in which we find ourselves. But in the modern world, where the suprasensible "has lost its effective force in history" (Heidegger), order has been undermined, "incompossible" eventualities intrude and confabulate our own, and not even the dead can be counted on to remain that way (in the modern era, what is memory if not resurrection?). This explains Deleuze's consistent recourse to Resnais, whom he considers the cine-philosopher par excellence because, like all philosophers—those who "have passed through a death," who are perched "between two deaths" (past and future)[175]—Resnais creates images that have returned from the dead, whether from the Holocaust (*Night and Fog*), the atomic blast (*Hiroshima, mon amour*), war (*Muriel*), or some other, unspeakable trauma (*Last Year at Marienbad*). The image is an aftermath of the trauma, the shattering of the present into so many shards that, like flaneurs, we labor to collect, each of us consigned to tracing different, incommensurable lines of this distended world-memory. In *Last Year in Marienbad*, for instance, different characters assume different presents, "so that each forms a combination that is plausible and possible in itself, but where all of them together are 'incompossible', and where the inexplicable is thereby maintained and created."[176]

Forced to try to reconcile incompossibilities, to make common sense, the dogmatic image of thought begins to suffer from contradiction, from disjunction (no longer either/or but both either and or). Regularity has been deranged, triggering the transformation that Éric Alliez explores in the second essay in this section, "Midday, Midnight: The Emergence of Cine-Thinking." Alliez begins by returning to Deleuze's reading of Bergson, but in so doing he explains that Bergson has effectively become the occasion for Deleuze's own philosophy, that Deleuze's is a "Bergsonism beyond Bergson."[177] This perfectly encapsulates Deleuze's sense of philosophical "apprenticeship" and his own immanent philosophical method: what appears to be the explication of another philosopher (or an auteur, in the context of certain directors in cinema books) is in fact a kind of free indirect discourse, a philosophical ventriloquism whereby Deleuze speaks through another. The point at which Deleuze and Bergson diverge, according to Alliez, involves not only the cinema but its promise as a "thinking image": whereas Bergson retreats from it, Deleuze gravitates toward the cinematographic image because its affect *"relates thinking to a perception that no longer passes into action."* When perception encounters pure optical images, images it cannot recognize or explain, the heterogeneity of affect refuses the conversion into action; the continuity from perception to action is disrupted, as in an irrational cut, and suddenly we find ourselves thinking the affect itself—thinking the virtual, the outside.

This transformation is tantamount, as Alliez suggests, to the shift from delimited affection to self-affection, the latter of which is, not incidentally, Kant's formula for the subject. For Kant, the old unity of the subject (Ego = Ego) has given way to a subject divided by time (as Rimbaud affirms, "I is another"), such that the subject is compelled by the interiorization time to think or affect itself. The problem of this design, which is no less the problem of Kant's metaphysics, is that the interiority of time still permits the possibility of compartmentalization, for the subject can withdraw part of itself (apperceptive unity) from the flux of the world. Whereas Heidegger in his own way attempts to overcome this organization from the inside by smuggling time into the above (faculty of understanding),[178] Deleuze suggests that the inside must be opened to the outside so that it is no longer time that is inside of us but we who are inside of time—folded in its crest, like a surfer riding its wave down into a pipeline of "pure virtuality which divides itself from itself in two as affector and affected, 'the affection of self by self' as definition of time."[179] Indeed, when the wave of time curls over, thought is thrust into a perilous yet invigorating interval, a feeling of life (élan vital)—belonging to no moment yet carried by the momentum, we share in the dynamism of a flow by which we are affected and which we affect, yet which we are also "in between."[180]

Deleuze calls this the "pure force of becoming," the result of a profound loss of ground (deterritorialization) that releases thought from the principle of identity / unity, that is, a return to the same place or repetition without difference. In *A Thousand Plateaus*, Deleuze and Guattari already linked becoming to an interval, the "substance" of which is affection, such that with each thought the thinker is altered (principle of mutation/multiplicity);[181] but in the cinema books, Deleuze returns to and refines the notion of becoming according to the way images are combined. Tom Conley's essay, "The Film Event: From Interval to Interstice," considers a number of Deleuze's texts (as well as Montaigne's) in order to explain this complex notion of the linking, and delinking, of images. Like Alliez, Conley dwells on the "nonactualizable" aspect of the image, or "event," as the point at which the image must be thought. In classical cinema, the event is the interval, though it is an interval that has been circumscribed, rendered the regulative mechanism that both divides and links series of images; rather than open up to becoming, the interval is relegated by the sensory-motor schema to the contrivance of commensurability or what Deleuze calls, in the mathematical sense, "rationality." Deleuze writes that "whatever the importance of the discovery, this interval [*écart*] remained subject to an integrating whole which was embodied in it, and to associations which traversed it."[182] The interval, in short, was remanded by the schema to rationally linking images, thereby making it the accomplice of action, which itself linked spaces and situations: such is the logic of montage that "constitute[s] the whole rhythmic system and harmony of classical cinema."[183] Indeed, classical cinema produces an image-track the linkages of which are sufficiently predictable to overcome even moments of aberrance (say, the crossing of the 180-degree line in *Stagecoach*); but, as Conley explains, the logic of the interval radically changes in modern cinema.

At the point when the sensory-motor schema begins to lack conviction, cinema begins to waver from established rhythms. To begin with, pure optical and sound images (opsigns and sonsigns) no longer function as mere instances of aberrance that can be overcome, but now function as the very terms under which modern cinema operates: there is no action that can broach the interval. Images cannot be linked spatially, and so there emerges a system of false continuity whereby "the cut begins to have an importance in itself. The cut, or interstice, between two images no longer forms part of either of the two series: it is the equivalent of an irrational cut, which determines the non-commensurable relations between images."[184] As Conley writes, "The interstice is the interval turned into something infraliminary in a continuum in which an event can no longer be awarded the stability of a 'place' in the space of the image." The distinction here between the delimited interval and the interstice that opens up in modern cinema—a distinction that lies at the heart of becoming—can be grasped along the lines of Deleuze's occasional references to a Markoff chain. "Distinguished from both determined linkages and chance distributions," a Markoff chain "concern[s] semi-accidental phenomena or mixtures of dependency and uncertainty."[185] The "determined linkages" correspond, of course, to the sensory-motor schema, in which the interval is made the mechanism for the rational succession of images. In other words, the sensory-motor schema establishes a feedback loop that produces a regular image-flow, but modern cinema delinks and deframes images, severing the feedback loop from any sense of predictability. The Markoff chain introduces chance into the image-flow, such that the between of images precludes anticipative expedience. Deleuze is careful to distinguish this from purely accidental linkages; like the rebel commander in Woody Allen's *Bananas* who launches a successful revolution and then declares, as his first order of business, that "all children under the age of sixteen years old are now officially sixteen years old," purely accidental linkages reduce thought to arbitrary judgment, to the absurdity of random whim, whereas what interests Deleuze is precisely the way chance introduces invention into thought. In the Markoff chain, each new image retroactively introduces a new relation among the series of preceding images, and so the image to follow is subjected to rules that must be constantly reinvented; the rule is—*improvise*.

No longer the circumscribed event, the between of images becomes the event of thought; as Deleuze explains, this "is the method of AND, 'this and then that,' which does away with all the cinema of Being = is."[186] The identity in which being, or beings, rested is deterritorialized by time and its concomitant powers of the false, the result of which is a "being of becoming"—the loss of a priori ground or, more precisely, the positing of chaos as the a priori. In the last essay in this section, "The Imagination of Immanence: An Ethics of Cinema," Peter Canning attempts to gauge this deterritorialization, not only in terms of the cinema but also in terms of the loss of stable (moral) subjectivity. Canning follows deterritorialization as the trajectory from schematic assurances to the terrifying liberation to which modern (and postmodern) life is increasingly drawn. In the beginning, the sensory-motor schema is organized by the categories of representation, which Canning identifies with the signifier; as he explains, "The sign-image chain is an endopsychic (internalized) theater of intensities produced by semiotic elements arranged to perform social structures." Subject and society are organically organized by the signifier, which generates a logic of deprivation and exceptionality: identity is procured by scapegoating those outside the pale, the result of which is a narrative or group psychology at once dependent on yet sworn to destroy the anomaly. Canning thus extends the organicism of classical cinema to a "hidden narrative" of community and fantasy, but the trajectory of cinema suggests that the story of our century is the contrapuntal dwindling of this narrative efficacy and the foreclosure of the signifier that conditions it. The modern cinema is thus the avatar of an "ethico-aesthetic" experiment, for deterritorialization means this: the annihilation of transcendental underpinnings, of any sense of preexistent structure.[187]

This separation of life from ground ("the earth") is what we find in the schizophrenic—the "body without organs." Deleuze's consistent recourse to schizophrenia is by no means a simple advocacy, nor a "question of opposing to the dogmatic image of thought another image." Rather, schizophrenia expresses a "possibility for thought"[188] that lies in the abolition of the dogmatic image—a possibility that, as such, also lies at the heart of modern cinema and its derealization of illusions. On the face of it, this is a terrifying outcome, an exile to an outpost of suffering where endless attempts to "pull things together" are measured against the inevitable disinheritance of the world of meaning, of that symbolic "credibility"[189] without which life always threatens to unravel (as in Cassavetes' *Woman under the Influence*). In this awful purgatory "Eros is dead," the world is infected by disbelief, and faith (or, in Freudian terms, libido) is withdrawn from the institutions that structured human life: it is in this hallucinatory light that we see that factories are prisons, that "children are political prisoners" (Godard), that the cogito is a fraud—but what or where does that leave us? As Deleuze writes, "in our universal schizophrenia, *we need reasons to believe in this world.*"[190] This is the real task of modern cinema—to return to us the world, *"this world."* To do so requires that we refuse to nominate knowledge as the medium through which that return takes place, for knowledge reinvokes the whole logic of territorialization, of clichés, of illusions, of globalizing explanations (as Lacan says, all knowledge is paranoid); rather, the link to this world must be "an object of belief."[191] What this means is the end of divine or structural mediation—in Canning's words, "learn[ing] to *think without Law,* without Father, to develop an *absolute ethics* that begins where symbolic-moral mediation leaves off and an aesthetic experience of nonrelation begins." We must learn, then, to affirm a landscape where lying and trickery mingle with "grace and chance,"[192] for these are the elements of a world devoid of Truth.

Just for a moment, then, forget about the subject, quit looking for the old metaphysical-moral compass, stop worrying that the "center cannot hold," and imagine a world where "force no longer refers to a centre, any more than it confronts a setting or obstacles. It only confronts other forces, it refers to other forces, that it affects or that affect it."[193] This world, as Robert Musil once wrote, "of qualities without a man"[194] unfurls and folds, refulgent with singularities, the constituents of images and signs that filter through us, affect us, such that "we" are diffused into the flux, "our" molecules seeping into "all the names of history" (Nietzsche). We have returned to the place, or plane, of immanence with which we began, a metacinema where we extract ourselves from chaos, where life is always in the process of becoming, of creating, of thinking. Such is the sentiment with which Deleuze concluded his own oeuvre, and the one with which our investigation of the cinema begins: "L'immanence: une vie . . ."[195]

NOTES

A great deal of what I have said here is indebted to conversations I have had with Peter Canning; also, I would like to thank Gregg Lambert, whose expertise and patience I have drawn on continually.

1. Gilles Deleuze, *The Movement-Image*, trans. Hugh Tomlinson and Barbara Habberjam (Minneapolis: University of Minnesota Press, 1986), 3.
2. Gilles Deleuze and Félix Guattari, *Anti-Oedipus: Capitalism and Schizophrenia*, trans. Robert Hurley, Mark Seem, and Helen R. Lane (Minneapolis: University of Minnesota Press, 1983), 91.
3. Nietzsche's statement is drawn from a section of *Ecce Homo*, "The Untimely Ones," in which he pauses for a moment on Stendahl. One suspects that Nietzsche had in mind Stendahl's famous statement: "I have drawn a lottery ticket whose first prize amounts to this: to be read in 1935." See *On the Genealogy of Morals* and *Ecce Homo*, trans. Walter Kaufmann (New York: Random House, 1967), 280.
4. Serge Toubiana, "Le cinéma est deleuzien," in *Cahiers du cinéma*, no. 497 (December 1995): 20.
5. As early as 1976, Deleuze had established a relationship with *Cahiers du cinéma* when the magazine interviewed him about Godard's television series *Six fois deux*. See Deleuze's "Three Questions on *Six Times Two*," in *Negotiations, 1972–1990*, trans. Martin Joughin (New York: Columbia University Press, 1995).
6. It should be pointed out, though, that in crucial ways the tendencies of French film studies followed a route laid out by Deleuze himself, most notably with Félix Guattari in *Anti-Oedipus*. The antistructural and, indeed, antipsychoanalytic

thrust was one in a series of backlashes against a kind of thinking dominated by the signifier—backlashes that can be traced back to the events of May 1968, one of the slogans of which was "la structure ne marche pas." See "Gilles Deleuze and Félix Guattari on *Anti-Oedipus*," in *Negotiations*, 13–24.

7. Deleuze makes ample reference to all three, and he eventually wrote the preface to Daney's collection, *Ciné-Journal* (the piece is reprinted as "A Letter to Serge Daney: Optimism, Pessimism, and Travel," in *Negotiations*). What Deleuze finds in each is a kind of thinking that moves away from psychoanalytic and structuralist models.
8. D. N. Rodowick, *Gilles Deleuze's Time Machine* (Durham, N.C.: Duke University Press, 1997), ix.
9. I borrow the phrase from the impressive collection *Gilles Deleuze: une vie philosophique*, ed. Éric Alliez (Luisant: Synthélabo, 1998).
10. As D. N. Rodowick claims, "There has been little sustained dialogue on the place of the cinema books, either as interventions in contemporary film theory or as part of Deleuze's larger philosophical project.... Deleuze's study of film has had comparatively little impact on contemporary anglophone film theory" (*iris* 23 [spring, 1997]: 3). It also seems to me that part of the problem for English audiences may have been the unofficial title of the two volumes, "the cinema books"—a title that likely developed as shorthand for the confusing variety of ways the books are cited in English but that has finally come to seem suited to the audacity of Deleuze's enterprise.
11. See Jonathan Rosenbaum, *Placing Movies: The Practice of Film Criticism* (Berkeley: University of California Press, 1995), 180–81. Rosembaum reserves a fair amount of blame for Deleuze's translators, though his criticism of Deleuze, especially his passages on Orson Welles, seems to me excessive.
12. The phrase here is a play on Foucault's description of *Anti-Oedipus* as an "Introduction to Non-Fascist Life." See Foucault's preface to *Anti-Oedipus*, xiii.
13. Gilles Deleuze and Félix Guattari, *Kafka: Toward a Minor Literature*, trans. Dana Polan (Minneapolis: University of Minnesota Press, 1986), 27.
14. See Gilles Deleuze and Félix Guattari, *A Thousand Plateaus: Capitalism and Schizophrenia*, trans. Brian Massumi (Minneapolis: University of Minnesota Press, 1987), 133.
15. Gilles Deleuze, *Difference and Repetition*, trans. Paul Patton (New York: Columbia University Press, 1994), xxi.
16. Deleuze, *The Movement-Image*, ix.
17. Gilles Deleuze and Félix Guattari, *What Is Philosophy?*, trans. Hugh Tomlinson and Graham Burchell (New York: Columbia University Press, 1994), 54.
18. Gilles Deleuze, *The Time-Image*, trans. Hugh Tomlinson and Robert Galeta (Minneapolis: University of Minnesota Press, 1989), 130; emphasis added.
19. Gilles Deleuze, *Kant's Critical Philosophy: The Doctrine of the Faculties*, trans. Hugh Tomlinson and Barbara Habberjam (Minneapolis: University of Minnesota Press, 1984), viii.
20. Gilles Deleuze, Foreword to Éric Alliez, *Capital Times: Tales from the Conquest of Time*, trans. Georges Van Den Abbeele (Minneapolis: University of Minnesota Press, 1996), xii–xiii.
21. *The Movement-Image* constitutes a powerful analysis of the forces that drive narrative, especially classical narrative, toward globalizing consummation. According to Deleuze, Hollywood cinema is especially conspicuous for creating narratives that revolve around such a totalizing resolution: when the equipoise of life or community is disturbed, action satisfies the desire to reestablish order. What Deleuze (following Noël Burch) calls the "large form"—a narrative that moves from situation to the demand for action to new situation (SAS')—can be understood in an

integral sense to invoke the Aristotelian understanding of narrative, namely, the affective (even cathartic) power of the plot vis-à-vis the spectator. See especially chapter 9 of *The Movement-Image*, 141–59.

22. Deleuze, *The Time-Image*, 6.
23. Ibid., xi.
24. Deleuze, *Negotiations*, 65.
25. This notion that possibility—the aesthetic creation of possibility—lies at the heart of the plane of immanence, which begins to emerge in later works of Deleuze, is one I owe to Peter Canning.
26. See Deleuze's comments in "Doubts about the Imaginary," in *Negotiations*, 64.
27. See Deleuze's chapter "What Is a Concept?" in *What Is Philosophy?*, 15–34.
28. Jean-Luc Nancy, "The Deleuzian Fold in Thought," in *Deleuze: A Critical Reader*, ed. Paul Patton (Oxford: Blackwell, 1996), 110.
29. Deleuze and Guattari, *What Is Philosophy?*, 60.
30. Deleuze and Guattari, *A Thousand Plateaus*, 134.
31. Deleuze and Guattari, *What Is Philosophy?*, 2.
32. Friedrich Nietzsche, *Untimely Meditations*, trans. R. J. Hollindale (Cambridge: Cambridge University Press, 1983), 60.
33. This term, which is meant to echo the "linguistic turns" that academia experienced in the 1960s and 1970s, I owe to Dudley Andrew and Steve Unger.
34. Deleuze, *The Time-Image*, 21.
35. Deleuze, *The Movement-Image*, 209.
36. Deleuze, *The Time-Image*, 280.
37. "Grand theory" refers to David Bordwell and Noëll Carroll's collection *Post-Theory: Reconstructing Film Studies* (Madison: University of Wisconsin Press, 1996), xiii. "Is this book about the end of film theory?" the two ask in their introduction. "No. It's about the end of Theory, and what can and should come after." My sense, however, is that the cognitivist gambit merely replaces Grand Theories (semiotics, psychoanalysis, Althusserian Marxism) with its own quasi-Aristotelian, quasi-Kantian schematism. Cognitivism may not produce allegories as obvious as those of its theoretical predecessors, but that should not be taken to mean that it has eluded totalization—only that it is deeply and deceptively unaware of its own habitus. What cognitivism calls science and, better yet, common sense are the accumulation of conventions whose schematization we have yet to significantly interrogate. Fortunately, to a certain degree Deleuze does this for us: above all the Kantian schemata, Deleuze suggests, is the expression of power, the aim of which is to tame visibility. See Gilles Deleuze, *Foucault*, trans. Seán Hand (Minneapolis: University of Minnesota Press, 1988), 68–70. For a clear summary of cognitivism, see David Bordwell, "A Case for Cognitivism," *iris* 9 (spring 1989): 11–40.
38. Gilles Deleuze, "On *The Time-Image*," in *Negotiations*, 58.
39. Deleuze, *The Time-Image*, 280.
40. Deleuze and Guattari, *What Is Philosophy?*, 9.
41. See, for instance, Gilles Deleuze, "On *A Thousand Plateaus*," in *Negotiations*, 31–32.
42. See, for instance, Stuart A. Kauffman, *The Origins of Order: Self-Organization and Selection in Evolution* (Oxford: Oxford University Press, 1983).
43. Deleuze and Guattari, *What Is Philosophy?*, 37.
44. Ibid., 41.
45. Deleuze, *Difference and Repetition*, 138.
46. Gilles Deleuze, "The Exhausted," in *Essays Critical and Clinical*, trans. Daniel W. Smith and Michael A. Greco (Minneapolis: University of Minnesota Press, 1997), 158.
47. See Deleuze's discussion in *Difference and Repetition*, chapter 3.

48. See Deleuze's preface to *Kant's Critical Philosophy*, xi–xiii.
49. Daniel Smith, "Deleuze's Theory of Sensation: Overcoming the Kantian Duality," in *Deleuze: A Critical Reader*, 33. Smith's piece and Gregg Lambert's essay in this collection, "Cinema and the Outside," are, to my mind, two of the most profound and extensive readings of Deleuze's relationship to, and departure from, Kant.
50. Deleuze, *Difference and Repetition*, 139.
51. Gilles Deleuze, *Proust and Signs* (New York: George Braziller, 1972), 1.
52. Deleuze and Guattari, *What Is Philosophy?*, 77. As Deleuze and Guattari write, "The philosophical faculty of coadaptation, which also regulates the creation of concepts, is called *taste*."
53. Ibid., 16.
54. Deleuze, *The Movement-Image*, 85.
55. This is one of the most difficult aspects of Deleuze's philosophy. As Constantin Boundas so clearly puts it, "Beginning with the intensive singularities of a 'pre-human' world ... Deleuze–Bergson will have to account for the formation of a closed, 'extended' or 'cool' system inside the open-ended, intensive *chaosmic* virtual" ("Deleuze–Bergson: An Ontology of the Virtual," in *Deleuze: A Critical Reader*, 84–85). This perfectly describes the trajectory of this section of the Introduction, if not *The Movement-Image* itself.
56. Gilles Deleuze, *The Deleuze Reader*, ed. Constatin Boundas (New York: Columbia University Press, 1983), 193.
57. The article that invokes Schelling is, in fact, an article about Bergson. See "La Conception de la différence chez Bergson," *Études Bergsoniennes* 4 (1956): 77–112.
58. Gilles Deleuze and Claire Parnet, *Dialogues*, trans. Hugh Tomlinson and Barbara Habberjam (New York: Columbia University Press, 1987), 15.
59. Deleuze, *The Movement-Image*, 56–66.
60. Henri Bergson, *Matter and Memory*, trans. N. M. Paul and W. S. Palmer (New York: Zone Books, 1991), 17. For Bergson, this aggregate of images is the plane of immanence; unlike Deleuze, for whom the plane is virtual, Bergson sees the plane and its images as actual, though insofar as all images act and react on each other, insofar as all images "prehend" (Whitehead) each other, one could argue that there is a virtual aspect to Bergson's plane.
61. Deleuze, *The Time-Image*, 27.
62. In this respect, the first chapter of Bergson's *Matter and Memory* really figures most prominently in the fourth chapter of *The Movement-Image*.
63. Bergson, *Matter and Memory*, 28–29.
64. Gilles Deleuze, *Bergsonism*, trans. Hugh Tomlinson and Barbara Habberjam (New York: Zone Books, 1991), 23.
65. Gilles Deleuze, *The Fold: Leibniz and the Baroque*, trans. Tom Conley (Minneapolis: University of Minnesota Press, 1993). See especially chapter 6, "What Is an Event?"
66. Ibid., 25.
67. Deleuze, *The Movement-Image*, 62.
68. The notion that Deleuze has displaced the archaeological aim of cinema studies onto philosophy was originally suggested to me by Steven Miller.
69. Deleuze, *The Movement-Image*, 59.
70. Ibid., 3.
71. For a discussion of movement and thought, see Deleuze, *Negotiations*, 122–23.
72. My brief discussion here is partly guided by Michael Hardt's introduction to *Gilles Deleuze: An Apprenticeship in Philosophy* (Minneapolis: University of Minnesota Press, 1993), though I cannot do justice to the complexity of the matter. Indeed, my sense is that the relationship between Hegel and Deleuze is much more involved than Deleuze himself would like to admit, though Deleuze's minor philosophy, as Hardt shows, irreconcilably divorces itself from Hegelianism.

73. Deleuze, *The Movement-Image*, 4.
74. Ibid., 4.
75. Henri Bergson, *Creative Evolution*, trans. Arthur Mitchell (New York: Henry Holt and Company, 1911), 355.
76. Deleuze, *The Movement-Image*, 2.
77. Deleuze, *The Deleuze Reader*, 191.
78. Ibid., 189.
79. Deleuze, *Essays Critical and Clinical*, 1.
80. Deleuze, *The Time-Image*, 156.
81. Deleuze, *The Movement-Image*, xiv.
82. Ibid., 215.
83. Deleuze, *Negotiations*, 55.
84. Deleuze, *The Movement-Image*, x.
85. Ibid., 64–65.
86. Deleuze, *Bergsonism*, 106.
87. Deleuze, *The Movement-Image*, 3.
88. Ibid., 66–70.
89. Ibid., 59.
90. Ibid., 61.
91. Ibid., 83.
92. Ibid., xiv.
93. Deleuze, *Negotiations*, 46.
94. See chapter 2 of *The Time-Image*, especially 25–30.
95. Deleuze, *Negotiations*, 47. It should be noted that the reality of the cinema books does not always meet this expectation; indeed, Deleuze's investment in Peirce seems, at moments, to waver. But Peirce is also the figure that Deleuze calls on at perhaps the most crucial moment, that is, the moment of "crisis" out of which arises the cinema of the time-image.
96. Deleuze, *The Time-Image*, 29.
97. See ibid., 29, 262.
98. Ibid., xiii.
99. Deleuze, *The Movement-Image*, xiv.
100. D. N. Rodowick, "A Genealogy of Time: The Nietzschean Dimension of French Cinema, 1958–1998," in *Premises: Invested Spaces in Visual Arts and Architecture from France, 1958–1998* (New York: Solomon R. Guggenheim Museum/Paris: Centre Georges Pompidou, 1998).
101. Deleuze, *Negotiations*, 46.
102. Deleuze, *Foucault*, 47–69.
103. Michel Foucault, *Discipline and Punish: The Birth of the Prison*, trans. Alan Sheridan (New York: Vintage Books, 1979), 200.
104. Deleuze provides a beautiful explanation of the *dispositif* in *Michel Foucault: Philosopher*, trans. Timothy J. Armstrong (New York: Routledge, 1992), 159–68.
105. For an more extended discussion of this new society, see Deleuze's "Postscript on Control Societies," in *Negotiations*.
106. Deleuze, *Foucault*, 64–65.
107. In an interview with Toni Negri, Deleuze explains, "Becoming isn't part of history; history amounts only [to] the set of preconditions, however recent, that one leaves behind in order to 'become,' that is, to create something new" ("Control and Becoming," in *Negotiations*, 171).
108. Deleuze, *Negotiations*, 67.
109. Two important points should be noted here. The first is that, though Deleuze's cinema books are literally marked by the predominance of certain images (movement-images or time-images), these images are symptomatic of broader systems and conditions (organic and crystalline). The second point is that while Deleuze

develops and describes these systems, more or less dividing them between the two books, the perspective from which he writes is the latter, genealogical one, and this may explain the sense one gets in the cinema books of always anticipating the emergence of the time-image. András Kovács makes a similar point in his contribution in this collection.

110. Deleuze, *Negotiations*, 67.
111. Deleuze, *The Time-Image*, 29.
112. Deleuze, *Negotiations*, 59.
113. Ibid.
114. Ibid., 51.
115. In one sense, Deleuze's own refusal of pat chronology frustrates any such demarcation; to take the most obvious examples, Renoir's *Rules of the Game* and Welles's *Citizen Kane*, two of the most prominent and important examples of the time-image, are produced in a period before any such break, a period of relentless action-images. Nevertheless, these films were unique for their time; they appeared before their time, as if to presage the transition that was to come—again, the essence of a thing appears "in the middle." As Angelo Restivo notes, the format of the cinema books literally suggests this trauma as the gap or interval between the two volumes, an unrecorded or unrecordable moment after which the schematic illusions no longer quite function.
116. Deleuze, *The Movement-Image*, 206.
117. The "uses and advantages" of Deleuze for the study of gender/sexuality, no less feminism, are limitless, though their pursuit is limited to relatively few texts and scattered suggestive comments. One might begin by consulting Rosi Bradiotti's "Towards a New Nomadism: Feminist Deleuzian Tracks; or, Metaphysics and Metabolism," as well as Elizabeth Grosz's "A Thousand Tiny Sexes: Feminism and Rhizomatics," both of which appear in *Gilles Deleuze and the Theater of Philosophy*, ed. Constantin V. Boundas and Dorothea Olkowski (New York: Routledge, 1994); see also Camilla Griggers, *Becoming Woman* (Minneapolis: University of Minnesota Press, 1997); and Steven Shaviro, *The Cinema Body* (Minneapolis: University of Minnesota Press, 1993). On the concomitant relation between Deleuze and psychoanalysis, a relation that is largely misunderstood, see Eduardo A. Vidal, "Hétérogénéité—Deleuze—Lacan," in *Gilles Deleuze: une vie philosophique*, and Peter Canning, "Transcendental Narcissism Meets Multiplicity (Lacan: Deleuze)," in *Thinking Bodies*, ed. Juliet Flower MacCannell and Laura Zakarin (Stanford, Calif.: Stanford University Press, 1994).
118. Deleuze, *The Movement-Image*, 200.
119. Ibid., 205.
120. Notably, Deleuze invokes Agnès Varda to suggest that, in the crystalline regime, "[d]escription stops presupposing a reality and narration stops referring to a form of the true at one and the same time" (*The Time-Image*, 135).
121. André Bazin, *What Is Cinema?*, vol. 2, trans. Hugh Gray (Berkeley: University of California Press, 1971), 52.
122. Deleuze, *The Time-Image*, 7.
123. Deleuze, *The Fold*, 93.
124. Deleuze's discussion of the actual and the virtual is especially prominent in chapters 4 and 5 of *The Time-Image*, though the entire volume is in some sense a meditation on the virtual.
125. Deleuze, *The Time-Image*, 99.
126. The diagram that Deleuze borrows from Bergson to illustrate this contraction is, notably, reproduced in Jean-Clet Martin's essay in this collection.
127. Deleuze, *The Time-Image*, 68.
128. Ibid., 79.

129. In *The Time-Image,* Deleuze notes that this means that there are in fact "two possible time-images, one grounded in the past, the other grounded in the present": the crystalline regime comprises both crystal-images qua time-images related to the present, and also a second cluster of images, "peaks of the present and sheet of the past," which are time-images related to the past (98). In actuality, though, there are three types of time-images: time-images of the present, time-images of the past, and a third kind, "which brings together the before and the after in a becoming, instead of separating them; its paradox is to introduce an enduring interval in the moment itself" (155). Indeed, the reader will find this last species of time-image discussed in the final section of this Introduction, in conjunction with reflective judgment.
130. Deleuze, *The Time-Image,* 147.
131. Ibid., 38. Deleuze is quoting an interview Godard gave with respect to *Passion* that appeared in *Le Monde,* May 27, 1982.
132. Deleuze, *The Movement-Image,* 206.
133. Ibid., 211.
134. In his introduction to Serge Daney's *Ciné-Journal,* Deleuze suggests, in Riegl's sense, that we are in the midst of a third cinematic moment ("A Letter to Serge Daney," in *Negotiations*).
135. Deleuze, *Negotiations,* 77.
136. Deleuze and Guattari, *Kafka: Toward a Minor Literature,* 16.
137. Deleuze, *The Time-Image,* 220.
138. Deleuze and Guattari, *A Thousand Plateaus,* 381. Nomadism can be understood, Deleuze suggests, as a release from monadism; the monad is, for Leibniz, a room without doors or windows, one of an infinite number of such prison-perspectives on the universe that are organized by the God-monad, the organizing idea that must be presumed. To release the inhabitants of the prison, then, is to make monad into nomad, to conceive of a thought without an overarching image.
139. Deleuze takes up the "problem of thought" in the chapter "Thought and Cinema" in *The Time-Image.* Notably, the question of Deleuze's general relationship to Heidegger is one that, in many respects, remains to be sorted out. See Deleuze's "Note on Heidegger's Philosophy of Difference," a peculiar little addendum to the first chapter of *Difference and Repetition,* 64–69.
140. Benjamin writes: "Our taverns and our metropolitan streets, our offices and furnished rooms, our railroad stations and our factories appeared to have us locked up hopelessly. Then came the film and burst this prison-world asunder in the dynamite of a tenth of a second, so that now, in the midst of far-flung ruins and debris, we calmly and adventurously go traveling" ("The Work of Art in the Age of Mechanical Reproduction," in *Reflections,* ed. Hannah Arendt [New York: Schocken Books, 1968], 236).
141. Deleuze, *The Time-Image,* 3; translation slightly altered.
142. Consider Thomas Pynchon's description of John Dillinger, who went to his death having just seen *Manhattan Melodrama* and who thus "found a few seconds' strange mercy in the movie images that hadn't quite yet faded from his eyeballs . . . there was still for the doomed man some shift of personality in effect—the way you felt for a little while afterward in the muscles of your face and voice, that you were Gable, the ironic eyebrows, the proud shining snakelike head" (Thomas Pynchon, *Gravity's Rainbow* [New York: Viking Press, 1973], 516).
143. Deleuze, *The Time-Image,* 20. The Kantian reference here to things in themselves (noumena) should, in a sense, be taken literally, as I suggest later in this section, though Deleuze's revaluation of Kant must also be taken into account. Contra Kant's "transcendental idealism," Deleuze calls his philosophical method

"transcendental empiricism," a kind of prelude to constructivism that begins by "overturn[ing] the image of thought" (Deleuze, *Difference and Repetition*, 137).

144. In particular, it is possible to see Deleuze's diagnosis of the sensory-motor schema as a kind of redux of the notion of "suture," which such film theorists as Kaja Silverman borrowed from Lacanian psychoanalysis (more precisely, from Jacques-Alain Miller). The analogy fails, however, when we consider that suture itself is based (like Metz's semiotics) on an analogy between the signifier and the image, which Deleuze dismisses; what Deleuze does seem to grant is that sensory-motor schema is a consequence of a moral vision founded in the signifier qua representation—the power of an utterance to explain and thus determine the image. The image is not a signifier, nor does it function like a signifier, though it is prey to the power of the signifier. See Peter Canning's essay in this volume for an insightful discussion of the question.
145. Deleuze, *Foucault*, 68–69.
146. Deleuze, *Difference and Repetition*, 148.
147. Deleuze, *The Time-Image*, 133.
148. These days, of course, the old imperative to "be good" has been supplemented by a psychopharmaceutical imperative; with the inundation of "cosmetic pharmaceuticals" like Prozac and even Ritalin, which temper and chemically alter personality, the new exhortation is to "behave." The question of chemical transformation is altogether pertinent to Deleuze's work, not only because it relates to the forbidding question of "control" (Burroughs), but also because the possibilities of *experimenting* with perception, with the Man-Form qua God-Form, loom in a future yet to be thought, as the future to be thought. See Deleuze's "Appendix: On the Death of Man and Superman," in *Foucault*. For an interesting explanation of the new pharmaceutical culture, see Peter Kramer, *Listening to Prozac* (New York: Viking Press, 1993).
149. Deleuze, *The Time-Image*, 133.
150. Deleuze and Guattari, *Anti-Oedipus*, 39.
151. See the 1800 preface to Wordsworth and Coleridge's *Lyrical Ballads*, ed. W. J. B. Owen (Oxford: Oxford University Press, 1969), 158. As for Romanticism's debt to the sublime, Deleuze suggests that the *Critique of Judgment* is the "foundation of Romanticism" (*Kant's Critical Philosophy*, xii).
152. Deleuze, *The Time-Image*, 20.
153. See the first section of Jameson's *The Geopolitical Aesthetic* (Bloomington: Indiana University Press-BFI, 1995). The promotion of the conspiracy narrative in Jameson's work is a particularly privileged aspect of a larger affiliation with Lukácsian totalization. Like Lukács, Jameson favors a kind of totalizing narrative that, in our postmodern world of global capitalism, contrives to "know the whole" (Hegel). Notably, Deleuze does discuss conspiracy in *The Time-Image*, arguing that the plot, in every sense of the word, is tantamount to money, "the international conspiracy that conditions it [the cinema] from within, as the most intimate and most indispensable enemy" (77).
154. Deleuze, *The Movement-Image*, 210.
155. Deleuze, *The Time-Image*, 20.
156. Ibid., 18.
157. Deleuze, *Kant's Critical Philosophy*, 60. Also see Immanuel Kant, *Critique of Judgment*, trans. Werner S. Pluhar (Indianapolis: Hackett Publishing, 1987), 204 and 209 (original pagination). For a description of the schemata, see Kant's first chapter, "Transcendental Doctrine of Judgment," in *Critique of Pure Reason*, trans. Norman Kemp Smith (New York: St. Martin's Press, 1965); indeed, Kant himself admits that the schematism is "an art concealed in the depths of the human soul" (B180, original pagination).

158. See Deleuze, "On *The Movement-Image*," in *Negotiations*, 53.
159. Deleuze, *The Time-Image*, 276.
160. Ibid., 20.
161. Ibid., 1.
162. André Bazin, "The Myth of Total Cinema," in *What Is Cinema?*, vol. 1, trans. Hugh Gray (Berkeley: University of California Press, 1967), 21. Bazin's argument is made with respect to the cinema's capacity for attaining realism, but the spirit of the argument strikes me as altogether akin to Deleuze's.
163. Deleuze, *Negotiations*, 60.
164. Michel Foucault, "Maurice Blanchot: The Thought from Outside," in *Foucault/Blanchot* (New York: Zone Books, 1990), 15–16.
165. See Deleuze, *The Time-Image*, 158.
166. Ibid., 210.
167. Ibid., 164. With respect to cinema, we typically tend to see these as separate, if not qualitatively different, ideological spheres, but Deleuze insists that the cinema's neural network, its sensory-motor schema, was equally at work in "Hollywood and Hitler": as Lambert explains, the State and sensualism rely on an automatism borne along by clichés that tap into our most aggressive drives.
168. Ibid., 166.
169. See Deleuze and Guattari, *What Is Philosophy?*, 16.
170. Deleuze, *The Time-Image*, 167.
171. Deleuze basically dismisses the better part of postwar American cinema at the conclusion of *The Movement-Image*, 205–11. Although some of this discussion is novel, there are moments—particularly the denigration of Altman—that strike me as overreaching. Notably, the two prominent American directors to show up in *The Time-Image* are Welles and Kubrick, effectively Hollywood outsiders (Cassavetes also appears, but to a lesser degree).
172. Deleuze, *The Movement-Image*, 206.
173. The question of production, of economy, of money, is crucial for Deleuze and deserves more exegesis than it receives here. In *The Time-Image*, Deleuze aligns classical montage and its image-circuit (SAS') with Marx's formulation for the exchange of capital (M-C-M), but in neorealism (and later in the New Wave and new German cinema) these regularities are deregulated. The image-circuit, the methodical flow of the sensory-motor schema, is disrupted, and the integrity of organic narrative implodes; in disillusioned and demolished zones left by the war, a new practice of the cinema takes shape. In Italian neorealism, for instance, the demolition of fascism and the collapse of its institutions provide the conditions for a new sense of cinema, the constituents of which are familiar enough by now: the practice of filming on location, the sense of creative improvisation in both the screenwriting and the filming (the shift from plots to the informality of "sketches"), the use of nonactors, and so on. Although one could explain all of these eventualities in practical or even technological terms (location shoots, for instance, were made easier by lighter, more portable cameras), Deleuze's point is that the production of such images is the expression of a life ripped from its habitus, of a force of deterritorialization qua capitalism. When Deleuze says in this context that "time is money," he does not simply mean that more money buys more time (though this is true), but rather, that "*the cinema confronts its most internal presupposition, money, and the movement-image makes way for the time-image in one and the same operation*" (one thinks, for instance, of the opening of Godard's *Tout va bien*) (*The Time-Image*, 78). See also John Beasley-Murray, "Whatever Happened to Neorealism?—Bazin, Deleuze, and Tarkovsky's Long Take," *iris* 23 (spring 1997): 43.
174. Deleuze, *The Time-Image*, 81.

175. Ibid., 208, 209. The notion of a "between two deaths" echoes a phrase of Lacan's that applies, appropriately, to psychosis. The psychotic experiences a "symbolic death," and so inhabits the derealized limbo in between the death of representation (i.e., signifying meaning) and physical death.
176. Ibid., 101.
177. As Alliez explains in a crucial passage, Bergson is a philosopher of intuition, whereas Deleuze is a philosopher of concepts, but "Bergsonism is the *paradoxical cause of the Deleuzian concept.*"
178. See Martin Heidegger, *Kant and the Problem of Metaphysics*, trans. Richard Taft (Bloomington: Indiana University Press, 1997).
179. Deleuze, *The Time-Image*, 83.
180. The question of the relation to time is so extraordinarily complex that it can only be touched on here. D. N. Rodowick's *Gilles Deleuze's Time Machine* offers a lengthy account of Deleuze's relationship to time, as does Peter Canning's "The Crack of Time and the Ideal Game," in *Gilles Deleuze and the Theater of Philosophy*. Notably, the latter's description of the "ideal game" informs my own description of the modern image-series.
181. Deleuze and Guattari, *A Thousand Plateaus*, 478.
182. Deleuze, *The Time-Image*, 211.
183. Ibid., 213.
184. Ibid.
185. Ibid., 319 n. 36. The subject of the Markoff chain arises in reference to Andrei Bely's novel *Petersburg*. For a more extended explanation, see Ilya Prigogine and Isabelle Stengers, *Order Out of Chaos* (New York: Bantam Books, 1984), 236–38, 272–77.
186. Deleuze, *The Time Image*, 180.
187. Consider in this context that while Deleuze often uses deterritorialization to describe the deregulation of philosophy, the term comes to the fore in *Anti-Oedipus* to describe the tremendous upheaval effected by capitalism. In this first volume of *Capitalism and Schizophrenia*, Deleuze and Guattari depict capitalism as unleashing vast, new "flows"—"flows of property being sold, flows of money that circulates, flows of production and means of production making ready in the shadows, flows of workers becoming deterritorialized" (223). The deterritorialization of life and labor effectively overrides the organizing principle of feudal and monarchical regimes, the organization of life on earth (*terre*); as the authors admit, "One sometimes has the impression that the flows of capital would willingly dispatch themselves to the moon, if the capitalist state were not there to bring them back to earth" (258). This is why Deleuze and Guattari argue that schizophrenia is the limit of capitalism, its tendency but also the point at which it loses all control. Inevitably, capitalism undertakes the process of bringing these flows "back to earth"—a process of axiomatization, coding, and regulation that is largely described in *A Thousand Plateaus*. In this sense, the trajectory from *Anti-Oedipus* to *A Thousand Plateaus* describes a shift from deterritorialization to reterritorialization, whereas the cinema books reverse this trajectory: the transition is toward deterritorialization, though the prospect of new "societies of control" always looms in the future, waiting to bring us "back into line."
188. Deleuze, *Difference and Repetition*, 148.
189. The question of the "credibility" of the world is, as Willy Apollon has argued, the crucial problem in psychosis (and, in a different sense, in schizophrenia as well). Having found a "flaw" or "defect" in the symbolic order, the psychotic ceases to have "faith" in the world. See Willy Apollon, Danielle Bergeron, and Lucie Cantin, *Traiter la psychose* (Québec: Gifric, 1990).
190. Deleuze, *The Time-Image*, 172.

191. Ibid.
192. Ibid., 175.
193. Ibid., 139. Deleuze adds, "Power . . . is this power to affect and be affected, this relation between one force and others."
194. Robert Musil, *The Man without Qualities,* vol. 1 (New York: Capricorn Books, 1965), 175.
195. Gilles Deleuze, "L'immanence: une vie . . . ," *Philosophie* 47 (September 1, 1995).

Approaching Images

Chapter 1

Of Images and Worlds

Toward a Geology of the Cinema

JEAN-CLET MARTIN

Translated by Frank Le Gac and Sally Shafto

It is difficult to accurately define the fate Deleuze wished to reserve for what he called the "image of thought" if we do not grasp from the outset the profound kinship between image and thought. It is therefore out of the question to deal, on the one hand, with the process of the image and, on the other, with that of thought. There is no dualism that would permit one to posit them each on opposite sides. As we know, Deleuze never begins by positing terms that would be exterior to one another. Doing philosophy is to be conceived starting off in the middle. We start off neither with the image nor with thought, but in the middle, where each melts with the other one into a common plane, the plane of immanence. It does not matter that this fold of the one upon the other is not identical in philosophy, in science, or in the domain of art. Each elaborates its respective plane in a middle where image and thought correspond according to modalities that need to be specified every time.

Whence the importance of beginning with examples. Image and thought are not abstract and separate entities. They actualize themselves in examples that mark their fusion and that provide an occasion for them to individuate themselves through a series of moments and figures whose history is no longer at all chronological but stratigraphic, foliated. This is why Deleuze's philosophy is a concrete philosophy: it is sensitive to the concretion of images and of thoughts or, more specifically, to the concrescence of their dimensions at the heart of an interpenetration that opens them to one another along axes or on planes that are called "Nature" and are consolidated in the course of a natural history. That Deleuze reactivates, under the sign of the conjunction of image and thought, a philosophy of Nature, a *Naturphilosophie,* lost since Schelling, might seem strange; but this is a hypothesis that comes out of Deleuze's own discourse, for we know how insistently he wished to prolong *What Is Philosophy?* with a new thought of Nature. However, the task should not be considered done, even if its lineaments are everywhere available.

Let us then gather these scattered lineaments, starting off with an example liable to actualize their concrescence—albeit one that momentarily takes leave of Deleuze's work (more than once, as we shall see: into Leibniz, urbanism, architecture, and painting, on the way to cinema). Deleuze often said to me that his work would only function at the price of such leave-taking: for those who traverse its lines of flight (just as the *clandestine* fish uses, even as it deterritorializes them, the lines traced by the edges of rocks to effectuate its own lines of flight). We gain an initial experience of this clandestine line if we take Bergson's way, into the circumvolutions that his *Matter and Memory* projects on the cerebral membrane of the world into which cinema first lets us trace an entry.

There are utterly spellbinding books of philosophy that never fail to catch us off guard, even after we have long had the habit of reading them and have slowly attempted to accommodate them. Nothing is to be done. No reasoned explication can encompass this strange feeling which hints to us that, despite our best efforts to make intelligible, the initial incomprehension will subsist. Understanding such books cannot mean anything but this: to harmonize oneself with the central incomprehension that carries the work to the heart of the darkness that it confronts, not existing as such except through this confrontation, through this gesture that penetrates the night knowing that the writing of this night will serve as testimony—testimony to the existence, deep within us, of what does not allow itself to be clarified without disappearing, and of which the mere index, the mere trace will only be realized if one dares to say the impossible, the incomprehensible in its state of absolute uncertainty.

How else should we understand the astonishing pages that open *Matter and Memory,* the most difficult to read of Bergson's works? Is one sure, after a few pages, about the subject matter of this book that one holds firmly in one's hands, or about the place toward which it transports us as if against our will? Everything begins, without ever reassuring us, with an incredible demand: We are asked to pretend! Just for an instant! That is, for the time it takes to have us penetrate into the heart of this night from which one does not return without the feeling that something in our everyday sureties and certainties has been damaged, has been broken off at a number of unlocalizable points . . . We are asked to close our eyes. To close our eyes as if they had never been opened before! As when one blacks out. What happens when finally one's eyes open? It is not me who opens them! I don't know yet where I am! I don't know what came over me, what happened! I don't know right away that it is I who sees! It takes time to get our wits about us again, to recover the thread of memories that constitute our habitus and, as such, the feeling of our identity.

We must place ourselves as if before the dawn of the world, at the moment when still anonymous perception awakens itself from its own stupor, from its own birth. What happens at this inaugural moment? Nothing but images! Everywhere are manifest fluorescent colors, figures, surfaces in an explosion of vibratory images. As soon as I open an eye, there are images and affections of images. All—my body, matter, trees, blackbirds—is given in moving images. Prior to any consideration, prior to any analysis, reality presents itself in images. The body sets itself going and there before it, beside it, and within it, it perceives a succession of paintings that connect according to characteristic laws. Hands and feet placed one in front of the other, memories and impressions that traverse the body and envelop themselves within it, do not escape this luminous and kaleidoscopic animation.

As soon as my senses open, a luminous breach shocks perception, unsealing this still absent gaze with the force of a continuity of flowering images, each reacting upon the others in an order that Bergson takes it upon himself to progressively unravel:

> Here is a system of images which I term my perception of the universe, and which may be entirely altered by a very slight change in a certain privileged image—my body. This image occupies the center: by it all the others are conditioned; at each of its movements everything changes, as though by a turn of a kaleidoscope.[1]

As it happens, there is no mark that would distinguish image and reality. Each image will be considered real from the outset, each expressing the others out of its place, the locus of which constitutes its transcendental principle. Indeed, the place can never be reduced to the site. The site is characterized by the delimitation of land. It lays itself out in a situation, defined by its particular geography, with reference to which buildings are to be implanted, and complex architectures elaborated, up against which one could beat or shatter oneself. In this respect, a city presents itself as a characteristic site, the map of which is traceable and whose packed arteries are navigable. The place, on the contrary, envisaged in the form of the locus, obeys principles that no longer arise from the situation congested with materials rooted to the land. The place is something immaterial without being an ethereal abstraction. It is, moreover, what, at the heart of the site, opens a perspective, a particular *point of view* upon the whole—not unlike in a theater where the same scene is multiplied, perceived differently depending on one's assigned seat. My neighbor, from the place allotted to him, will not see exactly the same thing that I do, his perspective being necessarily off in relation to mine. Nevertheless, it is the same—hard and unmoving—theater that opens these incommunicable loci that diverge at every point.

An analogous problem is obviously posed in the conception of the city. The same city, though taken to be a definite and materially invariant site, could nonetheless enter into a variation begun from different necessarily immaterial points of view. Indeed, a point of view never resolves itself into matter. It is to be conceived more as a way of being than as the form of a being. It places itself more on the side of "memory" than of "matter"—to use Bergson's terms. Each urban complex presents itself as a set or a "block." It designates a finite grouping of elements, of cataloged, numerable buildings. On the other hand, what will necessarily exceed the enumeration of elements is the infinite figure of possible perspectives that this city could offer us depending on the point of view from which one considers it. There is something like an unfurling of loci that open in the midst of the site and that will cut in the sky a singular array of rooftops, a composition of relations organized along sight lines that are characteristic every time.

This is, indeed, what Leibniz had posited as a principle of his system when he wrote to Thomasius that "a city appears with a physiognomy, if one considers it from the center," but "appears differently if one accedes to it from the outside . . . The external aspect of the city itself varies depending on whether one approaches from the East or from the West."[2] A single city, a single material site rises up in a space that will be multiplied to infinity by variable places and points of view. There is thus an expansivity to the *local* not covered by the extension of the *global*, an expansion of perspectives the immensity of which does not have to do with the extended space of the site. In space, there is a multiplication of places that no longer exactly arise from the situation. In logical terms, one would say that these places *do not belong* to the site. They are not elements of the site, but incorporeals, in the sense that the Stoics reserved for this term—events of the cut, or the cut out, surfaces piled up or planes superimposed in a way that depends on the displacement of the observer (or of the locutor), on the variation of the adopted points of view: something volatile that undoes itself with the rapidity of movement and the successive shifting of perspectives.

Logic provides us with precise operators to formalize satisfactorily the relation between the real and the virtual. As for the real, we necessarily *belong* to it insofar as it is a presence actually numerable in the present. It lays out in a site the set of elements that it contains in a stable, numerically determinable relation to one another. A certain building or a certain pavilion has an incontestable belonging to a certain site. Nonetheless, between the parts that compose this urban situation there is another form of relation than the one determined as belonging. If a certain building belongs to a certain city, it can nevertheless enter into relation with a certain house from a local point of view, thereby developing a perspective whose overloading will be purely virtual and modifiable upon adoption of another place of observation. This perspectivist composition will behave as a subset that opens in the initial set a number of possible rearrangements, superior to the hard elements of the site, which can intersect in an impressive variation of profiles. There will obviously be more possible perspectives on a city than there are buildings considered. The points of view on the city approach infinity while the architectural components remain essentially numerable. Without belonging to the site in a stable manner, this virtual combinatory of perspectives inhabits the site in the mode of *inclusion*. More numerous than the elements of the site, the perspectives escape it, hover over it in proliferating series that must nevertheless be included in the site itself.[3] Thus, the perspectives will not be real by the same rights as the hard elements of the set. Rather, they come within a special reality—a virtual reality!

The perspectives, thanks to which I perceive how streets and houses cut themselves out—these volatile points of view that multiply wildly as they correspond to the anarchy of my errant perambulation—never reside in the city as things that I could touch. It is a question of simple aleatory sight lines that do not depend on the site except in an inclusive or virtual manner. There is always an excess of places (*loci*) with respect to the site (*situs*)—as one would say in Cantor's language. Would one then go so far to say that all these virtualities, these points of view on the city, are simply fictive? Is the view that I have from this bridge, or this bench, unreal? This is to formulate the question badly because each perspective reveals a determinable aspect of the city, or cuts out a characteristic image. The view that I unfurl using myself is a kaleidoscopic set of images superimposed all along a line that cuts through the city. The least modification of place leads to a redistribution of the landscape in its entirety. It takes only a slight shift in the line cut through the city to develop another composition of images. There are images and piles of images, a matter and a memory. The least perception is already an overload of images and supposes memory as the law of their superimposition. In this sense, there is nothing unreal about a view—regardless of the place at which planes join, or from which the landscape gets cut out. But for all that, the point of view will not allow itself to be touched, handled like a pebble or a brick. Therein lies all the difference between the world as it has consistency and the world as it is experienced, traversed by a perspectival cut that persists in memory—that is to say, in this accumulation that tears mobile landscapes out of the world.[4]

In this regard, neither the profile of a city, variable to infinity, nor the construction of a panoramic territory refers to a state of things. Rather, they refer to an errant line that runs through space as a scaffolding of relations, a maze of depths, relative to the more or less typical place that one occupies—which implies that every landscape is a virtual construction in relation to a memory able to stock piles of images in all their encroachments upon one another. The human universe is open to a variety of changing perspectives, adjusted according to the axis of the gaze that cuts through the city, accumulating facades, stockpiling walls along the axis of a depth that is already memory. So there contracts a découpage of images, cut out upon the blue background of the sky, which is nothing like an objectively realized solid. Laws of affinity and contrast solicit these effects of juxtaposition all along a sight line that itself plays on the trajectories of memory. Each time, the place that I occupy juxtaposes and happily *accumulates* shadows and light according to virtual coincidences, pilings of planes—the individuation of which will be a function of the site and the place, of the matter and the memory that the image makes solidary and inseparable (*continuum*).

Memory for Bergson is nothing other than an *expansum* of dimension, the expansivity of which is internal, immanent, and intensive—and, consequently, will not be truly spatial, but rather, ideal [*idéelle*][5] at the very place where matter itself could not be profiled, mapped out, and put into perspective without the profound trajectories that memory realizes. The intensive "trajectivity" of memories necessarily comes to redouble the extensive "trajectivity" of perception. Without memory to suspend itself above perception there would be no landscape articulated along the depth axis, as if, finally, depth of field was only possible thanks to a purely intensive depth! What I see superimpose itself outside of me holds together only given the occasion of a piling up of levels, the relations between which are internal and the synthesis noematic. Which is why all the perspectives on the city are more in memory than in the site that they exceed. The infinity of possible points of view, all of them incorporeal, finds its immaterial cartography in memory, as illustrated by the figure of a cone that presents itself as "a pyramid ... standing on its apex."[6]

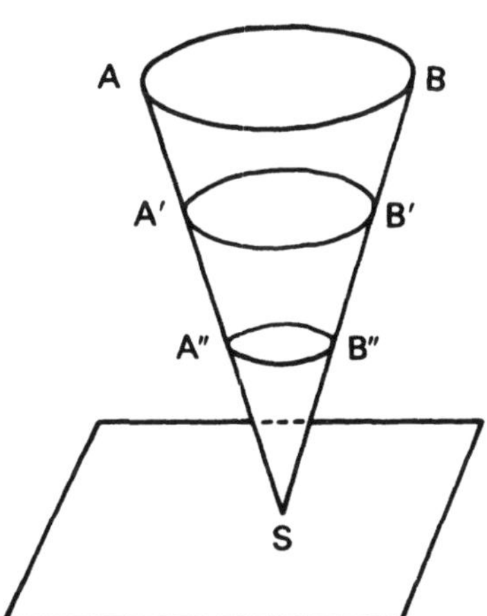

The point of the cone, directed toward the outside, launches the sight line, while the enormous base contains all the virtual depths, the tangle of perspectives that the city, for example, can include. The point traces the cut; the base accumulates the planes in depth and strings them together into a landscape that is mental before being spatial.

For Bergson, then, there are two perfectly real dimensions. The first is actual—the sharp point of a gaze that cuts through matter; the second is virtual, cumulative, and it connects along the lines of a paradoxical perspective the elements that perception isolates. In such an apparatus, the virtual no longer opposes itself to the real. We might, if need be, oppose *virtuality* to *actuality,* but not to *reality,* the contrary of which turns out, in fact, to be *possibility.*[7] The virtual could also perfectly well be envisaged on the side of the real, even if it is not actual, that is, effectuated on the plane of actuality. The domain of what is actual comes within perception. It is a material plane that Bergson symbolizes using the presence of an extensive site. The virtual, on the contrary, does not come within this plane, within this site. It does not reside there but redoubles it and prolongs it in depth. The virtual is, more than a set of elements, the infinite sum of their relations, an assemblage, an arrangement of parts or a composition of relations—which Bergson puts on the side of memory.

Matter presents itself like a plane, memory like a sequence of planes strung together, a rearrangement of the elements in the sequence that memory will thus complicate with a cone. The cone is an enveloped plane, wound in on itself, around an oriented tip, promising volume and promising the interiority that the cone initially lacked and now has only owing to this envelopment. Indeed, the cone is only the surface enveloping itself. And this envelopment will always wind around a tip; it is a folding back ever tighter upon itself that orients space—as if it were oriented for a gaze in the process of sharpening, or for a progressive adjustment, of which the telescope or, rather, the photographic *zoom* would provide the best example.[8]

It is this mutual penetration of the two dimensions, actual and virtual, that founds the richness of our lived experience. Let us make an obstinate return to our example of the city. The city spreads out, let us say, on a plane, a site. There one enumerates elements that perception materially distinguishes into houses and buildings. On this plane, each element separates from the others. They have not yet been enveloped in one another. One can pass horizontally from one to another the way one goes from one room to the next room or, as when one herborizes, from one flower to another. Which is why one should, with Bergson, distinguish between two forms of attention, or rather, two types of recognition: the one form of attention that permits associating images along a horizontal axis, such that each representation is juxtaposed with the previous one; and the other form of attention that, more attentive, opens each image to its depth, hollowing it out with a virtual double.[9] The image will then be affected with an envelopment that makes it resonate with the whole of memory. It is not, therefore, the elements situated in the solidity of external space that envelop one another; those elements are content to remain set in their hard immobility. Only points of view are liable to be enveloped in a conical dimension rather than a planimetric one, a spiritual rather than material one.

In this respect, it is in the mind where points of view superimpose themselves on one another—there where, at the level of matter, houses and their images do not get lost in a continuous amalgam but remain content with a horizontal juxtaposition lacking depth. The image—considered on the side of matter, or as the site on which elementary recognition exercises its pinpoint beam, the horizontal order of contiguities—has no virtuality. The city is there, laid out in numerable neighborhoods, such that one is unable to discover anything but what is offered to the perception of contiguities—beyond which we rarely go further, absorbed as we are in practical exigencies, or in the rush to get the last metro or the first train that takes total hold on us, dragging us from one sidewalk to the next, from a stairway to an underground tunnel that leads to a platform, to the tracks, to the cars, and, at last, to a place to sit. But then, within the boredom or patience of the trip, begins another type of landscape recognition, an attentive recognition that draws each image into the axis of resemblance or, perhaps better, of similitude, leaving behind the axis of contiguities.[10] Upon the horizontality of sensory-motor sequences and active images is suddenly superimposed the verticality of image-memories, the unmoored depth of memory. The city that I contemplate, from my immobilized position in the train, is directly found to be enveloped in the circuits of memory, in the leaves of perspective, and to be saturated with virtuality there where what is still this same city gets cut out along sight lines that are different each time and completely immaterial.

There is, then, a kind of cone—a field of perspectives—that opens above the perceived city, much as, above the chessboard, there unfolds a set of possible moves that only memory can condense in the mind of the player. And the city only becomes a veritable entity with the memory of one who cuts through it when it is animated by the trajectory and rhythm of continuous crossing—a combinatory of relations that vary with the place one occupies. Such is, perhaps, the sense of Nietzsche's formula that there are as many cities as there are adopted points of view. There would be so many cities, not only through horizontal variation, but also, at each point along the way, through a vertical variation attentive to the depth of perspective that plunges as much into ourselves as toward the heart of the city.

Where, then, should we place all these cities within the city if not along this incorporeal cone that is like the city's living memory? Where are all these circumvolutions enveloped that Bergson traces upon the first schema that *Matter and Memory* attributes to attentive recognition? And further, where are we to situate this virtual depth that exceeds the materiality of the city, if not at the heart of a dimension, without expanse or matter, shot through with crystalline images that penetrate and copenetrate one another without any resistance?

From the place in my seat on the train next to the window, within the wait imposed on me by travel, tired of having nothing to do, images no longer follow one upon another in view of prolonging action. Waiting [*attente*] turns into attention; images are folded in half and redoubled in a memory that piles them up in depth, often in a paradoxical manner—as happens in Proust, with the bell towers of Martinville or the trees of Hudimesnil, where reminiscence redoubles to infinity, according to incommunicable and contradictory planes, when one is surprised by the jolt that prompts one to set their brilliant points free into the nebulosity of the enveloping perspectives. Likewise, for Bergson, memory does not move in a straight line. It always conceives itself around a tip, whirling around a brilliant point. It is a vertiginous siphon of fluid turbulences, a flux and not a juxtaposition of atoms, undulatory rather than corpuscular. Memory is a siphon of divergent perspectives that hang over the city I now perceive. And each time my perception launches its tip in a given direction, my memory takes off, and contracts its lens of remembrance in the direction of this cone, just as a telescope trains upon ever more numerous stars a gaze able to discern them. Each perceptive pointing, in cutting through the landscape toward the exterior, hones itself toward the interior that will pick it clean of perspectives in order to form a continual and durable volume:

> these systems are not formed of recollections laid side by side like so many atoms. There are always some dominant memories, shining points around which the others form a vague nebulosity. . . . The work of *localization* consists, in reality, in a growing effort of *expansion* by which the memory, always present in its entirety to itself, *spreads out* its recollections over an ever wider *surface* . . .[11]

The manner in which memory cuts across a landscape concerns a *surface* of invagination that is not analogical. In its essential possibility, perception is not, for Bergson, of the order of representation, nor of reproduction, nor (more simply) of the resemblance of an image faithful to a supposedly exterior pattern. Perception does not conform to a model that it would exactly refigure. The image is not an analogical copy but presents itself initially as the numerical texture of the real. Perception designates—to lift a concept from the *Essay on the Immediate Data of Consciousness*—a numerical multiplicity, the metric of which obeys the intermittent flares of matter. The perceived image obeys a numerical construction subsumed under the sensory-motor organization of consciousness, which Bergson often compares to the nets of arithmetic or to the meshes of geometry. But this numerical construction of perception depends on a more profound multiplicity, an intensive multiplicity that Bergson places on the side of memory or of intuition, and which, far from being analogical, pertains to an intensive, virtual construction, without which the orthonormal net of perception would lose all its depth.

The manner in which memory cuts across a landscape, which it does not reproduce by analogy with a supposedly objective model, but rather creates in its volume and connectedness—this system that envelops every perspective around certain intense points, this accumulation of planes [*plans*] that only exist in me, as a function of the place that interiorizes them and from which they superimpose themselves upon one another—such an incorporeal arrangement supposes, at a deeper level, an "expansion" on a "surface" that, ever wider, does not occupy any site and will hardly take up any room in extended space.

We must return to Leibniz to discover such a virtual expansivity depending entirely on the interiority of a point of view—that point of view he called the monad. Every image envelops a numerical series, an intertwining of series, the inflections of which are not truly spatial, but rather pertain to intensive and absolutely spiritual magnitudes. Indeed, there is in Leibniz a spiritualization of space that is interior to the soul. Space, supposedly exterior, is only a numerical projection of embryonic differentials from the bottom of the soul, a space unfolded along the lines of a surface immanent to the life of the mind. It is thus that all space braids itself along a conceptual surface. One finds in Leibniz volumes of ideas (monads) that, without belonging to a durable and solid extension, nonetheless adopt a place, a determinate locus—as if the totality of the visible world had finally been reduced to the immaterial extension of an ideal world. Or rather, one should say, a world of ideas—in which one idea could divide itself into another idea or, on the contrary, find itself thwarted by the other one, while the next idea could prolong itself in one certain direction and find other access denied.

As a result, we have to recognize what Plato already knew, that one idea is distinguished from another by a certain contour and prolongs itself upon a given vector, upon a branch that can divide to the left or to the right (*Sophist*). An idea presents a limit that makes its definition possible, and on the edge of which it comes into contact with neighboring ideas or, to the contrary, detaches itself from them out of repulsion, resistance, or impenetrability (*Parmenides*). If such volumes remain, in Plato, subsumed under the analogical model of representation, they find themselves, in Leibniz, elevated for the first time to the level of an entire reality—a virtual reality that bears within itself the force of projection and configuration allowing it to actualize itself in integral images. It is this system of images indurated into a singular point of view that Leibniz unfolds in the concept of *monadology*—a whole ideal *expansum* of series and combinatory networks, the very ones that, today, the computer reactualizes even as it extends into immensity the field of their influence and confluence, something that Leibniz would formalize with the concept of the *immensum* or spiritual immensity![12] This is how we should envisage a volume and a field for the image: as a place and a perspective without real extension. There is a spiritual, or mental, milieu—which can be neither seen nor touched—where ideas cross with one another, or run up against one another thanks to a contour that distinguishes them. We will call this milieu *the world of ideas,* this phrase bearing witness to the understanding that philosophy is inseparable from a world, the construction of which is not perhaps entirely foreign to what we have just clarified with the words *virtual reality,* even if the totally intensive texture of the former cannot be reduced to the three-dimensional metric of the latter, which, we must admit, is not very far from the ideality that Kant, following Leibniz, attributes to space and time.[13]

The world of ideas is what is proper to philosophy, which is, as Deleuze liked to say, inseparable from an image of thought.[14] But it was not until very late in the history of philosophy that this image became virtual to the point of defining the régime of perception as an innervation that becomes the complete idealization of space and time (which culminates, for example, in Fichte). The importance of a thought will, in every case, be measured against the image of the world that it traces: an image is unfolded in an eidetic milieu no longer ascribable to the human eye, but rather to the volume of the concept capable of delivering the "epiphanic" scale and dimension of the world. It is difficult to read Plato's *Timaeus* or Plotinus's *Enneads* without the feeling of crossing unmoored spaces, the *expansum* of which has nothing to do with the extension of a material site. It is a question of an intensive surface—like that which Grosseteste, for example, in the thirteenth century, deployed in the form of a sphere of light. We might say that, very early, the concept manifested itself in the form of a volume hollowed out from inside, a three-dimensional volume that, as distinct from natural perception, must address things out of the hollow of their immanence, visualizing them within the virtual movement of their epiphanic genesis.

We owe to Henri Focillon the idea that between the Roman basilica and the sphere of light conceived by Grosseteste there is a mutual copenetration in which the concept confronts its own visibility, developed in a form of a three-dimensional inherence that was only accessible in architecture during that epoch. Architecture is a visual montage in which the world gets called into existence in the form of the ideality of a space that remains phenomenal, a world totally interior to the edifice that thereby ceases to be perceived simply from the outside. A space is born that is not reducible to exteriority; instead of condemning us to see things from the outside, it clarifies them from within. Everything works toward this clarification according to the immanence of a point of view with which philosophy necessarily enters into relation. Between the volume of an idea and the volume of an architectural form there is an interior spark that comes to idealize a thoroughly spiritual contour.[15]

Architecture appears to philosophy as one of the first volumes liberated of the site, with a visibility entirely conceived to be unfolded from within, forcing us thereby to plunge our gaze toward ourselves, in keeping with a "Copernican revolution" (as Kant would say) through which space becomes ideal, and ceases to be envisaged dogmatically from outside. The Abbey of Cluny: a mental design laid out in an interlocking series of vaults, the center of which is everywhere and the periphery nowhere.

This architectural milieu is not only the site of a possible stroll, but a volume with which philosophy communicates, if only through the need to call on a characteristic *expansum*—as Plato does in invoking the cave, as Saint Anselm does in taking the monastic cell as enclave of the spirit, and, closer to us, as Leibniz does in calling on the image of a windowless room (or a baroque chapel, as Deleuze says in *The*

Fold) to define the contour of the monad: a projection of thought upon the inner face of a peripheral wall! Rolling one's eyes back into one's head makes of architecture the skull of philosophy.[16]

The image and, in the image, philosophical contemplation are born on the occasion of a rupture with the geographical site, the occasion of a gathering able to illuminate things in a space not to be confused with the exteriority of the parts it was believed to separate—a space that rather allows things to be taken from "inside." What we need is a gaze liable to develop itself from the interior, encircled by the mass of a wall that presents itself as a volume swollen with light, so that images and thoughts, crypts and tombs may be born. This is true to such an extent that philosophy, in its entirety, must define itself—as the inverse of science—by an invagination or a turn of the gaze up into the head, by this indefatigable desire to explore an imperceptible world, taking as its only guide the internal architecture of a problem, if not the volume of a particular concept, caught in the net of memory more than in the exteriority of matter. This clear madness that bears thought toward a view without exteriority, caught in the ornamental cockpit of an interior that illuminates itself by itself—we come upon this same madness in van Gogh's paintings, in the form of an utterly characteristic movement distanced at every point from classical representation.

In the composition of *Las Meninas,* Velázquez presents us with precisely the duality at the origin of the classical work of art. On one side, we have the painter, placed behind the canvas, and, on the other side, the model for the painting, who is no less occulted by the contraposition of the easel. Either we see the painter but we no longer perceive the object of the work, except by way of the subtle mirror game that Velázquez exploits, placing the object behind the painter, or we perceive the object of the canvas but we no longer perceive the painter, nor the gaze he directs upon the real that the classical painter had cultivated as the blind spot of the work—its surrogate origin [*origine nourricière*], necessarily invisible, withdrawn into obscurity, veiled beneath what it unveils, just as Being is occulted under the beings it sustains. By contrast, van Gogh's *Bedroom in Arles* defines a totally other movement. This painting gives the feeling of a cramped perspective, as if the painter's eye were directly opened in the middle of things. It is occasion for a turning of the eye into the head, and it integrates the seen into the seer through a dive toward the image, an innervation at the heart of the work where the gaze passes beyond the limit, the border separating subject and object. With the work, we feel ourselves live in things even as things come to live in us according to a radical immanence.

The wall that Vincent dreamed of passing through, of patiently eroding, this was finally the limit separating inside from outside, the surface of the painting that turned its back on things. Now this border is over with, since the brain is becoming world even as life enters painting. The membrane separating the seen from the seer has opened up, absorbing things into the heart of the eye that contemplates them. As one can see, otherwise, in the last episode (dream) of Kurosawa's great film *Dreams*, devoted to van Gogh: in this scene, the eye has penetrated to the heart of the canvas, giving way to a traveling shot, which Vincent had already elaborated on the level of accelerated perspective, and which it remained for the resources of the cinema to rediscover. The world bathes in the brain in the form of mental landscapes, landscapes that the hand must seize with colors, the associations between which happen with the speed of flicking neuronal synapses. Such are the emotions, the affects of our nervous system that order the perception of landscapes and put them into perspective. Emotion is the regulation of images, the intensity able to hone their clarity or to activate their blurry zones.

Emotion is a force that hones perception, even as it activates the gestures with which the painter strikes the canvas with disordered brush strokes, blows delivered at lightning speed. This is the only way that the painter is able to seize life alive, in the form of a living work, a cerebral membrane upon which the difference between outside and inside fades away. The emotions take possession of the landscape with all the power of the nerves that elongate themselves while the entirety of nature switches into a dream, into a mental image charged with affirmation of the heaviest risk, the madness of one who turns his or her body into a painting studio. Van Gogh's painting reaches its maturity when each painting behaves as a membrane upon which emotions no longer distinguish themselves from reality. The canvas becomes the surface on which the artist's vision projects itself and where the texture of the world is woven together; it realizes a plane where it is no longer possible to distinguish dream from reality, the cerebral from the perceived image. It is a surface on which thought and being interpenetrate, physical and mental reality cross, without there being the least wish to separate them. The thing seen is only visible thanks to the emotions that deform it, or to impressions that accentuate its contour; it is interior to the painter's sight line from the moment he accepts to take leave of himself, to capture the murmur of an anonymous existence—impersonal existence, exterior to the intentions of consciousness.

It is not consciousness that permits us to take leave of ourselves, to plunge in the thing's direction, or to breach the limit of perception. To do this, we need an abandonment of the ego that will, too often, draw all things back toward the self, or, perhaps, a breach through which the ego liberates itself of its interiority in order for the difference of subject and object to be abolished on a common membrane, this membrane on which the brain enters the world at the same time as the world penetrates into the milieu of the brain. There is nothing dialectical about an ecstasy of such amplitude; for it pertains to a fusion in which things and colors are already thoughts, while thoughts have ceased to refer back to the ego (situated behind the canvas, in order to get lost back there) upon contact with elements whose concrescence they follow, whose mixture and tensive loves they accentuate. In short, the brain becomes world and the world invades the brain at the juncture of the canvas, which is as much a material as a spiritual membrane, a psychophysical entity made of extension and thought, matter and memory, flesh and spirit. The canvas is an intermediate reality between nature and the idea, a compound of being and thought that has detached itself from the one its author designates, though not without having forced him to take his wayward mind for a walk in the texture of things. This is what fatigue means: the nervous exhaustion that drives the author to collapse, to lose his grip, exhausted from having to walk upon a plane as virgin of traces as the sea. The cerebral membrane de-subjectifies itself, turns itself into a painting, alters itself to become a canvas of the world while the texture of the painting makes itself cerebral—a painting inside the head for a head become painting. And this can only occur there where the ego absents itself and, solitary, gets itself lost in giving way to the eye of things.

It is indispensable that the ego efface itself in order to let the murmur of the flowers express itself, which, van Gogh writes, "by its vibration will make you think of the gentle rustle of the cornstalks swaying in the breeze."[17] Accession to the pure image of things is only possible on condition that the ego is abstracted, the painter's mind diluting itself into an anonymous membrane, common to both thought and being. Therein lies the profound mysticism of van Gogh, who seeks to lose hold of himself on the way to the *Istigkeit* (beingness) of existence, a vibratory beingness, very different from what one customarily envisaged as Being, and which opens up within the Scotch plaid fabric of the world, on the surface of this cerebral membrane where mind and matter interpenetrate. On the rebound from such an absence, it is good not to remain alone, to be able to renew ties with oneself, to come to one's senses after having lost them. But this is not possible for van Gogh: he looks for alcohol to keep him company, while tobacco gives him back the power to make his head swim. In the neuter beingness of the world, tobacco presents itself as a substance that gives things back a contour. It is at the origin of an emotion, of an anonymous dizziness that allows one to profile the wind in the flowers. Absinthe, for its part, first acts as a will to return to oneself after a prolonged absence in an impersonal calculus—even if, ultimately, alcohol leads to difficult and erratic morning blackouts.[18] But both tobacco and alcohol function as means to withstand the furnace of conception, to breach the wall, patiently to erode it up to the doors of perception: "It is at times like these that the prospect of not being alone is not disagreeable. And very often I think of that excellent painter Monticelli—whom they said was such a drinker, and off his head—when I come back myself from the mental labor of balancing the six essential colors, red—blue—yellow—orange—lilac—green."[19]

The arduous and harrowing work of equilibrating colors is the work of the painter-weaver who repairs torn threads. Color matter is torn into pieces. The difference of its threads should not be lost in the uniformity of middle grey. The artist thus has the arduous task of breaching the little faults that separate each color, each thread, realizing an equilibrium that occasions a vital color—a vital plaid—there where difference does not abolish itself into homogeneity. Breaching the tiny distances that slip in between every color, keeping them at a distance from one another instead of abolishing their separation, is furious work, a work that concedes nothing to oneness, to unity of color, to a solid hue. Color is torn into pieces by the *places* that differentiate it, preventing it from lapsing back into uniformity, and that pull its threads toward poles that stretch it out and swell it up in opposing directions. Color must be broken up, torn into incompatible threads, the intervals between which the mind of the painter will breach in the work of subtle equilibration—an equilibration that, instead of deteriorating into middle grey, creates a vibratory, plaid entity, alive with life. This equilibration can only occur on the level of the eye of he who contemplates the lacing of the torn threads, or in the brain that seizes them and holds them together on the sensitive membrane of contractable nerves.

This plaid color is finally a mental color, an equilibrium produced in the mind of he who perceives it. And this exigency to work over the painting in its swarming ruptures, in the electric dismemberment of its hues, the equilibrium of which amounts to a trembling, dappled color, alive with life—this exigency will remain van Gogh's constant preoccupation until the very end. To unite the incompatible, to create broken hues [*couleurs rompus*],[20] or the impossible equilibrium of what bifurcates in every direction along tartan lines, this is the only means of hearing the murmur of the cypress tree, of realizing this membrane where a few cornstalks, or poppies, enter into concrescence with "a blue sky like a piece of dappled Scotch plaid, the former painted with a thick impasto like the Monticellis, and the corn field in the sun, which represents the extreme heat, very thick too."[21] The difficulty of equilibrating the six threads of color amounts to a madness, and brings on cerebral fatigue, given the impossibility of coming to rest amid solid hues. It is incumbent upon the mind to keep open the state of mutual strain out of which arises the rupture of the colors, to engage itself in the interval between an infinity of nuances, each one of which turns away from the previous one even as it contrasts with it in a unique impasto, an overall plaid effect. In short, the equilibrium is not given, available beneath the repose of unequivocal or unified colors: it must be produced, extracted from a jumble of threads, the continuity of which should remain in perpetual negotiation, a kind of "sheer work and calculation, with one's mind strained to the utmost, like an actor on the stage in a difficult part, with a hundred things to think of in a single half hour."[22]

Between the six threads of painting that all turn their backs on one another under the injunction of very different places, the mind must leap from one to the next, breach their heterogeneity in favor of a broken hue that can create equilibrium, though not without straining the mind to the utmost toward all the discords that cause it to bifurcate in every direction, requiring the thousand and one precautions without which this broken hue would not exist. Besides, where could there exist such a broken hue, such a plaid entity, if not in the mind of he who collects its torn threads? Such a hue is not to be perceived within the very colors it equilibrates. It does not reside in them as an objective given: in the object, there are only threads, grains of color that do not resemble the vaguely orangish or greenish hue that hovers over it. It is not even a subjective donation, because the attention of a subject able to scrutinize it up close disperses the effect, which is more likely to be obtained in the vacuity of distraction, with an abstracted gaze, drowning in a thousand details. This color deploys itself somewhere between subject and object, on this psychophysical membrane that is not an attribute of the ego, nor of solid things, but that comes between thought and being, which it imbricates and renders indiscernible—as François Rouan has so powerfully experienced, today, in a totally unclassifiable work in progress.[23]

This mystical perception is not therefore the result of attention, reflexivity, or an effort of concentration. It arises thanks to an evasive, a-subjective contemplation, the meditation of an "impassive cow," quite far from the ascetic exercise of monastic seclusion because it emerges by virtue of an excessive nature—excess of alcohol and tobacco, emotions and forces, there where monastic visions rely on fasting and the diminution of all vitality. Indeed, "the only thing to bring ease and distraction, in my case and the other people's too, is to stun oneself with a lot of drinking or heavy smoking. Not very virtuous, no doubt, but it's to return to the subject of Monticelli. I'd like to see a drunkard in front of a canvas or on the boards."[24]

Alcohol and tobacco only come into play after the process of creation, which is itself already too intense to allow for stimulants, unless these substances can stave off the even greater trouble of madness, thereby making it possible for the wayward mind of the painter to pass through the wall of common perception, even as he gives perception back an equilibrium—that surprising equilibrium of the alcoholic who walks straight ahead beneath the onslaught of the storm. Perhaps absinthe allows him to cut a narrow wake in the outside that would permit the ego to stray without getting lost—a lost sentry able to give proof of vigilance amid the chaos of a color storm, a vigilambulist liable not to go under there where all the references of common perception have faltered. And it is perhaps the only way to enter into the plaid of existence without passing out completely, maintaining sufficient vigilance to manage a little distance from madness. The floating that alcohol procures is like a sieve that emerges when the wall of our senses breaks open to the beingness of things (*Istigkeit*):

> Monticelli, the logical colorist, able to pursue the most complicated calculations, subdivided according to the scales of tones that he was equilibrating, certainly overstrained his brain at this work, just as Delacroix did, and Richard Wagner. And if perhaps he did drink, it was because he—and Jongkind too—having a stronger constitution than Delacroix, and more physical ailments (Delacroix was better off), well, if they hadn't drunk—as I for one am inclined to believe—their nerves would have rebelled, and played them other tricks: Jules and Edmond de Goncourt said the very same thing, word for word: "*we used to smoke very strong tobacco to stupefy ourselves* in the furnace of creation."[25]

When the membrane breaks that separates the seen from the seer, or the inside from the outside, then tobacco appears as a means to float within the furnace without going up in flames, while absinthe restores some of this lost sentry's vigilance, a vigilance that confers equilibrium on the rupture of hues. Alcohol is a factor of equilibrium within vertigo, an equilibrium of the unstable, necessary when all is reeling—a posture quickly conquered, as quickly as possible before the fall, when one is closest to falling and must calculate in advance the speed of recovery:

> Don't think that I would maintain a feverish condition artificially, but understand that I am in the midst of a complicated calculation which results in a quick succession of canvases quickly executed but calculated long beforehand. So now, when anyone says that such and such is done too quickly, you can reply that they have looked at it too quickly.[26]

The sunflowers: bent down by a balancing neutral eye, not without themselves mutating into eyes that make you feel them watching you. The sunflowers, from their vase, scrutinize and contemplate you with the round irises of live yellow beasts. They come to life as if they were captured in the absolute acceleration of their germination. One among them moves so quickly its contour blurs, effaced by the speed with which it bends and observes you, orange on a green ground, quivering in all its limbs. The one gazed upon becomes the one who gazes, the eye slips outside me toward the thing it touches, as if the difference between the I and the not-I no longer existed, reality having gone over to mind, not without mind itself having passed into every last twig, "with the pale smile of a last rose."[27] There is a whole philosophy of nature animated in the texture of the canvas, a plane of thought and being whose conjunction philosophy has pursued since Aristotle under the sign of a *Naturphilosophie*, on which the name of Schelling eventually conferred a certain nobility. There is an identity of nature and mind that Vincent's painting seeks to recover beyond the abstract distinction that has posited, there in front of the easel, objective reality and, behind its dark side, the subjective reality out of which projects the perspective of every possible point of view. It is this difference, this unbreachable rampart, imposed by the sieve of the common consciousness that the *Sunflowers* come to ruin as they bear perception toward the tension between colors that have become seeing colors, eye-catching colors [*couleurs voyants*]: colors that see and invite us to see what, finally, they alone can give to be seen, like as many human eyes placed at the heart of things. The sunflowers cease to be things seen from a distance that would place them outside of us. They come alive with a life able to take hold of us and contemplate us without averring any separation. But if nature and mind conjoin in a common membrane, this fusion does not amount to a dismal identity wherein every difference would merge into the uniformity out of which, as Hegel would say, nothing ever emerges. At stake here is not a night when all the cats are grey, but a live surface, cavernous and differential, streaked with holes and lights.

The immanence of being and thought is not a fall into the indiscernible, the equalization of all tensions in a lifeless, homogeneous soup. It is more of a metastable surface in perpetual variation, a surface on which matter and memory touch and conjoin one another, an intermediate canvas where images begin to flicker. What is an image that is not this psychophysical encounter of thought and nature? Where to situate an image, if not upon a common membrane, neither of pure spirit nor of pure matter but, rather, the intermediate fringe on which they blend? An image cannot be reduced to the cold, objective reality of independent matter, but neither is it the simple subjective survey of my mind as it exacts a look at the inaccessible back of things. The image is born in the middle, between the two, in the crucible of being and thought, as a new reality, an entity that comes to live an autonomous life that is impossible to place in me or outside of me. Images are floating souls, souls of the world that science knows precisely nothing about. That images rise up between spirit and matter, on a common surface, does not imply an empty identity, the One of Parmenides, the absorption of all tension into the vague grey that Hegel uses to reproach Schelling. The image, envisaged in the form of a live membrane, is not a dead plane, an undifferentiated mix where both I and not-I are abolished and "all the cows have become grey." In truth, the univocity in which being and thought conjoin, the image that articulates them, instead of fading into the One, unfurls as a complex multiplicity of broken hues, cracked ideas, explosive affections.

The image of the flower, such a simple thing at the heart of which the blossoming of nature coincides with the contentment of spirit, presents itself as a veritable psychophysical labyrinth. No relation to what Heidegger says of Silesius's poem, whose "rose" finally "asks not whether it is seen."[28] To the withdrawal of the rose into the obscure uniformity of Being, we prefer van Gogh's sunfloral clouds—clouds reminiscent of this haiku by Shiki that Huxley cites in *The Doors of Perception*:[29]

> Roses:
> The flowers are easy to paint
> the leaves, difficult

The rose might in fact blossom all in one absolutely simple image; it might in fact enjoin the immediate conjunction of spirit and matter in the form of the manifest splendor of flowers, but this takes nothing away from the more subtle miracle of its foliage. Simplicity is not grey, solid grey. It is not to be confused with the neutralizing One. To understand it, one only has to go back to the sunflowers that Vincent painted during the Parisian period. Here again are eyes that contemplate us, eyes of fire culled from a blue furnace, edged with orange flames. Nothing exists of the flower but its complex foliage, a surface where the mind gets lost, absorbed by the thousand little granular losenges laid out in a circumflex labyrinth. The flower is a cavernous body, shot through with chasms—as close as van Gogh came to this plaid that he had been pursuing at least since he was in Nuenen. If spirit penetrates into matter, gets lost in it, and becomes indistinguishable from it, if the I and the not-I are brought together in the unity of nature and thought, the result cannot be the Absolute Identity floundering in the uniform greywash of Being. The result can only be a live fusion, that of the image in whose crucible all explodes and is consumed by fire, allowing there to hatch myriad gold nuggets engorged with worlds, whose souls the painter invites us to explore. This is what the event is: a passage through the wall that leads thought and nature to intertwine, regaining the common surface on which they become images. The event, as Huxley will say, "is a succession of doors opening on furnaces of an azure blue, separated by abysses of unfathomable gentian."[30] A succession of doors and abysses, a labyrinth of textures as complex as the lobes of the brain, the twists and turns of paths whose bifurcation is much like the chasms that Vincent creates at Saint-Rémy with *Les Peiroulets Ravine*.

It is this ravine of the image that opens between thought and being that Deleuze has us discover through his books on cinema, no less in his detour through Bergson and Leibniz. From this entanglement of the mental landscape that the monad unfolds, and from the cerebral texture of the world inaugurated by cinema, is born the image of thought as Deleuze unfolds it in his essay on philosophy as plane of Nature, the plane that grasps being and thought on a common diagram of immanence. To conclude, then, let us weave the threads of our clandestine argumentation back into the texture where it gains clarity and pattern, there where Deleuze launches it, borne toward the future of those whom it now forces to think without his presence, calling out to us with an unforgettable sentence written in these precipitate words:

> The world has become memory, brain, superimposition of ages or lobes, but the brain itself has become consciousness, continuation of ages, creation or growth of ever new lobes, re-creation of matter as with styrene. The screen itself is the cerebral membrane where immediate and direct confrontations take place between the past and the future, the inside and the outside, at a distance impossible to determine, independent of any fixed point.[31]

NOTES

This translation is indebted to Steven Miller, without whose advice and acumen it would not have been possible.

1. Henri Bergson, *Matter and Memory*, trans. N. M. Paul and W. S. Palmer (New York: Zone Books, 1988), 25.
2. The metaphor of the city often recurs in Leibniz's writings. See, in particular, his complete works, published in German, part 1 (19, 20), part 2 (19), and his *Discourse on Metaphysics*, §14.
3. Alain Badiou developed the excess of this inclusion in quite a different way throughout *L'Être et l'événement* (Paris: Éditions du Seuil, 1988).
4. This construction of the landscape was developed in my analysis of medieval space in *Ossuaires* (Paris: Payot, 1995), plate 6.

5. The French adjective does not stem from *idéal* (ideal) but from *idée* (idea), a difference that does not come across in the English adjective.—*Trans.*
6. Bergson, *Matter and Memory*, 173.
7. This is the central concern of Deleuze's study on Bergson, *Bergsonism*, trans. Hugh Tomlinson and Barbara Habberjam (New York: Zone Books, 1991).
8. On the cone, the telescope, and photography, see Bergson, *Matter and Memory*, chapter 3.
9. For the analysis of attentive recognition, see ibid., 103–5.
10. On the difference between similitude and resemblance, metaphor and metonymy, see the sixth plate of my *Ossuaires*, 143–46.
11. Bergson, *Matter and Memory*, 171.
12. See Gottfried Wilhelm Leibniz, *New Essays on Human Understanding*, ed. and trans. Jonathan Bennett and Peter Remnant (Cambridge: Cambridge University Press, 1996), chapter 11, §6.
13. This actualization of Leibniz in computer circuits has been a constant assumption throughout Michel Serres's philosophical project since *Hermès I* (Paris: Éditions de Minuit, 1968–77). Also note that this was the occasion for my *L'Image virtuelle* (Paris: Kimé, 1996).
14. On the image of thought, see chapter 2 of Gilles Deleuze and Félix Guattari, *What Is Philosophy?*, trans. Hugh Tomlinson and Graham Burchell (New York: Columbia University Press, 1994), as well as my commentary in *Variations* (Paris: Payot, 1993), 1.
15. Henri Focillon, *L'Art des sculpteurs romans* (Paris: Presses Universitaires de France, 1988), 220. See my analysis of Focillon in *Ossuaires*, plate 1, as well as in *Variations*, 167–76.
16. I am indebted to Raymond Bellour for this idea of an internalization of the image, which he developed in a beautiful text, "La Chambre," *Trafic* 9 (P.O.L. Editions) (winter 1994).
17. Vincent van Gogh, *The Complete Letters of Vincent Van Gogh* (Boston: New York Graphic Society, 1975), vol. 3, 287.
18. Here the French phrase "évanouissment de matins" is ambiguous and could be read in two ways: to indicate either the painter's morning loss of consciousness or the loss, the vanishing, the passing away, or the "blackout" of the morning itself.—*Trans.* (based on the author's indications).
19. Van Gogh, *The Complete Letters of Vincent Van Gogh*, vol. 2, 606.
20. See Ralph Mayer, *The Artist's Handbook: Of Materials and Techniques* (New York: Viking Press, 1985), 161: "The three colors mentioned so far are called primaries; when any one is mixed with another a secondary color effect is produced: green, violet, or orange. This system of color mixing is known as the subtractive process, because the second color subtracts and absorbs still more waves from the white light than the first color did. When three or several more pigments of different color are mixed, *tertiary or broken hues are obtained*."—*Trans.*
21. Van Gogh, *The Complete Letters of Vincent Van Gogh*, vol. 3, 188.
22. Ibid., vol. 2, 606.
23. It is François Rouan's work in its entirety that places itself under the sign of such a problematic; it is a palimpsestual work, a surface woven with almost transparent strips of cloth that provoke the rupture of hues wherever they overlap and cover each other, a surface made into an ossuary of fragments about which I shall shortly publish a study.
24. Van Gogh, *The Complete Letters of Vincent Van Gogh*, vol. 2, 606.
25. Ibid., 606–7.
26. Ibid., 607.
27. Ibid., vol. 3., 524.

28. Heidegger's discussion of this poem figures in *The Principle of Reason*, trans. Reginald Lilly (Bloomington: Indiana University Press, 1991), 41.
29. Aldous Huxley, *The Doors of Perception* (New York: Harper, 1954), 53.
30. Ibid., 49.
31. Gilles Deleuze, *The Time-Image*, trans. Hugh Tomlinson and Robert Galeta (Minneapolis: University of Minnesota Press, 1989), 125.

Chapter 2

Cinema Year Zero

Gregory Flaxman

> *We have fixed up a world for ourselves in which we can live—assuming bodies, lines, planes, causes and effects, motion and rest, form and content: without these articles of faith, nobody would now endure life. But that does not mean they have been proved. Life is no argument. The conditions of life might include error.*
>
> —Nietzsche[1]

Ever since Plato's *Republic*, philosophy seems to have been the labor of "master builders": Descartes demolishes all prosaic assumptions about the world to lay the groundwork for his first principles, Kant fashions the exquisite proportions of his first *Critiques* as a propaedeutic to metaphysics, and even Hegel's professed dislike of philosophical preludes grounds his *Phenomenology of Spirit*.[2] We have come to expect our philosophers to build by design, pausing at the outset to reflect on the construction, and so it is all the more astonishing how Gilles Deleuze opens his cinema books. Never mind the brief, almost capricious preface that adorns *The Movement-Image* (or the slightly more cogent preface that was added to the English translation): to read the cinema books is to lapse, almost in medias res, into Deleuze's assurance that "Bergson does not just put forward one thesis on movement, but three."[3]

Of course, this is no assurance at all, but the moment at which we begin to lose our bearings, thrown from one strange milieu—what is billed as a philosophy of the cinema—into another: the theses of Henri Bergson. So disorienting is all of this that we are likely to gloss a remarkable discrepancy, for although Deleuze draws extensively on Bergson to elaborate his cinematographic philosophy, Bergson himself was not particularly impressed by the cinematograph. Deleuze appeals to Bergson's *Matter and Memory* (1896) to suggest that the cinematographic image can surpass "the conditions of natural perception,"[4] but Bergson's allusion to the cinematograph in *Creative Evolution* (1907) was intended to illustrate the *"mechanism of our ordinary knowledge."*[5] Thus, the inspiration for Deleuze's cinematographic philosophy is also likely to inspire our skepticism. Beyond even Deleuze's project, we might well ask: is there really anything *extra*ordinary about the cinema?

The question is as old as cinema itself, but in the context of Deleuze's claim that the cinematographic image so departs from normal perception as to compel philosophy to create new concepts, the question reaches a kind of critical mass. Surely, Deleuze believed as much, for, having recounted Bergson's cool reaction to the cinema, he immediately proceeds to offer an explanation. The cinematographic image that Bergson had witnessed, Deleuze explains, was the product of technology still struggling to unleash its potential (*agencement machinique*), to conquer "its own novelty."[6] The cinema had yet to really come into consciousness of itself; Lumière, for example, did not really grasp the possibilities afforded by the cinema, and Deleuze figures this initial blindness as the first, and perhaps founding, instance of the "long martyrology" that is the history of cinema.[7] More recent developments in the historicization of "early cinema" notwithstanding, the period is "primitive" for Deleuze because its images are still on a par with human perception. Not only was the cinematograph "fixed," withholding the pans, cranes, and assorted other movements that the cinema would thereafter discover, but the technical "combination" of camera and projector impeded any significant montage.[8] Deleuze grants that, as a contemporary of this early cinematograph, Bergson was bound to dismiss the device; rather, Bergson's real failure lay in never having envisaged what the cinematographic image could *become* . . .

For a moment let's consider the drift of Deleuze's argument, which aims to trump the philosopher of *Creative Evolution* with a theory of evolution. To do so, Deleuze intimates that, by dismissing the potential of the cinematograph, Bergson understood (or misunderstood) the technology to "imitate normal perception."[9] No doubt, Bergson draws the analogy between cinema and perception, but Deleuze seems to distort the terms of the analogy: cinema does not imitate normal perception; rather, it reveals the "mechanism" of perception. By perceiving, Bergson writes, "we hardly do anything else than set going a kind of cinematograph inside of us."[10] At first glance, the point may seem trivial, but failing to recognize it, we miss the regrettable origin of cinema and philosophy, the first of what will become, as Deleuze points out, a sorry history of missed encounters.[11] Whereas phenomenologists such as Merleau-Ponty at least entertained the notion that the cinematic image was abnormal, differing qualitatively from human perception, Bergson likens the cinematograph to perception because both are so conventional, so normal, and so secure. The cinema is only degraded, then, insofar as it is analogized to perception, and this is what should interest us, because Bergson has retreated from his former, more radical notion of perception, the notion on which Deleuze seizes in the cinema books. Bergson himself sums it up: "Instead of attaching ourselves to the inner becoming of things [the postulate of the earlier *Matter and Memory*], we place ourselves outside the things in order to recompose their becoming artificially" (the postulate of the later *Creative Evolution*).[12]

In effect, Deleuze takes Bergson to have misunderstood the cinema given certain philosophical presuppositions, but something else has happened in the meantime (behind our backs, as Hegel would say): Bergson has reformulated those presuppositions. The discussion that follows is largely concerned with this "Bergsonian turn," particularly the way in which the mechanism of stable perception acquires a kind of philosophical security, and so one might justifiably ask what this has to do with the cinema at all. My answer is that, by following this line of thought, we actually advance to what Deleuze himself deems the "essence" of the cinema: for Bergson's reversal constitutes a retreat from the potential of the cinema to transform perception, to "deregulate sense," and to compel a revaluation of philosophy itself.[13] On the one hand, this argument has the superficial advantage of correcting a lapse in Deleuze's argument in order to affirm its overall rigor; but my hope, on the other hand, is that something more profound will appear—perhaps, with respect to cinema and philosophy, both a sense of our penchant for regularity and our potential to think *differently*.

"Yes, if cinema does not die a violent death," Deleuze writes in *The Time-Image*, "it retains the power of a beginning."[14] That power consists in opening an "interstice" for thought to emerge, an "in-between" where image-affects are linked in an "adventure of movement and time."[15] By contrast, an investigation into Bergson's philosophy struggles to understand how he managed to recoil from this "adventure." How is it possible that Bergson, whose *Creative Evolution* relies on a cinematographic analogy, actually retreats from the cinema? To begin with, Deleuze rightly points out that Bergson's seemingly self-evident metaphor is flawed: though perception seems to proceed by stringing together immobile sections like so many photograms (frames) of film, what the cinema "gives us is not the photogramme: it is an immediate image, to which movement is not appended or added."[16] In other words, while perceptions are ostensibly abstracted "above" into "mobile sections" that are, in turn, strung together like "a kind of cinematograph inside us,"[17] the movement-image produced by the cinema is already strung together, already "corrected." Bergson depends on the cinema to demonstrate normal human perception, but he does so by concealing the abnormal nature of the cinematographic image; he attends to the mechanism, refusing to acknowledge that the image it produces is exceptional. Even as the cinematograph is advanced as the endgame of Bergson's argument, as Deleuze assumed, the rhetorical sleight of hand—the metaphorical appropriation of a technology that represses its effective repercussions—suggests a very different kind of logic, namely, that the cinema may have agitated the philosophical retreat in the first place.

To consider why the cinematographic image should prove threatening in this sense is not to court a "psychological" reading, at least not in any traditional sense. The question, rather, is that of our "anxiety before the image," for the cinema threatens to foreclose metaphysical certitude. Indeed, it is precisely this certitude—the adequation of subject and object on which philosophy traditionally rests—that preoccupies Bergson in *Creative Evolution*, to the point that he embarks on an exegesis of Platonic (or, as he calls it, "Greek") philosophy. The Greeks, Bergson reminds us, generally reconstituted the movement of images, à la Xeno, from eternal presuppositions. To do so, Platonism split the plane of intelligibility off from the vicissitudes of the sensible world, from images. One finds the dualism consecrated in language itself: although the Greek "idea" derived from the verb "to see" (*eido*), the Platonists forged a distinction whereby "Idea" became *Eidos*, or suprasensible reality, while "image" became *eikon*, the impression or likeness of an idea.[18] Bergson explains that "[e]xperience confronts us with becoming: that is *sensible* reality"; in the case of the Greeks, though, "*intelligible* reality, that which ought to be, is [considered] more real still, and that reality does not change."[19] The Platonic dualism privileges the intellectual mechanism, which strings together our stable views of the world on a "becoming abstract," and so it is only a logical step to the assertion that Platonism constitutes the cinematographic philosophy par excellence (as Plato put it, the world is a "moving picture of eternity").

In light of what we have already said, the conclusion is dubious—and even more dubious given the situation of the argument itself in the context of Bergson's philosophy. Indeed, *Matter and Memory* expressly critiques this sort of philosophical dualism; in the introduction, Bergson begins by explaining that the book "deals with body and mind in such a way as, we hope, to lessen greatly, if not overcome, the theoretical difficulties which have always beset dualism."[20] As Deleuze aptly wonders, "Had Bergson forgotten it ten years later?"[21] The question lingers at the opening of the cinema books, waiting for an answer or even a conjecture; but Deleuze is not really interested in providing one. For him, the question is the pivot on which his own philosophy turns: Deleuze begins with and then quickly dispenses with *Creative Evolution*, rapidly shifting to *Matter and Memory*, on which he draws to develop both a cosmology (the brain as cinema, the world as metacinema, in the first volume) and a model of world-memory (the cinema as brain, in the second volume). However understandable Deleuze's predilection, it assures that the "Bergsonian turn" remains a mysterious one. But what if one were to work forward from *Matter and Memory* to *Creative Evolution*, from the book that anticipates cinema to the one that degrades it? Could we begin to understand this reaction differently, perhaps even as a withdrawal from the possibilities of cinema itself? And, finally, could we see this retreat as the germ of the development that Deleuze himself sees, writ large, as the "history" of the cinema?

In order to answer these questions, let us begin by acquainting ourselves with *Matter and Memory*, both as a radical critique of dualism and as a theory of the image to which this critique gives rise. With deceptive straightforwardness and ease, *Matter and Memory* opens by describing the unsatisfying set of alternatives into which philosophy has lapsed. In the terms of dominant philosophy (contra Deleuze's renowned "minor philosophy," what we might here call "major philosophy"), Bergson finds that one is forced to choose between realism and idealism. The concrete examples of this split are revealed, on the one hand, in Descartes's geometrical extensity and, on the other, in Berkeley's pure mentalism. One either treats matter as "a thing able to produce in us perceptions, but in itself of another nature than they" or else as "the perception we have of it."[22] Although the choice is dualistic, the options in themselves maintain a kind of divide because both effectively mistake matter for something other than what it really is. In other words, by misunderstanding the nature of matter, realism and idealism invariably insist on a separation between matter and perception. "Of these two opposite doctrines," Bergson explains, "the one attributes to the body and the other to the intellect a true power of creation, the first [materialism] insisting that our brain begets representation and the second [idealism] that our understanding designs the plan of nature" (181).

What is remarkable in all of this, Bergson says, is that philosophy should have failed so completely to heed common sense, which discovers something different from—or, more properly, *in between*—these alternatives. As Bergson states, "Here I am in the presence of images, in the vaguest sense of the word, images perceived when my senses are open to them, unperceived when they are closed" (17). Matter should not be regarded, then, as that which is represented nor that which provokes perception, for both alternatives insert some variety of mediation. Bergson's "common sense," which is, philosophically speaking, altogether uncommon, consists in eliminating mediation, thereby realizing the identity of matter and the perception of matter. An image is the expression of matter, its *consistency* in movement, and not the re-presentation of that matter; indeed, when Bergson speaks of an image, the connotation is not of an illusion but of an affective intensity. Matter is tantamount to perception, and Bergson maintains that images themselves are the expression of this confluence: matter = movement = image = perception.

But in this string of equivalence, which precludes any dialectical opposition, any possibility of setting ourselves apart from (and thus totalizing) the universal flux, what do we mean by perception, by thought, and what would we mean by something like a "subject"? For Bergson, the world is an "aggregate of images" which coagulate and disperse, act and re-act on each other in a universal variation (22). Scientists speak of a Brownian buzz, a faint murmur of molecular popping experienced by young children whose eardrums have not quite solidified: images are just as much these vibrations, the ceaseless movement of matter in its endless convolutions. Matter is "the identity of image and movement," thereby rendering perception, usually a point of origin, always already *included* within the flux of images (matter). As Deleuze puts it, "can I even, at this level, speak of 'ego', of eye, of brain and of body?"[23] For Deleuze, this "level" figures within an ontogenesis of images or what amounts, in *The Movement-Image*, to a cosmology.[24] In the gaseous state of matter, the universe is primeval chaos, one that exists before the development of what physicists describe as strong or weak forces. "It is a state of matter too hot for one to be able to distinguish solid bodies in it," Deleuze writes; and as such "there are neither axes, nor centre, nor left, nor right, nor high, nor low . . ."[25] At this stage, the world consists solely in the convolutions of light, as if the eye had been spread into the infinitely trembling surface of things. Each unique image opens onto the vastness of a world-image; it is "a road by which we pass, in every direction, the modifications propagated throughout the immensity of the universe."[26]

For this reason, we cannot extract a subject from the universe of images as we might deduce it, in Kantian terms, from universal conditions. Rather, *the subject is the extraction*, the process of drawing order from this "chaos of light" as if through a sieve. Already this implies a "cooling down" of the universe, for the world of images has begun to settle into a semblance of "bodies" and "rigid lines."[27] Movement remains immanent to images—what is life if not movement?—but this "infinite set of images," or what Deleuze calls the "plane [*plan*] of images,"[28] no longer suggests a swirl of gaseous light, a chaos so accelerated as to prove inhospitable to life. Rather, the plane of immanence is that which distinguishes itself from chaos and in whose membranous pleats the friction of this extraction emerges (evolves) as thought (self-affection). "Like a formless elastic membrane, an electromagnetic field, or the receptacle of the *Timaeus*, the screen makes something issue from chaos, and *even if this something differs only slightly*."[29] To traverse the infinite set of all images is thus to transform infinity into a set by taking a shot (*plan*) of the infinite;[30] at the same time, though, each such point of view remarks a subject as that which "prehends" (Whitehead) the universe.[31] "If the world is in the subject," as Leibniz's monad implies, "the subject is no less *for the world*."[32] In a sense, the subject is a point at which the universe sees itself: the subject synthesizes the world from a particular point of view, but the subject also derives from that world, each perspective constituting a self-synthesis—the "*concentration, accumlation, coincidence of a certain number of converging preindividual singularities*."[33]

What we first grasped as a perspective on the universe emerges now as an interval (*écart*) in the universal flux, as if the universe itself had selected certain space-times in/at which to "fold," thereby enveloping the world inside itself. Consider that the very synthesis of an image presumes, in Bergson's famous phrase, that "consciousness *is* something"—a brief stoppage in the swirl of images, as if a photographic plate had been introduced into the flux.[34] This involution we can call the brain-body, and though it is one image among countless others, it is special. Because there is no difference in kind between images, the affections experienced by the brain suggest a difference in degree, a temporal dimension that opens up a moment of/in/for thought. Perception constitutes the dark surface on which the ceaseless flow of images is momentarily captured and thereby transformed into a set. Indeed, this point of view on chaos is precisely the process of "framing" which Deleuze describes in *The Movement-Image* as the formulation of a set (*ensemble*)—a set that opens onto other sets, other reframings as if we were tugged along a "line of time." But even so, the subject as such implies an essential ordering or "subtractive" function. "Consciousness," Bergson explains, "shows us our body as one image among others and our understanding as a certain faculty of dissociating, of distinguishing, of opposing logically, but not of creating or of constructing."[35] The subject is a synaptic gap in the aggregate of image in which a flickering of thought emerges to trigger the motor movements of a body:

> Of course, perception is strictly identical to every image, in so far as every image acts and reacts on all the others, on all their sides and in all their parts. But, when they are related to the interval of movement which separates, within *one* image, a received and an executed movement, they now vary only in relation to this one image, which will be called "perceiving" the movement received, on one of its sides, and "carrying out" the movement executed, on another side or in other parts.[36]

While all images, naturally, collide with other images, the brain introduces an interval in which thought stimulus occurs, thereby provoking actions. Actions, in turn, translate perception-images into new images, a process whereby the subject moves to acclimate to the exigencies of situations. One perceives by selecting from the image what one can *manage*, converting the "vibrations" of matter "into practical deed."[37] An onrushing train, the prick of a pin, a bidding gesture: images give rise to the movements of the body, to actions that are increasingly confident and practiced, engraved in memory.[38] The space-time of cognition, of the image-sensations that affect us, we call a sign, though because at this juncture signs are re-cognized we must be clear about the limitations on which Bergson's philosophy is careful to insist. In other words, though we cannot deduce subjectivity as such, we have deduced a system of habitual response that takes hold of us—and this "education," to use Hegel's word, constitutes a subject.[39] For his part, Bergson calls this system of habitual responses a sensory-motor schema (SMS), a deliberate mechanism that adapts the body to the vagaries of images, that litigates over signs to assure their regularity, their "common sense." In precisely this way, though, one discovers the divided allegiance that marks *Matter and Memory*, and this contradiction occurs under the aegis of the very motivation for Bergson's argument—common sense. The common sense to which Bergson first resorts in order to insist on the materiality of images gradually motivates the very apparatus that so accustoms us to images as to remove us from that constitutive common sense. Put another way, the understanding of the world as an "aggregate of images" conditions the development of a commonsensical system of actions that, in turn, renders that antecedent understanding increasingly inconceivable.

Hesitation, instances of excruciating self-doubt, those hallucinatory occasions when we cannot be sure what we see or how to formulate any responsible action, when we are pushed not only to look but to *think* awry: the SMS reflexively avoids these moments. The stream of action and reaction gravitates to the regulated equipoise of any feedback loop, whereas the breakdown of this machine would threaten, Bergson says, to deprive the subject of not only efficiency but, indeed, normality: "That which is commonly held to be a disturbance of the psychic life itself, an inward disorder, a disease of personality, appears to us, from our point of view, to be an unloosening or a breaking of that tie which binds the psychic life to its motor accompaniment, a weakening or an impairing of our attention to outward life."[40] If only briefly, Bergson hits upon the possibility that the SMS might be unhinged, though he immediately links the possibility to "disease," to abnormality. But what could disturb the sensory-motor linkages in such a manner? To this point, we have seen that the SMS develops to react to our consistency within the field of images; indeed, by virtue of that reaction, it comes to imagine itself as a "center of action." No longer "any-point-whatever" in the aggregate of images, the SMS constitutes our "anchorage" in a world that we perceive to surround (*englober*) us. The shift might be compared to the grafting of Euclidean geometry on the aggregate of images, a conceptual mapping that intimates what I would call a "soft dualism"—not so much a difference in kind between perception and images, which Bergson persistently rebuts, but the *belief* in such a difference, the infiltration of a moral-metaphysical ideology.[41]

Against the flux of images, the endless modulation and variation of the world, Bergson holds out an SMS that is not qualitatively different but habitually so. What this means is that the "unloosening" of the SMS necessarily entails rending the subject from its habitus as a "center of action." Now this is precisely the cinema's "great advantage"—in Deleuze's words, the absence of any "centre of anchorage and of horizon."[42] Although the cinema often actualizes images that reinforce centers of action, a question to which we will have occasion to return, cinematographic images do not naturally encompass such centers of action. Indeed, the cinema's system of identification is a posteriori the labor of a certain "tendency of the cinema," to lift Truffaut's phrase, which is not simply given, as many critics would have us believe. It has become a commonplace, especially among cognitivists, to consider the cinema's own patterns of narrative, from its images to the linkages of those images, from shots to scenes to sequences, as a condition of the cinema qua representation that is by definition suited to our own schemata; but Deleuze's point is that, though they arise immanently out of the cinema, schemata are not the essence of cinema. Rather, the classical patterns of narrative cinema—for instance, all the mechanisms of continuity editing—emerge from our own habit of treating the cinema as an extension of perception. In fact, the very impetus of cognitivism to take the cinema as naturally conducive to our systems of meaning-making or schemata actually reinforces those systems as natural, whereas Deleuze begins from an entirely different, acentered, and one could say "nonhuman" perspective within which the human emerges as a center of indetermination.[43] Because this center is not presupposed and does not exist prior to the world, the possibility exists that the cinema may allow us to return to an acentered perception. For this reason, Deleuze constantly gravitates in the cinema books to moments, "as for example in Renoir, when the camera leaves a character,"[44] because such moments reveal a movement-image unfastened from any center of action. This cleavage of camera and character (center) suggests the way the cinema surpasses human perception: what we discover is not perception, but rather a means to "rid ourselves of ourselves."[45]

Beyond Renoir, who also turns up in *The Time-Image* under a different guise, the trajectory of this special "forgetting" (Nietzsche) is tracked through a number of filmmakers, from Joris Ivens (*Rain*) to Samuel Beckett (*Film*) to Dziga Vertov (*Man with a Movie Camera*). What these examples share in the context of Deleuze's work—and, it must be noted, in varying degrees of persuasiveness—is a means of making the cinematographic image into an "any-point-whatever" in the universe of images, an "any-perspective-whatever" from which to enter that universe. The anchorage of early cinema, which is essentially tied to that of ordinary human perception, is thus forsaken in a new exploration of perceptual possibilities. "Instead of going from the acentred state of things to centred perception," Deleuze reasons, the cinema "could go back up towards the acentred state of things, and get closer to it."[46] And yet, precisely at this point of "getting closer," we would naturally leave behind the assurance of the SMS: *we would leave behind our belief in that stability which constitutes identity itself.* Could Bergson have glimpsed as much? Could he have glimpsed the tentatively proffered possibilities of *Matter and Memory* looming in the cinema?

The question is impossible to answer, seeming as it does to lead us away from philosophy and into the tangles of conjecture. What is fairly certain, though, is that between *Matter and Memory* and *Creative Evolution*, two things happened: the cinema emerged and Bergson reformulated his notion of perception vis-à-vis images. As to the latter, Deleuze speculates that it was

> because Bergson was here working out new philosophical concepts relating to the theory of relativity: he thought relativity involved a conception of time which it didn't itself bring out, but which it was up to philosophy to construct. Only what happened was that people thought Bergson was attacking relativity, that he was criticizing the physical theory itself. Bergson considered the misunderstanding too simple to dispel. So he went back to a simpler conception. Still, in *Matter and Memory* (1896) he'd traced out a movement-image and a time-image that he could, subsequently, have applied to cinema.[47]

But if, as Deleuze believed, Bergson was on the cusp of realizing the cinema's philosophical potential, then the reversal that *Creative Evolution* stakes out is all the more surprising. With this in mind, let us momentarily return to Bergson's own suggestion that the normal functioning of perception precludes abnormal or "untimely" (Nietzsche) thought, for this allows us to see how the performance of his own philosophy was inextricably involved with this dilemma. In *Matter and Memory*, Bergson had reached a fantastic juncture; he had managed to entertain the possibility of a universe of images in which we ourselves move as images—that is, of a chaos of images from which we extract ourselves, yet in whose ecstatic movements we partake. Insofar as cinema offered the possibility of realizing that a-subjective ontology, Bergson's own philosophy would necessarily, though perhaps unwittingly, enact a choice: to assume the (un)common sense of images or to pursue the common sense of order. *Creative Evolution*, then, constitutes that choice.

Whereas *Matter and Memory* endeavors to deduce "normality" from the aggregate of images, *Creative Evolution* begins by assuming normality, the site of which is a perceptual-cognitive system. Indeed, when Bergson does reach the point of discussing subjectivity in *Creative Evolution*, perception and intellect are now *assumed* and the "becoming" of images must be sought. Even Bergson's exhortation that "we must accustom ourselves to think being"—let us say, images in their becoming or duration—"directly"[48] is symptomatic of such a shift: whatever its aim, the exhortation discloses a perception that is already sequestered from images and that is, ostensibly, immune to aberrance. Bergson has chosen the common sense of perception and the exigencies of normal action.

Take Bergson's example of an "indirect" or "incorrect" measure of images, Xeno's famous arrow. Xeno proposed to reconstitute movement from the collection of points that describe an arrow's trajectory. Bergson counters that movement is indivisible: as soon as we begin dividing up the arrow's arc, we miss real movement—movement whose duration defies (even metronomic) divisibility. "The movement slips through the interval, because every attempt to reconstitute change out of states implies the absurd proposition, that movement is made of immobilities."[49] What is of interest here, however, is not Bergson's correction; Xeno's paradoxes had been refuted in the past and, as Deleuze notes, the discovery of the subordination of space to time is clear enough in Kant's first *Critique*.[50] Rather, what is of interest is that Bergson refutes Xeno while, at the same time, claiming that Xeno's model of movement—movement as the reconstitution of stable moments, positions, or states—nevertheless expresses the practical and necessary mechanism of our perception. Here, then, we discover Deleuze's oversight with regard to Bergson, the very point with which we began. Deleuze notes that Bergson gives the ancient formula for movement (immobile sections + abstract time) a "modern and recent name,"[51] the cinematograph; but Deleuze does not concede that, having refuted the formula, *Bergson nonetheless affirms its necessity*. Bergson's almost spiritual appeals to "install ourselves within" the duration of movement-images are played against a predominant refrain, the necessary removal of perception from movement-images. As he explains, "If matter appeared to us as a perpetual flowing, we should assign no termination to any of our actions."[52] In order to act, then, a kind of distantiation is required: "from the mobility of the movement we turn away as much as we can" (303).

Two broad developments follow from this. The first concerns the reconstituted nature of perception, and the second concerns the imperative for this reconstitution or, broadly speaking, the demands of action. Such are, of course, the two sides of the sensory-motor schema. Bergson writes:

> Sensory organs and motor organs are in fact coördinated with each other. Now, the first symbolize our faculty of perceiving, as the second our faculty of acting. The organism thus evidences, in a visible and tangible form, the perfect accord of perception and action. So if our activity always aims at a *result* into which it is momentarily fitted, our perception must retain of the material world, at every moment, only a *state* in which it is provisionally placed. (300)

This coordination implies the "normal" functioning to which Bergson alluded in *Matter and Memory*, though the anxiety attached to normality—what if the SMS were "unloosened"?—is notably absent. As we have seen, Bergson suggests in *Matter and Memory* that the SMS developed from the exigencies of recognizing images. In *Creative Evolution*, though, the SMS's potential to conventionalize perception and, in turn, action has itself become a convention. The "accord" has become "perfect," so algorithmically exacting as to defy most any disturbance.

Under what auspices has the SMS become so secure? The answer is complicated, but we can begin to see its outlines when we grasp that perception is kept in check by the "results" for which it prepares. In other words, Bergson says that it is action that keeps perception interested in a "state"—"the unmoveable plan of the movement rather than the movement itself" (303). By "action," though, Bergson seems to mean two different (albeit related) things. There is, strictly speaking, the action of our "motor organs"; the body is even more certainly a "center of action" than it had been in *Matter and Memory*. But the demand for motor action dictates the action of the sensory faculty, and in so doing it constitutively changes perception. Consider Bergson's assertion that

> [a] man is so much more a "man of action" as he can embrace in a glance a greater number of events: he who perceives successive events one by one will allow himself to be led by them; he who grasps them as a whole will dominate them. In short, the qualities of matter are so many stable views that we take of its instability. (301–2)

The recourse to masculinity underscores physical action as the imperative of Bergson's system, the aggressive mastering of space-time; but that action is also translated into activity at the level of perception. No longer open to movement-images, the sensory faculty is charged with the very *production* of images conducive to motor action. No longer open to molecular variation, perception "photographs" the world, leaving to an overarching intellect the work of piecing these images together. "We take snapshots, as it were, of the passing reality," Bergson says, "and, as these are characteristic of the reality, we have only to string them on a becoming abstract, uniform, and invisible, situated at the back of the apparatus of knowledge" (306).

By virtue of this withdrawal, perception forsakes imagistic reality for objective views of the world, for "molar" (Deleuze) certainties: perception "marks off the boundaries of bodies." This, Bergson continues, constitutes the "*fortunate inertia of our perception*" (302; emphasis added). The phrase is remarkable for a number of reasons, not the least of which is its sympathy with the very tradition of philosophy that Bergson had critiqued in *Matter and Memory*. If perception has the good fortune to linger behind images, this is not because of any congenital retardation; perception actively labors under the yoke of anticipation, compelled not simply to take pictures, but instead to take certain kinds of pictures that are conducive to action. As Bergson explains, our "stable views of instability" are aligned with "three kinds of representations: (1) qualities, (2) forms or essences, and (3) acts." Indeed, "[t]o these three ways of seeing correspond three categories of words: *adjectives*, *substantives*, and *verbs*, which are the primordial elements of language" (303). In effect, what we find here is that Bergson has refashioned the sensory-motor schema: whereas images once acted upon a receptive perception, now they are acted upon by perception and thus "re-presented" according to its presuppositions. Ultimately, we are inured to any moment that would unloosen the constraints of recognition because a purpose precedes this encounter.

This difficult point is perhaps more easily understood according to what Godard avouched as his desire for cinema, a formula that

Deleuze often repeats: "not a just image, just an image" ("pas une image juste, juste une image"). Just images—good, moral images—are the result of a sensory-motor schema that, having been internalized, ensures regularity, dependability, and the semblance of totality. In the cinema, the great example of this schematism is classical Hollywood because there the presupposition of a "destiny" organizes images organically:[53] milieus gives rise to modes of behavior that rise above (sublate) those milieus, thereby creating a new spatiotemporal arrangements. In this cinema, action is preordained as the translation from one situation to another, the result of which is the trajectory of traditional narrative: "the hero only acts because he is the first to see," explains Deleuze, "and only triumphs because he imposes on action the interval or the second's delay which allows him to see everything."[54] What follows from this, for Deleuze, is a typology of images that align with Bergson's categories. Situations present essences (*perception-images*), which give rise to actions (*action-images*), while the interval (*affection-images*) marks the moment between the perception and action.[55] Strung together, images are linked by regular patterns of action (movement), which, as in Aristotle's understanding of narrative emplotment, takes precedence over character. In the Aristotelian narrative schema, for example, any ethics to speak of emerges from (rather than motivates) action, as Paul Ricoeur has pointed out.[56] When, say, John Wayne is faced with an unendurable situation (*The Searchers*), a corrupt town (*Rio Bravo, El Dorado*), or a brute necessity (*The Green Berets*), his impetus, whether expressed or assumed, is that "someone's gotta do it." Perhaps we could describe the ideology of classical Hollywood cinema as one of "manifest destiny."

The point here is not that Hollywood simply illustrates the SMS, but rather that the American mode of production paradigmatically developed from this moral-metaphysical relay or image-automaton. How does this relate to Bergson? Although *Creative Evolution* is not innately cinematographic, the upshot of Bergson's categories, like those of classical narrative cinema, is to ensure a predictable, even causal, chain of images. The links that Deleuze draws between the SMS and classical narrative cinema reveal that the efficiency of action is conditioned by a fundamental optimism. Unfailingly working through this sensory-motor machinery toward action and, thence, resolution, Bergson's system, like classical narrative cinema, affirms a kind of "transcendental idealism." Naturally, the phrase suggests the indefatigable confidence with which these systems are able to reconstitute (or rise above) situations—in Bergsonian terms, dominating "successive events." But "transcendental idealism" also describes the nature of Kant's first *Critique*, in which an investigation of previous philosophy gives rise to a categorial system "above" empirical vagaries. Isn't this the logic that Bergson ultimately advocates in *Creative Evolution*? Consider his reasoning: as we have seen, Bergson's philosophy is intent on changing situations (images) by appealing to action—but this action would be impossible were it not for the active nature of perception itself and, indeed, its gravitation to certain categories. Action is the imperative for perception, which is itself the condition for action: to return to John Wayne, his ethics derive from action, the ability to act upon images, but those images have already been acted upon (perceived, i.e., re-presented) in such a way as to already demand action. One follows the circular logic of action and perception only to discover that the marker of its assurance is ultimately held by transcendental categories, the guarantors of good, common sense.

From *Matter and Memory*'s critique of dualism, then, we now find ourselves firmly lodged in the logic of dualism, of intelligible and sensible realities. It is hardly surprising, in this light, that when Bergson reaches the point of analyzing Platonic Ideas in *Creative Evolution*, he finds that his own categories (qualities, essences, acts; or, alternately, adjectives, nouns, verbs) are completely synchronous with Platonic *Eidos*. As Bergson explains, though we translate Plato's *Eidos* by the broad term "Idea," it actually has a "threefold meaning":

> It denotes (1) the quality, (2) the form or essence, (3) the end or *design* (in the sense of *intention*) of the act being performed, that is to say, at bottom, the *design* (in the sense of *drawing*) of the act accomplished. *These three aspects are those of the adjective, substantive and verb, and correspond to the three essential categories of language.*[57]

Such categories divide perception from the sensible world. In other words, the categories presume that normal perception cannot be surpassed, that no manipulation (or production) of images could possibly move the determination of perception. It is with this distantiation in mind that Bergson alludes to the cinematograph, for its mechanism seems to offer the model of a perceptive mechanism sequestered from sensible reality. As we have seen, though, the analogy works by attending to the mechanism rather than the movement-image it produces; that is to say, the resulting image is an "intermediate" image, one whose prior "correction" allows it to slip past the determinations of our schematism.

Bergson's pronouncement on Platonism finally describes his own philosophical turn: "As becoming shocks the habits of thought and fits ill into the molds of language, they [the Greeks] declared it unreal."[58] Having migrated into the brain, then, the SMS has colonized thought to the degree that disturbances can be ignored, shunted aside, "declared unreal." What Bergson accomplishes in *Creative Evolution* is to assert a transcendental plane in forcible harmony with the sensible realm. The contrivance of this harmony between "above" and "below" is a matter of schemata, a linkage devoted to *regulating* the flow of images. Kant himself defined schemata as "rules of determination," thereby tacitly acknowledging what we discover full-fledged in Bergson: that the predictable flow of images presupposes a subject that is itself predictable, anchored to an identity. As Nietzsche famously explained, in order to think of the world predictably "[m]an himself must first of all have been *calculable, regular, necessary,* even in his own image of himself."[59]

We are now in a position to see what happened between *Matter and Memory* and *Creative Evolution*, for the tendencies of the SMS elaborated in the first book became, ten years later, such an orthodoxy as to appear, even to Bergson himself, the norm with which philosophy begins. The Bergsonian action of *Creative Evolution* is, in the final analysis, not only a "reaction"—it is "reactive" (Nietzsche), the subject having been meticulously calibrated to adhere to an orderly standard. Such is the "grammar" by which we are determined, providing a kind of circuit breaker that staves off the vagaries of images, of aberrant signs that would produce a "disorder of all the senses" (Rimbaud). Images ride along the spokes of so many determinations in a methodical flow, such that the exuberant promise of *The Movement-Image*, to "rid ourselves of ourselves," has become impossible—not only in Bergson's philosophy but, more broadly, in the cinema of movement-images. By force of habit and education (for they amount to the same thing), the regularity of the SMS migrates into the supposition of a fixed and transcendental ego whose internalization secures identity by acting upon images rather than being acted upon by images.

But if the route back to the unbridled images of the plane of immanence has been closed off, the hopes of cinema and philosophy are, as we find in *The Time-Image*, cast with a new project: to trigger the deregulations of the sensory-matrix itself, to disrupt the certainty of the image-relay, and finally to assemble the intensities of the plane of immanence on the body itself. The new procedure can be understood along the lines of what is called an "embolism," a term that we normally understand to be a clotting or an occlusion, as in a blood vessel; but this interference is linked to another, and even more primary, definition of embolism, that of intercalation, the process of altering the calendar, of "messing" with time. We begin to disrupt the normative functioning of the body when we begin to disrupt the normative flow of time; such is the modern project of cinema—to make irregularities (false continuity), to unleash unspeakable durations (becoming), so that the sensory regularity of our organs (SMS) can be transformed into a "body without organs" (BWO). *Pars destruens, pars construens.*

To get back to the images that Bergson had intuited—this becomes the aim of cinema, but under a new guise. By unloosening the constraints that had been thrust upon it, the cinema unloosens the sensory-motor schema: "not just images, just images," that is, images ripped from the moorings of determinations. Whereas Bergson's trajectory is one of retrenchment, Deleuze's trajectory in the cinema books charts not only cinema but, indeed, thought from its categorial optimism to a contrapuntal "deterritorialization," the (dis)juncture at which thought is rended from the world (*habitus, terre*). Let us end this essay, then, at the moment when *The Time-Image* begins, after the war, with Italian neorealism. The images of this cinema verge, Deleuze tells us, on the "intolerable";[60] scanning the ruins of the war, the cinema captures images to which we can no longer react—images, as in *Germany Year Zero*, that trigger an "upheaval" of thought. In Rosellini's remarkable film, a young boy, Edward, kills his father; despairing, he takes to the war-torn, apocalyptic streets of Berlin. We find ourselves in the midst of an almost lunar landscape, a deterritorialized zone par excellence, as the boy moves aimlessly, drifting amid a swell of images. Deleuze terms this aberrant movement the *bal(l)ade*, both a ballad qua story and a kind of voyage, a "tripping" wherein there is no longer any destination. What can one do; how can one act? Such images induce the imagination itself to take a trip: evading any schematism, thought is pressed to the point of encountering itself, a precipitous "self-affection" wherein transcendental identity gives way to an ecstatic stream of self-syntheses. Such a line of thought—or "flight," as Deleuze calls it—marks the schizophrenic's stroll, the hither and thither of one who has left the world of reconstituted, metronomic, or even calendar time for the world of the time-image. The year is 1947, but what's the use of a year? Images, thought, life, and philosophy have begun anew: cinema year zero.

NOTES

1. Friedrich Nietzsche, *The Gay Science*, trans. Walter Kaufmann (New York: Vintage Books, 1974), 177 (aphorism 121).
2. Hegel's is perhaps the crucial moment for the philosophical preface, as it is for the placing of all philosophy in contact with thought, even if under the auspices of the regularizing, predictable dialectic. While there should be no preface, then, it is only appropriate that the denigration of a preface should preface the work, serving to establish its first (negative) moment. See G. W. F. Hegel, *Phenomenology of the Spirit*, trans. A. V. Miller (Oxford: Oxford University Press, 1977), 1: "It is customary to preface a work with an explanation of the author's aim, why he wrote the book, and the relationship in which he believes it to stand to other or contemporary treatises on the same subject. In the case of a philosophical work, however, such an explanation seems not only superfluous but, in view of the nature of the subject matter, even inappropriate and misleading. For whatever might appropriately be said about philosophy in a preface—say a historical *statement* of the main drift and the point of view, the general content of the results, a string of random assertions and assurances about the truth—none of this can be accepted as the way in which to expound philosophical truth."
3. Gilles Deleuze, *The Movement-Image*, trans. Hugh Tomlinson and Barbara Habberjam (Minneapolis: University of Minnesota Press, 1986), 1.
4. Ibid., 2.
5. Henri Bergson, *Creative Evolution*, trans. Arthur Mitchell (New York: Henry Holt and Company, 1911), 306.
6. Deleuze, *The Movement-Image*, 3.
7. Ibid., xiv.
8. Ibid., 3. Surprising here is how Deleuze reveals his allegiance with Bazin, who believed in the natural technological capacities of the cinema, rather than the likes of Jean-Louis Comolli, for whom the technology was always already ideologically determined. Indeed, Deleuze largely departs from film theory's more traditional understanding of ideology—specifically, how technology is historically constrained. Despite Deleuze's ostensible affinity with Foucault, with a history in which the power of statements seems to determine technology and effectively manufacture sense, the cinema suggests something different—if not an innate, then a constitutive possibility. Indeed, certain adaptations of Deleuze along Foucauldian lines, such as Jonathan Crary's *Techniques of the Observer: On Vision and Modernity in the Nineteenth Century* (Cambridge: MIT Press, 1990), all but elide images in favor of statements whose power determines the field of visibility; yet, to read Deleuze on cinema (no less on Foucault) is to grasp that power never entirely determines the visible and that, in fact, cinema holds the possibility of prolonging such disjunctions into the indeterminacy of thought—that is, thought recoiling upon itself to discover its own improvisatory groundlessness.
9. Deleuze, *The Movement-Image*, 3.
10. Bergson, *Creative Evolution*, 306.
11. The question of the "missed encounter" between cinema and philosophy is taken up by Deleuze in chapter 4 of *The Movement-Image*, when he compares the Bergsonian position vis-à-vis consciousness with the phenomenological (primarily Husserlian) position: "It is true that Bergson, as we have seen, apparently found the cinema only a false ally. As for Husserl, as far as we know, he never mentions the cinema at all (it is noteworthy that Sartre too, much later, in making an inventory and analysis of all kinds of images in *The Imagination*, does not cite the cinematographic image). It is Merleau-Ponty who attempts, only incidentally, a confrontation between cinema and phenomenology, but he also sees the cinema

as an ambiguous ally" (56–57). Although phenomenologists like Merleau-Ponty granted an abnormality to the cinema and, thereby, a certain privilege, this abnormality exists within a régime of normal perception, which is anchored and centered. On the other hand, Deleuze gravitates toward Bergson because, despite his professed disdain for cinema, he insists on the possibility for an acentered perception that Deleuze conceives as essentially cinematographic.

12. Bergson, *Creative Evolution*, 306.
13. As Deleuze says of the cinema, "The essence of a thing never appears at the outset, but in the middle, in the course of its development, when its strength is assured" (*The Movement-Image*, 3).
14. Gilles Deleuze, *The Time-Image*, trans. Hugh Tomlinson and Robert Galeta (Minneapolis: University of Minnesota Press, 1989), xiii.
15. Ibid.
16. Deleuze, *The Movement-Image*, 2.
17. Bergson, *Creative Evolution*, 306.
18. See F. E. Peters, *Greek Philosophical Terms: A Historical Lexicon* (New York: New York University Press, 1967), 46–51.
19. Bergson, *Creative Evolution*, 314.
20. Henri Bergson, *Matter and Memory*, trans. N. M. Paul and W. S. Palmer (New York: Zone Books, 1991), 9.
21. Deleuze, *The Movement-Image*, 2.
22. Bergson, *Matter and Memory*, 9.
23. Deleuze, *The Movement-Image*, 58.
24. This is essentially a repetition of the point made at the outset of the essay, namely, that Deleuze wants to trump Bergson with his own "story of evolution."
25. Deleuze, *The Movement-Image*., 58.
26. Bergson, *Matter and Memory*, 28–29. See also Gilles Deleuze, *The Fold: Leibniz and the Baroque*, trans. Tom Conley (Minneapolis: University of Minnesota Press, 1993), 26. There Deleuze explains that "because the monad is for the world, no one clearly contains the 'reason' of the series of which they are all a result, and which remains outside of them.... We thus go from the world to the subject, at the cost of a torsion that causes the monad to exist currently only in subjects, but that also makes subjects all relate to this world as if to the virtuality that they actualize."
27. Deleuze, *The Movement-Image*, 60.
28. Ibid., 58–59.
29. Deleuze, *The Fold*, 76.
30. As Deleuze was often heard to say, the cinematographic shot, also expressed in French by *plan*, is "conscience."
31. Although Deleuze analyzes the "plane of immanence" in relation to the cinema in *The Movement-Image*, the consummate accounting of the plane of immanence is Gilles Deleuze and Félix Guattari's *What Is Philosophy?*, trans. Hugh Tomlinson and Graham Burchell (New York: Columbia University Press, 1994), 35.
32. Deleuze, *The Fold*, 25.
33. Ibid., 63.
34. Of the duality of "images and movement, consciousness and thing," Deleuze says that "[t]wo very different authors were to undertake this task at about the same time: Bergson and Husserl. Each had his own war cry: all consciousness is consciousness *of* something (Husserl), or more strongly, all consciousness *is* something (Bergson)" (Deleuze, *The Movement-Image*, 56).
35. Bergson, *Matter and Memory*, 181.
36. Deleuze, *The Time-Image*, 31.
37. Bergson, *Matter and Memory*, 44.
38. As Bergson's title notes, the obverse of matter is memory—or, better yet, memory

is the other, virtual side of matter (images). This point is perhaps the most difficult in Bergson's book, and it is no less difficult (or essential) in Deleuze's cinema books. Indeed, Bergson's entire ontology relies on memory, but for that reason it seems that its formation must be either presumed or exhumed, that is, absolutely investigated. I have opted for the former, in large part because several essays in the collection (Jean-Clet Martin's, Laura Marks's, Peter Canning's) linger specifically on memory.

39. Hegel affirms that the "growth in the universality of thought is the absolute value in education," such that (like Rousseau) Hegel seems to indicate that education is the effacement of nature. See G. W. F. Hegel, *Philosophy of Right*, trans. T. M. Knox (Oxford: Oxford University Press, 1952), 116–17.
40. Bergson, *Matter and Memory*, 15.
41. Belief is, as I later suggest, a crucial element of cinema and, perhaps, the point at which Bergson retreats from its potential. The evolution the cinema would undertake—discovering new movements, new kinds of images, inflicting upon the body new kinds of signs—tends toward the expression of time, which, as Deleuze tells us, "has always put truth into crisis" (*The Time-Image*, 130).
42. Deleuze, *The Movement-Image*, 58.
43. On the other hand, it is equally important to distinguish Deleuze's notion of acentering or deterritorialization from the sense of "countercinema" that developed in the 1970s. Countercinema is essentially a Brechtian operation of defamiliarization, one that is aligned with experimental cinema generally and Godard specifically. Deleuze himself looks to experimental cinema (from Vertov to the New York avant-garde of the 1970s), but not simply because this cinema counters or exposes the so-called codes of realism. The question of experimentation and, indeed, deterritorialization goes beyond any sense of stylistic codes to reveal the nature of normal perception, within which realism is naturally contained and to which it naturally contributes, as the product of a system of regulation and control.
44. Deleuze, *The Movement-Image*, 23.
45. Ibid., 66.
46. Ibid., 58.
47. Gilles Deleuze, *Negotiations, 1972–1990*, trans. Martin Joughin (New York: Columbia University Press, 1995), 48.
48. Bergson, *Creative Evolution*, 298.
49. Ibid., 308.
50. "Time is no longer related to the movement which it measures, but movement is related to time which conditions it: this is the first great reversal of the *Critique of Pure Reason*" (Gilles Deleuze, *Kant's Critical Philosophy: The Doctrine of the Faculties*, trans. Hugh Tomlinson and Barbara Habberjam [Minneapolis: University of Minnesota Press, 1984], vii). In *The Time-Image*, Deleuze further suggests that, in *Matter and Memory* especially, "Bergson is much closer to Kant than he himself thinks: Kant defined time as the form of interiority, in the sense that we are internal to time," whereas Bergson also saw that "[t]ime is not the interior in us, but just the opposite, the interiority in which we are, in which we move, live and change" (82).
51. Deleuze, *The Movement-Image*, 1.
52. Bergson, *Creative Evolution*, 300.
53. Deleuze, *The Movement-Image*, 127.
54. Ibid., 70.
55. Ibid., 68.
56. Paul Ricoeur, *Time and Narrative*, vol. 1, trans. Kathleen McLaughlin and David Pellauer (Chicago: University of Chicago Press, 1984), 37. Aristotle, explains Ricoeur, gives action priority over character, "such that character emerges from action rather than the reverse." The possibility that "character studies" thoroughly

distort the sensory-motor schema remains, in this sense, a crucial and underdeveloped area of film analysis.

57. Bergson, *Creative Evolution*, 315.
58. Ibid., 314.
59. Friedrich Nietzsche, *On the Genealogy of Morals*, trans. Walter Kaufmann (New York: Random House, 1967), 58. Notably, it is within this context that Deleuze invokes the "schizo." In other words, Deleuze does not advocate schizophrenia (nor, for that matter, drugs), but he does look to the schizophrenic experience as a model of thought and life that forces us to look beyond the confines of our own limited notion of reality. One sees this specifically in Deleuze's discussion of neorealism in the first chapter of *The Time-Image*, hence my use of Rosellini's *Germany Year Zero* at the conclusion of the essay.
60. Deleuze, The *Time-Image*, 18.

Chapter 3

Escape from the Image

Deleuze's Image-Ontology

MARTIN SCHWAB

In his two cinema books, *The Movement-Image* and *The Time-Image*, Gilles Deleuze offers an aesthetic and historical account of the cinema based on an unfamiliar and intriguing ontology—an ontology of images. Objects, qualities, processes, actions, even the brain: all are images in a dynamic universe of images. In this "image-world," art—specifically, the cinema—emerges as something not ontologically distinct from the rest of the world. Indeed, Deleuze's theory amounts to the simultaneous dynamization and de-Platonization of the cinema. Deleuzian "image-art" is neither semblance (*Schein*), nor the coming to the fore of a separate and "artificial" world, nor the becoming sensible of the idea or of the forms, nor a fabric of marks engaged in a constant process of destabilization. Such views imply that art is ontologically distinct and functionally privileged, whereas Deleuze privileges art over other phenomena of the image-world because, quite simply, it shows more clearly and more overtly the depth or even surface dynamics of the world.[1]

In the discussion that follows, I present Deleuze's image-ontology in its abstract and conceptual development. To my mind, this is a dynamic ontology in which the more differentiated items emerge from and stabilize the less differentiated ones. Given this understanding, I use one of Deleuze's most integral and strategic examples, Samuel Beckett's *Film*, to show how this ontology applies to the cinema, at the same time expanding my focus to critically analyze the aesthetic theory implicit in the image-ontology.[2] My negative thesis is that, however tempting, Deleuze's image-ontology remains insensitive to the specificities of cinema. But in the final section of the essay I add a positive thesis: I propose modifications to those parts of the theory that deal with semiotics and subjectivity. Ultimately, my aim is to outline how a modified theory might deal with film and its history as a medium.

IMAGE-ONTOLOGY[3]

In general, we think of images in semiotic terms. Images are signs or, more precisely, signs that present their meanings in an iconic mode, traditionally understood as representation via similarity or resemblance. What a picture or image shows us, it does by presenting us with a structural analogue (it re-presents something). But this is not Deleuze's understanding of images. Deleuzian images do not primarily belong to aesthetics or semiotics, at least not in any traditional understanding of those categories. His world of images is neither a special field, nor a particular state of the mind, nor a regional ontology. One must insist on this point at the outset because Deleuze's many references to Peirce may mislead readers into thinking that images are a special case of being.[4] For Peirce, the field of semiotics is a special region of being in general, singled out by the category of thirdness. In other words, for Peirce (unlike Deleuze), not everything that possesses determinacy also possesses the kind of being peculiar to images.

In this sense, we can begin by understanding that Deleuze's ontology is not Peircean but, as we will see, Bergsonian.[5] In fact, it is so deeply Bergsonian that it is adequately called a "Deleuzian–Bergsonian ontology." It is not an ontology of semiosis or signification, but a general ontology of the universe—the universe of images. Being—being itself, without further qualification—is conceived as imagehood; all being is "image-being" and/or "being-image." As a general and comprehensive ontology, this theory applies to traditional semiosis as well as to other fields. But what is it to be an image in this general, ontological sense? Imagehood is a determination pertaining to a dynamic, relational Being whose ascertainable kinds of being are differentiations within a chaotic, motional cosmos. To be "imagistic" is a universal ontological feature of everything that *is*. The most general imagistic trait is to be a dynamic kind of relation or relatedness, though I use relation here in a different sense from that which Deleuze suggests. By "relational Being" I mean a relation that is *internal* to Being and not *external* to the relata.[6]

The most basic image is the movement-image.[7] Pure movement-images—that is, movement-images that do not simultaneously partake in another type of image as well—do not (indeed, cannot) occur, at least not for us. *Our* world is always more and otherwise differentiated than such pure movement-images, and our world possesses features for which movement-images alone cannot account. Ontologically, movement-images are thus a metaphysical or transcendental construct: they play their main role in Deleuze's theory by dynamizing the cosmos and conferring derived status on the other images. They are nevertheless the basic kind of being in Deleuze's dynamic ontology. Indeed, Deleuze calls movement-images "matter" in order to emphasize their underlying status as that which receives (or is continually receiving) form.[8]

Movement-images are images by virtue of relating to an environment in a specific way.[9] The movement-image thus presupposes a difference between the image and its environment or differences internal to a somehow distributed medium. This is not to say that difference as such constitutes a division or a separation between movement-images; we could not, for instance, say that the movement-image *is* something *and* relates to some other thing. The movement-image exists as a relation, as relating to or in a given milieu; indeed, it seems to exist *only* by virtue of relating. To be an image is to organize being in a specific relational way.[10] Deleuzian–Bergsonian imagehood is a relation without relata that are distinct and different from the relation—a "pure" (dynamic) relation! Imagehood seems to be a self-constituted or emerging difference within a potentially undifferentiated universe. As such, the difference between an image and its environment is entirely an emerging one. No constitutive contribution from anything already determinate and in place can be established (fall from some original undivided oneness, lack in being, etc.).

The relations to which movement-images give rise seem to be further determined as "effectuating" relations. Like "relating" above, "effectuating" holds for all images on all occasions: "Every thing, that is to say every image, is indistinguishable from its actions and reactions."[11] "Effectuation" is a first dynamic aspect of the ontology of images, and, as Deleuze indicates, it is bidirectional. On the one hand, an image is effectuated by factors originating from what is, will be, or counts in this respect as its environment; the image receives or *is* those effects—a reaction. On the other hand, the image is itself the origin or originator of effects; in this respect the image effectuates toward its environment, perhaps *in statu nascendi*—an action. To be an image is thus to be a form of exchange or interaction—action and reaction—between something and its environment, and to have or to constitute being and determinacy as such a form.[12] Exchange operates in both directions, from the environment toward the image, from the image toward its environment. Images are (by) being in exchange with the milieu—a milieu that is, of course, imagistic. Effectuating exchanges take place both across and beyond the boundaries of a particular image, for exchanges always take place in more comprehensive webs relating a plurality of images. Indeed, all movement-images interact all the time with all the other images,[13] and there are no nonimages.

The movement-image is "the way of being in a world of universal variation, of universal undulation, universal rippling."[14] Insofar as the image exists by virtue of its relation to other images, the world of images is always in motion. Interactivity and this motion are the first two dynamic essences and features of Deleuze's motional cosmos. This motion is again ontological in nature, and as basic to the imagistic character of the cosmos as was interaction. The world *is* (of) pure movement; it *is* motional! Bergson's "model," writes Deleuze, would be "a state of things which would constantly change, a flowing matter in which no points of anchorage nor center of reference would be assignable" (*The Movement-Image,* 57). Or, as the title of a section in *The Movement-Image* indicates: "The identity of the image and the movement" (56), "a world where IMAGE = MOVEMENT."[15] Everything that appears is "image." Nothing with any determinacy whatsoever is of a nonimagistic kind. All images are motional through and through. In a world of movement-images, it is impossible to distinguish what is in motion from the motion itself; indeed, we must stop looking for "the thing" qua substantive matter—which, however complex and internally in motion itself, we are tempted to think of as the enduring and independently identifiable substratum that is in motion. In our everyday understanding, the substratum of a motion is not itself engaged in the motion that is predicated of it. But in Deleuze's image-world, the absence of all "points of anchorage and center of reference" precludes the determinacy of something or other whose determinacy would be distinct from its movements. To this, one must add as a further feature that *"every image acts on others and reacts to others, on 'all their facets at once' and 'by all their elements.'"*[16] The activity of images is a global and universal event possessing a determinacy of its own, although there are "neither axes, nor centre, nor left, nor right, nor high, nor low . . ." (*The Movement-Image,* 58). The organization of space requires a system that provides a basis of reference for its coordinates, but the space of undivided movement-images is not originally oriented—neither in itself nor because of the emergence of movement-images in it.

As long as the perspective of "pure" movement-images prevails, space is no more than a "plane [*plan*] of immanence" (58–59), one "entirely made up of Light."[17] The same would be true of time. Movement-images, bundles of actions and reactions in that space, are the diffusions of light propagated without resistance, without decrease in intensity, and, as I understand the theory, without directional or temporal constraints ("without resistance and without loss" [60]). Obviously, Deleuzian–Bergsonian light is not physical light as we know it, which is to say, light that travels along foreseeable trajectories and at a constant speed. Rather, Deleuze's idea of light, of unimpeded and random flux, underscores a light that, above all, behaves whimsically. Now, what I just said of light holds for all Deleuze's basic concepts, which are always deployed with a spin intended to differentiate them from standard definitions. "Movement," "light," "life," "object," "image": they are all implicitly and internally defined by the process-ontology they articulate. As a consequence, the Deleuzian–Bergsonian model of the world is so different from ours that it is sometimes hard to imagine what it is really like. Distinct and localized seeing devices (eyes, cameras), for instance, are impossible in a universe of pure movement-images. Without reflection or refraction of light, the function of the eye is physically unrealizable.[18]

In any event, the movement-image is the basic image that underlies other types of images. Other images seem to be differentiations and differences of movement-images.[19] Not surprisingly, then, the connection between the primary world of undifferentiated movement and the secondary world of image types is not easy to determine, for the differentiated world both *is* and *is not* the world of the movement-image. Whereas perception-, action-, and affection-images are "varieties [*variétés*] of the movement-image,"[20] the differentiated images are also described as "avatars" of the movement-image[21]—that is, transformative results that come about by a change in form, the outcome of metamorphosis. On the one hand, the "original" and "pure" movement-image is differentiated into various other images, and thus it ceases to exist when they are realized. On the other hand, the movement-image *itself* metamorphoses into—or takes on the form of—perception-, affection-, and action-images. Movement-imagehood is, one could say, preserved in the more differentiated world as the "matter" of the formed world. It remains the underlying depth reality, present in those forms not "in person" (Husserl) but "indirectly."[22]

Consequently, we are left with a somewhat ambiguous relation between the primary and secondary worlds. If the three differentiated images do not dispense with the movement-image, then perception, action, and affection only introduce a second system or frame of reference—a second *régime*—into the image-world. This second régime is added to but also alters the first régime, namely, the movement-image. Perhaps we can think of the relation between the two régimes as we think of energy and the state of its organization in our cosmos, or of chemical reactions and their patterning into (and by) forms of life. Because of the "double régime," we beings of the secondary world can conceive of two perspectives. One is the point of view of the movement-image, which is without a center and which decenters what is centered. The other is the point of view of discreteness and selectivity, which is oriented and centered by subjectivity and by categories of thingness. The two régimes are constitutionally connected because the differentiated images (perception, action, affection) are all "avatars," that is, embodiments of the movement-image.[23]

I will begin, then, by reconstructing the order of the differentiated world. First of all, how do the "avatars" arise from the movement-image?[24] Deleuze suggests a genetic view of the image-world. At the beginning, the world consists in movement-images. The differentiated world takes form by cooling and slowing down, thereby producing distinctions in the originally undivided cosmos. But time, which is a condition of this genesis, belongs to the differentiated world only. Perception, action, and affection—the secondary images arising from movement-images—must therefore not be conceived as evolutionary events, neither from one secondary image to the other nor in relation to the movement-image. They are interdependent, perhaps mutually constitutive of each other. Their emergence is not of a temporal order, for we need a nontemporal order and hierarchy of emergence or constitution. The second (and related) difficulty stems from the ambiguous status of life and the subject in the image-cosmos.[25] One finds in Deleuze the intimation that the subject is a late evolutionary event, at least one that is placed at a highly derived spot in the hierarchy of emergence. At the same time, though, there is the suggestion that subjectivity is a *condition* of perception, action, and affection, that is, something approaching a transcendental subjectivity. As a result, the philosophical problem of constitution engenders a problem of presentation. Are perception, action, and affection to be represented as results of a transition or merely as secondary to movement in an atemporal hierarchy of constitution? Is the subject an ontologically "late," perhaps already outdated figure given our point in history, or is the subject the condition of the possibility of all the differentiated images? Deleuze seems to adopt one attitude in one context, another attitude elsewhere. In this discussion, I have opted for the following order of representation: First, I introduce what seems to ground the whole of the differentiated world, whether it is inanimate, animate, or subjective; in doing so, I follow Deleuze's own use of the language of development. Second, I present thinghood and subjectivity without taking any position as to the question of whether things require subjects; perception, action, and affection are dealt with more than once, depending on the places where they play their respective roles. Notably, this order of presentation should *not* be read as suggesting an order of constitution.

In Deleuze's ontocosmology, the differentiated images of the secondary world result from two—related, even concomitant—kinds of changes or variations. The first variation is that the "plane of immanence cools down," and the world of originally free and infinitely fast motion slows down. The second variation is the decisive "event" in the constitution of a world of objects in our sense: intervals appear, gaps open between the action and the reaction.[26] On the basis of such intervals or gaps, our world emerges and differentiates itself. It is the world as we know it, which is to say, the world that includes the full range of semiotic and cognitive modalities. It is a world of "things," "life,"[27] "living beings," "closed systems," and "tableaux" (*The Movement-Image*, 61). Note that, from the ontological point of view, the different kinds of determinate being are not more dense or more highly organized areas in the dynamic cosmos, but are *less* dense, *less* determinate, *less* dynamic than the medium in which and from which they emerge. *What looks to us as more differentiated and as a gain in complexity and being is, again, ontologically, and from the perspective of movement, a profound loss.* In comparison with pure movement, our world is characterized by loss of plenitude, by diminution of effectuation, mobility, and connectedness.

The appearance of life has three important and interconnected consequences. First, divisions split the field of universal and "all-sided" (Marx) effectuation. In the divided field, effectuation is selective and restricted. For living beings, some effects matter, others do not. Selected sets of causes lead to specific consequences, occur at specific places and times, while others are "made indifferent and pass through them [i.e., beings]" (62). "Centers of indetermination" arise that serve as poles of reference and attribution, for instance, of causes and effects. Relative to such a center, the selection of received effects is *perception*, and the item that is thus perceived, the thing constituted by the gap in the universe of movement-images, is a perception-image (64). Perception-images are a second kind of image in the image-world, and also the first kind of differentiated image. The second consequence of the emergence of life is that when the interval is established between it and its environment, then a gap also opens between an incoming effectuation and the response to it. This makes the response of the "live image" (not Deleuze's term) an *action*. The first two images or achievements—perception and action—are closely connected: perception is "only one side of the gap, and action is the other side. What is called action ... is the delayed reaction of the centre of indetermination" (ibid.). After perception and action, we record a third consequence of the interval: a specific internal response arises as an "in-between" perception and action. "*Affection* is what occupies the interval" (65; emphasis added). The specificity of the affection-image lies in a difference between afferent and efferent effectuation ("perception" and "action"), that is, as an internal transformation between the two ("affection"). Obviously, the being or emergence of one species of differentiated image depends on or contributes to the being or emergence of the other species. The three kinds of differentiated images are ontologically or genetically co-dependent. Take, for instance, the affection-image: whereas the affection-image "adds" the difference or distance between internal and external processing to the selectivity of perception and action, that affective interval makes possible the boundaries that separate the living from its environment and allows for the distinction between input and output.

Let us now add Deleuze's concepts of "thing" (*la chose*) and of "subject" (*le sujet*) to that of "life," and we will have assembled the basic constituents of the Deleuzian–Bergsonian cosmos. Life and thinghood are likewise constituted by the gaps that emerge in the original continuum of the pure image-world. In the case of thinghood, however, the gaps constitute the distance between *one* thing and *another* thing, and the boundary each thing maintains between itself and its environment. Things arise from the "cooling down" of the fluid, hot cosmos of movement-images.[28] This cooling is "correlative to the first opacities, to the first screens obstructing the diffusion of light. It is here that contours of solids or rigids and of geometric bodies would be formed."[29] We must bear in mind that in Deleuze's relational ontology things are perceptions as well: "The thing and the perception of the thing are one and the same thing."[30] To possess thinghood is, among other things, to perceive light (in the special sense of "perception" introduced above), for resistance to penetration is defined in terms of resistance to transparency or translucency, the unfettered spread of light-energy.[31]

By contrast, Deleuzian subjectivity is not a "non-thing" (Descartes through Sartre), but rather, a special case of thinghood, for it is defined as a thing that relates to other things in a particular (or peculiar) way. What distinguishes the subject is that it constitutes a "centre of indetermination"[32] and, thus, possesses a subtractive power: subjectivity "subtracts from the thing whatever does not interest it."[33] As suggestive as the definition may be, however, Deleuze's understanding of the subject remains obscure in the cinema books. On the one hand, the subject is just one item among other items, and what distinguishes the subject as such is solely its "subtractive" capacity; in other words, the subject has no privileged position vis-à-vis the world. On the other hand, the subject seems to play an important role for "perception proper,"[34] and by extension for the formation of action-images as well as affection-images; indeed, Deleuze's subject seems to be the privileged place of perception, action, and affection. In this regard, we might say that Deleuze finally combines transcendental and nontranscendental conceptualizations of subjectivity, but he does so without addressing the problems incurred by such a combination.[35] Perhaps Deleuze believes that his distinction between the "objective" and "subjective" version of the secondary images, as well as his doctrine of the two régimes, offers a theoretical solution to these problems.[36] *Subjective* perception is anchored in a specific being, the "subject," and such a perspective disregards everything that does not correspond to the particular perspective of that subjective being. *Objective* perception is the specific causal selectivity of things. Some things "perceive"—that is, respond to each other by being transformed through an encounter with each other (X rays leave traces on photographic film)—while others do not.

Once the subject is at hand, then, perception, action, and affection take on their subjective forms.[37] The perception-image arises when "we go from total, objective perception, which is indistinguishable from the thing, to a subjective perception which is distinguished from it by simple elimination or subtraction," a perception "related to a centre of indetermination."[38] The perception-image proper would then be an encounter, a product, a superposition of two kinds of perception, one objective and the other subjective. By means of its centering pole, the subject renders itself insensitive to certain effects that would in principle reach it from the objective pole. The subject also connects and unites the effects it selects in the form of a *frame* or *tableau*. Originating from a center of indeterminacy, each selection is only one of many possible perception-images for one and the same objective source. The action-image, the second metamorphosis of the movement-image, is closely tied to the perception-image: "one passes imperceptibly from perception to action."[39] Action is nonetheless different from perception; for action is not "elimination, selection or framing, but the curving in of the universe, from which result together the virtual action of things on us and our possible action on things."[40] Action- and perception-images have in common that they occur in a universe of things and subjects, relating the two. But in the case of the action-image, the effectuation "relates movement to 'acts' (verbs) which will be the design for an assumed end or result."[41] Such a "curving in" is, as I understand it, the result of a comparison between a world trajectory as it would occur without the intervention of a subject and the different, "roundabout" trajectory that results from the intervention of interests and procedures specific to subjectivity.[42] Recall that affection, the third of the differentiated images, takes (its) place in the "in-between," in the gap or interval; it is "what occupies the interval, what occupies it without filling it in or filling it up" (*The Movement-Image*, 65). In other words, affection "takes the place of the interval," just as when I take a seat that place is taken. Affection "surges in the centre of indetermination, that is to say in the subject, between a perception which is troubling in certain respects and a hesitant action" (ibid.). The affection itself is said to be a coincidence of subject and object—a felt feeling, or the manner in which the subject perceives itself, has "a feeling" for itself, or a perception of itself. Like perception and action, affection results from a transformation of energy-in-motion that has come to be embodied. The coincidence of subject and object is peculiar to affection and sets it apart from perception and action—but affection is also pure quality, perhaps of the kind Kant calls an "intensive quantity." Under conditions of subjectivity, affection is located in and attributed to a "centre of indetermination," where it may be differentiated into degrees of intensity, for instance, in form of pain or pleasure. The most "interior" of images, affection may well also be the subjectivized urge of something transcending the "closed form" of the subject. In that case it would be a representative or derivative of nonsubjective forces within the subject. However this may be, the affection-image "relates movement to a 'quality' as lived state" (ibid.).

APPLICATION AND CRITICISM

The true application of the image-ontology is, of course, the wealth of analyses offered to the reader in the roughly six hundred pages that constitute *The Movement-Image* and *The Time-Image*. In order to even begin to discuss this application, I want to simplify my task by focusing on just one film out of the nearly one thousand—namely, *Film*. Deleuze mentions *Film* in the first of his two cinema books, and confers on this example an originary and ontological significance. Produced in 1964 by Samuel Beckett and Alan Schneider, it is a silent, black-and-white short "starring" Buster Keaton. In fact, Keaton plays O, one of the two main characters, who is pursued by the other, E, who is in turn "played" by the film camera itself. Whence the major trope of *Film*: we see Keaton's O while E remains invisible.

Obviously, my choice of *Film* for a discussion of the image-ontology is not altogether arbitrary, for Deleuze himself uses it, somewhat tongue in cheek, as a paradigm case for his theory.[43] O, short for "object," is a character from whom self-perception has been severed. E, short for "eye" = the camera, is O's split-off self-perception. The drama of *Film* remains obscure unless one grasps the set of extreme ideas and conventions that determine it. The guiding idea is that O tries to attain nonbeing by getting away from all the gazes that "hold in being." The guiding convention is that E, the camera, moves behind O, always at an angle not exceeding forty-five degrees with respect to O's back. Whenever E leaves that space, in which it is unknown to O, O feels this presence as *anxiety*. Moreover, whenever someone looks into E's eye from up front, then that person falls into *agony*. Both anxiety and agony are a matter of O's "perceivedness."

Film opens with a shot of a huge unblinking eye. Cut to a street scene, where the camera's E watches out for and catches Keaton's O, who tries in turn to avoid all gazes. When E transgresses the forty-five-degree angle for the first time, O reacts anxiously to being perceived, and E quickly withdraws into the invisibility of his space of immunity. In the next scene, O is in the staircase of an old house, while E, still unknown to O, pursues him from behind. There follows the second transgression of the space of immunity by E and the second moment of anxiety on O's side, and so we begin to see that O's anxiety actually encourages E's transgression. O enters a room, locking it carefully behind him, but he is too late—E has already slipped in behind O. Now O proceeds to eliminate all gazes, signs of gazes, and memories of gazes from the room, in order to bring about the desired transition to nonbeing. Among other things, he destroys photos that show him in various phases of his life. Finally, he settles into one of those Beckettian rocking chairs, and rocks himself to sleep. This is E's opportunity, and he moves around the sleeping O, turning to look straight at his face. When O wakes up, he looks at E and experiences the full-fledged "agony of perceivedness." At this moment we see, for the first time, what O sees: in E, O sees the features of his own face, although the expression is different. The O who looks up shows agony; the face to which he looks, or, if one prefers, the face that looks down on him, shows intent awareness and emotionless scrutiny. O closes his eye, covers his face with his hands, falls back into the chair. He remains in that position while the rocking dies down. Cut to the close-up of the eye that opened *Film*. In its pupil we read: "Film by Samuel Beckett."

Film is a paradigm case for the image-ontology because, first of all, it exhibits all the aforementioned types of images. Moreover, in so doing it also follows a specifically imagistic path: *Film* ostensibly traces the way back from more differentiated to less differentiated images, which is also a trajectory through modes of *being*.[44] Its dramatic trajectory begins with an action-image (the street scene), continues with a perception-image (the staircase and the preparation of room), and then proceeds to the affection-image (the agony of perceivedness when O confronts E). Hence, *Film* comes to an end just before it reaches the movement-image.[45] Let us turn, then, to Deleuze's own characterization of the image-trajectory of *Film* and its three "moments" in *The Movement-Image*.

FIRST MOMENT—ACTION-IMAGE

"In the first, the character O rushes forward and flees horizontally along a wall; then, along a vertical axis, tries to climb a staircase, always sticking to the edge of the wall. He 'acts' [*agit*], it is a perception of action, or an *action-image*" (67).

SECOND MOMENT—PERCEPTION-IMAGE[46]

"The second moment: The character has come into a room.... O perceives (subjectively) the room, the things and the animals which are there, whilst OE perceives (objectively) O himself, the room, and its contents: this is the perception of perception, or the *perception-image*, considered under a double régime, in a double system of references" (ibid.).

THIRD MOMENT—AFFECTION-IMAGE

"Then O can be installed in the rocking chair and rock gently with his eyes closed. But it is at this moment, the third and last, that the greatest danger is revealed: the extinction of subjective perception has freed the camera of the forty-five degree restriction. With great caution, it advances beyond, into the domain of the remaining two hundred and seventy degrees, but each time wakens the character who regains a scrap of subjective perception, hides, curls up and forces the camera to move back again. Finally, taking advantage of O's torpor, OE succeeds in coming round to face him, and comes closer and closer to him. The character O is thus now seen from the front, at the same time as the new and last convention is revealed: the camera OE is the double of O, the same face, a patch over one eye (monocular vision), with the single difference that O has an anguished expression and OE has an attentive expression: the impotent motor effort of the one, the sensitive surface of the other. We are in the domain of the perception of affection, the most terrifying, that which still survives when all the others have been destroyed: it is the perception of self by self, the *affection-image* . . . death, immobility, blackness" (67–68).

The criticism that follows concentrates on two aspects of Deleuze's interpretation, namely, representation and subjectivity. Specifically, I raise two problems: Does Deleuze's image-ontology adequately account for the manner and modes in which *Film* presents its story (O's enterprise of unbecoming, E's successful confrontation of O in the final scene)? Do O's project and E's role fit into the imagistic ontology and the dynamic thesis of the "way home," which is also a trajectory away from the conditions of subjectivity? The first problem is of an aesthetic nature and suggests doubts with respect to how well the image-ontology accounts for the complicated aesthetic devices of the film. The second problem concerns the theory of the subject and doubts as to whether the image-ontology is useful for the analysis of the subject and its vicissitudes, especially insofar as Deleuze often recommends his theories as a kind of "tool box."

To begin with, Deleuze claims that *Film* offers viewers a sequence ordered into three segments, subsumable under the three image-concepts of the differentiated motional cosmos. The first "moment"—the street scene—is said to be an action-image. O hurries along a wall and eventually up the stairs inside a building. Indeed, the background conditions for action-images seem to be in place. There exists an obvious subjective center in the form of the agent O, and O's behavior is teleologically oriented; O pursues goals, among them to pass from being to nonbeing, and to avoid being seen. O hurries and keeps close to the wall in order not to be exposed to gazes. The situation is presented from the point of view of a call for action, for everything we see—events, scenes, actions—receives its specific meanings from the point of view of O's goals and thus his subtractivity. For O, gazes are threats, his itinerary a path toward nonperceivedness, the room a "sanctuary."

We should note in passing that a differentiated Deleuzian–Bergsonian cosmos consistently, albeit trivially, fulfills the Beckett–Berkeleyan postulate of *Film* that "esse est percipi." "Being" coincides with "being-image," and "to-be-an-image" is "to-be-perceived" as well as "to-be-perceiving." Things, subjects, actions, perceptions, affections—ultimately, all are perceptions of light or energy. In the objective sense, then, all differentiated being is perception, at least under one aspect; only freely moving light would be perceptionless.[47] Ontologically speaking, it is therefore not the perception anchored in a gaze that "holds in being." In a Deleuzian–Bergsonian universe, O's project is even more absurd than in a Cartesian world (if that is possible), because, to get rid of perception, O would need to be able to dispose of the organization of energy that constitutes his own determinate being. And yet, O's project *does* make sense when we grasp it as the more limited project of eliminating subjective perception and the specific subtractive condition of the subject. It makes sense, that is, if one accepts the premise that subjects "are held in being" by subjective perception. The success of such a project depends on O's ridding himself of the centering and subtracting devices proper to subjectivity. O would thus attempt to do away with the differentiation and limitation of his image-being that are specific to subjectivity, and he would accomplish that aim by means of an action that suppresses or eliminates those constraints. The negative teleology of O's de-subjectivization is, again, best conveyed in Deleuze's own words: "How can we rid ourselves of ourselves, and demolish ourselves?"[48]

Nevertheless, the question also reveals a problem for the image-ontologist. Does Deleuze not imply here that the differentiated item or sphere of subjectivity forms a project and pursues an action to go beyond *itself*, to become movement of a purer motional quality—all by drawing on its own resources? We can imagine Nietzsche articulating the problem of *self-transformation* in these terms, but on the basis of his very different ontology of centers of will-to-power. By contrast, O's action aims not at self-overcoming but at overcoming the self; his goal is to return to a lesser degree of imagistic differentiatedness. The problem here is that this return is presented as the project of a being who has the form of subjectivity. In Beckett's *Film*, O—the subject—rejects subjectivity and acts in order to rid himself of himself. In Deleuze's terms, O is subjectivity, a centering indeterminacy "incurving" the universe at the place where he is, acting to abolish its centering and selecting. O's activity in *Film* would thus need to be, simultaneously, a curving in *and* a curving out. The paradoxical problem is this: *O's action seems to be an action that includes the conditions of its own failure among the conditions of its success.*

A strangely dialectical light begins to emanate from Deleuze's analysis of *Film* and its action-image. The source of this light, I would argue, is not so much the material to which Deleuze's theory is applied as the theory itself. O acts, and his action is attributable to a subject. The same act possesses subjectivizing power *and* is intended to move away from subjectivity. De-subjectivization takes the form of a centering gesture and is performed by an agency with all the prerogatives of subjectivity. The problem is most palpable when we see O systematically and thoroughly eliminating all sources of perception while "preparing" the room for his passage to nonbeing.[49] In doing so, O displays a remarkably pure (and highly comical) form of centering subjectivity.[50] Given as much, one could argue that Deleuze's thesis about the action-image does not sufficiently appreciate O's subjectivity as embodied—that is, manifested and sustained—by O's action. The imbrication of de-subjectivization and subject-based agency in O poses for Deleuze the general problem of how subjectivity can be simultaneously a form of differentiation qua diminished freedom of energy, as well as a force that pushes toward de-differentiation.[51] The problem is by no means restricted to subjectivity. How does one reconcile the action of differentiating and de-differentiating tendencies in a Deleuzian–Bergsonian universe?[52] What is needed is more than the idea of the prison house of form and a contra puntal liberation by de-differentiation; in other words, the theory also needs to account for differentiation and to explain the resistance to entropy.

As I have suggested, this problem has a representational aspect as well. The aesthetic project of Beckett's *Film* is also an action, and thus equally subject to the problems of self-defeating activity. If *Film* is a paradigm case for the Deleuzian–Bergsonian theory of images, then the work is or represents an action that articulates the longing for pure movement, and accomplishes a leg in that journey back, but also expresses the anxiety aroused by such a risky adventure—at least from the point of view of organized subjectivity. Let us assume as much for the purpose of our discussion. Does *Film* then also show "how to extinguish the three varieties"[53] of images? Does *Film* itself contribute to the extinction of the three secondary varieties of images? Or, more generally, what is the activity of showing or performing "a return" (*retour*) or "an extinction" in terms of the Deleuzian–Bergsonian process-ontology? The answer cannot come from O and his project, and so I believe that we need to turn toward the images of the movie and the writing of the script. How are we to conceive of the differentiated images, modes of showing, that is, the presentational arrangements of *Film* in terms of the image-ontology? Do the iconic elements participate in the de-differentiating itinerary? Do they perform a differentiating motion, perhaps even a counterpoint to de-differentiation? Are those pictures plurivalent cathexes or expressions, forces that de-differentiate *and* differentiate at the same time and in one and the same gesture? Does the aesthetic item and image *Film* participate in the movement it is said to (re)present?

Representation and subjectivity present the same kind of fundamental problem for Deleuze. Both seem to manifest specific differences when compared to their nonrepresentational and nonsubjective environments. If "representation" shares its ontological traits with an englobing reality, how do we account for the plurivalence of a "representation" that seems to move in opposite and incompatible directions—differentiation and de-differentiation—in one and the same movement? This is not to say that the image-ontology has encountered an insurmountable problem; rather, it is to suggest that there is a problem, and that I have not found an account of the aesthetic specificity of *Film* from the point of view of a "return" toward the movement-image, or, more generally, of the status of art in the image-world.[54] Both are missing from the cinema books. Deleuze is either not aware of a problem, or—more likely—he chooses to ignore it. As a consequence, Deleuze fails to account for the specifically aesthetic character of his object(s) in terms of his basic ontology, or, by denying that there is such a specificity, he misses some of the potential of the work. After all, does not all being have a tendency to return to the free mobility and universal sensitivity of the movement-image? Is art merely one of the many forms that are subject to this universal tendency? Or, to ask Nietzsche's question from the *Birth of Tragedy*, does art have a special power to confront us with the underlying reality of movement-images, and, if so, how?

The next critical point concerns the relation between O and E, and pertains even more intimately to subjectivity. For Deleuze, the antagonism between O and E is a struggle between objective and subjective perception. The two forms of perception are opposed because subjective perception, the more differentiated of the two forms, obstructs the path and movement toward objective perception, which is less differentiated.[55] Things, living beings, subjects—all impose or superimpose their own specific forms or modes onto the more fundamental forms or modes of other images. An increase in differentiation is thus inversely related to power; the more differentiated forms impose their own mode onto the less differentiated forms. Organizing forms of differentiatedness must lose their organizing power before the "compound" (*ensemble*) can return to the more "primitive," but also more "pleasurable," condition.[56] Applied to *Film*, this idea provides the ontological reason why, in Deleuze's interpretive perspective, alert subjective perception (O) blocks objective perception (the camera, E) in its return to the movement-image. O's internal de-subjectivizing tendency fails to materialize as long as, and because, he is awake. The more differentiated image O, a subject, cannot relate to himself in the mode of the less differentiated image or "objective perception." If the subject is to de-differentiate itself, then its transformation presupposes an internal change in the hitherto dominant type of imagehood, which is that of subjectivity. The image-ontology requires that the dominant mode must weaken before it can be transformed—or transforms itself—into the hitherto dominated mode.[57] This is what the image-ontology requires. Nevertheless, this "narrative" seems to reverse the order of the drama presented by *Film*. The work suggests that it is O, the "subject" without self-perception, who follows the trajectory traced by *Film*. How can that subject *also* and *simultaneously* block its own way? The blockage would need to be performed by something of the order of unconscious resistance. And, if O does simultaneously block what he seems to be pursuing, how can we avoid dialecticizing O, who now acts to achieve one thing but simultaneously prevents its success? In neither of the two cases would one of the modes be standing in the other mode's way, as Deleuze claims. Indeed, it is difficult to believe that there is, in the subject, an objective element striving to transcend and get away from the subjective bind.

Perhaps my criticism, however, is turned around. If the objective element is not O or one of his integral parts, then perhaps the desubjectivizing force is located in E, the disintegrated part. What, then, is E's contribution to the return? For obvious reasons, I here present E as Deleuze sees him.[58] Prima facie E's role in *Film* shows the features of a complex action-image. If E has the status of an independent agent, then his perception can be expected to be subjective in Deleuze's sense. For Deleuze, however, E embodies objective perception because E is identified with the camera, the apparatus of cinematic recording. If E manifests subjectivity, then the confrontation between O and E would take place between two representatives of subjectivity—the classical, antagonistic couple since Diderot and Hegel.[59] But Deleuze does not want to adopt a dialectical model. Consequently, he reads the image-antagonism into *Film* by virtue of denying or neglecting those elements that testify to the subjectivity and agency of E's gaze. Deleuze's interpretation does not make room for the subtle and strange personification of E, the way E hides behind O, the way E pursues O, E's strategic decision to circle O with averted eye, E's confrontation with O in the final scene. Deleuze thus misses a whole dimension of *Film* in which the camera is fictionalized into the agency E, and takes on a life of its own in the form of a character: E is a hybrid, a subject-object or in-between. By the same token, Deleuze also blinds himself to the aesthetic implications of a fictionalized camera.

In order to highlight a further difficulty with objective perception, let us once more follow Deleuze and assume that there is a return toward the movement-image, and that its trajectory is divisible into three "moments" that correspond to the action, perception, and affection-images. Is the camera, understood as "objective perception"—that is, as merely a recording device—a facilitator, an inhibitor, or merely a neutral element on that path? The presentational modalities of *Film* do not seem to change as the film progresses. Would not some perceivable changes in cinematic attitude be necessary if objective perception were the agent or event that comes to play a prominent role in the last part of *Film*, a role that it did not play before? *Film* performs its cinematic gestures in a typically Beckettian style, with great precision and a wealth of significant (though barely noticeable) internal variation. But there is very little global transformation as the drama unfolds. If there is an evolution toward de-differentiation, then the film we see does not participate in it.[60] In sum, *Film* is not on its way back to the movement-image.

The Deleuzian reading is thus forced to treat *Film* as a work of *representation* that presents to us, the readers and viewers, something—the return of the images along a trajectory of diminishing differentiatedness—in which it does not participate. Against his will, the theoretician of a monistic ontology is led to a classical dualism in the aesthetic domain of being. Everything is image, but some things (for instance, *Film*), *represent* images and trajectories of images that they do not *exemplify*. In other words, form and content are distinct and follow different logical paths. Gradually, a gap in Deleuze's interpretation of *Film* has become evident. Deleuze fails to interpret the aesthetics of the work in terms of his own imagistic ontology. This is all the more surprising insofar as Deleuze's whole enterprise in his cinema books is a self-proclaimed classification ("taxonomy") of procedures and styles used in the cinema, a classification carried out in the terms of his ontology, whereas *Film* is actually analyzed in terms of its content. In other words, Deleuze uses the content of *Film* in an effort to exemplify his division of images: each scene is read as representing a type of image and a transition from one type to another, but the cinematic modalities of the work remain unexplored. Had Deleuze turned to the *form*, he would probably have met with even greater resistance. The work rescinds via its medium what Deleuze claims that it demonstrates via its content, that is, a performance showing "how to extinguish the three varieties" of image.[61]

REVISIONS

What could be done to avoid some of the difficulties that I have elicited? Recall that there are two interconnected sets of problems. One concerns subjectivity and the action to "rid ourselves of ourselves, and demolish ourselves." The problem is that subjectivity—Deleuze's very special subtractive, indeterminate, selective subjectivity—is not adequately understood as the imprisonment of an energy alienated into the form of the incurving center of indetermination. Traditionally, such theories of essential alienation have a hard time with questions such as the following: How and why has the alienated subject become what it is? How and why does the subject formulate a project to rid itself of its form and burden? What is the alternative to "essential" alienation? What would be a model of non-alienation? The second difficulty concerns the place of art and representation in the image-ontology. Deleuze's ontology seems hard pressed to accommodate a well-known duplicity of symbolic action, which is to be able to show one kind of thing and, simultaneously, perform a gesture normally thought to be incompatible with what it shows. In Deleuze's reading, Beckett's *Film* shows de-differentiation of images but it *is* or *does* that by way of highly differentiated images. How can *Film* be a case of de-differentiation when it displays refined differentiation? The Deleuzian–Bergsonian image-ontology frees itself from the idea—indeed, the oppressive idea—that all images are false because they are not what they claim to be; but how does it account for the highly desirable capacity of images and other signs to generate a surplus of meaning from a lesser degree of being, or to show what they are not? The theory does not seem to make space for differences between two kinds of being, one that signifies, and another one that does not.

However, if a genuinely Peircean[62] triadic model of the sign is substituted for Deleuze's dyadic model, Deleuze might be able to more convincingly make his claims with respect not only to *Film* but, indeed, to all films. In Deleuze's model, basic characterizations of the differentiated images of perception, action, and affection are all cast in terms of two-pole relations between images. Consider the perception-image,[63] which is said to vary by "receiv[ing] the action of the other images on one of its facets and react[ing] to them on another facet."[64] The two dynamic relations—acting upon and being acted upon—are both dyadic, even if bipolarity adds the necessity of the other to each of the two relations. By contrast, Peirce—the subject of ample reference in the cinema books if not the source of "real" guidance[65]—built his complex semiotics on the assumption that semiotic relations are fundamentally and irreducibly *triadic*; these relations belong to the category of "Thirdness."[66] In one of many definitions, Pierce claims that a sign is that which represents something (a meaning) to something or other (an interpretant). In this relation between three positions, the interpretant stands in *two* significant relations. The sign relates the interpretant to its meaning by connecting with the interpretant via the sign. What makes this relation essentially triadic is the idea that the different relations are dependent on each other: the interpretant's connection with meaning would not exist, nor be what it is, without its specific relation to the sign that functions as its "bearer." If *Film* is a complex sign in Peirce's sense, then the differentiated images and the perception of the cinematographic images (relation 1: sign-interpretant) can convey to the interpretant the meaning that a constituted subject such as O acts (relation 3: interpretant-meaning) "to rid himself of his subjectivity." At the same time, there is no need to conceive of the relation of *Film* to its meaning (self-annihilating subject; relation 2: sign-meaning) along the same lines that the viewer (interpretant) relates to *Film* (the sign; relation 3: interpretant-meaning). The sign can be what its meaning is not, that is, differentiated and without being on its way toward the movement-image. Could it not be the case that we need something like an incurving subject with a high degree of determinacy in order to operate the complex triadic structure of Peircean semiotics?

Instead of continuing to explore further the Peircean model of the sign, let us turn again to Deleuze himself, for what we need we can find right there in the cinematographic toolbox of his cinema books. The specific concept I have in mind is "free indirect discourse,"[67] a concept originally refashioned for the cinema, as Deleuze points out, by Pier Paolo Pasolini. In effect, what Pasolini and Deleuze have in mind is a cinematographic discourse that does two things by performing a single gesture. "A character"—let us say, the O of *Film*—"acts on the screen and is assumed to see the world in a certain way. But simultaneously the camera sees him, and transforms the viewpoint of the character." Deleuze's description here fits the Peircean model, but it also provides the desired difference between O's project of unbecoming and the complex cinematographic strategies of *Film* itself. To this add the fact—and here I use words that Deleuze borrows from Pasolini—that "the director has replaced wholesale the neurotic's vision of the world by his own delirious vision of aestheticism." The only word here that does not ring true for Beckett's aesthetic project is the term *delirious*; otherwise, *Film* is "a pure form which sets itself up as an autonomous vision of the content . . . a correlation between a perception-image and a camera-consciousness which transforms it."[68] It would appear to me that Deleuze's free indirect discourse is capable of being theorized under a triadic semiotics, but does not find its home as readily in the Deleuzian–Bergsonian image-ontology. Let us note the reason, namely, that indirect discourse possesses the duplicity we need to understand *Film*. It is *one* discourse at work within *another* discourse, and the duplicity of the two discourses is clearly marked in the discursive genre itself. By the same token, indirect discourse is of a higher degree of differentiation than direct discourse.

The reader may ask how I can claim to have proposed a revision here when Deleuze himself seems to propose the elements that I purport to add to his theory. Note that my thesis was not that the cinema books contain nothing that is of help in reading *Film*. Indeed, my essay to this point has defended the much more restricted thesis that the theory of the image-ontology as sketched by Deleuze does not really provide the conceptual map for the complex landscape and behavior of images that we find in *Film* (and, by extension, other films). There is a gap between, on the one hand, Deleuze's detailed accounts of films qua his history of the cinema—broadly construed, his aesthetics of cinema—and, on the other, Deleuze's ontological views as expressed in the theoretical sections of the two books. The image-ontology needs to establish its cinematic credentials by offering insight into the specific workings of the "Seventh Art." Free indirect discourse is a fruitful cinematographic concept, but it is not accounted for ontologically.

With this in mind, I want to turn to the second proposed modification. From a merely ontological perspective, either all the differentiated images are diminutives of freer forms of energy, or they result from the freeing of energy in a shift from the more strongly bound to the less strongly bound types. Their dynamic is that of either forming (*composer, générer*)[69] or undoing and extinguishing (*éteindre*) the varieties: restriction or liberation. Still, ontologically, the theory does not seem to value things such as "happily moving through a variety of images," perhaps in a free variation of different forms, or "happily forming more differentiated out of less differentiated images." Deleuze's ontology does not offer us a theory of self-differentiation, of its status and its possible values. We are not told why the cosmos slows down and differentiates itself, nor does differentiation ever appear in an ontologically positive light.[70] In an even more general vein, the fact that unrestricted free energy is underlying a cosmos of restricted forms—forms that also bind energy—orients and polarizes the whole Deleuzian–Bergsonian cosmos. It prescribes two, and only two, principal directions to the dynamics of that space: one toward increasing differentiatedness, the other toward decreasing differentiatedness. The resulting, quasi-Manichaean grid of two tendencies in perpetual struggle appears too simple. As I said earlier, not all comparisons between images are suited to the terms of decreasing or increasing proximity to movement-imagehood; we need "happy" differentiation as much as "unhappy" de-differentiation. *Film*, films, art, and the world at large call for a more complex categorical apparatus than the one provided by this image-ontology.[71]

The second revision I propose, then, is the addition of an undirected and value-indifferent differentiation to the ontology. Directions and evaluations would not have to disappear from the critical machinery, though they would cease to be global and ubiquitous features of being. Instead, they would become local and situational events. The "Crisis of the Action-Image,"[72] for instance, would lose its liberating underpinning and appear as a historical event that can be analyzed and evaluated in a number of different ways—for instance, as an epistemic change (Foucault), as a transformation of the superstructure (Marx), or as a transformation of the semiotic structure owing to a change in the dominant mode of stratification of Western societies (Luhmann). The change can be the happy differentiation of aesthetic modernists, or the "unhappy de-differentiation" of more traditionally minded critics such as Stanley Cavell.[73] Differentiation need not be tantamount to alienation—it could be *jouissance* or even progress! The evaluation of changes becomes a question whose frame of reference is internal to the differentiated world, and not one to be decided on a priori grounds. Revisions of the kind I propose should be all the more acceptable to Deleuzians insofar as Deleuze himself defended similar ideas in his earlier writings such as *Difference and Repetition*, *Anti-Oedipus*, and *A Thousand Plateaus*.[74]

My third modification is a corollary to the first two and concerns subjectivity. Naturally, ontological and semiotic alterations affect the status of Deleuze's subject. That subject is subtractive, incurving, and a center of indetermination—in short, a being that operates under the dominance of the sensory-motor schema. Now, the triadic semiotics provides a basis for the philosophical account of the subtractive, incurving, indeterminate traits of that subject, and gives us the freedom to evaluate them anew. But a subject whose mental and behavioral performances and attitudes are actualized in terms of triadic complex signs is no longer relegated to the gap or interval between afferent and efferent effectuation, which, in the Deleuzian–Bergsonian image-ontology, accounts for the indetermination of the subject. Indetermination at the place of the subject is not merely the effect of a randomizing mechanism that injects irregularity into the stream of predetermined events. Sign-using subjects *generate* order and disorder in their environment; indetermination and incurving occur, but only from the very specific point of view of a subjectless cosmos. From the point of view of the whole, though, the order of the cosmos *includes* subjects. The place of the subject is the location of unexpected order and disorder, not because of some break or rupture in that order, but merely because the world at large is so constituted at that place. The subject is not an anomaly—it is cosmic normality, however unlikely its emergence.

This generative function of (if one likes) small satellite orders is rooted in the semiotic orientation of the subject, which, while using signs for its sensory-motor purposes, is also endowed with the competence to re-create the universal connectedness that movement-images had "before" the cosmos coagulated into the secondary modes. Peircean signs are parts of a sign world of universal connectedness—or better yet, connectibility—of all signs with all signs. But there is a restriction: the mode of connectedness is of the special triadic kind and requires complex sign-operating images. What matters in our context is the fact that the sign-world is not bound and limited by the constraints of the sensory-motor condition and therefore, historically, did not need to wait for the cinematographic turn to the time-image to rid itself of that constraint. Nor does a Peircean sign need to "stop being related to an interval as sensory-motor centre" for "movement [to] find its absolute quality again, [such that] every image reacts with every other one, on all their sides and in all their parts."[75] Both the movement-image and the time-image are realizations of one basic competence, which is that of a sign-oriented comportment and attitude.

When subjects conceive of a world and of themselves, they do so in semiotic terms—terms that are not adequately conceptualized by incurving and indetermination, which represent a view from the outside. Subjects introduce into the world a place where that world is viewed. The reflexive idea of such an inside view is absent from Deleuze's ontology. It is, however, by no means alien to Deleuze, theorist of cinema. Whenever he has reasons to distinguish specifically "subjective" achievements from images that do not rely on an incurving subject, he introduces a duplicity into those achievements. We have seen this most clearly in his reading of *Film* (*The Time-Image*, 18–19). The "sign" is not merely an image that displays its features, but "a particular image that refers to a type of image" (32; see also 42). It looks as if images were not signs per se but first only "signaletic material [*matière signalétique*]" (33). When this matter—for instance, a perception-image—is a sign, then there is not just perception, but "perception of perception" (32).[76] Although the difference between the "subjective" and the "objective" is never systematically worked out in the cinema books, the subject proposed by my modifications adds to the world the "features of expression that compose and combine ... images, and constantly re-create them, borne or carted along by matter in movement" (33).

Consider once again Beckett's *Film*. O's project is not the expression or translation of an ontological alienation into a project of unbecoming. Rather, this is O's *ideology;* his world model is based on "esse est percipi." The idea and the use O makes of it belong to the image-world of *Film*—but Beckett's script makes amply clear that O's ideas about the world and himself are ill conceived! In its free indirect cinematic discourse, *Film* shows us a *specific* subject and that subject's perceptions, actions, and affections. O is not a general but a very specific subject, situated in the specific context of a specific and failing project. O does show us something about the general subject, but he does so in the indirect mode.[77] Most important, this particular subject's misconception is both a mistake about the world and a fact of that world. It is generative by being the source of the strange comportment and particular order of the events that we witness in *Film*.

Ultimately, the subject is the place where a certain differentiatedness achieves the status of self-feeling and projects a world-picture. Everything characteristic of that place is ipso facto also a feature of the cosmos. In addition, there is no reason to think of the advent of the subject as catastrophic. Rather, the subject is the complex image where the cosmos, as it were, has decided to "curve in" and to become "indeterminate." We can, of course, think of such an event in affective terms, as cosmic pleasure or pain. But do we really have reasons to think that the cosmos acts, enjoys, or suffers because of the changes it undergoes? Do we really have reasons to think of the condition of subjectivity as either the telos of history or as its greatest accident? For O, as for other Beckett characters, and perhaps even for the cinema, the problem of one's essence and trajectory does not correlate with into the terms of such an ontology. Finally, the three revisions I propose remove the Neoplatonic and Romantic idea that our world has fallen and that subjectivity is an alienated condition.

NOTES

I would like to thank Gregory Flaxman for his editorial expertise and assistance, without which this essay would not bear its present form. Having said that, of course, the usual reminder: he is not responsible for any of the theses I express in this essay.

1. This is a Schopenhauerian and Heideggerian trait of Deleuze's theory. Together with the fact that "showing" is achieved through the "becoming sign" of the images, this would accord to the cinema (and art) a particular revelatory function vis-à-vis being.
2. Samuel Beckett, *"Film": Complete Scenario/Illustrations/Production Shots. With an Essay "On Directing Film" by Alan Schneider* (New York: Grove Press, 1969).
3. I rely primarily on two texts for my discussion of Deleuze's image-ontology: Gilles

Deleuze, *The Movement-Image* and *The Time-Image*. (Minneapolis: University of Minnesota Press, 1986 and 1989, respectively). My discussion of the image-ontology is limited in two ways. I take Deleuze's image-ontology to be the philosophical theory concentrated in chapter 4 of *The Movement-Image*, and, to a lesser degree, in chapters 2–4 of *The Time-Image*. This is where the theory is introduced as a separate ontology, not merely used in interpretations of films. Hence, when I speak of the Bergson–Deleuzian image-ontology, I mean the theory as presented in these passages. One of the theses of this essay is that there is a gap between the image-ontology and the critical/historical observations on film in the two cinema books. In his interpretations of films, Deleuze uses the *terms*, but very often not the *concepts*, of his ontology. The second limitation is that the image-ontology in *The Movement-Image* is presented in the form of a general and comprehensive ontology; but when Deleuze writes *The Time-Image* (published two years later), he has formed ideas about the cinema that are even more difficult to subsume under his original image-ontology than those of the first book. He makes a halfhearted attempt to adapt the earlier image-ontology to his ideas about modern cinema, but without devoting great energy to the task. As a result, the interpretations in *The Time-Image* are even further removed from the image-ontology than those of *The Movement-Image*. These are reasons why my discussion of the ontology focuses on *The Movement-Image*, with only an occasional glance at the theoretical chapters of *The Time-Image*. I do not address the differences between the two books.

4. See Deleuze, *The Movement-Image*, 98–99 and 197–98. Compare the remarks on Peirce in *The Time-Image* (30), which offer a more comprehensive view on Peirce than the applications in the first volume. In *The Time-Image*, Deleuze introduces Peirce's ontological categories ("firstness," "secondness," "thirdness"), but avowedly not in Peirce's sense. For Deleuze, imagehood is ontologically universal; for Peirce, to be an image pertains to thirdness only, and thirdness is not a universal category. The concepts of the image and of the sign are thus differently determined in Peirce and Deleuze.
5. For a more independent assessment of the Bergsonian ancestry, see Gregory Flaxman's insightful contribution to this volume: "Cinema Year Zero." Deleuze makes his "no" to Peirce clear in *The Time-Image*: "We therefore take the term 'sign' in a completely different way from Peirce" (32).
6. Deleuze's sense of relation emerges most clearly at the beginning and the end of *The Movement-Image* (10 and 197), when he says that "relation is always a third, being necessarily external to its terms."
7. The status of the time-image and its relation to the movement-image are not clearly determined in the two cinema books. There is little mention of the time-image in *The Movement-Image*. The few places where it is invoked are in relation to *cinematographic* versions of images (23, 29, 68–69). The context indicates that Deleuze thinks that the cinematographic movement-image relates to time only in an indirect way, and that there is a contrasting direct way, which is that of the time-image. Both cinematographic images are based on movement, and would therefore be variants of the *ontological* movement-image. In the preface to the English edition, the "direct" time-image is said to be a "reversal in the movement-time relationship" (ix). In *The Time-Image*, Deleuze emphasizes the difference between the two images. Here he says that "the movement-image does not give us a time-image" (270). But the tie to movement is never broken: the time-image "carries out a direct presentation of time by reversing the relationship of subordination that time maintains with normal movement" (37). Is the time-image an image side by side with the movement-image, or is it a variety of the movement-image? The answer is complicated by three factors: Deleuze does not always make it clear whether he speaks of images in the ontological or cinematographic sense. In

cinema, the two types of image are alternatives and one takes the place of the other. I think, however, that the time-image is a movement-image, *ontologically* speaking. Here the other two factors enter to cast doubt. Deleuze does not discuss the place of time in the ontological picture; and he does not really introduce the time-image in an ontological way in *The Time-Image* in his "Recapitulation of Images and Signs" (25–43). As a consequence, the ontological status of the time-image remains vague.

8. Deleuze, *The Movement-Image*, 59: "This in-itself of the image is matter." Also compare *The Time-Image*, 33. To receive form is not necessarily a passive status.
9. Strictly speaking, an environment seems to be constituted only at the more complex stages of differentiation when "the universe is incurved and organised to surround it" (*The Movement-Image*, 64). That would require subjects. But, apart from "creatio sui et ex nihilo," effectuation implies a difference, however continuous, between an effectuating and an effectuated pole. Therefore, everything involved in effectuation has an environment.
10. Deleuze is somewhat more guarded in *The Time-Image* in a context where he is concerned with Peirce and the contrast between the movement- and time-images: "from the point of view of the movement-image: this is framed by the relations which relate it to the whole that it expresses, so much so that a logic of relations seems to close the transformations of the movement-image" (33–34).
11. Deleuze, *The Movement-Image*, 58. This is only *one* of at least two "systems of reference" (63).
12. We may compare this to Nietzschean wills-to-power, but we need to notice that the central notion of *power* is missing in Deleuze. *Overpowering* is not part of the basic relation of image to image.
13. This model is, of course, reminiscent of the ancient materialists' conception of icons (idols, simulacra) as material films (!), "effluences" that emanate from the objects, travel toward the sense organs, "influe" on those organs, and are perceived when these are transformed by the iconic matter. The materialists also held that matter constantly lost in emission was constantly regained by the acquisition of small particles from the environment. Bergson and Deleuze have generalized, ontologized, and, above all, dynamized this idea. Their basic "matter" is not corporeal, but energetic. See *The Movement-Image*, 58, for a clear allusion.
14. Deleuze, *The Movement-Image*, 58.
15. Ibid., 58. This idea applies to the world of differentiated images: "The movement-image is the object; the thing itself caught in movement as continuous function" (*The Time-Image*, 27).
16. Deleuze, *The Movement-Image*, 58. Deleuze himself emphasizes this sentence. The passages to which he refers can be found in Bergson's *Matter and Memory*.
17. Ibid., 60. Here Deleuze follows Bergson.
18. See *The Movement-Image*, 59 and 60. The more differentiated the images, the more comprehensive the sentience of items, both of other items and of themselves. Differentiation is thus also a path toward enhanced sentience *of* the cosmos *in* the cosmos. The Stoics, the seventeenth-century mystic Jakob Böhme, and Denis Diderot thought along these lines.
19. This is another analogue to ancient materialism.
20. See Deleuze, *The Movement-Image*, chapter 4 ("The Movement-Image and Its Varieties"). It becomes clear very quickly that there are movement-images in the differentiated world, and that to be a movement-image is a character of films. See *The Time-Image*, 27–29. Is the time-image also an "avatar" of the movement-image? Deleuze seems to think that the time-image *is not* a cinematographic movement-image: "The movement-image of the classical cinema gave way, in the post-war period, to a direct time-image" (*The Time-Image*, xi). I have claimed above that the cinematographic time-image is, indeed, *ontologically* a movement-image See note 7.

21. For the perception-image, see *The Movement-Image,* 64; for the action-image, see 65; for the affection-image, see 65.
22. For an earlier model of that same relation, see Gilles Deleuze, *The Logic of Sense* (New York: Columbia University Press, 1994). One thing (here the movement-image) underlies something else (here the three differentiated forms of images, which are simultaneously transformations of the first *and* modes of being of the first).
23. Questions Deleuze does not address: If the differentiated world is an embodiment of undifferentiated energy, why is there an immanent tendency in the differentiated world to *return* to the undifferentiated, that is, to *abolish* the differentiations into which that energy has first coagulated? Or, to ask the same question differently: why does the cosmos of pure and purely mobile energy slow down, cool down, originate differences in density, intervals, and so on? Why are there *two* régimes rather than one or many? Are the two régimes co-originary, or are they the result of a split or division of an originally undivided cosmos?
24. Deleuze's language is often temporal and evolutionary, as if the differentiations arose in a temporal fashion. The considered theory, however, requires an untemporalized hierarchy of ontological constitution and ontological dependencies. The "cooling down" is a particularly temporalizing expression, and therefore highly problematic. Deleuze uses an evolutionary qua temporal *and* structural qua atemporal perspective side by side, but does not address the problem of their relation. The movement-image is both the image from which the more differentiated images emerge (differentiation) *and* something that assumes the specific form of the other images (specification of a matter). Cf. *The Time-Image,* 29 and 33. More generally: the history and the ontology of the image-world present a number of problems that Deleuze chooses not to address (which is not to say that he does not address problems of this kind in other writings).
25. Compare to *The Movement-Image,* where life and the subject seem to be accorded transcendental functions (61–63).
26. Ibid., 61.
27. Again, and in line with Deleuze's ontology, "life" is a "gap." The place of the living being is a gap. Sentience and mental functions will be equally anchored in the "interval." "Life," as here introduced, is not based on a previously formed and otherwise constituted matter that falls into organic or self-regulating patterns. Once again, life here depends on the ontology of the theory and is not meant to reconstruct and match current conceptions of life. The specific form of *organic* life is only a special case of more englobing living matter (Diderot) or living cosmos (the Stoics).
28. This is a place where life and the subject do not seem to have a contribution to make to thinghood. Things seem to be presented as early differentiata in the history of the cosmos.
29. Deleuze, *The Movement-Image,* 63.
30. Ibid. With the qualification: "in one system of reference."
31. Here we seem to encounter subjectless perception; or perception that is not bound to the senses as we conceive of them.
32. Deleuze, *The Movement-Image,* 64.
33. Ibid., 63. Do "things" not do the same—that is, accept effectuation from certain kinds of items, but not from others?
34. Ibid., 64. See also 65.
35. Is it perhaps even constitutive of the world of things? Some of Deleuze's remarks point in that direction. Or is the subtractive subject ontologically later than the world of things, more subtractive than the things of that world, an additional "incurving" of a cosmos primarily of things ontologically earlier than the subject?

36. This will be important later in this essay. I think that the distinction between objective and subjective modes presupposes conceptual models of the different kinds of beings, rather than accounting for them. The difficulties ancient materialists have with perception and thinking are instructive.
37. I have not been able to find any clear indication whether these are second-order differentiations—perception, action, and affection in their subjective embodiment—or whether they are primary. In the first case, we will have objective and subjective versions of the differentiated images, in the second, perception, action, and affection depend on the subject and bear its mark.
38. Deleuze, *The Movement-Image*, 64. Deleuze does not pay much attention to the concept of "objective perception." What distinguishes subjective and objective perception? Are they two kinds of images? Is objective perception not "subtractive"? Is only that perception a perception-image proper which is the result of subtraction?
39. Ibid., 65.
40. Ibid.; translation altered. Compare the original wording in *The Movement-Image*, 65.
41. Ibid., with a reference to Bergson's *Creative Evolution*.
42. I believe that Deleuze's image is borrowed from physics. Black holes (analogue: subjects) make the light curve in.
43. The section on Beckett's *Film* is inconspicuously included in chapter 4 of *The Movement-Image*. It is the section 3 of that chapter (97–101 in the French original; 66–70 in the English translation). I quote its full title from the table of contents (French 296; English vi): "The reverse proof: how to extinguish the three varieties (Beckett's *Film*) / how the three varieties are formed." A shorter, but much less developed account of *Film* under the ironic title *Le plus grand film irlandais* can be found in chapter 4 of Deleuze's *Critique et clinique* (Paris: Éditions de Minuit, 1993).
44. The title of the chapter that contains Deleuze's reading of *Film* is also instructive: "The Movement-Image and Its Three Varieties: Second Commentary on Bergson" (*The Movement-Image*, chapter 4).
45. For a more detailed analysis, see my *Unsichtbares—sichtbar gemacht*. Zu Samuel Becketts Film (Munich: Fink, 1996).
46. The English text uses "E" for "eye." But Deleuze follows the French translation of the scenario, published in Samuel Beckett, *Comédies et actes divers* (Paris: Éditions de Minuit, 1969). The translation renders "E" as "OE." At first sight, this appears appropriate, because "eye" translates into *œil*. But "OE" also suggests that E is a version of O: "O as E," or even "O who is inclusive of E." The French word *œil* lends itself to this move. Unfortunately, it is not supported by Beckett's script and the film. Beckett does not suggest that E is a part of O. What the script does state is that O and E are divisions of one protagonist. When Deleuze's *The Movement-Image* is translated into English, Beckett's text returns to its original medium, but imports into it what it has acquired on the passage through French. Beckett's "Eye" remains "OE" in the translation of *The Movement-Image*. I will continue to speak of "E," losing the subtle point of "OE," but also freeing the text from a misleading suggestion.
47. Here, the reader must recall what I have said about the difference between "objective" and "subjective" perception.
48. Deleuze, *The Movement-Image*, 66 (English); 97 (French): "Comment nous défaire de nous-mêmes, et nous défaire nous-mêmes?" The English translation loses the connotation of "uncoming," an event that has inner reasons and is passively endured as well as being actively enacted, both by one and the same agent and in the same action.
49. "This room sequence falls into three parts. 1. The preparation of the room ..." (Beckett, *Film*, 23).

50. These observations would also hold for the modified concept of the "action-image" used in *The Movement-Image*, chapter 9, "The Action-Image: The Large Form," and *The Time-Image*, 33. Here, to be an action-image is to be determined by the interplay of behavior and milieu. The modification does not touch the decisive intentionality of O's action, which is "to rid O of O."
51. The Freudian "death drive" aims at dissolution from beyond the organized form of subjectivity, but poses the same problem: why does it allow or even promote free energy to be transformed into cathected energy, when it opposes itself to the cathexis at the same time? Freud and Lacan have tried to avoid the problem by letting the dissolute forces act *against* the form of subjectivity and in an *unconscious* manner. What acts on the subject is the *Other* of the subject located in the subject. This does not solve the problem of genesis: why, how does "free" energy contribute to becoming "bound" energy?
52. Nietzsche, for example, avoids the difficulty by operating with a *duality* of destructive and constructive effects when he evaluates cultural events and forms—for instance, asceticism or "bad conscience." See Friedrich Nietzsche, *On the Genealogy of Morals*, second essay, nos. 16 19; third essay, no. 11.
53. Deleuze, *The Movement-Image*, 66.
54. When Deleuze turns to modern cinema and proposes the time-image as its paradigm in *The Time-Image*, there is some anchoring of the cinematic transformation in changes in the social environment of the medium. But the linkages look representational to me. What do the crisis of the cinematic action-image and the advent of modern cinema mean in the ontological history (*Seinsgeschichte*) of the image-world? Hegelians and Heideggerians would answer: the becoming self-conscious of the image-world (Hegel); the end of the era of "forgetfulness of being" (Heidegger). Deleuze, not wanting to draw conclusions of this kind, prefers to leave a gap in his theory.
55. Deleuze does not develop how this more aesthetic "return" is related to the trajectory of the character O.
56. These are not Deleuze's words. The quotation marks indicate that the notions "primitive" and "pleasure" do not apply.
57. The logic of Darwinism has left its trace here, as it did in Nietzsche. Images have supplanted living beings, and the struggle for "survival" transmuted into a struggle for dominance and existence. Deleuze also draws on earlier social philosophy, in particular Hegel's (historical formations of the spirit) and Marx's (historical modes of production).
58. I see E as the self-perceiving part of the subjective apparatus split off into a separate agent seeking self-objectification vis-à-vis the rest of the self to which it belongs, that is, O. See my *Unsichtbares—sichtbar gemacht*, 92–104.
59. I do not think that *Film* exemplifies the Hegelian scheme of a struggle between two consciousnesses. For Diderot, compare *Jacques the Fatalist*; for Hegel, *Phenomenology of Spirit*.
60. Deleuze's basic idea sounds more appropriate for Pynchon than for Beckett. Pynchon's *Gravity's Rainbow*, for example, can be read as participating in the de-differentiation of its plot and characters.
61. Deleuze, *The Movement-Image*, 66; also vi. The full title of the section: "The reverse proof: how to extinguish the three varieties."
62. Deleuze, *The Time-Image*, 30.
63. In the "recapitulation" of the image-ontology in *The Time-Image* (31 and 32), Deleuze calls the perception-image a "degree zero in the deduction which is carried out as a function of the movement-image" (31).
64. Deleuze, *The Movement-Image*, 62; see also Deleuze, *The Time-Image*, 31. In *The Time-Image*, the binary character of Deleuzian signs is particularly marked: "We

therefore take the term 'sign' in a completely different way from Peirce: it is a particular image that refers [*renvoie*] to a type of image, whether from the point of view of its bipolar composition, or from the point of view of its genesis" (32).

65. The most concentrated reference is in *The Time-Image*, 30–34.
66. Deleuze mentions and uses "Thirdness," Peirce's ontological category of semioticity. As noted earlier, Deleuze has his own understanding of thirdness, for he distinguishes it from affection and action which, for Peirce, would fall into the realm of thirdness because of their symbolic character. See *The Movement-Image*, 197, and *The Time-Image*, 31.
67. See *The Movement-Image*, 74–76.
68. Ibid., 74.
69. See *The Movement-Image*, 20; *The Time-Image*, 32.
70. I want to emphasize once more that this is not true of Deleuze's historical ideas about the evolution of film or of its criticism. It is quite possible to read the "crisis of the action image" (*The Movement-Image*, 197) and the emergence of the "time-image" (*The Time-Image*) as being (also) a process of differentiation. More adequate, however, would be an understanding that does not rely on the one-dimensional schema of greater or lesser differentiatedness.
71. Chapters 4 and 5 in Gilles Deleuze, *Difference and Repetition*, trans. Paul Patton (New York: Columbia University Press, 1994), discuss examples that could be interpreted as "happy differentiations" in my sense.
72. Deleuze, *The Movement-Image*, chapter 12.
73. See Stanley Cavell, *The World Viewed* (Cambridge: Harvard University Press, 1979).
74. Whatever the reasons in the development of Deleuze's thought, the darker ontology is or would also be an impediment in the analysis of films. Luckily, Deleuze leaps beyond the limitations of the leading ideas of his image-ontology when it comes to reading films and the history of cinema. It is interesting to note that Deleuze's idea about the historical trajectory of the medium—from the movement-image and its three varieties to the time-image—parallels the trajectory that *Film* describes in Deleuze's reading. But, again, the time-image is a highly differentiated cinematographic mode.
75. Deleuze, *The Time-Image*, 40; translation slightly altered. It is *not* the case either that the "régime of universal variation ... goes beyond the human limits of the sensory-motor schema towards a non-human world ... or else in the direction of a super-human world which speaks for a new spirit" (ibid.).
76. Similarly, in Deleuze, *The Movement-Image*, 67: "O perceives (subjectively) the room...: this is the perception of perception, or the *perception-image*, considered under a double régime, in a double system of reference"; or, with reference to Hitchcock, he "introduces the mental image into the cinema. That is, he makes relation itself the object of an image, which is not merely added to the perception, action and affection[-]images, but frames and transforms them" (203).
77. With regard to representation, indirectness is a major concept in *The Time-Image*.

Chapter 4

The Eye of Montage

Dziga Vertov and Bergsonian Materialism

François Zourabichvili

Translated by Melissa McMahon

Perhaps we will teach, in two hundred years, that twentieth-century philosophy ended with two hieroglyphics: *The Movement-Image* and *The Time-Image*. A misunderstanding surrounds these books: they rightly fascinate film lovers, even though they are expressly books of philosophy. As for philosophers, they find little interest in them, or else read them while leaving cinema aside, even though Deleuze considered that he could not have written them except through contact with cinema. What could have determined, in Deleuze's work, such an encounter between philosophy and cinema?

The misunderstanding in the reading is perhaps linked to an extreme difficulty: the theoretical instrument that is used to problematize cinema. By drawing on the first chapter of Bergson's *Matter and Memory*, Deleuze chooses the accursed text of an accursed author. A triple provocation, because (1) he recognizes in Bergson, going against all current trends, the contemporary philosopher par excellence, the only recent author whose thoughts are new, have not yet been thought, and are capable of completely changing our way of thinking; (2) the famous ontology of images, often recognized as the summit of Bergson's meditation, also comes across as an obscure, even sophistic text, upon which commentaries regularly stumble; (3) Bergson is after all known for his contempt for cinema.

And no doubt Deleuze offers a marvelous analysis of Bergson's text—but in a style that is as limpid, dense, rigorous, and virtuoso as Bergson's own.[1] Dazzled, the reader remains with his or her difficulties, for the beautiful style is not always enough to carry him or her along. Nevertheless, one cannot understand *The Movement-Image*, and, consequently, *The Time-Image*, without in the first place mastering the Bergsonian theory of images. And even if the theory is mastered, another difficulty awaits the reader: the meaning of the parallel with cinema, and the type of philosophical effects that follow.

We will venture a brief analysis here, in the hope of contributing to the prehistory of a genuine reading of the cine-philosophical work of Deleuze. What interests us is the special status of the pages dedicated to Dziga Vertov (*The Movement-Image*, 39–40, 80–84). The book's fundamental proposition is the following: "The material universe, the plane of immanence, is *the machine assemblage of movement-images*. Here Bergson is startlingly ahead of his time: it is the universe as cinema in itself, a metacinema. This implies a view of the cinema itself which is totally different from that which Bergson proposed in his explicit critique" (59). But here we find cinema giving its own presentation of Bergson: "The materialist Vertov realises the materialist programme of the first chapter of *Matter and Memory* through the cinema, the in-itself of the image.... It is, first, a machine assemblage of movement-images" (81).

On a first level, "machine assemblage of movement-images" seems to be the very definition of a film: the montage of a series of shots. De facto, the movement-image is indeed the real definition of the shot; any shot whatever, in this sense, is a movement-image (22). But the case of montage is more complicated: it is an assemblage, but only "in one of its aspects" (70). The word will be reserved for Vertov, in the same specific conceptual sense as in *A Thousand Plateaus*. Everywhere else, the generic term corresponding to montage is the whole (*le tout*) (conceived as open, in contrast to the set [*l'ensemble*] which is not affected by duration). A machine assemblage of movement-images is thus not just any film, but an experimental film: a film that experiments on its own conditions.

What is astonishing, in Bergson's text, is the way in which, starting from human perception ("Here I am in the presence of images . . ."),[2] he reaches an impersonal field that overflows this perception and is no less constituted of images and special, acentered, a-subjective perceptions, in order to finally reengender human perception starting from this field ("when we have placed ourselves at what we have called the *turn* of experience . . . [this] marks the dawn of our human experience" [185]). What authorizes the initial overflowing is both, it seems, commonsense experience (there is no doubt that for each person, what he or she perceives exists in itself, and as it is perceived) and the very fact of science (which itself only deals with images, but treats them objectively). From which comes the surprising, and at first glance monstrous, concept of an "image in itself," in that it amounts to the same thing to speak of matter or of image. One of the difficulties of this text is perhaps that we tend to only conceive of the identity of the two by favoring the image, by bringing matter back to the image, without realizing that the operation must equally work in the other direction: it is less easy for us to renounce the traditional concept of the image than the traditional concept of matter. It is true that on the question of matter, Berkeley prepared us long ago; but this is precisely why Bergson insists on the insufficiency of Berkeley's conception (10).

Whatever the case may be, Bergson can henceforth distinguish two régimes of perception: a human, centered perception, and an acentered perception that merges with all physical interactions. The first misses the real in dissociating matter from movement, whereas the images in themselves are pure movements. It remains that this acentered perception—a kind of perception that leads Bergson to say that "the photograph, if photograph there be, is already taken, already developed in the very heart of things and at all the points in space" (38)[3]—presents difficulties. It is nevertheless at the heart of Deleuze's reasoning, which will find an equivalent for this acentering in Vertov's "cine-eye" (*kinoglaz*).

A certain ambiguity can be noticed in Deleuze's use of the notion of the "movement-image": on the one hand, cinema merges with the production of movement-images ("[t]he shot is the movement-image" [22]); on the other hand, the glossary at the end of first cinema volume defines it as "the acentred set [*ensemble*] of variable elements which act and react on each other" (217), which cinema achieves only in experimental conditions; and even more confounding, if *Man with a Movie Camera* is the paragon of experimental cinema, this is because it goes beyond an initial conception in which Vertov "went no further than the movement-image" (82). However, these contradictions are only apparent: they disappear when we understand that the image, whichever perceptive régime it is related to, remains in itself a movement-image. The cinematic image can indeed appear to be distinct from the movements it shows, a pure frame, an image *of* movement. But what makes it, by right, a movement-image, is that it can be assembled (*montée*). If Deleuze sees in montage (much more than in the moving camera) the very signature of cinema, it is because montage provokes a complete change in perspective: the image is no longer only in tune with moving things, it extracts and autonomizes the movement of these things, in order to link them to other movements, of the same things or different ones. Whence the two-sided character of the shot: as a *framed* image, it contains the movements between the different parts of a set; as an *assembled* (*montée*) image, it merges with these movements, which become valid for themselves, separated from their worldly supports ("The shot is movement") (20). In one instance, movement is subordinated to its parts; in another it subordinates them to itself in order to enter into an assemblage with other movements. The concept of the "movement-image" is thus inseparable from a multiplicity.

Only, in a certain way, the "movement-image" does not take on its full autonomy, and continues to be subordinated to something other than itself: as centered, it counts as either a perception, or an action, or an affection. Formally extracting pure movements using the subjects to which they were attributed in the natural conditions of perception (cinema "suppresses both the anchoring of the subject and the horizon of the world" [57]), images nevertheless continue to presuppose this natural perception, this external world, like a background that distinguishes itself from them. They redirect the system of attribution to the superior plane of a global finality: the characters, their perceptions, actions, or affections. We are still in the conditions denounced by Bergson, of an image separated from movement, or of a movement-image separated from itself because it is relative to a privileged image (the character), center of perception, action, or affection.

In short, cinema has not conquered the conditions of a genuine immanence. And no doubt it can only do so in experimental conditions, because the spectator remains a human subject: it is a matter of making visible what the spectator cannot see. The good thing is that cinema is capable of creating these limit conditions (that are attained in Bergson by intellectual "intuition").[4]

In fact, *The Movement-Image* describes several operations of overcoming (*dépassement*), of raising to the limit (all of which are put into play in Beckett's *Film*) (*The Movement-Image*, 66–68). Thus, for the movement-image, we have the close-up (chapter 6) and the any-space-whatever (chapter 9): the emergence of the possible and the event as such in cinema. In the same vein, the action-image is put into crisis by the mental images created by Hitchcock, namely, the emergence of the relation (chapter 12). But the stakes of bringing the perception-image to its limit, as Vertov does, are quite different: movement-images are perceptions of perception, perceptions of action and perceptions of affection. Cinema thus confronts its own conditions, the perception of the camera, the perception of the spectator. Whence the double operation at the beginning of *Man with a Movie Camera* of including the cameraman and the audience in the film, both becoming movement-images interacting with other movement-images, those of the film properly speaking. There Vertov realizes, literally, the "cinema in itself" or the "metacinema" attributed to Bergson in the introductory proposition.

In order to tackle the pages on Vertov, let us first of all recall where the difficulty lies. If one admits Bergson's initial slide from the images that are revealed to my gaze toward the images in themselves that interact among themselves, the difficulty then becomes focused on the status of this interaction, which governs the image of the "photograph already developed in things." Apparent contradictions are often the best indication of a difficult idea: in this case Deleuze, faced with the paradox of the image in itself, begins by asking, "how is it possible to speak of an Appearing [*Apparaître*], since there is not even an eye?" (59), in order to conclude on the following page that, "In other words, the eye is in things, in luminous images in themselves" (60). But Bergson already spoke of a photograph that was already developed, although "never ... revealed."[5] The solution is of course to invoke a nonhuman eye (Bergson, for his part, speaks of a "translucent ... photograph," lacking a black screen),[6] but in what sense?

These images in themselves, writes Deleuze, are "lines or figures of light," in other words, "blocs of space-time."[7] The preceding analysis, which defined the cinema image as pure movement, liberated from the moving object, is no longer enough; for this movement is also light. Such a notion is, at first glance, very ambiguous: we move surreptitiously from physical light to the *lumen* of the classics. Obviously, we are dealing here with the cinematographic image, which has its own light, in contrast to painting or photography. But "light" signifies above all a condition of visibility or of appearing. It is no longer enough to posit a material world as "virtual perception of all things":[8] the status of the image still presupposes the form of a transcendent consciousness, in such a way that the identity of matter and the image is not originary (the image preexists itself as primary matter, which consciousness informs). Identity implies that matter, or the movement-image, comprises its own condition of visibility. It is thus necessary that perception, even in the absence of man, be entirely actual, and Bergson can thus restore the true problem: "*What you have to explain, then, is not how perception arises, but how it is limited*"

(40; emphasis in original). In cinema, it is by diminishing the atmospheric light that the luminous projected image is distinguished from the white screen. But above all, we understand in what sense we can arrive at "a consciousness by right [*en droit*], which is diffused everywhere": consciousness does not emerge in opposition to the world, as an instance of a different nature (61).[9] If Vertov can reach a pure machinic assemblage, in which images interact with each other, then its light is no longer that of a human consciousness that would condition the images and their montage from the outside, even virtually: they comprise their own condition of visibility, they are figures of light.

Dziga Vertov's "cine-eye" is, in the first place, an idea: that of creating, with images, an interaction between any given point in the universe with any other given point. It is the emergence of a "nonhuman" eye, which is supposed to correspond, in the Deleuzian commentary, to Bergson's translucency. But how can Vertov lay claim to a nonhuman gaze? It is not an improved human eye, whose capacities would be augmented technologically (*The Movement-Image*, 81). Nor is it the eye of an animal, which is to say a point of view other than that of man (ibid.). In both cases, in effect, "the images vary for a single one": they are centered, relative to a subject identical to itself that perceives them. Finally, it is not even the eye of the camera, even though certain viewing angles may be unusual (on the ground, from the tops of roofs, canted), and certain filming procedures show what the human eye, in normal conditions of perception, does not see: slow motion, fast motion. The image, in any case, still remains centered, relative to a center of perception; the shot (*prise de vue*) is still human, all too human. Or else the nonhuman eye is indeed that of the camera, but insofar as this eye infiltrates everywhere, multiplies the points of view, makes each point of space a point of view: perception becomes internal to matter, relations of distance pass into the image, become relations between images. On the one hand, this already presupposes montage; on the other hand, the Bergsonian world of movement-images assumes that the points of view change in nature when they pass into each other. Interactive perception is acentered; it dissolves points of view.

On this point, whatever the case may be, comes a first proposition by Deleuze concerning Vertov: *the nonhuman eye is montage*. Double exposures, miniaturization, animation, inversion: the principal procedures refer to montage. For what montage shows is not "life caught unawares" ("la vie à l'improviste"), the impasse of Vertov's early years, which is of no interest to Deleuze. Or, rather, the life of movements as images can only be restored or extracted, and seen as such, by assembling the image with at least one other image, because movement is henceforth valid for itself.

In this respect, *Man with a Movie Camera* testifies to a conscious struggle of Vertov with himself, or with who he already no longer is: is capturing life really what the camera does when the camera is put to voyeuristic ends, say, when surprising a woman waking up or in the process of dressing? Or is it rather the montage of a naked back with other naked backs, elsewhere and in different circumstances, in such a way as to extract pure visual and dynamic values (for example, the mud-baths scene)? Voyeurism is immediately denounced by spectacular false continuities, which put the image into relation with an outside that is not its immediate out-of-field (*hors-champ*): the awakening of a young woman coincides with the noisy passing of a locomotive that she nevertheless can neither see nor hear; we then go from her naked back to a camera, which we see aimed in its direction, but which is nevertheless located elsewhere, somewhere in the town, targeting other objects. As for the athlete engaged in high jumps, he will not come into contact with the javelin, even though he appears to be within the same trajectory in the montage.

Thus a second proposition of Deleuze's concerning Vertov: *it is in the intervals of matter itself that nonhuman vision emerges*. These intervals are created by montage through the "correlation of two images which are distant (and incommensurable from the viewpoint of our human perception)" (82). Or again, the same example of the young woman dressing, even if such correlations are also obtained through superimposition: the image is decentered, subtracted from its subjective condition, since the eye is taken away from the voyeur or the camera operator without for all that being attributed to another operator, the spectator perceiving the falseness of the continuity. For false continuity has an objective effect: that of opening the image onto a point of view that is not its own, and insofar as it is not its own. Each image thus interacts with other images, instead of organizing itself according to the conditions of the centering of "natural"—that is, subjective—perception. And it is in this sense that Vertov *rejoins* the "world before man," or the material world of movement-images: he starts with necessarily centered images (pointing the camera), which he submits to an operation of decentering (montage). The limits of this operation are those of cinema, by nature subjected to the conditions of human perception, whether at the beginning of its process (the eye of the camera) or at the end (the eye of the spectator). The world before man can only be constructed, though "[i]t is not surprising that we have to construct it since it is given only to the eye which we do not have" (81).

Still, there is another way of starting from the shot (*prise de vue*) in order to rejoin the conditions of a nonhuman perception, a way that Deleuze judges to be the most profound and that justifies a third proposition: when "montage is introduced into the very constituent of the image" (82), we reach the photogram as "the *genetic element* of all possible perception" (83). It is a second power of montage and a deepening of the notion of the interval that Vertov only attains in *Man with a Movie Camera*. It is often said that this film presents variations on the theme of animation from beginning to end, from the immobile town at dawn to the animation sequence properly speaking. But this beginning and this end only make sense as a function of the sequences in which the very operation of montage (and not its result) is shown: when Vertov relates the image with its constitutive photograms to the screen. The photogram is then revealed as a real constituent of movement, its differential or its genetic element, and not, as Bergson believed, a simple instantaneous cut or "immobile section." It is the second sense of the interval, according to Vertov: "the point which changes, and which makes perception change" (83). The change is not simply from one photogram to another, it is in the photogram. The freeze-frame (*l'arrêt sur image*), far from fixing movement, exhibits its condition. Immobility thus takes on a new sense, which has retrospective repercussions on the beginning of the film, this town at dawn which henceforth appears to us as a vast assemblage of photograms: its immobility is already movement.

"In Vertov the interval of movement is perception, the glance, the eye" (39–40). The eye figures twice in montage: once, because the nonhuman perception presupposes the interaction of human, all too human images; a second time, because the image itself is revealed as a montage. These are the two correlating ways of reaching the nonhuman.

And why must we "rid ourselves of ourselves, and demolish ourselves"? (66). Because this nonhuman perception is *our* dawn, following the image shared by Bergson, Cézanne, and Vertov. It is indeed a matter of making life burst forth as such on the screen, but this is not "life caught unawares," prisoner of the all too human impasse of voyeurism: it is "the molecular child, the molecular woman," who only exist in interaction, the child and the woman grasped insofar as they receive and give back movement, themselves movement-images (39). It is in this way that cinema realizes what Bergson described, by confronting its own conditions: a machine assemblage of movement-images. What Vertov admired in machines was not the mechanization of life, the too human conception of the machine; it was their *precision*, a theme that he shares with Bergson: machines are only movement, and connections of movements. But subjectivity separates man from his movements and, for this reason, Vertov wanted neither the actor nor acting (*jeu*), but actuality. He wanted to give man back to his movements, to make perceptible the movements that traverse him and make up his prehuman life: an unattributable humanity, involving an acentered perception.

There is much that is surprising in the Bergson–Vertov collage. When Soviet cinema attains materialism, on Deleuze's account, it is not the materialism that one would think: the subversive thought of the century is that of Bergson, fresh and still to be thought, and if Vertov is revolutionary, it is as a Bergsonian, not as someone who "splits skulls," according to Eisenstein's formula (indeed, Eisenstein reproached Vertov for neither understanding this "splitting" nor desiring to undertake it). It is hardly surprising that Bergson was the target of a similar charge, which originated, in particular, among Marxists (notably Politzer); we will simply remark that Deleuze's political thought is in many respects a meditation on Bergson, in particular on his category of the possible.

NOTES

1. Gilles Deleuze, *The Movement-Image*, trans. Hugh Tomlinson and Barbara Habberjam (Minneapolis: University of Minnesota Press, 1986), chapter 4.
2. Henri Bergson, *Matter and Memory*, trans. N. M. Paul and W. S. Palmer (New York: Zone Books, 1988), 17.
3. Also quoted in *The Movement-Image*, 60.
4. Bergson, *Matter and Memory*, 186–87.
5. Ibid., 36; also quoted in *The Movement-Image*, 60 and 61.
6. Bergson, *Matter and Memory*, 38–39.
7. Deleuze, *The Movement-Image*, 61.
8. Bergson, *Matter and Memory*, 39.
9. One can notice this idea already emerging in Gilles Deleuze, *Difference and Repetition*, trans. Paul Patton (New York: Columbia University Press, 1994), 220.

Mapping Images

Chapter 5

The Film History of Thought

András Bálint Kovács

Translated by Sándor Hervey

The purpose of this essay is not to attempt a general reconstruction of Deleuze's philosophy of cinema, but only to shed light on the traces of a certain—possibly unintentional, sedimentary, and in any event undeveloped—way of thinking about the history of cinema in his work. One has to agree with the opinion of virtually all serious commentators on Deleuze that the purpose behind the two volumes this philosopher wrote on cinema is not purely film-theoretic, nor is it directed at the history of cinema. Rather, Deleuze turns to the cinema as a means of expression for certain philosophical problems he encounters. The complexity of these problems refuses any neat reduction, but perhaps we can accept D. N. Rodowick's assertion that "Deleuze's larger objective is not to produce another theory of cinema, but to understand how aesthetic, philosophical, and scientific modes of understanding converge in producing cultural strategies for imagining and imaging the world."[1] As Rodowick adds: "Reduced to its simplest form, the question informing Deleuze's cinema books is this: how does a sustained meditation on film and film theory illuminate the relation between image and thought? . . . Among aesthetic practices, Deleuze argues, cinema concretely produces a corresponding image of thought, a visual and acoustic rendering of thought in relation to time and movement."[2]

Despite this general aim, though, one cannot help but notice that, owing to his theoretical starting point, as well as to his analytic methods, Deleuze inevitably discusses his subject matter in historical as well as taxonomic terms. The fact is that Deleuze is not seeking an answer to the question "What is cinema?" but to the question "Into what form(s) of thinking does cinema develop?" Deleuze's cinema books as such do not belong to any single discipline. But the qualities that, from the point of view of "strict science," make his books objectionable (to the extent that Christian Metz was not even prepared to enter into debate with them) may from another point of view—notably that of the history and development of a theory of cinema—produce radically new insights. Deleuze's cinema books appeared at a time when film studies had just reached the state of an "established science." The institutions growing up around this discipline were just beginning to firm up, certain accepted methods of analysis were gradually acquiring wide currency, and the production of cinema studies was becoming a "major industry" on both sides of the Atlantic. One of the main symptoms of this process was a turn away from "pure theory," which was paralleled by a renaissance of historical research. Perhaps it was no accident that at this distinct moment an "outsider" should have appeared with a program whose theoretical assertions are thoroughly interwoven with the threads of a peculiar conception of the formal history of cinema.

Of this program, Deleuze wrote in 1986: "The task that I hoped to complete in my two books about film ... was the categorization of crystals of time."[3] The question posed in this essay is as follows: how does a historical mode of thinking find its way into, or emerge from, this self-proclaimed taxonomy ("categorization")?

The answer is to be found in Deleuze's particular approach, and in the nature of his categories. The historical character of his system is determined right from the outset when he sets himself the theoretically novel aim of defining the cinematic image in a way that makes it possible to handle image and movement simultaneously. This, in effect, is the very reason why he turned his interest to the cinema: he realized that the conceptual unity of duration and image, which is one of the cornerstones of Bergson's philosophy, is the constitutive element of the cinema. The fact that the image cannot be divorced from time lies at the heart of Deleuze's understanding of the cinema, as is often pointed out, but my point is that it also lies at the heart of his methodological project. If time is included in the image by definition, Deleuze concludes that the cinema is always in some sense narrative, that it cannot avoid telling a story—though the kind of story it tells will vary radically, as we shall see. Indeed, it is the very mutation of storytelling that informs Deleuze's categories. He defines his categories qua different types of images according to the different narrative conceptions that emerge during the history of cinema. Images are made up of different kinds of signs whose "combinations" render different kinds of narratives. As such, Deleuze's categories find their place not only in a kind of "periodic table of the elements" but also in a historical world that suggests a cinematic trajectory. Deleuze's analyses are as much individual stages of a historical-logical process as they are the product of a protoscientific method. In contrast to Metz's semiological system, which, in principle, is applicable to any film-historical concept, Deleuze's cinematographic philosophy cannot be divorced from real history, from the history of the transformation of various "movement-images" (in classical cinema) into various "time-images" (in modern cinema). Thus, the same categories describe a synchronic system and a historical evolution.

To define movement, as I have said, Deleuze borrows the concept of duration (*durée*) from Bergson. Duration suggests that temporal change inheres in things, in the state of things. This changing state is what Bergson and Deleuze call the whole, such that movement expresses "the change in duration or in the whole."[4] As Deleuze writes, "The whole creates itself, and constantly creates itself in another dimension without parts—like that which carries along the set of one qualitative state to another, like the pure ceaseless becoming which passes through these states. It is in this sense that it is spiritual or mental" (10). Because the whole escapes the determination of any fixed set (*ensemble*), it is defined as "open"—and Deleuze intimates that the mental and open natures of the whole are closely correlated, if not identical. "It is widely known that Bergson initially discovered duration as identical to consciousness," Deleuze notes. "But further study of consciousness led him to demonstrate that it only existed in so far as it opened itself upon a whole, by coinciding with the opening up of a whole" (9–10). In contrast to Hegelian totality, which is both teleological and organic, Bergson's sense of the whole has the following four major attributes: it is a system of reference for all change; it is a mental category; it is open-ended; it is ceaselessly becoming.

Deleuze deploys the whole to explain how movement-images are created and linked together, though given the image of history that arises out of this concept, it must be pointed out that not all the Bergsonian criteria are satisfied. As described by Deleuze, the cinema is not entirely a ceaseless becoming of movement-images through which the whole would pass as a "history" of images because, at its outset, the cinema bears a strong element of organic evolution.[5] Deleuze distinguishes two phases of film history: the classical, which he calls organic, and the modern, which he calls crystalline. More than merely chronological, the relationship between the two is historical, and this broadly comes to light in what Deleuze asserts was a "crisis" of the movement-image. Following the organic conventions of the classical cinema (the chains of perception and response that Deleuze calls the sensory-motor schema), modern cinema emerges as a mental image, that is, a crystalline system of direct time-images that arise from mutations of the organic movement-image. The categories that Deleuze uses to define modern cinema—as I suggested, mental images or direct time-images—were already given at the beginning of cinema, virtually present in the image. As Deleuze writes, "The direct time-image is the phantom which has always haunted the cinema, but it took modern cinema to give a body to this phantom."[6] Indeed, we have to agree with Alain Ménil's comment that Deleuze considers the time-image "the object of a singular conquest, the point at which the cinema would come into possession of its essence."[7] As much is announced at the conclusion of *The Movement-Image*:

> Certainly, people continue to make SAS and ASA films: the greatest commercial successes always take that route, but the soul of the cinema no longer does. The soul of the cinema demands increasing thought, even if thought begins by undoing the system of actions, perceptions and affections on which the cinema had fed up to that point. . . . A new kind of image is born that one can attempt to identify in the post-war American cinema, outside Hollywood.[8]

The incarnation of the time-image, then, is also the incarnation of a goal (*telos*) in the broad cinematographic evolution, the point at which cinema arrives at its own consciousness and discovers its "essence." For Deleuze, who writes from this perspective (or retrospective), consciousness is the constitutive element of both the new image and cinematographic history. Even though he never says outright that film history is tantamount to the emergence of modern cinema, that this is the "aim" of film history, Deleuze's entire taxonomy anticipates the shift from classical to modern. *The cinema books are by definition written from the point of view of the modern.* In the first volume, especially, Deleuze regards the various image-types as successive forms in ever more cerebral developments, developments (i.e., the history of cinema) that lead to the mental images of modern cinema. As he understands movement with regard to the whole, Deleuze is committed to seeing not only each film as a whole but, finally, to rendering film history itself as a whole—a whole that retrospectively gives meaning and sense to the image of movement that makes up individual films. Each film, then, is a kind of "image" made up of movement-images and time-images (an image, that is, of the cinema), but at the same time the cinema itself is an image or "system of crystal-images"—in other words, an image synonymous for Deleuze with modern cinema, such that this history depends on its own imagination of history as having culminated.

This means—and herein lies the essence of Deleuze's approach—that the definition of a cinematographic sign is not given independently of the history of cinema. In other words, *films and their constitutive signs have no definition outside of film history.* Cinema cannot be described with the aid of abstract definitions of linguistic or communication theory (in this sense, indeed, there is a sharp opposition between Deleuze and Metz). Deleuze explains that "cinema itself is a new practice of images and signs," and so the philosophy of the cinema is an *immanent* conceptualization of this practice and not, conversely, the application of some abstract theory from outside.[9] It follows, therefore, that cinema is defined by film history (practice) itself, through the transformations that are inherent in its sheer technical particularities.[10] One can see this in Deleuze's treatment of Bergson, who condemned the cinema because, as he argued in *Creative Evolution*, the technology attempted to grasp movement abstractly without taking duration into account.[11] Deleuze retains Bergson's argument in its entirety, but declares that what Bergson failed to notice was that, far from refuting his thesis, film constitutes its most positive demonstration. Of course, Bergson could not have seen this, because his theorization appeared at the cinema's earliest moments, that is, when its techniques had yet to fully unfold. As Deleuze explains, "The cinema would rediscover that very movement-image of the first chapter of *Matter and Memory*."[12] From this perspective, the history of cinema is a series of the images of movement that have been successively brought into being in the course of time by deploying these inherent technical potentials.

Needless to say, Deleuze is aware that his work is open to a historically slanted interpretation. The opening sentence of his preface—"This study is not a history of the cinema"[13]—bears witness to this awareness, and the issue is raised again in later discussions. In "Sur le régime cristallin," Deleuze compares the historical logic of his approach to that of Wilhelm Worringer: "With respect to the arts, Worringer showed a long time ago the opposition between an organic 'classical' system and an inorganic or crystalline system ... Here we are dealing with two stylistic stances about which it cannot be said that one is 'more valid' than the other."[14] Deleuze claims that his own classification is more exhaustive, but it should be noted that Worringer's is an account of the periodic alternation of two methods of artistic creation. In other words, Worringer is not developing an art-historical taxonomy (as did, say, Wölfflin) but, rather, a conception of the history of art. Indeed, the categories Worringer deploys are psychological, not historical. In his view, these two types of art constantly alternate with one another over time, such that their manifestations in ever newer styles do not constitute anything like a linear progression. By contrast, the two types of cinema described by Deleuze belong to two successive eras: roughly speaking, one runs from the cinema's birth up to the 1940s, and the other runs from the 1940s on. In good conscience, one cannot ascribe to this duality an alternation because Deleuze constantly implies a progressive shift from one régime to another. Although films are still made in the Hollywood tradition, for instance, Deleuze suggests that there will never again be a classical art of the cinema. Whether we like it or not, Deleuze's model is linear. If we insist on comparing it to models in art history, its concepts of movement-images and time-images are more reminiscent of Wölfflin's "categories," while its division into eras is more akin to Schiller's dichotomy between "naive und sentimentalische (Dichtung)," which gives an account of classical and modern aesthetics, that is to say, of two different eras in the philosophy of art.

What is it, then, that the historical aspect in Deleuze's work has to offer? In my view, the contribution is twofold: concretely historical and methodological. As far as the concrete historical contribution is concerned, this does not consist in uncovering new facts, nor in reclassifying old ones. On the contrary, in his historical analyses Deleuze makes few original assertions, always citing others and interpreting their commentaries in terms of his own concepts. When he does make independent historical assertions, these tend to be superficially documented, conveying as they do a sense of having resulted from intuitive hunches. For the most part, Deleuze conceives of the history of cinema as a totally abstract process in the course of which we see, first of all, the genesis of variants of the movement-image (in classical cinema) and, subsequently, the mutation of the various configurations of the time-image (in modern cinema). Putting it in "cinematographic" terms, first comes the formation of those types of the movement-image that actualize different aspects and interrelationships of events, of action; then, as a result of a "crisis," those image-types come into being that are capable of handling time apart from events or action and that actualize the world of action in the scattered form of a crystalline structure. This rather abstract schema is neither determinate nor complete as a historical process. Deleuze makes no effort to set up correspondences between the well-known periods of film history and the individual stages of the transformative process that movement-images have undergone. At best, he occasionally identifies particular stylistic trends or schools with particular types of images (for instance, naturalism with the "impulse-image").[15] Again, Deleuze is not writing a history of the cinema, and so it is all the more striking when he does finally posit a paradigmatically historical moment relative to which he classifies every other phenomenon in film history as belonging to this or to that stage of cinema, as belonging to the classical or to the modern era. This unique period of transition is none other than the turning point of the late 1940s and the early 1950s, that is to say, Italian neorealism and the beginning of the "great period" of Hitchcock.[16]

One may ask why, if Deleuze insists on dividing the history of cinema into two major eras, he should make this the cutoff point. Why not designate as the watershed the far more obvious shift from silent film to sound film? There are two main reasons for this. On the one hand, Deleuze is simply joining the tradition of French film criticism and film history according to which, after André Bazin, Italian neorealism constitutes the most important influence on the emergence of modern cinema.[17] On the other hand, if Deleuze's concept of the movement-image and its permutations devolves in relation to a whole (the cinema—or, better yet, the "idea" of cinema), then the process of this devolution is, to some degree, always already conceived with an end result in mind. This end result is, Deleuze claims, the modern cinematographic form in which events are divorced from action. Indeed, the first inclinations of this shift become visible around the time of neorealism (though it is true that they can already be observed in the second half of the 1930s, as Deleuze's discussions of Renoir make clear). However, Deleuze pays no attention at all to the extent to which modern cinema was built on the European avant-garde of the early 1920s, nor to the fact that surrealism, expressionism, dadaism, the Russian "montage" school, and the agit-prop film enjoyed a great period of renaissance just at the time when, granted, a version (traceable to certain neorealist influences) of modernism—

introspective, diffuse in plot, lacking in action and in hero, tending to build the passage of time into its very substance—was beginning to create new, hitherto unseen narrative forms and time-images. It is the latter development that preoccupies Deleuze and whose origins he seeks, and this largely explains why neorealism remains, for him, modernism's point of departure. In actual fact, neorealism only contributes certain elements to modernism, as did the avant-garde of the 1920s; the one is as much of an antecedent to cinematic modernism as the other. What is more, the emergence of the precursors of cinematic modernism coincides with the decline of neorealism—with, for instance, Dreyer's short film *They Caught the Ferry* (1948), Bergman's fourth independent production, *Fangelse* (1949), Antonioni's first film, *Story of a Love Affair* (1950), and Fellini's fourth production, *I Vitelloni* (1953).

Nevertheless, the quality that Deleuze singles out in neorealism is critical for the development of modernism. According to Deleuze, the significance of neorealism lies in the way it replaces situations embedded in action with "optical-acoustic" situations. In other words, the aim of neorealism is not the transaction of certain events, but the realization of the visual and acoustic space surrounding events. It is in this connection that the aimless loitering so indicative of, say, Rosellini and De Sica moves to the forefront of cinema, enveloping action in a kind of waiting (or, as Deleuze would say, "patience," even "exhaustion") that becomes, paradoxically, the "action" itself. Deleuze's observations provide an apt summation of the importance of neorealism from the viewpoint of the further development of the cinema, even if these observations do not give an exhaustive picture of neorealism itself. The reason why this style became one of the most significant paradigms of the ensuing thirty or forty years involves the way neorealism introduced the possibility of a story without a plot, without the schematic determinations and linkages of strict action (i.e., causality). Even if this development was never entirely consummated by neorealism, Deleuze locates its specific origin there: producing increasingly "plotless" narratives, neorealism lingers on situations in which action has become impossible. Indeed, Antonioni became the father of modern film, so to speak, because he consistently elaborated this fundamental affinity for "tirednesses and waitings."[18] One sees this most clearly in the trend he inspires (and which extends beyond modernism per se) in the likes of Jancsó and Angelopoulos, later in Wenders, Jarmusch, and Tarr, to name only its most important representatives. This trend is modernism's strongest, most universal current—a trend that is rooted in pure optical-sound situations, which is to say, the radical disjunction of action and situation.

The main consequence of events being replaced as the focal point of interest by the milieu is that the role of time in the cinema changes entirely. If time and space are split off from the logic of events, an abstract space-time dimension is created. This is what Deleuze calls an "any-space-whatever," namely, a dimension to which the only reality one can attribute is a subjective reality as part of some function of consciousness (because it is no longer determined by the logic of events). According to Deleuze, modern cinema means, on the one hand, the different variations of the composition of abstract time (in this respect he is in complete agreement with Tarkovsky, who calls film "sculpting in time"); on the other hand, it means a variable formation of images of subjectivity. A major tendency in modern cinema is to blur the boundary between fact and fancy, dream and reality. Modern cinema conceives of, and realizes ("virtualizes"), time in a totally Bergsonian sense: that is, in absolutely subjective terms. As such, time-images and forms of subjectivity converge, and one can see this in the visions, imaginations, memories, or failures of memory (amnesia, ellipses) that come to dominate modern cinema. All are time-space extensions of subjective consciousness, at the same time as being forms connected to time and to systems of time, whose deployment signifies a fundamental revolution with respect to narrative. In modern cinema, the narrative (or "storytelling") aspect no longer represents "reality," but concentrates on showing how the act of narration falsifies reality itself. This is why the central focus of narrative in modern film is what, after Nietzsche, Deleuze refers to as the "powers of the false."

At first sight this change may seem tantamount to the emergence of narrative reflexivity. That is to say, traditional narrative schemata disintegrate, or, in the case of French "New Wave" and its successors, they acquire the character of pastiche and parody. Yet Deleuze's formulation does show a certain originality, for he does not regard modern cinema simply as the disintegration, distortion, pastiche, parody, or ironic reflection of particular preexisting forms. Although he does not deny that these constitute a part of modernism, Deleuze's position cannot be said to be equated with the tautology "stories happen only in stories" (Wim Wenders, *The State of Things*). Modern cinema is not only a matter of crisis or intellectual reflection. Deleuze senses the appearance in modernism of a new way of thinking, a new way of looking at the world, which goes beyond the crisis in traditional narrative film and beyond the conflict between the mass-produced film industry of Hollywood and the genre of European intellectual art films. Classical cinema is, for Deleuze, a specific state of cinematographic thinking, which leads to another state (modern cinema), from a description of which we get glimmerings of yet another, further (postmodern) state.

In any case, for Deleuze cinema does not "represent" thoughts or modes of thinking. It is thought itself, the image of thinking:

> Cinema is not a universal or primitive language system [*langue*], nor a language [*langage*]. It brings to light an intelligible content which is like a presupposition, a condition, a necessary correlate through which language constructs its own "objects" (signifying units and operations). But this correlate, though inseparable, is specific: it consists of movements and thought-processes (pre-linguistic images), and of points of view on these movements and processes (pre-signifying signs). It constitutes a whole "psychomechanics," the spiritual automaton, the utterable of a language system which has its own logic. The language system takes utterances of language, with signifying units and operations from it, but the utterable itself, its images and signs, are of another nature. This would be what Hjelmslev calls non-linguistically formed "content" ... Or rather, it is the first signifiable, anterior to all significance, which Gustave Guillaume made the condition of linguistics. (*The Time-Image*, 262)

Because of its mechanical character, Deleuze regards film as a particular kind of thought machine or time machine that—though not unconsciously, yet without the mediation of language—makes visible the fundamental prelinguistic mechanisms and contents of thinking. This, in a nutshell, is Deleuze's conception of cinema. Thinking is inseparable from time, and modern cinema creates direct images of time, images divorced from practical ("sensory-motor") relationships and determined only by "optical and sound situations." "[I]n modern cinema ... the time-image is no longer empirical, nor metaphysical; it is 'transcendental' in the sense that Kant gives this word: time is out of joint and presents itself in the pure state" (271). The main characteristic of the direct time-image is the conflation of incommensurable units of time and space. That is why Deleuze terms the constructive principles of modernism, collectively, a "crystalline system," thereby opposing it to the "organic system" of classical cinema. According to Deleuze, modern cinema develops a mode of perception that makes it possible to sense virtual worlds, that is, worlds divorced from space-time built on the logic of practical action, worlds containing simultaneously the past, the present, and the future, the imaginary and the real. In the concept of the time-image, then, Deleuze does not see a movement away from narrative per se, but rather, the birth of a new kind of narrative.

It is from this vantage point that we can best appreciate just how much Deleuze's work advances former theories and historical accounts of modern cinema. Historians of modernism have always defined modern cinema according to the presence or absence of a "traditional" narrative, as if these terms were always opposed. Both the creators of modernism and its critics have regarded storytelling as a necessary evil, as a millstone worn around the neck of cinema, or simply as a form that has "become impossible." In Wenders's film *The State of Things*, for instance, we find a storehouse of commonplaces about the relationship between modern cinema and narration. From a technical point of view, there is no doubt that the problems of modern cinema crystallize around the issue of narrative, because, as Deleuze points out, the crisis of the action-image means that images are torn out of a "sensory-motor" relationship: which is to say that there is no automatic reaction to (or recognition of) an image. Contemplation takes the place of action—but this does not imply that narrative is no longer possible, nor that there are no longer any "narratable stories." In Deleuze's theoretical approach, "The cinema is always narrative, and more and more narrative, but it is dysnarrative [i.e., it creates a rift between narration and practical reality] in so far as narration is affected by repetitions, permutations and transformations which are explicable in detail by the new structure" (137). The opposition of classical and modern cinema does not imply a break between narrative and nonnarrative but, instead, between different *modalities* of narrative: the narrative principles in modern cinema are different from those in classical cinema. Indeed, the narrative principles of modern cinema consist in making possible the realization *of virtually existing supersensible worlds*. The aim of modern cinema as such is the creation of *mental images* that are independent of the logic of practical sensory experience. Nevertheless, such a notion already goes beyond modern cinema, as we shall see.

With an eye toward conceptualizing Deleuze's notion of cinematographic evolution, let us posit that, broadly construed, cinema inherited the narrative forms of the nineteenth-century novel. In Lukács's view, reduced to its essence, the classical novel's main principle is that the individual confronts a problem in the imperfect world, and by his/her own life creates an ethical perfection, a subjective counterbalance to the imperfection of the world. In Lukács's interpretation of the novel, it is the individual's life that ultimately gives ethical integrity to the world. This is basically how Deleuze characterizes the "big form" of the organic (classical) system (he, too, calls it "ethical").[19] Indeed, Deleuze's "cinema of action" seems to be a translation of the Lukácsian principle of the classical novel: the hero becomes a hero by virtue of his/her capacity to act, to respond to a situation, to bridge the gap in order to bring about a new, global situation. The task of the hero is the restoration of a global situation by creating a new order. To accomplish that task, the hero rises to the level of the global situation, and this can only happen if he/she represents something that is much bigger than himself or herself, that is, a community. "It is as representative of the collectivity that the hero becomes capable of an action which makes him equal to the milieu and re-establishes its accidentally or periodically endangered order," Deleuze writes.[20] To the classical form of the novel and the cinema, then, belongs a global situation that is broken but can be restored by an individual action that represents the values and aspirations of a community. The question of the classical cinema's narrative is this: how can an individual's action restore a corrupted situation? The underlying presumption here is that there is an order that can be restored, that there are values shared by a community, that there is a global situation that gives sense to any act (Deleuze mentions the "American Dream" in this regard, as if it is indicative of both the global situation of the classical form and the confidence—to "dream"—with which actions give rise to this situation).[21]

By contrast, modern cinema, and the modern novel for that matter, step back from this question. Their interest is not "how a gap can be filled in," but "how a gap can be detected and recognized," or even "whether any global situations exist relative to which a gap has a sense." In this respect, Deleuze says, modern cinema cuts one off from external reality, while it attempts to bridge the resulting gap on a different level. The real difference between classical and modern cinema is not that the latter lacks any global integrity. Rather, in classical cinema the gap is filled in by physical action within a plot, whereas in modern cinema it is filled in by different *mental* operations, which require the spectator's active intellectual participation. In a sense, the modernist auteur refuses, defers, forecloses his or her own answers, passing the project on to the spectator. This stance is well illustrated by one of Fellini's statements: "I think it is immoral to tell a story that has a beginning and a conclusion. A film has to be in a certain manner like life itself: it has to contain unpredictable events, errors. But at the same time, a film, and especially the one I want to shoot now, requires an absolute control."[22] To give unambiguous, final answers is not *impossible*—rather, it is *immoral*.

Modern narrative does not suppress the global situation of classical narration but, instead, examines its "truth conditions." For this reason, one could argue that what Deleuze means by modern cinema qua the crystalline régime actually exceeds the "high modernism" of the cinema. Although the crystalline régime does, of course, characterize some aspects of modern cinema, this régime also implies something other than (or after) the tendencies of European art cinema between the mid-1950s and the mid-1970s. But why doesn't Deleuze ever directly address a "postmodern cinema" in his book, or ever really even distinguish between phases or periods once the modern "turn" has been made? Perhaps we can understand this oversight in terms of Deleuze's own moment of production, for when he finished *The Time-Image* it was still possible to think of modern cinema as signifying the "intellectual art film" after, say, 1958. But this kind of art film now suggests a preparatory or even gestative phase for a postmodern phase in which the real crystals of time logically emerge: modern narrative prepares the "crystalline régime" rather than completing it, just as neorealism prepares the ground for Antonioni to represent real pure optical-sound situations.

In postmodern narrative, the dissolution prefigured in modern narrative comes to full fruition; the global situation disappears completely. The postmodern narrative does not endeavor to "restore our belief in the world," because the world—that is, *one* world—no longer computes. Gaps in the global situation do not exist anymore in the postmodern because the idea or the illusion of global "integrity" relative to which a gap would make sense has disappeared. In this situation, the crystalline régime can develop its potential by creating images that keep surfing from one narrative universe to another, always finding that fine thread which traverses "incompossible" worlds. Indeed, postmodernism knows about a plurality of worlds to the exclusion of any one, and as such Deleuze's crystalline régime is finally realized: incompossibility is, so to speak, finally possible. "The primary question for Deleuze is how thought can be kept moving, not toward a predetermined end, but toward the new and unforeseen ... Thus the organic and crystalline régimes are qualitatively different . . . the latter is the *creation* of concepts through difference and nonidentity in a continually open Becoming."[23] Whereas classical narration asserts identity and modern narration questions it, postmodern narration works through "difference and nonidentity."

Ultimately, Deleuze's insight suggests how narrative trends develop from classical to modern to postmodern cinema and digital culture. The concrete historical contribution of Deleuze's approach is a new analysis of modern cinema whereby the latter is shown as a transitional stage between prewar cinematic art and the aesthetic possibilities offered by a subsequently evolving digital audiovisual form of communication. But within this evolutionary framework, what is the methodological achievement of Deleuze's peculiar history? Insofar as his framework implies a shifting narrative "imagescape," perhaps we can say that this methodology consists in positively conjoining image and narration, or, more precisely, image and time. Implicit in this point of departure is the historical logic that regards the formal transformations within cinema not as mere alternations between different fashions, styles, techniques, or even "worldviews," but as the internal process of visual thinking itself—a process that operates not only with events and images, but always with the two of them together. By definition, the cinematic image always contains time, and time always contains some germ of narration. Indeed, it is meaningless to oppose the cinematic image to narrative. The transformation of modes of narrative necessarily entails the mutation of images; conversely, as images undergo mutation, the piecing together of time sequences is consequently altered. It follows, therefore, that a system can be built on the relationships between image and movement, image and time, and image and narrative by means of which one can mark out—again, the analogy would be a kind of "periodic table"—the logical place in film history of particular movement-images and time—images, no less (secondarily) the narrative modes, stories, or styles to which they give rise. As such, the changing relationship between image and time becomes the principal dimension of a film-historical analysis. Although this evolution often coincides with those divisions into periods or aesthetic movements that film studies traditionally asserts, there are other moments when Deleuze's approach cuts across (or flies against) conventional wisdom.

In this light, the transition from movement-images to time-images is the illustrated history of twentieth-century thinking about time and movement. Although this itinerary seems to isolate cinema from its cultural and social-historical context, questions of movement and time are conditioned by history and cannot escape it. Finally, Deleuze's is a kind of "inherent history of form" (Lukács), the likes of which had not been attempted since the fragmentary essays of André Bazin. It offers the possibility of writing a history of cinema in which the periods and schools of that history can be broken down in a new way using an analytic method that provides for the discovery of significant connections (in respects hitherto seen as incidental, or left entirely out of consideration) between works that seem to be worlds apart. Godard called this process the excavation of "the geological strata of the history of cinema."[24] In this sense, a given film belongs at one and the same time to several modes of thought, because it contains several different types of images, and, conversely, a given mode of thinking (movement-image or time-image) can find its realization in several different styles, using different techniques. Traditional film history uses a combination of criteria (for instance, technological and social history) as a basis for classifying works, thereby defining schools and establishing trends. The foundations of these categories are family resemblance in thematic, stylistic, or technical characteristics, and mutual connectedness in time and space. Deleuze's novel approach does not intend to modify existing classificatory categories, hence his acceptance of many received notions of film history; rather, his approach would break down received notions in order to bring to light deep, underlying connections far beyond superficial changes, "revolutions," or "innovations" in terms of which works hailing from different periods and schools are linked to, or differentiated from, one another with respect to the fundamental possibilities of cinematographic thought.[25]

Let us take an obvious example. One may well ask: what would 99 percent of the world's film critics and historians of cinema reply if asked whether Alain Resnais is a director more closely related to Alain Robbe-Grillet or to Orson Welles? There can be little doubt about the answer: after all, Resnais and Robbe-Grillet are not only colleagues and compatriots, but they have also collaborated to the extent that their work and careers were inseparable well into the 1960s. In spite of this, Deleuze ventures the statement: "Resnais is perhaps closest to Welles, his most independent and creative disciple," which he follows a few lines later with: "In this way we can also understand his [Resnais's] antagonism to Robbe-Grillet."[26] At first sight this seems to be film-historical nonsense, but Deleuze bases his assertion on criteria that allow us to see new affinities.

Given how Deleuze locates Welles in the history of cinema—namely, in terms of his experimentation with images of memory and reality (*The Magnificent Ambersons*) and his imbrication of past and present (*Citizen Kane*)—Resnais's interrogation of remembrance and trauma undoubtedly can be said to undertake Welles's project. No doubt, Deleuze grasps the difference between the two: in the case of Welles, there is always a solid and fixed point of reference that marks the status of memories of the past, and of visions, relative to a sphere of "reality." In Resnais's case, this fixed point of reference disappears such that Welles's incipient exploration of memory and image has evolved: it is no longer possible to determine the interrelations between images of the past and of the present. Resnais "attains a generalized relativity, and takes to its conclusion what was only a direction in Welles: constructing *undecidable alternatives* between sheets of past."[27] By contrast, there is no question of denying the spiritual alliance of Resnais and Robbe-Grillet: when we examine the history of cinema from the point of view of cultural and social history, the two of them belong to the selfsame period, school, and trend. But in the case of Robbe-Grillet, the lack of a fixed point of reference affects "sheets of the present" rather than those of the past, and it is this distinction that decides matters for Deleuze. The assertion is simply that from an individual historical standpoint—conceived by Deleuze as the history of time-images—an unexpected perspective opens up whereby Resnais's works are organized by different relationships and stages according to a new vector of thought.

The methodological significance of the historical aspect in Deleuze's work is that his approach makes possible a more unified, yet at the same time more pluralistic, view of a film history. This comes about because of the fact that, on the one hand, Deleuze touches on large-scale processes spanning long periods of time, while, on the other hand, he makes it possible to view these processes simultaneously in a number of dimensions. At a time of profound crisis in traditional film theory, when the majority of researchers in the domain of film studies continue to turn to concepts informed by a regimented history of cinema, or to interpretive theories with political applications, Deleuze reaches back to the roots of a philosophy of signs. His is, as he so adamantly avouches, a philosophy of the cinematographic image, but it is one that opens the way to a revolution in the history of ideas that ranks in importance with the appearance in nineteenth-century art history of historical theories of stylistics. Deleuze's work initiates a move toward a conceptualization of the great periods of history of cinema and, for that matter, of the formal transformations in the history of cinema, enabling us to understand, by way of philosophy, how modern cinema evolved.

Deleuze began to write his cinema books in the mid-1970s, at a time when talk of a crisis in modern cinema had exploded and, indeed, when the demise of "art cinema" was readily predicted. His book became, for this reason, a more or less latent critique of the theories proclaiming the death of cinema. This is not only because his sign-typology is in principle infinitely expandable, implying as it does the inexhaustibility of the cinema, but also because his analysis of modern cinema proves so revealing with respect to the future of audiovisual culture as a whole. What Deleuze underlines and conceptualizes vis-à-vis modernism are the very features that the digital culture of the 1990s has blown up and popularized to incredible proportions: namely, nonlinear, crystalline-structured narration, the coincidence of mutually exclusive worlds, and the constitutive rôle of the "any-spaces-whatever." All the more value is to be attached to the work by virtue of the fact that, in 1985, when the second volume appeared, little was as yet visible of the revolution in audiovisual techniques that was to take place over the next decade. Indeed, the fact that Deleuze's work has become the subject of increasingly intensive research now (more than a decade later) bears witness to the genuine nature of his insights: from modern cinema, we must put Deleuze's philosophy to the task of understanding the future of audiovisual culture.

NOTES

This essay is dedicated to the memory of its translator, Sándor Hervey.

1. D. N. Rodowick, *Gilles Deleuze's Time Machine* (Durham, N.C.: Duke University Press, 1997), 5. For a philosophical reconstruction of Deleuze's work with respect to the cinema, see ibid.
2. Ibid., 5–6.
3. Gilles Deleuze, "Sur le régime cristallin," *Hors Cadre*, no. 4 (1986): 45.
4. Gilles Deleuze, *The Movement-Image*, trans. Hugh Tomlinson and Barbara Habberjam (Minneapolis: University of Minnesota Press, 1986), 8.
5. Notably, David Bordwell does in fact call Deleuze's conceptualization of film history Hegelian. (*On the History of Film Style* [Cambridge: Harvard University Press, 1997], 117).
6. Gilles Deleuze, *The Time-Image*, trans. Hugh Tomlinson and Robert Galeta (Minneapolis: University of Minnesota Press, 1989), 41.
7. Alain Ménil, "Deleuze et le 'Bergsonisme du cinéma,'" *Philosophie* 47: 1 (September 1995): 29.
8. Deleuze, *The Movement-Image*, 206–7.
9. Deleuze, *The Time-Image*, 280.

10. The cinema itself is a sheer technical particularity, as Deleuze suggests, creating the "illusion" of real movement by a kind of "correction": as he writes in *The Movement-Image*, "is not the reproduction of the illusion in a certain sense also its correction?" (2). On the following pages he maintains the word *illusion* with respect to the cinema, but he makes the distinction between "ancient" illusion and "modern" illusion; which is to say that he concedes that cinema "is" the reproduction of an illusion, but by the same token it corrects the illusion and makes the movement real. On the other hand, cinema belongs to the "modern" conception of the reproduction of the illusion of movement.
11. On this point, Deleuze makes reference to two works by Bergson, *Matter and Memory* (1896) and *Creative Evolution* (1907).
12. Deleuze, *The Movement-Image*, 3.
13. Ibid., xiv.
14. Deleuze, "Sur le régime cristallin," 42.
15. Deleuze, *The Movement-Image*, 123.
16. Following the French tradition, Deleuze considers Hitchcock one of the main sources of modernism. At the end of *The Movement-Image* he discusses at length Hitchcock's role in creating the "mental image" (200–205).
17. See André Bazin, *What Is Cinema?*, vol. 2, trans. Hugh Gray (Berkeley: University of California Press, 1971). For the relationship between Bazin and Deleuze, see Jon Beasley-Murray, "Whatever Happened to Neorealism? Bazin, Deleuze and Tarkovsky's Long Take," *iris* 1 (1997): 37–52.
18. Deleuze, *The Time-Image*, xi.
19. As Deleuze writes, "[t]he milieu and its forces incurve on themselves, they act on the character, throw him a challenge, and constitute a situation in which he is caught. The character reacts in his turn (action properly speaking) so as to respond to the situation, to modify the milieu, or his relation with the milieu, with the situation, with other characters. He must acquire a new mode of being (*habitus*) or raise his mode of being to the demands of the milieu and of the situation" (*The Movement-Image*, 141–42). Such a form, Deleuze says, can be called "ethical": "it imposes itself in every genre, inasmuch as the ethos designates simultaneously the location or the milieu, the stay in a milieu, and the habit or the habitus, the mode of being" (144).
20. Deleuze, *The Movement-Image*, 146.
21. Ibid., 205–6.
22. Costanzo Costantini, *Conversations avec Federico Fellini* (Paris: Denoël, 1995), 94.
23. Rodowick, *Gilles Deleuze's Time Machine*, 85.
24. See Jean-Luc Godard, *Introduction à une véritable histoire du cinéma* (Paris: Albatros, 1980).
25. For a development of such a "deep, underlying connection," see my work on the connections between German Expressionism and French New Wave, "Metropolis, Paris" (Budapest: Képzõmûvészeti Kiadó, 1992).
26. Deleuze, *The Time-Image*, 116–17.
27. Ibid., 117.

Chapter 6

Into the Breach

Between The Movement-Image *and* The Time-Image

Angelo Restivo

The question was rather, what happens "in between."

—Gilles Deleuze[1]

Gilles Deleuze's work on the cinema is marked by a grand caesura, not only conceptually (movement-image giving way to time-image) and "historiographically" (World War II as the name for the historical moment of this giving way), but also, even, *materially*. Because this division materializes—one might even go so far as to say "dramatizes," or "flaunts"—what some consider to be the work's major flaw, an insufficient grounding in history, one could argue that perhaps this is a deliberate strategy. Perhaps, that is, the "space" between the classical cinema and the modern cinema occurs because what happened between the two is somehow unspeakable. In this light, "World War II" is as good a signifier as any to mark the site of a trauma around which our discourses invariably circulate but which they never pin down.

Of course, Deleuze is not "doing history," as he is the first to admit.[2] In the essay from which the epigraph above is taken, Deleuze uses popular sports to illustrate how a certain "energetic" conception of movement—which we see in sports such as javelin throwing, for example—has been replaced in more recently popularized sports by what we might call an ecology of movement—in surfing, for example, where one is not the point of origin of the movement, but rather where one puts oneself into the flow of already existing movement.[3] Might not the enterprise of "doing history" be looked at in the same light? On the one hand, master narratives, "origins"; on the other, wave after wave of details, pushed by the swell of some hidden trauma.

To jump into the gap, into the "in-between" of Deleuze's work on cinema, we wager that the contours of that trauma will somehow be made clearer. But we also embrace a kind of contamination, the kind implied by the notion of being "between" any two things. This essay proposes that we look at Deleuze through the "lenses" of three films—*Il grido* (Antonioni, 1957), *Psycho* (Hitchcock, 1960), and *Kiss Me Deadly* (Aldrich, 1955)—each of which falls historically within the chasm that, for Deleuze, separates the classical and the modern cinema. Of course, these three films of the late 1950s and early 1960s were not chosen casually, and as the essay proceeds, the reasons for looking at these seemingly unrelated films together will become clearer. At this point, what is most crucial to note is that all three are undergirded by a sense of having arrived at a limit. Each of the films invokes trauma, both within the film's diegetic space and in the film's spectatorial address (this latter most immediately obvious in the case of *Psycho*, where Hitchcock's injunction against latecomers was a deliberate strategy to preserve the traumatic effect of the film's opening act). Ultimately, I will argue that the traumatic in these films is manifested in remarkably similar ways: that they involve temporal disruptions that are accompanied by disruptions of *sound*, and particularly of voice in relation to the body. These films, in a sense, exhibit early symptoms of what Michel Chion would later dub the "quiet revolution" in the film's sound track, where the increasing density of the sound mixes creates a hyperreal cinematic space such that the boundaries between inside and outside are blurred.[4] These films thus are marked by an incipient postmodernity, even as they fall, paradoxically, between classical and modern cinema.

This paradox brings to mind Jean-François Lyotard's dictum that postmodernism is actually that which *precedes* modernism.[5] The point of Lyotard's inversion is to create a binary opposition within the enterprise of history itself, where an occluded past is juxtaposed against the moment "in its becoming." Now, the very phrase "quiet revolution" is striking in that it marks Chion's as a similar view of history,[6] for insofar as the revolution was "quiet," it is clear that it is something that Chion has retroactively constructed. Between point A and point B, something has happened, but that "something"—in this case, a certain aesthetic of the sound mix that became technologically feasible after Dolby in 1975 and became by the 1980s a standard Hollywood convention—is only apprehended in retrospect. The movement from point A to point B is imperceptible "in its becoming," whether that movement is from the photographic to the digital image, from the economy of production to the economy of consumption, or from *The Movement-Image* to *The Time-Image*. In other words—and this is central to the argument that follows—Chion adopts a theoretical structure that mimics, or repeats, the narrative economy of the "crisis cinema" exemplified by the three films under consideration here; the difference is that Chion, like Deleuze, has the benefit of hindsight, whereas the films are fully immersed in their own historicity.

These observations on historiography, finally, must be viewed alongside Deleuze's own strongly Foucauldian position. From Foucault, Deleuze uses not only the notion—evident in the very structure of the cinema books—of the "break," but the thinking that grounds such a notion of historical break: namely, the past as a "sedimentation" to be excavated by way of an archaeology, and the concomitant project to produce the "maps" of varying régimes of discourse and visibility. This produces an essentially *spatial* model. Thus, within any excavation of a discursive régime, statements are found to be distributed across a field held together by the force fields of power; but there always arise statements that begin to form a "divergent series," thus pointing the way toward a break in the *epistēmē*.[7] What is critical for Deleuze in this method is that one is able to see "emergences of the new," or what he calls the "outside of thought."[8] This promise of the new is precisely the stake in the time-image. For, as Deleuze argues, it is time itself that inevitably throws the truth into crisis,[9] so that the cinema of the time-image rejects a totalizing "view" of the world in favor of a radical openness toward the possible emergence of new thought, whether realized in terms of an image or a sound (a "speech act" that—in a purely performative gesture—constructs a purely strategic "truth").[10] The time-image *permits* this possibility of emergence because (as will be described in greater detail) it severs the classical connections between the cinematic images, and between images and sound. Thus, this essay will interrogate Deleuze by looking at very specific disjunctions of sound and image in the cinema of the 1950s. Specifically, I will subject those disjunctions to the procedure of a symptomatic reading, as a way of "forcing" the texts to reveal something of the historical moment of their emergence. In this way, perhaps, the limbo between movement-image and time-image can be illuminated.[11]

Of the three films under consideration, *Il grido* is the only one that can be said to fall entirely on "this side" of the Deleuzian divide, on the side of the time-image. In looking at *Il grido before* looking at the

American films, we uncover a constellation of symptoms that the American films anticipate or repeat, thus problematizing their positions within the régime of the action-image. Our argument, then, employs a kind of historical "retroactivity" in order to speak more fully about what remains in Deleuze a rather enigmatic moment of crisis, the moment when "the great genres of this [i.e., action-image] cinema, the psycho-social film, the *film noir*, the Western, the American comedy, collapse and yet maintain their empty frame."[12] Here, Deleuze alludes to the well-known hegemony that, by the 1940s, Hollywood cinema (with its "great genres") had established internationally; and yet there is a sense that as this hegemony collapses with the emergence of the modern cinema (beginning, let's posit, with Italian neorealism), so too does the attention to detail in Deleuze's own work, such that *The Movement-Image* falls into the same kind of fragmentation ascribed to the genre cinema. Hence, Hollywood cinema of the 1950s becomes a crucial site for interrogating Deleuze's argument, because Deleuze sees this cinema as already having been aesthetically superseded and thus not demanding close attention.

To begin with, though, we must trace out in broad terms some basic Deleuzian concepts regarding the action-image, the time-image, and the passage from the one to the other. For Deleuze, the action-image is what had governed filmic narrative, especially in the dominant mode of classical Hollywood cinema. Classical narrative cinema constructs itself from the interaction between space and protagonist, the images of both constructed in such a way as to connect them through a "sensory-motor" link.[13] The "action" in the cinema of the "action-image," then, is to be seen as a kind of analogy to the movement of the (biological) organism, where the latter is a kind of perceptual filter, or nodal point, or *screen*: in this way, an unproblematized link is created between sensation and movement. In a sense, this view of classical cinematic narration is eminently compatible with the "canonical" position of Bordwell, Staiger, and Thompson, namely, that narration is the construction of causal chains.[14] In both cases, narrative relies on the unproblematic bridging of gaps. We enter the modern cinema when this "bridging operation" breaks down: when a character such as Aldo in *Il grido* becomes a spectator to the very images he is immersed in, so that all he can do when his girlfriend inexplicably ends their relationship is wander through the mists of the Po Valley, taking odd jobs and drifting into casual affairs.

But what is important is that, for Deleuze, this severing of the sensory-motor link is not read as an allegory of the plight of modernity (which is, sadly, all too often the discourse in which Antonioni's films are framed); in other words, Antonioni is not diagnosing a postwar malaise. In fact, the demise of the action-image is what allowed the cinema finally to fully realize itself; liberated from the grip of narrative, the cinema was able to do *self-consciously* what it had always been able to do (if only in exceptional cases)—to give us aberrant movement, false continuity, so as to allow that which is seen to become charged with that which is unseen.[15] It is for this reason that the emergence of modern cinema prompted a total re-reading of the classical cinema. This is nowhere more evident than in French film criticism of the 1950s: the *politique des auteurs* was conceivable only insofar as it could articulate a notion of cinematic *écriture*, and this was possible only after the "naturalism" of the sensory-motor schema had begun to break down.

Il grido is a lesser-known work of Antonioni, even though it lies at the end of a solid decade of film production on his part. Deleuze mentions *Il grido* only once, in relation to Antonioni's wry comment to the effect that he was taking the bicycle out of neorealism.[16] Without that bicycle, of course, one gives up the thing that motivated Ricci's movement through Rome; in Antonioni, movement has turned into wandering. This formal development Deleuze calls the *bal(l)ade*, the "trip/ballad" that marks the point of crisis in the action-image. Indeed, in *Il grido* there is little sense of narrative causality: the film simply follows its protagonist, Aldo, as he hitches rides—sometimes with his daughter in tow—across the bleak, wintery Po Valley, revisiting an old lover, taking on new ones, until he finally returns to the town he left at the film's beginning. But even if today *Il grido* is seen as minor compared to the films Antonioni would direct immediately after it (the trilogy beginning with *L'avventura*), it nevertheless exhibits the formal qualities for which Antonioni would become famous: in particular, the construction of the cinematic sequence in such a way that the cutting preserves the temporal duration of the event the camera has registered. In this way, Antonioni's films can be seen as the perfect exemplar of what Deleuze calls "the time-image," where the cinema—having abandoned the sensory-motor schema of the action-image—is finally able to unleash pure duration. As Deleuze argues, in the modern cinema, the camera has liberated itself from dependence on the representation the image is registering, and so it creates what he calls a "pure optical situation."

In the case of Antonioni, these marks of the time-image are clearly evident, from his famous deployment of "dead time" before and after the characters are in the frame, to his use of what Pasolini called cinematic free indirect discourse. Each of these stylistic innovations is clearly dependent on the image liberated from its (nominal) representation, liberated, that is, from the characters' interactions with their environments.

But if these are the symptoms that mark the emergence of the time-image, then what is the *form* that this new cinema of severed sensory-motor links, or pure optical situations, takes? It is, Deleuze argues, the self-contained form of the image and its virtual double. To understand this, it will be useful to backtrack a bit, to look at some of Deleuze's basic presuppositions about the image. For Deleuze, the shot faces in two directions: toward parts within the frame, and toward a "whole" outside the frame.[17] The cinema, that is, always posits a virtual wholeness or continuum of the world (what Bazin calls "the myth of total cinema"), while at the same time necessarily—by the very requirement of the motion-picture camera—subjecting the whole to discontinuity, dissemination. This idea is central to Deleuze's project, for it is what allows the cinema to *function in the way that consciousness does*—dividing things up, reassembling things into sets, framing its interests, forming wholes. From here, we can now talk about the modes of consciousness that the cinema enacts. For example, Griffith's shots divide up into finite, discrete units or planes according to an organic conception of the relation of part to whole; from this come the characteristic marks of Griffith's découpage, such as parallel montage, insertion of the close-up, and so on. German Expressionism, by constrast, creates an infinite series of gradations of light and dark within the shot, leading to a Manichaean conception of the whole as split between two infinities, marking the everyday world as "fallen." And expressionist découpage—the distortion of the horizontal and the vertical, for example—derives from this posited whole.[18] It is this posited whole that then assumes an explanatory, or conceptually prior, position in relation to the *particulars* of expressionist filmmaking practice. For example, the distortions of the horizontal and vertical, or the extreme chiaroscuro, create a space in which the object-world is always "fallen" into subjectivity.[19] With the arrival of the pure optical situation, however, the shot no longer links to what has now become a shattered whole; instead, it seeks out its "virtual counterpart," with which it forms a "circuit." The final sequence of *The Lady from Shanghai*, in the hall of mirrors, can be taken as paradigmatic of this new form of découpage that results from the time-image.

In *Il grido*, this mirroring process is perfectly exemplified in the film's opening and closing sequences. *Il grido* is constructed as a near-perfect narrative circle: at the beginning of the film, Aldo descends the phallic tower to begin his vague wanderings through the squalid countryside of the Po Valley, only to end up returning (almost somnambulistically) to the place where he started, climbing back up the tower. The only "forward movement" in the film is Aldo's ambiguous fall/jump from the tower, which provokes Irma's "cry" or scream that the title promises us.

Interestingly, the temporal disruptions of *Il grido* are specifically linked to a phenomenon of sound and voice: the scream. When Aldo finally returns to his town after his wanderings, the sound track gives us two other types of "outcry" before Irma's final scream: the cry of a baby, seen through the window as Aldo passes Irma's house, and the various cries of the townspeople, who are engaged in a resistance to the (national) plan to raze part of the town to build an airport. The voices here present us with a radical ambiguity: on the one hand, voice marks the point at which historicity emerges in the text (in this case, Italy's economic miracle as seen only by a disastrous and incomprehensible local effect—the airport); on the other hand, the very diffuseness of the cries (which are mostly offscreen) renders them almost as unfathomable as the infant's cry. To put it another way, the film's very title sets up the anticipation, not only of an "outcry," but one that functions as a *point de capiton*, something that will enable us to pin down meaning. Irma's scream *is* that cry, and yet it puts under erasure any possibility of articulating the relationship between (narrative) action and the diegetic world of the film.

It is the severing of this relationship that lies at the heart of the time-image. And, as Deleuze astutely notes, the question that ends up being posed is, "[W]hat happened? How have we arrived at this point?"[20] Which is to say, the question being posed is precisely the question generated by trauma. Here, I am deliberately using the singular "question" to apply to the *two* questions Deleuze has strung together, because *Il grido*—for example—elides the two. The second question clearly refers to trauma at the collective level, whereas the first is ambiguous. We are at the level where public discourse and private experience radically diverge (which is the very point, we shall see, where *Psycho* leaves us).[21] Thus, the economic miracle—the reorganization of capitalism according to the logic of consumption—

must be seen as that which underlies the radical disjunctures in *Il grido*; and we can surmise that the same processes of the transition to neocapitalism will have produced similar effects in American cinema. It is striking nevertheless that in both *Kiss Me Deadly* and *Psycho*, we see the same conjunction of symptoms at the surface of the texts: namely, the foregrounding of "voice-events" combined with an involution of narrative temporality.

Deleuze does not really develop the notion of sound/image disjuncture until well over halfway through *The Time-Image*, particularly in chapter 9, "The Components of the Image," where he outlines a brief history of sound. If the talking picture introduces into the cinema the possibility for the presentation of the "speech act," this speech is at first firmly entrenched within the public, intersubjective (or "sociological") sphere. In the modern cinema (and in its precursors such as Bresson, whose "models" speak as if their words were coming from some strange and unknown place), speech becomes detached from the sphere of public action. It separates from the visual in order to become its own "image," the sound-image. But at this late stage in Deleuze's argument, he is far from the intimations of trauma that began the book. Instead, he is looking at the disjunctive speech act as "founding speech," speech that will performatively inaugurate the new—as, for example, in postcolonial cinemas that seek the empowerment of a new subject or people. Interestingly, though, when D. N. Rodowick attempts to unpack the sound/image disjuncture, he takes for his example *Shoah*, a film that Deleuze does not discuss and that takes as its subject one of *the* world-historical traumas.[22] What Rodowick uncovers here is the demand for *witnessing* that the cinema of the time-image confronts us with. Thus, if we return to the neorealist moment that inaugurates the time-image, we could plausibly argue that there, too, we experience the centrality of bearing witness to the incomprehensible event that has left the world in ruins. So far, this is in perfect keeping with Deleuze's earlier remarks, where the neorealist protagonist can only observe the "pure optical situations" that surround him/her. If witnessing, then, is a necessary middle term to open up the space for the new, what happens when there is no event to witness? For the economic modernizations of Western capitalism were exactly such (non)events: we need only compare the harrowing accounts of memories of the death camps to, say, Pasolini's "disappearance of the fireflies" as sign of a transformed Italy to see how vastly different the two situations are.[23] It is precisely for this reason that the sound/image disjunction in *Il grido* must be seen as a symptom: there is literally nothing for memory to recover, except for a disguise or a displacement. And in the two American films to be discussed next, this same symptom marks the point of trauma, with no possibilities (yet) for thought to move beyond it.

For Deleuze, Hitchcock is a liminal figure, "bringing to completion" the movement-image, anticipating the time-image. But it is clear that Deleuze wants to keep him on the side of movement, as is evident in the rhetoric of his final remark on Hitchcock: "What Hitchcock had wanted to avoid, a crisis of the traditional image of the cinema, would nevertheless happen in his wake, and in part as a result of his innovations."[24] One can object here that although Deleuze gets at something essential in Hitchcock, he does not attend to the profound changes we see as Hitchcock develops: something that, for example, makes Žižek group Hitchcock's work into five periods that move from classical to modern to postmodern.[25] But to begin our analysis, it is essential to understand just what Deleuze is getting at when he argues that Hitchcock perfects the movement-image, and that this perfection lies in his creation of a cinema of "pure thought." What is paramount in Hitchcock, Deleuze argues, is the *relation*; everything in the Hitchcockian universe is caught up in symbolic exchange (as Chabrol and Rohmer had already noted), and it is the symbolic positions, the "differentials," that concern Hitchcock. (This—we might conclude as an aside—might just be the reason why psychoanalysis, particularly Lacanian psychoanalysis, has found such a congenial theater of operation in the work of Hitchcock.) Hitchcock's cinema abounds in objects that exist only to ensure that the system of exchanges continues to function.[26]

But it would be perverse indeed to imagine the shower murder of Marion to be an act of symbolic exchange, rather than the (psychotic) mark of its foreclosure. Although *Psycho* is certainly so widely known that any plot summary seems superfluous, we can nonetheless recall that central to the spectatorial experience of the film is a radical rupture of expectations: we begin on the familiar terrain of the transgressive desires running beneath the complacencies of everyday bourgeois life, here marked by Marion's theft of a rich man's money in order to get her economically strapped lover to finally "make an honest woman out of her." But Marion is brutally and inexplicably murdered, thus shifting to an entirely different terrain those very issues of desire and guilt that have always been central to Hitchcock's work. In *Psycho*, the circuit of exchanges is marked by the stacks of money Marion steals; when that money sinks into the bog of quicksand, the circuit is not *closed* (as it would have been if the film had allowed Marion to go through with her decision to return the money), but rather *foreclosed*.

Foreclosure, as most fully developed by Lacan in his third seminar on the psychoses, is a concept devised specifically to differentiate the *repression* of some signifier (characteristic of neurosis) from some more radical condition where a key signifier never comes into being in the first place. Suffice to say that foreclosure is precisely that which prevents the psychotic's signifiers (or images) to cohere, to engage with the intersubjective dimension of a symbolic order. It is not that the psychotic do not have use of signifiers; it is just that they are unquilted from the symbolic order. They thus become islands of "intensities," to borrow Jameson's term for what he calls the "schizoid" experience of language in postmodernity.[27] This brief discussion brings to light, I think, an important affinity between this logic of the signifier and Deleuze's conception of the action-image versus the time-image; for the action-image is dependent precisely on a sequencing process in which the "meaning-effect" emerges out of the construction of a chain. Insofar as the time-image is "liberated" from this kind of enchainment, the hypothesis emerges that the time-image can be seen as the symptom of psychotic postmodernity.

Foreclosure also allows us to articulate a connection between Deleuzian history and the history of sexuality. This connection has in fact been argued (without the deployment of the concept of foreclosure) by Jaimey Fisher, who uses the German rubble film (and the centrality of the child's point of view in such films as *Germany Year Zero*) to connect the time-image to the postwar crisis in masculinity.[28] The Lacanian conception of foreclosure is linked to a failure of paternal intervention: in fact, the concept is developed out of a close analysis of the case history of Schreber, who fell into psychosis at precisely the moment when he was required to assume the position of the father. The hallucinatory "intensities" that accompanied Schreber's psychic dissolution are organized around a fantasy of penetration by God's "rays." Thus, the postwar collapse of the paternal function can be seen as subtending not only the case of Norman Bates in *Psycho*, where masculinity is clearly "in ruins," but also the more generalized paranoia that characterized American culture of the 1950s and that is so central to the logic of *Kiss Me Deadly*. The remainder of this essay, then, will attempt to draw out and expand the implications present in the preceding discussion of foreclosure: specifically, the connection between the Deleuzian "breach" and the emergence of a postmodernity characterized by certain specific failures at the level of the formal, the psychic, and the social.

But to return for the moment to the discussion of *Psycho*, what will be the next step in Hitchcock's cinema of thought, once we have reached the limit of the symbolic order? To answer this, we might start with one curious "voice-event" that happens while Marion is driving. We see her at the wheel, looking out the windshield onto the road, while the sound track provides a montage of voices (presumably from the office where she worked). This is the first instance in the film of the "acousmatic voice," the voice that emanates from the limbo between diegetic and nondiegetic space. Here a profound ambiguity is set up: are these voices the hallucinatory superego of Marion, or are they the actual conversations going on in Phoenix? The question is unanswerable at this point (although, as we shall see, this question returns in a different form in the penultimate scene of the film, when Norman and Mother "merge"). In any case, the voice of the millionaire at one point utters a strangely prophetic message, to the effect that he'll make Marion pay "with her own flesh." Thus, already we see that symbolic exchange is going to give way to the real of the body; that desire (which is based on the metonymy of the symbolic) is going to give way to drive (which is based on the repetition of the real); and that all this is connected to the emergence of a fierce, superegoic voice.

Thus, we must turn our attention to this shift from symbolic to real that occurs in Hitchcock's later work. If we look briefly at the symbolic logic of the mark/demark (which, for Deleuze, characterizes Hitchcock's "image-series"), we might note that the demark functions—within a field of signifiers—as the master signifier (or, to put it in the terms of Deleuze's own *Logic of Sense*, as the "esoteric word"),[29] as that which closes an open series. But if, on the one side, there are always too many signifiers, on the other side, there is always too little "reality." And, as Hitchcock moves through the 1950s, his work begins to focus not only on the symbolic exchange but also on the places within the visual field where "the reality effect" fades, where the image becomes "stained" by an unreadable blur (overhead shot of "Mother"), or an eruption of the interior onto the outside (the pecked-out eyes in *The Birds*, or the skull in *Psycho*), or a petrified monument that blocks the perspective openness of the image (Mount Rushmore, or the "hulk" at the end of *Marnie*). Once again, Žižek has been the one to uncover these "holes" in the Hitchcockian reality.[30]

After the shower murder, the two great images that speak of the presence of the real are "Mother" and the bog of quicksand—one the image of petrification (mummification), the other of the radical loss of form. This is, however, a "false" binary, insofar as it remains unmediated by any "third term." The film, that is to say, becomes short-circuited insofar as no image/idea exists that can break through the deadlock created by these images of a stasis lying outside narrative (and, thus, history). Henceforth, the narrative drive will be attenuated, dissipated among a host of minor characters whose fate we hardly care about—precisely because we have entered an entirely different temporal order, the secret of which lies in the short-circuit between the frozen body and the quicksand that "wraps itself around your face."[31] We have moved, that is to say, outside the realm of symbolically inflected time, which has been superseded by an "inorganic" time, the time of pure matter and its processes, which of course registers to us as a kind of timelessness. That this is indeed where the film is moving us is evident from the final scenes: of Norman, immobile, in a space so depleted that any possibility of movement is foreclosed; followed by the superimposed shot of Mother's skull, and then the bog (which, in its "exhumation" of the car, stages a perverse reenactment of Norman's crime).[32]

Although *Psycho* as narrative holds tenuously to the régime of the action-image, its form moves toward the virtual doubling characteristic of the time-image, with the circuit being completed by the superimposition of Norman and Mother. What must be noted is how this particular shot is a violation of the canons of classical realism, insofar as the image becomes contaminated by "surplus enunciation"—in other words, the image, strictly speaking, is nondiegetic.[33] This is why this culminating image is the correlative to the sound-montage discussed earlier, where the hyperrealism of the voice-over dialogue makes it impossible to place the voices "within" Marion. In both cases, the enunciative energy of the film pushes itself to the surface, obliterating momentarily the depth-effect of realism. This contamination of the boundary between the outer and the inner, or between the diegetic and the nondiegetic, stands in for a larger social breakdown, between the private realm and the public space. Not only do we see this diegetically—in, among other things, the prevalence of hotel/motel rooms that constitute a liminal space between public and private—but also, once again, in the enunciation: in, for example, what is called the film's "sadistic voyeurism," as when the camera seeks out the open window at the film's opening, from which it enters the aftermath of a sordid sexual scene.

Historically, this collapse can be connected to the reorganization of capitalism in the 1950s, insofar as the emergence of a consumer-driven economy was subtended by the reorganization of space around the itineraries of manufactured desire. This is the spatial system of commercial television, and thus it is not surprising that it was the political economy of television itself that provided Hitchcock with the means for shooting such an unconventional film as *Psycho*. Within the film itself, it is significant that—just as in *Il grido*—the film's historicity is marked by a structuring absence. The entire story is made possible by the construction of a highway (presumably an interstate) that destroyed the economic viability of such small businesses as the Bates Motel, the highway from which Marion made her fateful detour.

In the cinema books, Deleuze confronts the issue of the electronic image only at the very end, in relation to the experiments of directors such as Godard and Syberberg that attempt to construct new types of images whose "windows" no longer open onto a world, but rather open onto yet other windows, along the lines of a computer screen. Needless to say, this is a rather recent development. In 1950s America, the televisual system, though relatively new, was nonetheless so potentially all-encompassing that the cinema of this period—which Deleuze characterizes as the action-image in its death throes—attempted in fact to take the televisual into account.[34] But it did so not through the image so much as through the sound, which is why *Kiss Me Deadly* is such a crucial film with which to complete our argument.

Certainly, there is a critical consensus that with *Kiss Me Deadly* the film noir cycle reached its limit. But to look at the film as simply the sign of the breakdown of the sensory-motor link that had made possible the régime of classical realist cinema (in all its genres) is to miss the profound connections this film has to the other two discussed above. To my mind, *Kiss Me Deadly* is the film that most falls within the "gulf" between *The Movement-Image* and *The Time-Image* (and interestingly, perhaps inevitably, it is a film that Deleuze does not discuss in either volume).

Kiss Me Deadly is set solidly in the paranoia—complete with its concomitant homosexual panic—of Cold War America. All of its characters are driven by insatiable appetites for money or power, and even the "G-men" dispatched to impede Mike Hammer are the bureaucratic emissaries of some invisible government machine. Based on a hard-boiled detective novel by Mickey Spillane, the film follows the violent and hypermasculine Hammer as he cynically combs a deliriously expressionist Los Angeles in search of a highly valuable (and dangerous) "thing" that is ultimately revealed to be a postmodern Pandora's box. The power that is at the center of everyone's quest is literally unthinkable (and not visualizable except as a blinding white light, the limit point of the photographic image itself); perhaps what Frances Fergusson has called "the nuclear sublime" is the most apt expression for what lies at the heart of the film. In this sense, the film inscribes its own historicity, but at the same time it is the inscription of the unimaginable, the unfilmable, the unspeakable. Thus, when the top G-man attempts to get Mike Hammer to back away from this dangerous case, he can only produce a series of sliding signifiers: "the Manhattan Project ... Los Alamos ... Trinity ..."[35] This slide is halted only upon the production of the "esoteric word," "the Great Whatzit," which names the contents of the box the murdered engineer has called "the riddle without an answer." If the film's ending has aptly been described as an apocalypse, it is only because the energy within the box has been posited as beyond comprehension (as unfilmable); the burning beachfront house stands in for a total annihilation, just as the film finally brings us to the water that marks Los Angeles's end. Fredric Jameson has noted how, in the novels of Chandler, water marks the point where the Los Angeles space itself reaches its limit, brings us to "the very edge of Being"[36]—the ocean in Aldrich's film functions in precisely this way as well.

The sound that emanates from the box is also a kind of limit sound: a kind of white noise that sounds like the distortion of some horrible internal "breathing." In fact, of the three films we are considering, *Kiss Me Deadly* is the one in which sound—and particularly the disjunction between voice and body—is most central. The issue of the (dis)embodiment of voice in this film has been widely written about, but not in a way that connects this phenomenon with the particular historical moment of the film.[37] We might begin by noting the centrality of voice-recording apparatuses in the film. Even the small (but crucial) details that form the background to the narrative are connected to the introduction of a gap between voice and its point (or moment) of origin. Not only does the film present us with what is probably the first telephone answering machine on screen, but Hammer's sleazy law practice is based on the production of incriminating tapes. Hammer is a divorce lawyer who makes money by playing the husband and wife against each other, using his secretary, Velda, to get incriminating evidence on the husband while he gets the goods on the wife. That all of this is accomplished by tape recordings is revealed when Hammer casually mentions to Velda that he has lost the tapes of Velda's last "date" with a client, and tells her that she will have to see him again.

Thus, the emergence of a new technology (tape recording) radically undermines the capacity of sound to guarantee presence, and ultimately, truth. At the broadest level, we can say that, just as in *Psycho*, what lies underneath the radical disjuncture of image and sound in *Kiss Me Deadly* is the emergence of the televisual per se; if the electronic media have finally married sound to image in an inextricable way, then film will use its inherent separation of image and sound—ironically—to present the electronic marriage as fundamentally deceptive. This is made clear when, early in the film, Mike Hammer visits the chain-smoking man in the apartment on Flower Street: when the man opens the door, he alternates loud protests that he knows nothing with whispers of "stage directions" to Hammer—"force your way in!" and "make it sound good!"—even though there is no evidence that anyone else is in his apartment.

Within this régime of the deceptive reproduction—or of (why not?) the simulacrum—the panoply of voices in the film is spread across two extremes. One is, of course, the scream, which is omnipresent in the film and which, as in *Il grido*, posits authenticity at the same time as it erases meaning. The other is a limit point that the voices of the film approach only asymptotically: we can call it the voice of "pure logos," the voice as bearer of the pure signifier (which in cinema is traditionally the male voice-over narrator of documentary). Pascal Bonitzer argues that the voice of Dr. Soberin achieves this authority precisely because its point of origin (his face) is not shown until the end of the film, and when it is, he is almost immediately shot dead.[38] I am more concerned here, however, with the "grains of the voices" as we hear them; and in this regard, Mike Hammer's voice—clipped, aggressive, tight-lipped, and monosyllabic—comes closest to inhabiting this "ideal" of the voice that betrays no signs of its "interiority." This voice is, of course, the defense mechanism of a control freak, the character trait that Christina (Cloris Leachman) immediately seizes upon in the film's opening, in her snap psychoanalysis of Hammer. (And, as well, these opening sequences set up the binary opposition of voicings to begin with.)

But to assume that this binary opposition coincides with gender is to miss the very crisis of logos that is implicit in the voicings of the film. True, the voices of women in the film are, as Kaja Silverman puts it regarding Christina, "thick with body."[39] These are voices that register breath, musicality, interiority; and the enigmatic message that Christina leaves with Hammer—"Remember me," a message that circulates throughout the film—is actually the "voice" of a poem by Christina Rossetti. But the voices of men in the film are subjected to similar embodiments, and this is particularly true of the Mediterranean men conceived as "ethnic other." Nick, the Greek mechanic, has a voice that cannot contain the ejaculations of enjoyment ("Vra-vra-vroom!" "Pow!" etc.) he is prey to; and his last sound is the scream he emits as he is crushed by the car that is lowered onto him. The Italian at Christina's old apartment building has a voice thickly accented and musical (and always slipping unintentionally into Italian). And there's also the opera singer manqué who aspires to the voice of Caruso. In all these cases, the voice precludes the character from access to power: this is simply another trace of the film's historicity, insofar as any mark of alterity is perceived dangerous enough to require containment, and where the signifier "communist" served as the master signifier in this process of containment.

Within the delirious masculinism of Hammer's worldview, the voice's betrayal of any interiority is treated with contempt. This is, in fact, the mechanism by which the chief of the G-men makes himself superior to Hammer; he puts into his voice an unctuous, sneering musicality, but with an ironic distance that has the effect of "raising the stakes," throwing the loss of masculinity back to Mike Hammer. The no-win situation created by this particular voice strategy is a remarkably symptomatic moment in the film: historically, it mimics the dynamics of an escalating "balance of terror" in the arms race, while psychoanalytically, it mimics the dynamics of superego.

Thus, the scene of central importance in *Kiss Me Deadly* is the scene during which Mike Hammer's voice finally cracks, is finally reduced to the contentless noise of interiority; this scene is imagined as a homosexual rape.[40] Mike Hammer is bound spread-eagled and facedown (or, more pertinently, ass up) on the bed while the mafioso partner of Dr. Soberin gives Hammer an injection of "truth serum." The "truth" that comes out in this scene is entirely symptomatic:

the film's uncovering of the notion that, as Leo Bersani puts it, the rectum is the grave of masculinity. Significantly, when Hammer "comes to," the radio in the next room is blaring out coverage of a live prize fight that had been previously alluded to in the scene at the boxing studio; in that earlier scene, the black trainer stares lovingly at the (offscreen) sight of his new discovery, saying things like "Isn't he beautiful?" To all this, Mike Hammer replies that the trainer will sell him out as he did all his previous "boys," thus connecting the signifiers of capriciousness, promiscuity, and betrayal to a (pedagogical) relationship already charged with homosexual desire.

So far, then, our analysis of sound has uncovered a remarkably complex web of operations that organize the film around the binary opposition interior/outside, and for which the central fantasy is homosexual penetration. The logic of this fantasy is that of the "uneven exchange," so that it has the potential of throwing any masculinity into crisis. (This logic of uneven exchange is perfectly exemplified by the way Hammer manages to escape from the room: he knocks out the mafioso and secures his body to the bed in an exact duplication of his own earlier position; when the two thugs guarding the room come in, one of them pounces on top of the supine mafioso and plunges a knife into his back.) At the same time, however, it represents the point in the text when Hammer's voice is finally fully embodied, finally acquires its "grain." Thus the paradox: it is the very allure of the fantasy that, first, necessitates its repression, and second, allows it to then become the central organizing principle for all social interaction. Given the Los Angeles of *Kiss Me Deadly*, a place in which all social bonds have been abrogated, reduced to the economy of exchange (to the point where the film's central couple, Mike and Velda, are essentially prostitutes), the centrality of this fantasy is not surprising.

I have spent so much time on sound in the film not only because it is so insistent, but also because it establishes more clearly than the other two films the connection between sound dislocation and the particular historical moment of the film's production. It remains, then, to place these observations within the context of Deleuze, and particularly his notion of the crisis in the action-image. At first glance, *Kiss Me Deadly* is surprisingly linear in its narrative development, especially given the prevalence of the flashback in the noir genre. In a sense, though, we can say that in *Kiss Me Deadly*, the flashback function has been taken over by the letter that Christina puts into circulation at the beginning of the film: "Remember me!" Once again, as in *Psycho*, a woman is "dispatched" very early in the film, and the memory of her drives both narratives toward the unimaginable horror that lies at the core of the film. Is there, then, evidence that *Kiss Me Deadly* is organized formally around the principle of virtual doubling? Yes, but that evidence lies not so much in the images as in the *sound*, for, as we have seen, it is the basic premise of the film that technology has introduced a fundamental gap between the sound and its temporal origin. This instability creates an increasingly escalating series that reaches its internal limit in the monstrous sound that emanates from "the Great Whatzit."

In this sense, the sound in *Kiss Me Deadly* might be characterized by Lacan's neologism, *extimate*, which he employs to describe the strange topology of the subject, the way that a certain aspect of our being can be so exterior (outside) as to be our most intimate (interior) point.[41] Likewise, sound has become the foreign "body" that permeates the most private recesses of Aldrich's film. As Deleuze notes (in relationship to the films of Duras), this produces a fatal schism: in the exquisitely written final sentence of his chapter on the sound image, Deleuze writes that the image now presents us "with its two dissymetric, non-totalizable sides, fatal when they touch, that of an outside more distant than any interior, and that of an inside deeper than any interior, here where a musical speech rises and is torn away, there where the visible is covered over or buried."[42] This presence of sound as extimate also explains another curiosity of *Kiss Me Deadly*, the way its narrative lurches from one inconclusive action to the next, almost as if each event has become self-contained and separated by the barrier of the edit from its before and after. This is most evident in the character of Hammer: the world either thrusts things at him, or else he erupts into great violence (slamming the drawer on the coroner's hand; suddenly slapping the old clerk at the Hollywood Athletic Club), which, rather than being a sign of the integrity of the sensory-motor link, is the hysterical overreaction to its *failure*. Thus, when Hammer notices that he is being followed, he reacts by cornering the man in an alley and knocking his head against the brick wall almost to the point of death. Conventionally, the detective would want to take the occasion to get useful information; but when the tail picks himself up from the ground, Hammer proceeds to knock him down a vertiginous staircase. Ultimately, this dissociation—this feeling that the other is nothing so much as an obstacle—is why *Kiss Me Deadly* gives us the strange feeling that we are in a detective film in which there is no real *detection*, but just a kind of jerking forward of self-contained spasms of action. This is the mark of a world in which any notion of the social totality has been shattered.

Herein lies the trauma that falls between *The Movement-Image* and *The Time-Image*, and that is enacted symptomatically in all three films as a limit point, a point of unreadability or radical ambiguity. That these limit points are connected with temporal disruptions makes a case for Deleuze's conception of movement (or action) giving way to time; that they are also connected to sound and voice events makes a case that the trauma underlying the change is rooted in the transition to an economy of consumption. For the technology that drives and shapes this new economy is no longer the cinema at all, but rather the televisual; and television is a medium in which voice predominates over image. Under the incessant and omnipresent demands of this superegoic voice, public space is domesticated, and so gives way to the purely private itineraries of *jouissance*.

In his "Letter to Serge Daney," Deleuze articulates a view of television with important connections to the view developed here. Arguing that television's function, unlike that of cinema, is essentially *social*, he aligns the televisual system with "the new social power of the postwar period, one of surveillance or control."[43] But these are precisely the powers centrally mobilized by neocapitalism: surveillance in the form of public opinion measurement/management; control through marketing, advertising, and so on. Television, Deleuze argues elsewhere[44], should force us to revise the classic theory of information, which constructs a binary opposition between information and "noise." Rather, we should conceive information as falling somewhere between a different binary opposition, with "precepts" (the instructions and commands issued through various media) on the one end, and on the other end a kind of grasping toward the new, which can take the form of "stammering" or—significant in light of the films discussed here—the scream.

It is this "stammering" that connects to Deleuze's most overarching intellectual project: to arrive at the "unthought," in order for thinking to begin. We could thus argue that he is mobilizing the sublime in relation to the modern cinema. Many consequences flow from this, the most salient being that Deleuze returns the aesthetic question to cinema studies. This is an aesthetics in a precise, Kantian sense: as that which can articulate a connection between epistemology and ethics, between the world as known and the world as acted upon. As Rodowick notes, "the time-image asks us to believe again in the world in which we live, in time and changing, and to believe again in the inventiveness of time where it is possible to think and to choose other modes of existence."[45] Or, in Deleuze's own words, the time-image is redemptive: "the irrational cycle of the visual and the sound is related . . . to information and its overcoming. Redemption, art beyond knowledge, is also creation beyond information."[46]

NOTES

1. Gilles Deleuze, "Mediators," *Zone 6: Incorporations* 6 (1992): 281.
2. Gilles Deleuze, *The Movement-Image*, trans. Hugh Tomlinson and Barbara Habberjam (Minneapolis: University Minnesota Press, 1986), ix.
3. Deleuze, "Mediators," 281.
4. Michel Chion, "Quiet Revolution . . . and Rigid Stagnation," *October* 58 (1991): 69–80.
5. Jean-François Lyotard, "Appendix," in *The Postmodern Condition: A Report on Knowledge*, appendix trans. Regis Durand (Minneapolis: University Minnesota Press, 1984), 79.
6. All of these views of history are akin to that of psychoanalysis, in that they reject a simple historicism in favor of an indeterminate (because overdetermined) "moment" of *coupure*.
7. See Gilles Deleuze, *Foucault*, trans. Seán Hand (Minneapolis: University of Minnesota Press, 1988).
8. Ibid., 70–91 passim.
9. Gilles Deleuze, *The Time-Image*, trans. Hugh Tomlinson and Robert Galeta (Minneapolis: University Minnesota Press, 1989), 130.
10. Ibid., 243.
11. This procedure is not without its dangers: specifically, it leaves open the charge that, in introducing the symptom, one is introducing a negative discourse in order to reconstruct the very totalizing thought that Deleuze wants to supersede. Thus, one of the things I hope will emerge in the course of this essay is the recognition of an affinity between Deleuze's thought and recent psychoanalytic thinking. (Here I am indebted to Gregory Flaxman whose editorial suggestion that I simply let this affinity emerge helped me to see more clearly the contours of my argument.)
12. Deleuze, *The Movement-Image*, 211.
13. Ibid., chapter 9.
14. David Bordwell, Janet Staiger, and Kristin Thompson, *The Classical Hollywood Cinema: Film Style and Mode of Production to 1960* (New York: Columbia University Press, 1985).
15. Deleuze,*The Time-Image*, 41–43.
16. Ibid., 23.
17. Deleuze, *The Movement-Image*, chapter 2. One of the by-products of this view is that it allows us to sidestep the binary opposition "montage/mise-en-scène"—which, of course, the French term *découpage* accomplishes as well.
18. I am necessarily condensing here a complex argument, because I am focusing on later developments. See *The Movement-Image*, chapter 3, for the full and dazzling argument.
19. This is my own explanatory example, which I hope illustrates Deleuze's procedure. I would further argue that what Deleuze uncovers as the logic of expressionism has resonances with Heidegger's notion of unconcealment.

20. Deleuze, *The Time-Image*, 50.
21. This observation about *Psycho* was made by Slavoj Žižek, "In His Bold Gaze My Ruin Writ Large," in *Everything You Always Wanted to Know about Lacan, but Were Afraid to Ask Hitchcock*, ed. Slavoj Žižek (New York: Verso, 1992), 262; his point regards the inability of the psychiatrist's discourse to explain Norman/Mother.
22. D. N. Rodowick, *Gilles Deleuze's Time Machine* (Durham, N.C.: Duke University Press, 1997), 145–49.
23. For a discussion of Pasolini's deployment of the "disappearance of the fireflies" to stand in for the trauma of modernization, see Cesare Casarino, "Oedipus Exploded: Pasolini and the Myth of Modernization," *October* 59 (winter 1992): 27–47.
24. Deleuze, *The Movement-Image*, 205.
25. Slavoj Žižek, "Alfred Hitchcock, or the Form and Its Historical Mediation," in *Everything You Always Wanted to Know about Lacan, but Were Afraid to Ask Hitchcock*, 1–12.
26. The details of this process are fully elaborated in Žižek's essays cited above; see also Slavoj Žižek, *Looking Awry: An Introduction to Jacques Lacan through Popular Culture* (Cambridge: MIT Press, 1991), 67–122; and Mladen Dolar, "Hitchcock's Objects," in *Everything You Always Wanted to Know About Lacan, but Were Afraid to Ask Hitchcock*, 31–46.
27. On foreclosure generally, see Jacques Lacan, *Seminar III: The Psychoses*, trans. Russell Grigg, ed. Jacques-Alain Miller (New York: W. W. Norton, 1993). On Jameson's use of "intensities," see Fredric Jameson, "Postmodernism, or, the Cultural Logic of Late Capitalism," in the book of the same title (Durham, N.C.: Duke University Press, 1991), 27–32. Finally, it should be noted that Deleuze himself adopts a similar "logic of the signifier" in relation to the "esoteric word," in *The Logic of Sense*, trans. Mark Lester, ed. Constantin V. Boundas (New York: Columbia University Press, 1990).
28. Jaimey Fisher, "Deleuze in a Ruinous Context: German Rubble-Film and Italian Neorealism," *iris* 23 (spring 1997): 53–74.
29. Deleuze, *The Logic of Sense*, 42–47; 48–51.
30. See Žižek, *Looking Awry*, 102–6, on the "failed symbolization."
31. The allusion is to Lacan's description of the "lamella" as the real of the life force, as that which is beyond the pleasure principle (Jacques Lacan, *The Four Fundamental Concepts of Psychoanalysis* [Seminar XI], ed. Jacques-Alain Miller, trans. Alan Sheridan [New York: W. W. Norton, 1978], 196–98).
32. As Michel Chion notes in his essay on the film, "The Impossible Embodiment," in *Everything You Always Wanted to Know about Lacan, but Were Afraid to Ask Hitchcock*, 204.
33. *Marnie* is the film that will extend these "stains of enunciation," with the red suffusions, the visible back-projections, and so on, which were so anathema to the popular critics at the time of the film's release.
34. Here, I mean not simply the experiments in color and cinemascope but, more important from a Deleuzian perspective, the attempt to construct new images for a transformed world.
35. Robert Lang has noted this sliding of signification, in "Looking for the 'Great Whatzit': *Kiss Me Deadly* and Film Noir," *Cinema Journal* 27, no. 3 (spring 1988): 32–44.
36. Fredric Jameson, "The Synoptic Chandler," in *Shades of Noir*, ed. Joan Copjec (New York: Verso, 1993), 53.
37. This issue has, of course, been written about in the critical literature, especially by Pascal Bonitzer and Kaja Silverman. Although my reading has points in common with theirs, I believe that it moves the issue of sound to a fundamentally different place. See Pascal Bonitzer, "The Silences of the Voice," in *Narrative/Apparatus/Ideology*, ed. Philip Rosen (New York; Columbia University Press, 1986); and Kaja

Silverman, *The Acoustic Mirror* (Bloomington: Indiana University Press, 1988), 62–70. Finally, I should note that Robert Lang has written on the queerness of *Kiss Me Deadly* in "Looking for the 'Great Whatzit.'"

38. Bonitzer, "The Silences of the Voice," 323.
39. Silverman, *The Acoustic Mirror*, 62.
40. Once again, Robert Lang has stressed the centrality of this scene, and part of my analysis simply "fleshes out" what he has noted. He does not, however, deal with the *repetition* of the "rape," via the exchange of bodies, nor with the issue of voice, which is the central focus of my analysis at this point.
41. For a discussion of extimacy, see Jacques-Alain Miller, "*Extimité*," in *Lacanian Theory of Discourse*, ed. Mark Bracher, Marshall W. Alcorn Jr., Ronald J. Corthell, and Françoise Massardier-Kenney (New York: New York University Press, 1994), 74–87.
42. Deleuze, *The Time-Image*, 261.
43. Gilles Deleuze, "Letter to Serge Daney: Optimism, Pessimism, and Travel," in *Negotiations, 1972–1990*, trans. Martin Joughin (New York: Columbia University Press, 1995), 71.
44. Gilles Deleuze, "Three Questions on *Six Times Two*," in *Negotiations*, 41.
45. Rodowick, *Gilles Deleuze's Time Machine*, 200.
46. Deleuze, *The Time-Image*, 270.

Chapter 7

Signs of the Time

Deleuze, Peirce, and the Documentary Image

LAURA U. MARKS

Let us set this essay in Beirut, where documentary filmmakers have struggled to reconstruct the traces of the real—should any real still exist—buried under the heavy weight of discursive representations of their city. Beirut has been easily brought into discourse in Europe and North America, too easily, mostly thanks to the television news. In the erstwhile West, there is little sympathy for the complex history of the Lebanese civil war; the country's history has lapsed and collapsed into clichés, foremost of which is the image of a building shattered by bombs from the Israeli-occupied south. Such clichés would seem to call for a brisk volley of counterclichés, a standard documentary of what "really" happened in Beirut. Yet a number of works by Lebanese documentarists, both in that country and in diaspora, are marked by a simultaneous refusal to validate official discourse or to offer a coherent, activist rallying cry against it.

Many of these documentaries revolve around the moonscape of bombed-out Beirut, truly one of the "any-spaces-whatever" in which emerges what Gilles Deleuze calls the time-image. The Beirut of recent years is full of those "empty or disconnected spaces" that do not permit action as usual but invite contemplation.[1] From these spaces emerge the images of directors such as Jayce Salloum, Walid Ra'ad, Jalal Toufic, and Roula Haj-Ismail: a man's hands obsessively rearrange bullets on a bedspread; inmates at an insane asylum stare into space, traces of anger and intelligence on their slack faces; shot from a car window, the Palestinian refugee camp at Al-Shati blurs by, distinguishable as no more than a cloud of dust; from barred windows we stare into other windows . . .[2] Do these documentaries attempt to recuperate the chaos of this postwar city into a knowable whole, or do they see in the chaos "holes" that allow them to connect to an outside, where meanings cannot be pronounced with finality? On the one hand, these images struggle against the weight of prior pronouncements and, thus, ask to be reconnected to the "story of Beirut," brought into the organic embrace that Deleuze identifies with the movement-image; on the other hand, these images seek to deterritorialize memory, bringing what is remembered into contact with what cannot yet be thought, which Deleuze identifies with the terrible and liberating aperture of the time-image.

Deleuze himself pays little attention to the category of documentary; the conventional distinction on which documentary rests, the distinction between the constructed images of fiction film and the real-world images of documentary, is not really operative in the cinema books. The reason for this lies in Deleuze's own reconceptualization of "reality" in terms of a relationship between virtual image and actual images, both of which are real (the world—i.e., the concrete images we live among and which constitute us—is actual, but the actual is inextricable from a virtual domain that is no less real). The distinction between "documentary" images and "constructed" or "fictional" images is thus meaningless, because all of these images are actualizations of the virtual. Still, "reality" remains a crucial issue for documentary, and so we must ask: what is the real in Deleuze's philosophy of cinema? In what follows, I explore how Deleuze brings together Peirce's semiotics, Bergson's theory of memory, and Foucault's archaeology to describe the relationship between the real and its embodiment in cinema.[3]

First, I must stress that the connection between the image—that is, the Peircean sign, as Deleuze deploys it—and the real is not one of representation but one of *implication*. The sign never represents the real, in the sense of fixing the meaning of an event; rather, it enfolds or implies it.[4] As physicist David Bohm writes, in language recalling Leibniz, "Whatever persists with a constant form is sustained as the unfoldment of a recurrent and stable pattern which is constantly being renewed by enfoldment and dissolved by unfoldment. When the renewal ceases the form vanishes."[5] An image is the explicit, unfolded, or apparent form of a virtual that is implicit, enfolded, or latent; a single image may be the explicit form of an entire virtual universe. At every level of the sign, certain qualities, perceptions, actions, and thoughts are thus extracted from a virtual archive that includes, but is not limited to, memory, what is forgotten or unknown, and what is known only to the body. An image *is* the actualization—which is to say, the presentification, the making "now"—

of the virtual, and so the virtual itself remains largely "outside" the vast majority of cinematic images, comprising the "deserted layers of our time which bury our own phantoms."[6] But how do we get to this deserted layer, this "unthought" which Deleuze claims it is our task to try to think?

The question takes us to the heart of Deleuze's cinema books, and the distinction between the movement-image and the time-image. Conventional documentaries, which largely revolve around the movement-image, proceed with the belief that those images can reproduce the real, but because movement-images maintain a divide between actual and virtual, they effectively impoverish the image. The very assumption that there is a real to be re-presented dooms such images to a logic of diminishing returns, whereby the best attempts to counter the conventional wisdom (of, say, the situation in Beirut) degenerate into a new set of clichés. The time-image, by contrast, disintegrates the distinction between actual and virtual because it renders indiscernible the very distinction between present (actual) and past (virtual). As I have said, the image actualizes the virtual, but the virtual also exists as the reflection of the actual, a kind of "vast crystalline universe" of virtual images, of "[m]emories, dreams, even worlds" (*The Time-Image*, 81). Thus, each virtual image leads to "deeper and deeper circuits which are themselves virtual" (80), but at the most contracted of these circuits, past and present, actual and virtual, converge at a point of indiscernibity, a seed crystal from which the time-image germinates.

In the cinema, the time-image is catalyzed when images begin to plumb the archive of memory that is latent in the body and brain, for it is here that the empirically verifiable category of reality begins to lose its integrity. For Deleuze, the question is not to find images that approach reality; rather, it is to actualize the virtual by bringing thought into contact with a virtual image or sign, which is essentially "more real than reality." For this reason, Deleuze prefers Peirce's semiotics to Saussure's, as we find in his critique of Christian Metz, whose quasi-Saussurian semiotics effectively reduces images to linguistic utterances (25–29). Most semiotic theories tend to be theories of mediation, such that signs, typically linguistic ones, intercede between thought and reality. By contrast, Peirce's semiotics offers a flexible array of signs, of which language is only a category of the most general of signs, the *legisign*. Peirce's numerous categories of signs range from abstract and conventional signs, such as language, to the most emergent of signs, such as a physiological response to an event. Although Peirce maintains that the world can only be known through its signs, he also maintains that signs qua images are real, and therein lies his appeal for Deleuze (30).

The flexibility of Peirce's sign system is most useful for describing how documentary engages with events. Documentary does make generalizations about the world, but it also depends on an intimate contact with the world. Peirce suggests three different modes in which the real appears; he calls these three modes Firstness, Secondness, and Thirdness, though there remains a kind of "before of Firstness." "The present pure zero is prior to every first. . . . It is the germinal nothing, in which the whole universe is involved or foreshadowed. As such, it is absolutely undefined and unlimited possibility—boundless possibility. There is no compulsion and no law. It is boundless freedom."[7] As the material of the world is taken up in signs, this fecund field of pure possibility remains, and in it lies the hope of infinite, unimaginable signs to come. We shall see that this quality of limitlessness, the virtual reservoir that exists before a sign has been marshaled to particular uses, returns (in some sense) at the level of Thirdness, the most rigorous and abstract mobilization of semiotic material.

Firstness, for Peirce, is "a mere quality," such as "red, bitter, tedious, hard, noble."[8] This remarkable range of first impressions indicates that for Peirce sensibility does not distinguish between subjective and objective perceptions. Indeed, a documentary that aims to be "objective" is in fact screening out the experience of Firstness that does not accord with the dictate of objectivity. Firstness is something so emergent that it is not yet quite a sign, for it is perceptible only in the crowd of other signs: we do not perceive only the quality of red, or of melancholy; rather, we perceive these as a complex with other signs. It is a sign of possibility, "a mere may-be." Firstness characterizes the complex of possible images among which, according to Bergson, we selectively choose only those that interest us. Yet as soon as we perceive a sign (as soon as there is, in Bergson's term, a brain-image), it enters into action and into the sensory-motor schema. Peirce has a special love for Firstness: it is "predominant in the ideas of freshness, life, freedom."[9] Semiotic terms associated with Firstness are the sign itself, namely, the *qualisign*; the relation of the sign to its object, which is *iconic*, that is, the sign denotes the object by being like it; and how the interpretant represents the sign, as a *rheme* (Deleuze's *reume*), a sign of possibility. Deleuze translates Peirce's category of Firstness as the *affection-image*, an image of barely contained feeling or affect: "it is quality or power, it is potentiality considered for itself as expressed."[10] In the affection-image, a becoming-other occurs; for as soon as we have sensation or feeling, we change. Thus, in the affection-image there is an enfolding of perceiving self into perceived world.

Firstness, the realm of barely observed qualities, is where documentary films whet their whistles on the stuff of reality. Documentaries remain fascinated with qualities observed as they emerge fresh from the undifferentiated mass of the world. Indeed, this is one strength of documentary of which Deleuze takes little account. The gleam on the knife in *Lulu* and the luminous planet of Falconetti's face in *The Passion of Joan of Arc* are arresting affection-images, as Deleuze attests, but they are so partly because of the efforts of the lighting director and others responsible for the mise-en-scène. In a documentary, by contrast, we observe the birth of affection-images from the world itself, with minimal intervention by the filmmaker.[11]

The sense of possibility that characterizes the affection-image precedes perception, for affection conjures an anonymous quality of feeling. Zero in the Peircean categories. In perception, by contrast, certain aspects of the image are seized in their usefulness, and others ignored as blithely as the herbivore ignores all aspects of the grass that do not concern its appetite.[12] In the perception-image, then, a great narrowing of focus takes place; yet documentary maintains the advantage that other potential perceptions remain latent or implicit in the image. The image is still rich with qualities of Firstness and invites the viewer to bring them forth, to actualize them.

Secondness is for Peirce where the actual emerges from the virtual. Struggle enters the sign in Secondness, for here everything exists through opposition: this and not that, action-reaction, and so on. A feeling of unease may entail Firstness; a summons from the courthouse, which I may obey or not, may entail the symbolic domain of Thirdness; but the firm hand of the sheriff on my shoulder, Peirce writes, is a brute fact of Secondness.[13] Semiotic terms associated with Secondness are the sign itself, namely, the *sinsign* (Deleuze's *synsign*), an actual thing or event; the relation of the sign to its object, which is *indexical*, that is, the sign denotes the object through an existential connection to it; and how the interpretant represents the sign, as a *dicisign*, a sign of possibility. It is in the realm of Secondness, of "brute facts,"[14] that qualities become attributes of objects and events, which are perceived in their individuality and in opposition to everything else. This we might term the realm of the real. "Qualities and powers are no longer displayed in any-spaces-whatever, no longer inhabit originary worlds, but are actualised directly in determinate, geographical, historical and social space-times."[15]

Secondness is evidently the realm where the documentary is most at home. As the realm of the index, Secondness is certainly where the documentary places its chips. The pockmarks of bullet holes on Beirut apartment buildings (Toufic's *Credits Included: A Video in Red and Green*), or the scars that Arab prisoners gained in a prison camp in southern Lebanon (Ra'ad and Salloum's *Talaeen a Junuub*), produce a chill of recognition in the spectator, who knows she or he is witnessing indexical evidence. Secondness is the realm of relations—not of causality, but of brute matter in contact with brute matter—that the documentary must claim to accurately record. But no sign is an island: the evidence of sinsigns draws from the affective power of qualisigns when our observation of the scars is tinged with fascination, or a sense of the offhand way the former prisoner pulls up her sweater to show the scar to the camera. And by movement-image standards, it would be a poor documentary that did not posit relations between the affective response and the indexical evidence, introducing the Thirdness that observes general patterns (40 percent of prisoners in Lebanese jails are Palestinian, and 30 percent of them are journalists) and passes judgments of one kind or another. Hence, a Nietzschean sense of power already enters the sign at the level of Secondness, for as soon as there is action there are relations of power (not forces of destruction but inducements of movement).

Thirdness is where signs take part in mental operations that make general statements about qualities and events: it is the realm of interpretation and symbolization. Peirce's semiotic terms associated with Thirdness are the sign itself, namely, the *legisign*, an agreed general type; the relation of the sign to its object, which is *symbolic*, that is, the sign denotes the object through its relation to an interpretant; and how the interpretant represents the sign, namely, as an *argument*—for Deleuze, a *mental image* or *relation image*.[16] A mental image or *legisign* mediates affection-images or *qualisigns* (feelings, sensations) and action-images or *sinsigns* (facts, events) and builds an argument from them. This may be as simple as remarking upon a pattern or *habit* of natural relations, or it may consist of comparing two quite different images and abstracting from them.[17] Again, Peirce stresses that the relationship among the three is very fluid. Thirdness mediates Firstness and Secondness, and so it is no dry abstraction but is constantly "wet" by Firstness and Secondness.[18] Deleuze points out that the affection-image and the action-image already have elements of thought in them (the judgment implicit in choosing a course of action, for instance). What distinguishes the mental image is that "it is an image which takes as objects *of* thought, objects which have their existence outside of thought, just as the objects of perception have their own existence outside perception."[19] The mental image intervenes in the clichés of the sensory-motor schema by making us aware of the subtractive nature of perception.

I would suggest that the mental image may either reinforce clichés; or open the film to the whole; or open the film to the outside. In the best of cases, Thirdness tends back to a degree zero, as Deleuze remarks of Hitchcock: the mental image is not the final completion of the other images, but questions their very status.[20] Thirdness can exist comfortably within the realm of the movement-image, as when the mental image creates a relation between images, generating general laws, statements, and conventions from them, and thus producing a whole. Conventional documentaries, though they may engage with mental images, remain in the confines of the sensory-motor schema, which regulates these moments of thought. Such films might be termed *theorematic*. But the mental image can also create an *interval* between images, introducing elements from the outside that the film cannot answer. Such films might be termed *problematic*.[21]

We might distinguish mental images that reinforce clichés and those that introduce new thoughts by referring to Godard's statement, often quoted by Deleuze: "not a just image, just an image" ("pas une image juste, juste une image").[22] Just or correct ideas are those that conform to what is already known, Deleuze writes; the productive ideas are those that stammer, that confound answers, that take apart "any set of ideas purporting to be just ones and extracting from it just some ideas."[23] Such a stammering idea is Toufic's "gallery" of vernacular architecture in *Credits Included* . . .

With the mental image a film begins to reflect upon itself. Reflexivity has become a trope of documentary: the filmmaker including himself or herself in the image, framing revealing how an interview is staged, the use of on-screen text, and so on. Even television news now reflects on the means of its own production, for example, in upbeat establishing shots revealing the camera crew in the newsroom. Thus, it would seem that more documentaries are entering the realm of the relation-image. But I would concur with Floyd Merrell in suggesting that it is (or has been) the tendency of our age to hypostatize the symbolic, to ossify the mental image.[24] Deleuze remarks wearily that the world has come to resemble a bad film; even reflexivity has become a cliché. The breakdown in movement-image cinema leads back to Firstness and Secondness, but even these, as affection-images and action-images, seem destined to connect back into movement, leaving behind Peirce's degree zero where all things are still possible. Notably, Deleuze breaks with Peirce by claiming that the recycling of Firstness back to degree zero—as the legisign becomes the interpretant for a new sign—does not accomplish enough to break the cycle. Deleuze laments the dominance of an ossified Thirdness, for while the mental image builds a relation between other images, it may still subsume these into a theorem, rather than reveal these relations to be incomplete, problematic. As we shall see, Deleuze shifts to more Foucauldian language to describe this struggle, which becomes less the struggle between Thirdness and Firstness than that between discourse and the visible, on the one hand, and what is unsayable and unseeable, on the other. In our present Thirdness/symbol–saturated era, it seems urgent to look back for that source of renewal that is Firstness, to try to get past discourse to "things themselves." There are always elements of knowledge that cannot be mediated by Thirdness, that cannot be symbolized.[25] By forestalling symbolic action, however, the mental image begins to probe the affective components that are enfolded in the action-image, breaking the action-image down to its component affections.

The weighty premise of Walid Ra'ad's *Miraculous Beginnings: Part 1* (1998) is that Elias Sarkis, president of Lebanon from 1976 to 1982, sought to make a record of a momentous event by exposing a frame of film every time he believed he had brought the civil war to an end. After his death in 1994, his assistant found the exposed rolls of photographic film and developed them. We see the resulting movie: for about a minute, images flash by at the rate of twenty-four per second—street scenes, people casually snapped, plates of food, views from a window, all too quick to be deciphered. On the sound track we hear bells, whirring sounds, a cuckoo clock. Our retrospective reconstructions of these images as views, people, food are perception-images, attempts to organize the affect of the images. But really what we experience, after expecting a series of momentous occasions of state, are flashes of color—red, turquoise, the green of palm trees, figures silhouetted in the sunlight, the prospect of a meal, faces (and the suggestive faciality of all objects); the light tap of bells and the mocking of the cuckoo clock. This gentle barrage of luminous affection-images is all there is to witness the hundreds of times Sarkis believed he had brought peace to his land—and the joke is that he was wrong every time, the war proceeded after he left office. The mental image of the end of a war shatters into bright fragments, "miraculous beginnings."

Miraculous Beginnings: Part 1 is, like many works by Ra'ad and the other Beirut filmmakers I mention here, a fake documentary. Of course Sarkis did not expose these random images on those important occasions. But this tape exploits the rift between the (false) pronouncements of history and the fragments of the real contained in the affection-image. In an especially spectacular example of what many documentarists do more subtly, *Miraculous Beginnings* reintroduces subjectivity into the documentary. This subjectivity is not the earnest reflexivity of the documentarist who endeavors to include himself or herself in the frame (a mental image of subjectivity), but rather an opening to the flow of Firstness. As Patricia Pisters points out, cinema's becoming-time-image blurs the distinction between documentary and fiction, and fake documentaries are the current apotheosis of this tendency. Whether it is "moral" to fool the audience, she argues, is not the question: "Nietzsche taught us that it is better not to ask 'Is this true?' but 'What does it do?,' 'What forces are at play?'"[26]

Documentary's discursive stumbling block is the myth of objectivity. Deleuze critiques the "cinema of reality," the founding documentaries of Grierson and Flaherty, for the fundamental mistake of preserving an ideal of truth that is itself based on cinematic fiction.[27] Where documentary should be the model of opening to the outside—for we cannot know what is going to happen in the real world—classical documentary's ideal of truth is itself a fiction. It confuses truth with what can be said "objectively." In the documentary, the legisign dominates in the presumption that objectivity is the guarantor of truth. What might be called bias in the documentary prevents such objectivity and instead invites the transforming flow of the outside. A documentary whose underlying *affect* is "I love or I hate" invites the good that is "ascending, outpouring life."[28] Rhetoric, then, far from revealing the ethical inferiority of the "biased" film, invites the powers of the false into documentary. Rhetoric returns difference to documentary, as Bill Nichols argues,[29] by inviting others to intercede in the film's production of mental images.

It is interesting to note how film and television funding enforce the production of documentaries on the fiction model. Documentary filmmakers are usually dependent on some kind of public funding, such as from the Public Broadcasting Corporation in the United States or the National Film Board in Canada. To secure funding, they must submit support materials, such as a script, before they can make the film. Mainstream funding bodies, of course, tend to be suspicious of subjective documentaries. Further, a proposal for a vérité-style documentary, where the filmmaker plunges into the event with no foreknowledge of its outcome, is less likely to get support because funders cannot be sure whether the film will succeed. The funding process therefore biases documentary production to prejudge the world, rather than allow the world to flow into the film.

Deleuze devotes a fair amount of space to those documentary films that critique the dominant or colonizers' notion of truth through "creative falsification." Rather than hooking up with sensory-motor extension, the optical image connects with virtual images that are dreams, fantasies, the sense of a general past.[30] When the people's experience cannot be represented in discourse, *the story must be creatively falsified in order to reach the truth.* Jalal Toufic expresses this beautifully:

> What I dread when I am asked to bear witness is not only or primarily the pain of accessing extremely painful memories; and/or the pain of discovering all or part of what I thought unforgettable; but that I am asked also to definitively forget in order to release, this side of the event horizon, the created voice that can tell about a created but true event.[31]

Such documentaries are not in a position to posit a complementary and opposite truth to that of the dominant discourse, for such truth still lies dormant in experience. In Deleuze's example, the Québécois filmmaker Pierre Perreault represented the "people who do not yet exist" of the emerging Québec nationalist movement in the 1970s—not by claiming an opposite truth to that of the dominant Canadian narrative of Anglo-national unity but by telling stories.[32] These are not the filmmaker's individual stories, but the stories of intercessors, those whose tales falsify the filmmaker's own narrative.

As at every level of the Peircean sign system an enfoldment takes place, so every image enfolds a heterogeneous element. What Deleuze terms "peaks of present" are those points where two or more pasts are enfolded in an image. To unfold or explicate the image requires retracing each of these pasts into histories that are incommensurable with each other. Thus, to invite an intercessor into a film is to refold the sign according to another point of view, bringing out elements that were implicit, absorbing elements that were explicit. Falsified documentaries mobilize the stories of these opinionated tellers against official versions of history in absurd or poignant pairings, crystal-images that falsify the official story while respecting the partial views of the intercessors. It is conventional for a documentary to represent "diversity," for example, by including interview subjects of different classes and ethnic groups, but this is mere inclusivity. Intercessors speak in voices that break open the film's unity.

The political stakes of intercession are especially clear in Ra'ad and Salloum's *Talaeen a Junuub*. This video deals with the near impossibility of representing the Lebanese political situation to outsiders, particularly to North Americans, given the way "Lebanon" is circumscribed by North American political interests and cultural expectations. The video is composed almost entirely of interviews with numerous Lebanese political and cultural figures—figures who are not identified, in a refusal of talking-head authority. Their speech, in Arabic and French, is subtitled for an English-speaking audience, in long strings of words that rush along the bottom of the screen, often too quickly to be read. But there is enough information to know that their views differ widely with regard to the Lebanese political situation and with regard to the very possibility of representing it to North Americans. Ra'ad and Salloum invite their interviewees to reroute their project by questioning the videomakers' assumptions.

These intercessors unfold the implicit sentiments of sincerity and search for the truth that produced the action-situation in which filmmakers and authority figures face each other on opposite sides of the camera. One woman in particular refuses outright to discuss her opinions on camera, that is, to deliver her experience to the goal of narrative containment. "I know you will only use my words to make your own point," she says (in Arabic, translated in subtitles). "Even my refusal to speak you will use as part of your argument." By frustrating the videomakers' attempts to mobilize their opinions (with, one suspects, the videomakers' willing consent), the intercessors of *Talaeen a Junuub* delaminate the notion of balanced reportage that is a trope of official history. As it turns out, all the interviews in *Talaeen a Junuub* are staged, although there is not necessarily any way the viewer would know this.[33] About halfway through the tape, some people speak who have been jailed and tortured in Lebanese prisons. These images come as a pure shock, for the relation-images that might have connected them into a meaningful (and forgettable) narrative have been dismantled. *Talaeen a Junuub* is not resolved as a plea for human rights. It maintains a rigorous pessimism about communication throughout.

Following Foucault, Deleuze argues that experience cannot be represented directly and in its entirety, but only approached partially by the orders of the seeable and the sayable.[34] These orders cannot be reduced one to the other. They are two incommensurable forms that confront each other at a given historical moment. "'What we see never lies in what we say', and vice versa."[35] A given discourse must be broken open to find its implicit statements, which cannot be conceived of in the terms of the discourse. Things (not in the sense of objects, but of space that has been stratified in a historically particular way) must be fractured open to find the visibilities concealed in them. These have the emergent qualities of Firstness: "Visibilities are not forms of objects, nor even forms that would show up under light, but rather forms of luminosity which are created by the light itself and allow a thing to exist only as a flash, sparkle, or shimmer."[36]

Reading Foucault literally, Deleuze understands the cinematic image to correspond to the notion of the visible, the layer of things in which one can read about a particular stratum or historical formation. Thus it would seem that documentary film is in a special position to hear what is just beyond discourse and see the flash at the edge of known things; for, even in its most conventional form, documentary bears witness to the world and in so doing exceeds the instrumental, sensory-motor use (pedagogical, investigative, etc.) for which it was intended. Image and sound tracks usually corroborate each other, but they can also be used to undermine each other, to show the limit of what each is able to represent. "What constitutes the audio-visual image is a disjunction, a dissociation of the visual and the sound, each heautonomous, but at the same time an incommensurable or 'irrational' relation which connects them to each other, without forming a whole."[37] The time-image is distinct from the movement-image in that its relation-images do not reintegrate its First and Second elements but allow them to continue to destabilize each other. And in forms that break open the cracks in the sensory-motor schema, the suggestions implicit in discourse and the light implicit in things begin to emerge.

At points in his cinema books Deleuze conflates a "speech act" with a "sound image,"[38] but I would argue that the rift between seeable and sayable is not the same as the difference between cinematic image and sound. The sound track exceeds the sayable, for it contains far more than words and other kinds of symbolic sound. For that matter, some elements of the image track exceed the seeable, in that they are *not* perceptible (they are enfolded) in the dominant discourse. All these extradiscursive sounds and images appear as noise. What Deleuze's optical image does is "finally SEE" what has not been encoded in discourse—and finally hear it as well. In showing the disjunction between the seeable and the sayable, falsified documentaries reveal how power has constructed the contents of these categories.

Consider how D. N. Rodowick describes the evocative juxtaposition of incommensurable image and sound in Claude Lanzmann's *Shoah* (1985). Rather than attempt to reproduce the experience of the concentration camp at Chelmno according to the sensory-motor schema—to render the events of the Holocaust imaginable, containable, and cathartic—the film brings together the image-trace of the camp with the memory-trace of survivors. The camp is silent to what it witnessed, and the words cannot re-create the survivors' memories. Yet it is precisely in the asymptotic meeting between the two that the documentary establishes both that the Holocaust happened and that it is unimaginable, that is, beyond the confines of both discourse and visibility.[39] Rodowick suggests that Shoah "authenticates" the survivors' testimony. This, I would argue, is not something the time-image is capable of, if to authenticate means to testify to the truth of an event. Rather, *Shoah*, like the documentaries I discuss here, unfolds a sheet of past from a peak of present. The ethical nature of *Shoah* exists not in authenticating testimonies, but rather in demonstrating that some events are too terrible to be fully actualized, to be animated like puppets by the movement-image. As Paul Celan once cautioned, "Niemand zeugt für den Zeugen" ("No one bears witness for the witness"). The ethics of the time-image is that it allows inconceivable events to remain inconceivable, while insisting that they must be conceived of.

Time-image documentaries are "difficult"—not because they intentionally seek to frustrate the viewer, but rather because they seek to acknowledge the fact that the most important "events" are invisible and unvisualizable. A tape by Jayce Salloum and Elia Suleiman, *Muqaddimah Li-Nihayat Jidal (Introduction to the End of an Argument) Speaking for Oneself . . . Speaking for Others* (1991), laments the impossibility of representing the experience of the Middle East when that experience is already so utterly spoken for—that is, determined—in

Western contexts. Barely any of the footage is original: instead the tape is a jarring pastiche of images of Arabs borrowed from American movies, cartoons, and television news. What images are shot by the artists themselves are uninformative and thus resist being brought into narrative: landscapes filmed from a moving car so as to strip them of any picturesque quality; streetscapes shot at waist level; a handheld shot of Israeli souvenir T-shirts, emblazoned with menorahs and M-16s (the videographer, Salloum, asks, "Do you take American dollars?"). Similarly, Toufic's *Credits Included: A Video in Green and Red* (1995) presents the destruction, homelessness, and insanity that the Lebanese "civil" war produced, without suggesting any possibility of a return to normal life or normal speech. Much of the tape is shot in a southern Lebanon mental hospital, where men from a local village now live, driven mad by the incessant shelling, the loss of their homes, and the incomprehensibility that as Lebanese, not Palestinians, they would be imprisoned in their own country. The tape is filled with optical images that are forever stranded, refusing to be brought into movement by the memory of one who would make sense of them. In an ironic twist on Deleuze's notion of faciality, or the face-like quality of the close-up, lingering shots of the plastic dishes on which the inmates are served their lunch seem to search these ordinary objects for memories that are lost from the vacant faces of the insane.

Toufic draws a parallel between the destroyed buildings of Beirut and the men who have lost their minds: both have become any-places-whatever, terrible to behold, but also the place where new images might come into being in the rubble of the old. A segment of the tape is devoted to "An exposition of anonymous architecture, manifesting a revival of that art in Lebanon." The harsh screeches of John Zorn's guitar play over images of damaged walls that people have reterritorialized, by filling in the most gaping of the holes with bricks, cinder blocks, and plastic sheeting, so as to go on living in them. Similarly, Toufic witnesses the creativity of the mad in a long "interview" with a dignified man clutching his battered Koran. His rants, in which he conflates himself with the prophet Muhammad and even with the state of Lebanon, begin to have a ring of truth, to generate the kinds of mental images that only the rants of a schizophrenic can. Madness, *Credits Included* suggests, is not only the most logical way to respond to war; madness is also an image of ruin, an image that cannot be connected to memory, much less to chronology.

Deleuze's conception of time is drawn from Bergson, for whom time is based on a forking model: at each moment that the present passes it is doubled, and thereby preserved, in the past. Actual and virtual images are constituted around the splitting of time, and this indiscernibility, and our concomitant inability to designate either as the true image, is what Deleuze calls the powers of the false. This struggle over the truth is, of course, of paramount concern in documentary. But where a conventional documentary ultimately judges (or encourages the viewer to judge) that one image is truer than others, the time-image strategy is to create the conditions for new thought in this confrontation among incommensurable images. In other words, the past is preserved among various discursive strata that confront each other with, in Leibniz's term, incompossible truths. Time puts the truth into crisis, not in the sense of shifting cultural values, but in that we cannot know today what will come to pass tomorrow and thus must acknowledge the existence of more than a single world—one in which the event does occur, one in which it does not. As time passes, an actual image will be plucked from the field of virtualities; but in acknowledging all the virtual images, a film keeps open the idea that any of these may have been true and may come to be true. Elias Sarkis's fictional film diary in *Miraculous Beginnings* is a sweetly ingenuous example of the powers of the false, for it acknowledges that in every actual moment—whether one is eating or showering or blinking on the balcony—there are virtual events, such as the possible conclusion of the civil war.

Deleuze reminds us that the virtual image (what may or may not be recorded in memory) is opposed to the actual image (what was recorded), but not to the real—"far from it."[40] Such an indiscernible complex he calls the *crystal-image*: the original point at which actual and virtual images reflect each other produces a widening circuit of actual and virtual images like a hall of mirrors. Is it the end of the war or just a glance down the street (in *Miraculous Beginnings*)? Is it a prison camp or a mirage (in *This Is Not Beirut*)? Is this articulate interviewee an expert or an expert liar (in *Talaeen a Junuub*)? The powers of the false are at work when there is no single point that can be referred to as real or true—for example, when an intercessor's tale derails the unity of the film's story. The lucid madman in *Credits Included* is such an intercessor, and Toufic is utterly willing to allow this character to introduce the postulate (the mental image) that madness is the correct perspective with which to comprehend civil war.

Another way a documentary acts as this sort of catalytic crystal is by reflecting upon the obstacles to its own production, reflecting the film-that-could-have-been in the complex of its virtual images (*The Time-Image*, 76). A documentary that foregrounds how much money it cost to make, or mourns the shots it could not get or the rights to archival footage the filmmakers could not afford to purchase, reveals the real film-within-the-film: money. "Time is money" (77), Deleuze reminds us, and the poverty of many independent documentaries is a way of immediately bringing forth time-images. Toufic's *Credits Included*, for instance, begins with a scene in which a young teacher, who turns out to be Walid Ra'ad, discusses the finer points of video-making with students in a Beirut classroom. In fact, this class resulted from Jayce Salloum's efforts to bring video equipment and training to Beirut so that Lebanese students could give expression to the experience of the civil war. One of those filmmakers may well be Roula Haj-Ismail. Salloum's *This Is Not Beirut* includes a shot of Ra'ad animatedly discussing an extremely elaborate chart in which the filmmakers are planning the issues to be dealt with in *Talaeen a Junuub*. Such intertextuality suggests that this small group of Lebanese filmmakers are all each other's intercessors, that none need create a final statement, because each other's work will both complete and creatively falsify what has been said.

The difference between this collaborative work and Salloum's and Ra'ad's individual videos reveals two central documentary strategies, one archival and one embodied. Both are devoted to the question of how to evoke the contemporary state of Lebanon without fixing its images, but each deploys its own strategy to accomplish this. Salloum takes the archaeological approach in his work, frustrating efforts to carve a coherent meaning from the images by revealing their discursive construction at every turn; for instance, into *This Is Not Beirut* Salloum incorporates footage that he shot during the making of *Talaeen a Junuub*. Most of the images are public and street scenes of Beirut, but Salloum uses a battery of techniques to prevent them from signifying the city, or much of anything at all. Many shots are taken from a speeding car; jump cuts obliterate objects just coming into view and abort dialogue mid-sentence. The result is jarring and frustrating, and it effectively blocks the mental image that automatically links the affection-image "war-torn" with the index "Lebanon."

Meanwhile, Ra'ad was shooting footage of a quite different sort: not the public spaces of the city but the intimate and largely uninhabited interiors of his father's house and office in Beirut. While Salloum seeks to obliterate easy signification by fracturing images ad infinitum, Ra'ad attempts to do so by slowing images almost to stillness. In *Missing Lebanese Wars,* long takes slowly scan the furniture, objects, walls, and other mute interior surfaces. The objects seem to hold within them histories that Ra'ad is anxious to indicate, but he is hesitant to do so by narrating stories—stories of his family life in Lebanon, for example. Ra'ad's use of snapshots attributed to a fictional family heightens this effect. Autobiography is veiled in the restrained voice-over, which indicates merely that "Mrs. Zainab Fakhouri" transported seventeen objects, some of which are presumably those pictured, in her successive moves from Palestine to Jordan (1947), to Lebanon (1967), to Sierra Leone (1969), and again to Lebanon (1971) following her divorce.

Family snapshots, one would think, are introduced at such a point to explore the untold stories—by, for example, scanning the image of Mrs. Fakhouri's face for clues to her unhappiness. The camera does move into each image in three increasingly close-up shots, but instead of examining the family's faces, it slides over their shoulders to focus on a chair, a sculpture, or some other object, which we recognize as being the same things that populate Ra'ad's father's home now. It is the surface of these objects that the camera scans, with infinite slowness, as though seeking to massage forth from them the stories of his family's dispersal. The emergent quality in *Missing Lebanese Wars,* then, is of a tactile sort of perception. Ra'ad extracts affection-images from the photographs, in an attempt to evoke memories that seem unable to take shape any other way. Whereas Salloum excavates the image from the archive, Ra'ad returns to the body of the image.

A first videotape by Roula Haj-Ismail, *I Wet My Hands Etched and Surveyed Vessels Approaching Marks Eyed Inside* (1992), brings images to the limit of the seeable and, I would argue, into a Firstness located in the body of the viewer. This work is especially notable because Haj-Ismail, a philosophy student living in Beirut, is clearly suspicious of the ability of either the verbal or the visual to embody the experience she wishes to evoke. At one point the story spoken on the sound track is sped up so that it becomes all but unrecognizable, mere noise. The tape attempts to give form to the "inner scars" of both the artist and her grandmother, a Palestinian from Haifa, by exploring visible scars on the people and buildings of Beirut. "Death cannot be made visible or cast the shadow of its presence," the artist says in voice-over, as the camera slowly pans over images of suffering bodies—not Lebanese bodies, but European clichés of suffering, in the manner of a Philippe Halsman photograph of child whose face is covered with flies. Such images cannot give a sense of the wounds that constitute the experience of this community: this is an experience that can only be touched.

Images of bomb-pocked walls are common in films and videos about Lebanon, but Haj-Ismail's camera treats them like bodies, caressing the buildings, searching the corners of shutters and stone-latticed windows like folds of skin. Shot thus, these exterior scars increasingly resemble the image with which they are paired, a close-up of a woman's fingers, with red-enameled nails, repeatedly pressing into her Caesarian scar. "Everything around me is imperfect, broken, shattered, destroyed. Holy wars, broken windows, jagged edges. My world and I, we echo each other. We reflect upon each other: two broken pieces of another broken part." The devastation of Beirut, the brokenness and incompleteness of each person, family, and house, have forced a greater porousness among them, and Haj-Ismail reenfolds the images of the wounded city into her own body.[41]

Are these images affection-images, struggling to extend into movement and into history? Or are they opsigns and sonsigns, the motes of pure perception that for Deleuze inaugurate the time-image? Both are signs that do not *in themselves* connect to movement. Affection-images ask to be felt, and in being felt they often are actualized in movement. Opsigns and sonsigns, by contrast, ask to be *read*; they are characteristic of the lectosigns of the time-image, not comprehensible in terms of ordinary extension into movement but through contemplation. However, those affection-images that occur in any-spaces-whatever may indeed lead to contemplation, as Deleuze remarked of French impressionist cinema.[42] It is a bodily contemplation, however: neither the instantaneous reaction of movement, nor a purely intellectual response. If such images ask to be read, they ask to be read by a whole body. The affection-images of Haj-Ismail's tape, such as the long-nailed fingers caressing the Caesarean scar, invite a bodily response—a shudder, perhaps—but they do not extend into movement. Rather, they are followed by an irrational cut (to the windows, themselves like scars) that invites continued, embodied contemplation. Thus the affection-image is the domain of what Deleuze calls the ceremonial body.[43] It offers a time-image that is both experienced in the body and invites a direct experience of time.

Deleuze writes that cinema cannot give us back the body, but it can give us "the 'genesis of an unknown body' which we have in the back of our heads, like the unthought in thought, the birth of the visible which is still hidden from view."[44] The time-image "opens to the outside" because its images are connected to an unseeable and unsayable real. What is implicit in the image ruptures any continuity offered by its explicit face. This hole in the image connects to the body of the viewer, inviting us to complete in our bodies what cannot be said in the image. Thus documentary returns to the body to seek that degree zero from which experience might arise anew. Where the memories of the Lebanese war were found by Toufic to be concealed in madness and incoherence, and by Ra'ad to be concealed in the muteness of objects, Haj-Ismail elicits individual and common memories by appealing to the way those memories are embodied. She makes a hole in the image through which the scars speak. The excavation of the time-image has brought us to these scars, in which we witness a return to that "germinal nothing, in which the whole universe is involved and foreshadowed."[45]

NOTES

Many thanks to Gregory Flaxman for his illuminating comments in the course of this writing.

1. Gilles Deleuze, *The Time-Image*, trans. Hugh Tomlinson and Barbara Habberjam (Minneapolis: University of Minnesota Press, 1989), 272–73.
2.. Images from *Missing Lebanese Wars* (1996) by Walid Ra'ad; *Credits Included: A Video in Red and Green* (1995) by Jalal Toufic; and *This Is Not Beirut* (1994) by Jayce Salloum. As it happens, all these works are videotapes. Although Deleuze saw video as a medium quite distinct from film, I would argue that these works have more in common with film than not. The fundamental difference is the conditions of exhibition, that is, broadcast rather than projection; but most of these "art" videos are exhibited as single-channel works or projected, making their conditions of exhibition similar to film. Activist video has a lineage in the cinéma-vérité films of Rouch and Perreault that Deleuze discusses; video art has roots in the experimental films of Vertov, Snow, and others, which, he writes, permit a "gaseous" perception; and generally these works share the critical strategies of Godard and many other filmmakers in whose works Deleuze sees the inauguration of the time-image. The fact that video is less *visual* than film, literally harder to see, has interesting consequences for the status of the sensory-motor schema. Conventional video, such as most of what gets shown on TV, may encourage viewers to simply fall into clichéd perceptions with even less visual distraction than in conventional film. But this lack of things to see in video may also disrupt the sensory-motor schema and encourage viewers to draw imaginatively on their own resources. See my essay "Video Haptics and Erotics," *Screen* (fall 1998): 250–69.
3. I shall concentrate here on the role of Peircean semiotics in Deleuze's theory, as it applies to documentary. Elsewhere I have taken a more Bergsonian and Foucauldian approach to the time-image documentary; see Laura U. Marks, "A Deleuzian Politics of Hybrid Cinema," *Screen* 34:3 (autumn 1994): 244–64.
4. François Zourabichvili, *Deleuze et l'événement* (Paris: Presses Universitaires de France, 1994), 38.
5. David Bohm and Basil J. Hiley, *The Undivided Universe: An Ontological Interpretation*

of Quantum Theory (London and New York: Routledge, 1993), 357. Patricia Pisters discusses the fascinating confluences between rhizomatics and theoretical physics in a running countertext of footnotes to her "From Eye to Brain—Gilles Deleuze: Refiguring the Subject in Film Theory" (doctoral dissertation, University of Amsterdam, 1998).

6. Deleuze, *The Time-Image*, 244.
7. Charles Sanders Peirce, "Objective Logic," in *Collected Papers*, vol. 6, ed. Charles Hartshorne and Paul Weiss (Cambridge: Harvard University Press, 1985), 148.
8. Charles Sanders Peirce, "The Principles of Phenomenology," in Justus Buchler, ed., *The Philosophy of Peirce: Selected Writings* (New York: Harcourt, Brace, 1950), 77.
9. Ibid., 79.
10. Gilles Deleuze, *The Movement-Image*, trans. Hugh Tomlinson and Barbara Habberjam (Minneapolis: University of Minnesota Press, 1986), 8.
11. The films of Robert Flaherty, for example, dwell in Firstness: the white vastness of the snow in *Nanook of the North*, the gleaming lily pads on the bayou in *Louisiana Story*. Deleuze suggests that Flaherty's documentaries extend to Secondness but not beyond: this particular struggle between human and nature is their subject (ethology), more than a generalization about such struggles (ethnology), the realm of Thirdness (ibid., 143).
12. Deleuze, *The Time-Image*, 45.
13. Peirce, *The Philosophy of Peirce*, 79.
14. Ibid., 79.
15. Deleuze, *The Movement-Image*, 141.
16. Deleuze beautifully explicates the relationship among Firstness, Secondness, and Thirdness by observing them among the Marx Brothers: "The three brothers are distributed in such a way that Harpo and Chico are most often grouped together, Groucho for his part looming up in order to enter into a kind of alliance with the two others. Caught in the indissoluble group of 3, Harpo is the 1, the representative of celestial affects, but also already of infernal impulses, voraciousness, sexuality, destruction. Chico is 2: it is he who takes on action, the initiative, the duel with the milieu, the strategy of effort and resistance.... Finally, Groucho is the three, the man of interpretations, of symbolic acts and abstract relations.... he is the master of *reasoning*, of arguments and syllogisms which find a pure expression in nonsense: 'Either this man is dead, or my watch has stopped' he says, feeling Harpo's pulse in *A Day at the Races*" (*The Movement-Image*, 199–200).
17. Ibid., 197–98.
18. As Walter Benjamin noted—in terms that evoke the swirling of Firstness, Secondness, and Thirdness in Peirce's semiotics—even language contains the traces of a mimetic, relatively immediate, relationship to the world: "The coherence of words or sentences is the bearer through which, like a flash, similarity appears. For its production by man—like its perception by him—is in many cases, and particularly the most important, limited to flashes. It flits past" ("On the Mimetic Faculty," in *Reflections*, trans. Edmund Jephcott [New York: Harcourt, Brace, 1978], 335).
19. Deleuze, *The Movement-Image*, 198.
20. Ibid., 200–205.
21. Deleuze, *The Time-Image*, 174.
22. Gilles Deleuze, "Three Questions on *Six Times Two*," in *Negotiations*, trans. Martin Joughin (New York: Columbia University Press, 1995), 38.
23. Ibid., 38–39, 43.
24. Floyd Merrell, *Peirce's Semiotics Now: A Primer* (Toronto: Canadian Scholars' Press, 1995), 170–76.
25. Floyd Merrell gives the example that the wine taster, the jazz musician, and others with a nonverbal grasp of their art "*know more than they can explicitly tell*. A portion

of their knowledge will always remain at the level of Firstness and Secondness, unmediated and unmediable by Thirdness" (ibid., 116). In other words, the mental image may create a kind of closure in which some kinds of knowledge, especially embodied knowledge, are inexpressible.

26. Pisters, *From Eye to Brain*, 83.
27. Deleuze, *The Time-Image*, 149.
28. Ibid., 141.
29. Bill Nichols, "Film and the Uses of Rhetoric." Talk at the Society for Cinema Studies, San Diego, April 4, 1998.
30. Deleuze, *The Time-Image*, 55.
31. Jalal Toufic, *Oversensitivity* (Los Angeles: Sun and Moon, 1996), 46.
32. Deleuze, *The Time-Image*, 221–23.
33. The videomakers present such information selectively. For example, Ra'ad says that he presents the tape to Middle East specialists and historians as Lebanese history and to filmmakers and theorists as a meditation on representation. The former are not let in on the fact that the interviews are acted and (unless they speak Arabic) that some of the subtitles do not translate what is spoken; the latter are.
34. I believe it is also possible to talk of an order of the *sensible*, which, like the seeable and the sayable, is the sum of what is accessible to sense perception at a given historical and cultural moment. Just as we can only speak in the language that surrounds us, so we can only feel in the ways we have learned it is possible to feel.
35. Gilles Deleuze, *Foucault*, trans. Seán Hand, foreword by Paul A. Bove (Minneapolis: University of Minnesota Press, 1988), 64; quoting Foucault.
36. Ibid., 52.
37. Deleuze, *The Time-Image*, 256.
38. Ibid.
39. D. N. Rodowick, *Gilles Deleuze's Time Machine* (Durham, N.C.: Duke University Press, 1997), 145–49.
40. Deleuze, *The Time-Image*, 41.
41. Deleuze suggests that female directors deploy the body as one of these any-spaces-whatever through which they may "conquer the source of their own attitudes and the temporality which corresponds to them as individual or common gest" (ibid., 197). This argument is not as sexist as it first appears. Deleuze is privileging those whose bodies have been inhabited by legisigns, or who have been forced to embody a mental image (here, of woman), as agents of deterritorialization of those same signs.
42. Deleuze, *The Movement-Image*, 40–45.
43. Deleuze, *The Time-Image*, 190–91.
44. Ibid., 201.
45. Peirce, "Objective Logic," 148.

FILMOGRAPHY/VIDEOGRAPHY

Credits Included: A Video in Red and Green (Jalal Toufic, 1995). Distributed by Arab Film Distribution.

I Wet My Hands Etched and Surveyed Vessels Approaching Marks Eyed Inside (Roula Haj-Ismail, 1992). Distributed by V Tape.

Miraculous Beginnings (Walid Ra'ad, 1998). Distributed by Arab Film Distribution, Video Data Bank, and Video Out, under the compilation title *The Dead Weight of a Quarrel Hangs*.

Missing Lebanese Wars (Walid Ra'ad, 1996). Distributed by Arab Film Distribution, Video Data Bank, and Video Out, under the compilation title *The Dead Weight of a Quarrel Hangs.*

Muqaddimah Li-Nihayat Jidal (Introduction to the End of an Argument) Speaking for Oneself . . . Speaking for Others (Jayce Salloum and Elia Suleiman, 1990). Distributed by Heure Exquise, Vidéographe, Video Out, and V Tape.

Talaeen a Junuub (Up to the south) (Walid Ra'ad and Jayce Salloum, 1993). Distributed by Arab Film Distribution, Vidéographe, V Tape, and Third World Newsreel.

This Is Not Beirut (Jayce Salloum, 1995). Distributed by Arab Film Distribution, Vidéographe, and V Tape.

DISTRIBUTORS

Arab Film Distribution, 2417 10th Ave. E., Seattle, WA 98102. 206-322-0882. Fax 206-322-4586. info@arabfilm.com; www.arabfilm.com

Heure Exquise, BP 113, Mons en Baroel, 59370 France. 33-20-049574.

V Tape, 401 Richmond St. W., Ste. 452, Toronto, ON M5V 3A8, Canada. 416-351-1317. Fax 416-351-1309. video@astral.magic.ca

Video Out, 1965 Main St., Vancouver, BC V5T 3C1, Canada. 604-872-8449. Fax 604-876-1185. video@portal.ca

Vidéographe, 460, rue Ste-Catherine ouest #504, Montreal, PQ H3B 1A7. 514-866-4720. Fax: 514-866-4725.

Third World Newsreel, 335 W. 38th St., New York, NY 10038. 212-947-9277. Fax 212-594-6417. twn@tmn.org

Chapter 8

The Roots of the Nomadic

Gilles Deleuze and the Cinema of West Africa

DUDLEY ANDREW

> *... nomads are in fact people who don't want to move on, don't want to leave, who cling to the land taken from them, their* région centrale ...
>
> —Gilles Deleuze[1]

CLASSICAL, MODERN, AND NOMADIC CINEMA

If one were to take the Academy Awards and the Cannes film festival the way the newspapers do, one would believe that standard cinema is in good health. Global action pictures (*Independence Day*), more artistic passion pictures (*The English Patient*), and their perfectly stewed combination (*Titanic*) have appeared on screens around the world, firing the universal imagination the way cinema has since Griffith. These two types of cinema, which might be termed first and second cinema, seem to defy predictions that the century's end also spells the end of this century's mass art. Still, those tracking aesthetic and social developments realize that the "soul of cinema" (to use Gilles Deleuze's manner of isolating what is crucial in the medium)[2] moved beyond Hollywood, the first cinema, by World War II, and by 1975 passed beyond the alternative second cinema. The "soul of cinema"—what the cinema at any given moment permits those devoted to it to think—is on the move, and has moved elsewhere. Let's follow it ...

Deleuze's categorical elaboration of the powers of film involves one, and only one, historical break. Drawing on André Bazin's intuitive sense of cinematic development, Deleuze takes World War II to have utterly reconstituted cinema's cultural significance, and at all levels, from the kinds of films made to the way they were produced, exhibited, and discussed. After the war, the "classical" era, in which a stable studio system had mastered "movement-images" ceded the "soul of cinema" to the modernism of Japanese and European auteurs, the most worthy of whom fashioned "time-images." Ideally, once the time-image became "fashionable" (in the etymological sense of the term), the cinema was free to emit an indefinite set of temporalities, responsive not so much to history but to those auteurs who, each in his or her own manner, released the powers of cinematic production. Plotted along this axis of strong auteurs, however, Deleuze's "time-image" conceivably retards his philosophy of cinema from thinking beyond the modernism that was the legacy of auteurism—the modernism that many find sickly today.[3]

Why should we not entertain another shift in cinema, as complete as that which occurred at World War II, this time corresponding to the decay of auteurist modernism and the ascendancy of new conditions of exhibition and distribution? Fredric Jameson, for instance, suggests that such a break occurred around 1975, the end of the Vietnam War at home and abroad, when the promises of modernism, including the political ones of May '68, had soured.[4] Since then, the entire film complex has responded to expanded conditions of exhibition, distribution, and production (the era of "cinema without walls," as Tim Corrigan has dubbed it, alluding so nicely to Malraux.)[5] The VCR is the emblem of this apparent victory of consumers over producers, a victory that Deleuze, it would seem, could never (or would) recognize. His remains a theory devoted to the production (the creation) of images and the virtual temporalities they bring into existence; but in the age of the VCR, surely, authority in the cinema has been handed over by producers to viewers, who can literally alter the time of the image by manipulating the remote control. Cinema is no longer centered in Hollywood studios nor in the fertile minds of auteurs; without walls, it is centered nowhere.

The vertigo that this decentering has produced in film studies can also be experienced, I believe, as an exhilarating liberation, one that may not have been presaged by Deleuze's cinema books but that may well have Deleuzian consequences. Those who have tired of Hollywood and Paris, whose interests have migrated to Irish, West African, Québécois, and African-American films, for example, sense themselves running freely in an unpoliced arena, escaping—momentarily, at any rate—standard critical discourse and standard films. And so Deleuze's importance for cinema studies in the coming years may lie not so much in his volumes treating classical and modern films, respectively, but in the section of *A Thousand Plateaus* devoted to "nomadism" (hence postmodernity).

Can Deleuze's alluring concept of the "nomadic" be imported as an intercessor for cinema studies just as he imported it into philosophy?

Must we not be wary precisely because this term recruits a way of life, and by extension a category of human beings, for a presumed regeneration in European philosophy? Gayatri Spivak took Deleuze and Michel Foucault to task for this very gambit when she found them deploying "subaltern" peoples in their discussions with fellow philosophers, using such people, she suggested, like the slaves they have always been, but showing them off to effect and profiting from the display.[6] Undifferentiated desire can be conveniently attached to the subaltern as a "nonpeople" without history who become protagonists in Deleuze's drama of movement, repression, territory, and flow. To this Deleuze would surely admit that his is a Western drama played out on a Western stage. By invoking "intercessors" whose voices have not been heard, or, if heard, not really listened to (Spinoza in philosophy, Kafka in literature, and now the subaltern in history), Deleuze opens "thought" to movements and rhythms outside its traditional purview. Intercessors break open the walls of the theater of philosophy and allow thought to move in "lines of flight" beyond its traditions, beyond its history, beyond its identity. Spivak too would alter, indeed revolutionize, Western thought, but she reminds us that Deleuze's intercessors have a real history by which they are constrained;[7] in other words, she implies that these intercessors deserve to be taken as more than metaphors by French philosophers who are already free, who already have passports, money, and access to world communications systems.

Although nomadism is a principle of thought for Deleuze, it is also a metaphor, one that is attached to science when first evoked in *A Thousand Plateaus*.[8] Now, a metaphor is nothing other than a work of linguistic intercession, where, in Paul Ricoeur's terms, one field is redescribed by an inappropriate term imported from another domain.[9] In this case the domain is explicitly that of anthropology, whose "Arabs or Indians"[10] redescribe legal and scientific activities in the known civilization of the West. Finding nomadism everywhere, Deleuze nevertheless relies on what we historically know and imagine about Asian and African peoples: to our (Western) gaze their chief quality appears to be fluidity, and so they are used as intercessors to free up a tradition of Western philosophy that has been gridlocked for centuries in a strict hierarchy of concepts. Curiously, the nomadic does not directly reappear in Deleuze's writings on the cinema nor in the volume of commentary that D. N. Rodowick devoted to that work. Other, related concepts step in to perform a similar function, most notably the "time-image" and its components or aids such as "the serial form," "the minor," "fabulation," and "the oral";

but of nomadic cinema itself we hear nothing.[11] If only to take up this open invitation, let us explore nomadism in cinema by examining this metaphor in its seemingly literal emanations.[12]

Given his lexicon, Deleuze should have encountered difficulties just trying to identify an object named *cinema* so as to talk about its span, about its past and its prospects. For Deleuze, cinema might be conceived less as object or institution than as an assemblage within which images bubble into existence and fly off in vectors of power. But, of course, cinema is also an institution, often a state one, consisting of various constraints on images (technological, ideological, aesthetic). It exercises political and economic power that bends to its purposes the otherwise aimless power of images. In short, the "soul of cinema" must fight to emerge within the "state of cinema." On one level, Deleuze suggests that the cinema possesses a past to be parsed into the eras of, respectively, the movement-image and the time-image; on another level, the cinema also possesses something of an "essence," one that had not sufficiently emerged by 1907 for Bergson to properly understand it when he publicly disparaged it,[13] and one whose fullness was realized only after World War II (once the cinema, particularly in Europe, had been "deterritorialized").

Insofar as Deleuze looks for evidence of this essence, a virtual power that appears outside the classical norm, he can be said to follow the lead of André Bazin. Bazin attacked what might be called the Platonism of a system whereby a film exists first as a written script transcoded into a technical découpage, then realized (copied, in fact) in shooting and montage. In Renoir and preeminently in Rossellini, Bazin glimpsed a more directly corporeal approach to the making and watching of a film. In a wonderful analogy, he likens their existential approach to a ford discovered in the array of rocks strewn along a riverbed, which he opposes to the bridges that Hollywood writers and editors engineer for smooth passage.[14] In both cases, the spectator moves across the narrative to arrive at the other side; but whereas the ford presses the filmgoer to pay close attention to the idiosyncratic shapes of the individual rocks (and to risk getting splashed midstream), the bricks of the bridge, shaped uniformly from a mold, are secure and, hence, without interest.

Philosopher of difference, Deleuze too prefers the ford to the bridge and—because it must come to terms with fluid in the literal sense—the bridge to the roadway. He champions "nomad science" for which "matter is never prepared and homogenized [Bazin's brick] but is essentially laden with singularities [Bazin's rocks]. . . .

Nomad science which presents itself as much as an art as a technique ... *follows* the connections between singularities of matter and traits of expression."[15] Finding postwar cinema happily midstream,[16] Deleuze "affords" descriptions of the contours of virtual time-images in neorealist works, in Welles's *Lady from Shanghai*, in films employing a ballade structure, and so on. His cinema volumes comprise an extended application of "noology, as opposed to ideology ... the study of images of thought in their historicity."[17] Indeed, the central historical moment for Deleuze, as for Bazin, is World War II. In the wake of *Citizen Kane* and *Rules of the Game*, the cinema is transformed and a striking modification of the feature film emerges from the critical auteurs of the time.

That modification was visible to Bazin everywhere in the cinematic phenomenon, not just in feature films. Far more than Deleuze, Bazin focused on ideolects such as documentary, scientific, ethnographic, and art films, all of which lie outside the domain of the "normal" or the "standard." Bazin also wrote about changing methods of production and about new conditions and stakes of exhibition and reception, perhaps because he promoted his views in deterritorialized spaces such as cine-clubs, labor-union halls, film festivals, and cinémathèques. Deleuze, one would have to say, largely ignored these aspects to concentrate on his noology, but his views about films can be extended to the full cinematic phenomenon if one attends to his other writings, particularly the "nomadology" of *A Thousand Plateaus*. There Deleuze sponsors alternatives to capitalism, hence to the film industry, inevitably questioning the supremacy of Hollywood and Paris in search of more dispersed and multiple production situations. That search I now undertake, beginning with a brief survey of film history "outside the classical lines" and eventually alighting in West Africa, where one can locate both a subterranean mine of images ripe for noological analysis (à la the cinema books) and an alternative system of production and exchange—a unique assemblage or nomadic war machine surviving in the sahel despite a rapacious global image industry.

BEYOND *THE MOVEMENT-IMAGE* TO THE MOVEMENTS OF CINEMA

Deleuze partly takes up the tale of nomad cinema in his few remarks on documentary, but we can more fully elaborate the story. Consider that the Lumière brothers had teams of cameramen scattered across the globe taking pictures or "views" of locales that would be projected at other locales around the globe. The "view," the predominant genre in those early years, derived from the narrated slide shows of itinerant lecturers so popular at the turn of the century. With this version of cinema in mind, traveling fairs, ambulatory projection teams, and spontaneous showings in town centers and cafés should be taken as a proper rather than a "primitive" exhibition system. Only later would this variety be replaced by the dull consistency of the nickelodeon and, ultimately, by picture palaces where movies were meant to emulate such state-sponsored arts as opera and theater.

The progressive urbanization of the manufacture and distribution of films rationalized the crazy energy of those first years; the medium's hunger for the great outdoors was palliated by bringing everything into the studio kitchen. In effect, Hollywood films would allude to the outside world rather than be led to or by it. True, open-air footage found its way regularly onto the screen in the classical period; but it was always digested by the genres concocted in newsreel and short film bureaus whose job it was to fill out a bill dominated by the tailored look of the feature film. In Deleuze's terms, the sedentary studio empire protected itself by colonizing (territorializing) the uncontrolled spaces, times, and dramas beyond its walls. These processes of centralization and domestication were blatantly exposed in Paris at the Colonial Exposition of 1931, where the tradition of the traveling fair mutated into an august state fair. Here one of the pioneers of ethnographic cinema, Léon Poirier, who had trekked down the spine of Africa for his *La Croissière noire* (1925), presided in staid fashion over a continuous program of travel shorts and colonial features. In short, these films already constituted a *mainstream* genre;[18] one could say that by this time, the unknown world had been miniaturized and brought to the metropole to be experienced by tourists at leisure and according to conventional dramatic rules. Parisians had only to travel as far as the Bois de Vincennes to experience a safari—either on the little train constructed around Lac Daumesnil in the Bois or by sitting in a pavilion to watch the films Poirier had arranged to screen.

Against the background of a general homogenization of images, ethnographic cinema constitutes a contrary (or contrapuntal) cinematic tendency, one equivalent to a Deleuzian war machine. The ethnographic filmmaker rebuffs the empire of the norm so as to join the lives, spaces, and temporalities of other peoples. Such a cinema gallops across open terrain with a variable assemblage of personnel and materiel. Its production on location resembles logistics and tactics, ever the issue for ethnographic filmmakers, as opposed to the strategies (plots) that are of primary concern to producers in the studio system.[19] Take the 1925 effort *Grass*, where an actual nomadic people led Merian Cooper and Earnest Shoedsack to develop new ways of thinking about and shooting film. The incredible trek of an entire society across rivers and mountains compelled the use of long takes, long shots, and mobile cameras in a manner quite foreign to features of the time. Of course, whatever gains this and other ethnographic films made in formulating means adequate to their subject matter were quickly recruited by the studios for their own purposes. After the surprise of *Grass*, for instance, Cooper and Shoedsack made the semidocumentary *Rango* and then were paid handsomely to drag the wilds of the jungle inside RKO for *King Kong*.[20] Studios could not ignore reality, particularly the reality of far-flung exotic places; instead, they learned to let in the fresh air, fresh subjects, and fresh techniques of documentary but without losing control of dramatic scripts, consistent acting, and predictable shooting schedules. In short, Hollywood was fascinated by, though ultimately contemptuous of, the contrariness—the waywardness—of ethnographic film.

Look at Hollywood's, rather than Bazin's and Deleuze's, reaction to Robert Flaherty. Flaherty's distinctly inefficient method of editing (likened to the way Inuits carve away at a large piece of ivory until the seal believed to be within it slowly is "released")[21] corresponds to his equally inefficient production practices on location, far from the studio. Flaherty followed his subject rather than roping it in where it could be filmed in controlled conditions. In light of the "Treatise on Nomadology," one can recognize Flaherty as having thrived outside the walled city of Hollywood; he entered into an assemblage that made use of the camera in so different a fashion that it challenged the classical essence of cinema, whose codes were already written in stone in the 1920s. Indeed, in *The Movement-Image* Deleuze discusses Flaherty's attachment to an impervious milieu within which the subject acts not to change that milieu, as in standard films of the SAS' type, but to survive either its encompassing brutality (*Nanook*) or its equally encompassing benevolence (*Moana*).[22] Flaherty's SAS structure has the effect of making the main characters of his early films into accomplices through whom he explores, and exploits, incalculably rich landscapes, those eternal "situations" that are beyond politics and that inspire such awe.

Let's consider this assemblage: it consists of a portable camera plus tripod and photographic accessories, a mobile laboratory, a sled with dogs and additional items for a trek involving a single operator (Flaherty himself, likewise an element). The assemblage must also include Nanook, the Eskimo whose values and ways are meant to be captured and brought back to circulate as rare commodities in the image markets of the world. Nanook is linked to a technological array that includes kayaks, igloos, and flint, as well as implements for hunting and fishing. He expressly ties his life to that of the seal he hunts, the seal Deleuze would instantly have recognized as a mobile, subaqueous source of oil, that is, of energy and value. Brought to the surface through a complex relay, the oil ultimately can be said to have powered Nanook's lanterns as well as the projector (energy) and the screen (image) at the film's premiere in 1924. Appropriate to its process of production, *Nanook of the North* was distributed through an ad hoc mechanism, keeping Flaherty on the move even as he was organizing his subsequent projects.

One of those projects, *Man of Aran*, allows us to more rigorously gauge this documentary assemblage as it develops among elements in an unpredictable situation, once again distant from the centers of cinema. Unlike the independently organized *Nanook of the North, Man of Aran* was commissioned by a British film company; nevertheless, in recognition that his idea departed utterly from standard studio production, Flaherty received a flexible budget and a nearly open-ended shooting schedule. This time he set up his mobile lab on the Aran Islands and settled down with farmers on their large barren rock, intent on capturing their determination to battle and befriend an austere, sometimes hostile milieu. On the Aran Islands, a minimal ecology links people, land, and the surrounding ocean: the ocean washes up seaweed that the islanders gather into soil beds just thick enough to hold the roots of the potatoes on which they subsist. But potatoes are unheroic, and their growth undramatic; and so Flaherty focused instead on the ungovernable sea, and on a complex assemblage involving men, boats (with oars, harpoons, and nets), and the great sharks that intermittently feed off the coast.[23] The full assemblage includes women, lamps, sod huts, and huge kettles for rendering oil. Indeed, the fabulous sharks constitute another mobile source of oil to be dredged from the sea—not so much for the energy they provide as for the unforgettable image of danger they portend.

As it later came out, by 1933 shark oil no longer interested the islanders; they could buy other forms of energy cheaply from the mainland. The hunt was an artifact of the film, undertaken entirely for the images it could provide. In this breach of standard documentary ethics, Flaherty abandoned his project to record the lives of the islanders; instead—and altogether in the mode of Hollywood production—he *designed* his subject. He cajoled the islanders, who had never fished, to take up shark hunting in the manner of their ancestors. An elder of the island could still remember the technique well enough to instruct those who agreed to set out on an escapade for the film. Cynical as this seems, something quite authentic remains on celluloid, for the sharks we see were truly harpooned and landed by these men of the Aran Islands; their ancestral past reemerged in front of the cameras there in 1934, later to be projected on screens around the world.

Flaherty's sin, if sin it be, was habitual. For he would say of his first film that he was out to capture not "Nanook the man," but "the Spirit of the Eskimo"; of the Irish film that he was not out to capture the particular inhabitants of the Aran Islands, but the "Spirit of Islanders." According to Flaherty's romantic view, we are all, in some basic way, islanders ourselves, up against the elements even as we enjoy the film in urban centers where we no longer need to hunt anything. In taking on a subject as large and abstract as human nature, however, Flaherty's methods inevitably begin to resemble those of Hollywood. He may have pressed close to the texture of Nanook's existence during the seal hunt, but the Eskimo had to be taught to hunt the walrus as his father had done. Flaherty had predetermined to land images of men in contact with the walruses of the Canadian Arctic and of the sharks of the furthest coast of Europe, precious images of power and danger that he could market internationally.

No doubt, Flaherty's has become a familiar formula—to film exotic people and places in such a way that their difference ultimately loses its strangeness, allowing viewers everywhere to assimilate it, ingest it, and feel stronger after such a diet. His contract to deliver rare and presumably authentic images, increasingly difficult to fulfill, led him to take shortcuts, staging or restaging the lives whose authenticity he had originally sought. To make *Louisiana Story*, Flaherty actually worked for Standard Oil:[24] we glimpse rigs in several shots, alerting us to the rigging of the drama, and reminding us how disappointed André Bazin was in this film (for Bazin, this disappointment was condensed in the scene between boy and alligator, which Flaherty rendered in a prefab shot–counter shot routine).[25] Coming home under contract to work in his own country, Flaherty had relinquished the languorous narration, by turns indirect and aphoristic, that characterizes and sustains his early work. Now he simply was out to make a movie.

Even though he cut deals with corporations and studios for production funds and distribution guarantees, Flaherty still showed that during the constrictive period of Hollywood's monopoly a different cinema—a mobile one—might ignore many of the methods and principles of standard features. Although he compromised his mission, Flaherty has become an emblem for a nomadic cinema that today escapes an even more pervasive Hollywood that, under the conditions of a bogus "free-market economy," has colonized the world's screens. His mission lives on, for example, in a director otherwise so different from him, Werner Herzog. Like Flaherty, Herzog suffered and prospered in difficult voyages (to the Australian outback for *Where the Green Ants Dream*, and to the sahel of Niger for *Herdsmen of the Sun*). Like Flaherty, he unearthed strange ways of life that he could bring back to a "civilization" for which he has even more obvious contempt. To a greater degree than Flaherty, from whom he should have learned better, Herzog bears the guilt of catering to a questionable taste for something exotic, something "out there" that he was not averse to trumping up if it failed to emerge on its own.

Flaherty may have compromised the nomadic form he championed and he may ultimately have served the interests and the form of the cinematic status quo, but what of his pristine subjects, Nanook and his family, or the Aran Islanders? Does not their pure exteriority, and their relation to the harsh environment, provide, via cinema, a model of the nomadic assemblage? Perhaps. But unobstructed and unthreatened, we never see these ways of life in conflict with Flaherty or with the society for which, in an increasingly obvious way, he worked. Unopposed, they are also unopposing, hence unpolitical; they appear to be fully constituted bodies, bodies with consistent identities. Indeed, Flaherty was drawn to them in large part because of the timelessness of their ways of life.

By contrast, Deleuze's nomads are never quite constituted; always "coming into being" they take (and change) shape in relation to an already colonized environment that would define and place them.[26] Deleuze's metaphorical nomads compose an aesthetic and moral category that outruns its anthropological vehicle. Unlike Nanook, today's nomads cannot help but live alongside and within the states that are their antagonists. Deleuze might count among them, for example, computer hackers who, sedentary before their screens, gallop alone or with cohorts around the communications network, which they use, manipulate, or disrupt as the occasion demands, even whimsically.[27] Hardly the subjects or agents of traditional philosophy, they are "plugged in" to an assemblage through which they also pass as "effects" of power.

To think nomadic cinema with this in mind one should look less at the representation of lives lived in movement than at "movements" in which cinema participates. This includes directly political cinematic movements, such as the one proclaimed by Solanas and Gettino in "Toward a Third Cinema," and by Espinosa in "For an Imperfect Cinema," the grammar of whose title expresses the ontology of nomadism.[28] Deleuze takes up third cinema in *The Time-Image,* arguing for the deterritorializing of cinema in documentary and ethnographic practice. By lending support to the "minor" and "imperfect," he implicitly conjures up what is sometimes termed "oral cinema," that is, the use in situated practices of storytelling.[29] Associated with politically marginal cultures, as opposed to the studio spectacles of Hollywood (for which architecture would be the model) and auteurist European film (writing as model), storytelling connotes social action more than representation. A throng of anthropologists—not to mention Walter Benjamin—evoke the situation of the storyteller, who can now serve as prototype for a certain ethos of filmmaking on the margins.

The most visible such margin in recent years has been the one that marks the far western edge of Europe, where Irish cinema has produced enough storytellers not to need another Flaherty.[30] We imagine these filmmakers as children of a culture that for years has responded with accent and wit to the dull but hard realities of BBC news broadcasts. This is what William Butler Yeats had in mind when, actually invoking the spirit of the nomad, he distinguished Ireland as a place where tradition flashes up in transient images from the anecdotes of clever songs and poems. These forms are ideal for sniping at the thick novels and history books that anchor England.[31] Indeed, England was to Yeats what Hollywood is in this account, namely, the smothering status quo, heavy and predictable—the colonizing country that implemented in Ireland the first geological survey map ever commissioned so as to turn wild countryside into an extension of the striated logic of London. In response, Ireland engendered a nomadic mode of discourse, linked to its "traveling people" who (as in a film such as *Into the West*) recast their identity each night around the fire.[32] Those fires are now the xenon bulbs projecting Irish cinema, beckoning audiences to follow tales they will not encounter on the British airwaves or in Hollywood movies. Ireland turns out a score of films each year, some that could be said to constitute on the screen precisely what Deleuze identified as "minor" literature.

Let Hollywood colonize the globe and let nations erect the pretense of state television systems to protect their codified national cultures; the "soul of cinema" now emerges elsewhere, in movies assembled in scattered locations, then bicycled to outlying viewing sites and to diasporic cultures, the symbol of which is the film festival. The movies that today think the national beyond the nation travel from Rotterdam to Toronto to Berlin. Critics literally follow this moving camp to catch the rumor of cinema—and a rumor it is, for the "soul of cinema" is passed around as though by word of mouth, a transitional idea existing in passage.

BACK TO AFRICA

To the Deleuzian, the cinema is poised to begin its second century auspiciously, that is, as both oral and nomadic. Not an instrument to represent the world and to express the interior of man, it is a weapon of action (if not necessarily what Deleuze calls action-images), a machine to accumulate and transfer force in the purely exterior movement of the world. *Oral* and *nomadic* are words that aptly characterize even so quiet a film as Julie Dash's *Daughters of the Dust.* Determined to steer clear of Hollywood conventions, Dash's aspirations for the film differed from those of art films as well. As she proudly explained to bel hooks, her narrative technique emulates that of the African griot (traditional storyteller) in the indirection of the events, in the way her film moves languidly from one concern to another and then back again.[33] This is a migratory tale, she implies, told by a migratory people in transit from Africa to the United States. In the confidence and wisdom of its narration, *Daughters of the Dust* would calm and stabilize a dispersed and disoriented African-American society. It eloquently expresses the paradox of my title, for, although a tale of (and in) transition, it must at the same time be taken as a version of *Roots;* in other words, the film traces the migration of a lost nation back to its source in Africa, the birthplace of humanity. An American in flight from what America (and its image industry in Hollywood) has become, Dash looks to Africa as the source of what can only be called "rooted mobility."

Admirably, Dash never claims to adopt an African perspective; the griot serves only as an "intercessor" to encourage her search beneath the concrete surface of America where hidden pockets of heritage lie forgotten. Although Dash looked and listened to Africa for inspiration, many others have gone directly to Africa to locate and release images of untold power. Most have crassly exploited what I want to call the continent's "image mines" to startle the West from the outside. But even the most subtle and thoughtful traveling filmmakers run up against the conundrum familiar to ethnographers: how, as Westerners, to phase into a culture where these images are significant; how to appropriate images without expropriating them.

This issue, at once epistemological, ethical and aesthetic, touches on questions about the revered Jean Rouch, known by his biography as the "Cinematic Griot."[34] Despite the care with which Rouch approaches the peoples he so respects, his films nevertheless meddle in a culture that is not his. His trance films, for example, when projected in the villages where they were originally taken, have been known to provoke dangerous recurrences of the trance. Or consider the audacity of his determination to record the *Sigui*, the creation rites the Dogon people celebrate every sixty years. This ceremony has been passed on from elder to initiate for more than four hundred years, but now the Dogon peoples can dispense with their elders; they can watch the ceremony every Saturday night if they wish, and they can witness it as never before, from the high cliffs where Rouch perched his camera, taking in the full pattern of processions from a perspective they may never have imagined. Awed by the Dogon people, preserving this ritual out of respect for them, has not Rouch also endangered their cultural landscape and disturbed the process and perhaps the capacity of memory and orality? Cinema has altered Africa by exploring it, even when doing so conscientiously.

In different ways, Rouch and Dash raise the two-colored banner of nomadism and orality that would seem to link an African and a Deleuzian conception of cinema. Yet, neither filmmaker is African and both find themselves entangled in conundrums of borrowed or imagined identity. The site of so many early ethnographic films, Africa may destabilize conventional production, conventional imagery, and conventional film language, but Western notions always move in quickly to contain the continent's energy, usually pouring it into standard generic molds. In Deleuze's terms, Western encounters with an African aesthetic or spirit, even when inspired by the idea of deterritorializing Western notions, eventually reterritorialize the continent. Rouch certainly helped Africa discover its voice and its look through the films he made in concert with his subjects. Yet his position vis-à-vis African subjectivity is vexed. He may boast that he avoided stultifying documentary prescriptions with the surrealism of a form he dubbed the "ciné-trance," and he may claim to have instigated "ethnography in reverse"[35] by encouraging his African assistants to travel to Europe and record the odd habits and beliefs of the white natives in a style all their own; but Rouch nevertheless "turns Africans into insects," as Med Hondo and Ousmane Sembène once claimed.[36] Although Deleuze praises Rouch because "no one has done so much to put the West to flight, to flee himself, to break with a cinema of ethnology,"[37] should he be called the griot of a people to whom he does not belong? In fleeing the West, Rouch migrates to a culture that will never be his; indeed, Deleuze aptly argues that migrants have nothing in common with nomads because migrants leave a place they have come to doubt (Rouch leaving France) for one that promises more, whereas nomads cling to their land even when, as in the desert, it shifts under them.[38] Living on terrain, not territory, the nomad takes no account of borders. And if colonizers survey and coordinate the terrain, the nomad will reclaim it through lightning strikes that seem to come from nowhere[39] and from a "people who are missing" because they have yet to be "identified." The griot sings of such a land and to such a people, belonging to both. Rouch could only envy him, while Deleuze could find in him, as did Julie Dash, the ideal model of the filmmaker as agent or relay and of storytelling as emergent political act.

In tracking a nomad and oral cinema to Africa, if only to let these metaphors expand in the location they spontaneously call forth, one immediately encounters the filmmaker to whom the name "cinematic griot" was first applied, Ousmane Sembène. It is with him that one must begin.

ROOTING AROUND IN THE PAST

The one African filmmaker Deleuze discusses, Sembène took on the task of renaming a land and a people at the moment of decolonization. As André Gardies puts it, before Sembène, before 1960, "African cinema hardly belonged to the indigenous peoples. By the time of *Djeli* [1980], however, one could say that the continent had been spatially reappropriated by the native eye. The history of these twenty years shows the growth of cinema and the reconquest of space."[40] A man of incomparable influence and stature, Sembène set about identifying (and recoding) the agents, institutions, and practices of Africa once the French had been expelled. His films treat not just the wresting of the land from the French but its subsequent usurpation by a puppet class of Africans who succeeded them. For more than three decades Sembène has dramatized the struggle to decode African space, to deterritorialize it from interests that are literally entrenched. Deterritorialization forms the explicit topic of his last film, *Guelwaar* (1991), which concerns the exhumation of a treasured body (a martyr for the African cause who happens to be Christian) from even more treasured ground, a Muslim cemetery. The satire of Christians and Muslims arguing on opposite sides of a plot of land that neither can tread upon gives way to the film's more serious argument with regard to African dependency, an argument that the title character makes so loudly that he is killed for it. In the end—in the pithy and powerful final scene—the fight continues in Guelwaar's name, as the cart that bears his body grinds World Bank rice into the soil. Refusing to be bought off by a neocolonial politician, the Africans spurn the rice and spill it onto the earth that, as poor as they are, *belongs* to them; or rather, forms with the Africans an assemblage aimed at a future that will exclude the World Bank (a patronizing organization in any case).

To complement this defense of open terrain, Sembène simultaneously projects on the screen objects, people, and practices that had been invisible, because insignificant, to a colonial audience. Much of the comedy of *Mandabe* (1969), for instance, flows from the confrontation between the neocolonial bureaucracy and the indigenous gestures, habits, speech, and values of a character who had never been present in African cinema before. In "identifying" (naming) African practices and values, and in offering proverbial wisdom (shaming and praising), Sembène performs the role of the griot. Recognizing no boundaries, his oeuvre reconstitutes a moral and geographic landscape that had been confiscated by the French (and by others before them), a terrain on which gather "the people who are missing" as they shape themselves into a force.

Sembène's own paternalism, however, may blunt the force he wields. As I have argued elsewhere, Sembène's allegorical tales and proverbial, didactic style serve as homilies or illustrations of positions he has come to by way of politics, philosophy, and literature.[41] Indeed, he explicitly denigrates cinema in relation to literature, deigning to use it as the best available tool with which to broadcast his compelling Africanist views. Unquestionably, his mission to bring into view and to discuss social problems such as polygamy and religious intolerance has inspired the most ample strain of African cinema—numerous films on such pressing topics as the treatment of women, AIDS, governmental corruption, and so forth. As powerful and effective as these films may be, however, they do not point the way to an alternative cinema. Instead, in the mode pioneered in the Soviet Union, they employ variants of didactic cinema to help build an alternative society.

Still, an alternative cinema did sprout on terrain that Sembène sowed. In fact, two generations of African filmmakers since 1980 have ridden across this landscape with a camera that explores rather than broadcasts. They ride atop the cinema, often following its lead in an effort to discover and conceive a nation in the making. The sahel lies before them, unplotted, and they traverse it, sometimes following the shifting contours of sand and bush, sometimes taking ancestral paths, or sometimes picking their way at random. But invariably it seems they encounter a baobab, the great tree whose stature arrests the free movement of thought and cinema, turning filmmakers to a past represented by its roots. Ultimately, African cinema would yoke the dual impulses of liberty and identity, represented, respectively, by the open sahel and the rooted baobab.

Djeli inaugurates this second major phase of African cinema. In its elaborate pre-credit sequence, it projects the crucial constellation of elements that characterize this phase: a griot, accompanied by musicians, sings to a well-to-do family. He sings the legend of two brothers who, after wandering the sahel to the point of starvation, sit beside a baobab tree. One brother gives to the other something to eat; when the little meal is finished, the revitalized brother realizes he has partaken of flesh his sibling cut from his own body. This communion sequence under a baobab may stand to introduce not just *Djeli* but a strain of African cinema that would dominate critical writing for the next fifteen years.

Just two years after *Djeli*, Souleymane Cissé's *Finyé* (*The Wind*, 1982) shook ancestral spirits from just such a sacred tree. Up to this point Cissé's work had been, if anything, even more didactic than Sembène's in its direct, confrontational, anticolonial rhetoric. *Finyé* opens in the same vein, in the heat of a student revolt in contemporary Bamako, where ordinary politics, including revolutionary action, results in a familiar standoff. But suddenly Cissé sublimates this declarative mood into the interrogative and conditional syntax that would haunt his masterpiece *Yeelen* five years later. In this utterly new mood he embarks on a search for identity, looking for "a culture that looks like my people, like my country Mali ... [where] colonization is only an accident along the way."[42] He gives over his drama to the hero's grandfather, the last chief of his ethnic group, who, to save his grandson and the future of that group, calls up the forces of his ancestors to overwhelm contemporary political power. At the moment when all directly political options have been exhausted, this Bambara chief addresses the "Cosmic Tree" with cries that are echoed by those of invisible birds. On both sound and image tracks, the film shifts to a plane where the sacred can supervene in the injustice. To be sure, Sembène had occasionally represented magical powers, most memorably in the curse and fetishes of *Xala* (1974). But in that film he did so satirically, to ridicule an autocratic leader's impotence. In *Finyé*, on the other hand, Cissé shoots the tree ritually, to activate its power in order "to propose a sensual image of a mental image" that harbors a different kind of knowledge. Such knowledge is neither ethnographic (a description of an unfamiliar and fascinating religious rite) nor allegorical (a symbol for a complex notion).[43] It comes from elsewhere.

Cissé opens a door to such knowledge in the hermetic prologues and epilogues of his mature works. *Finyé*'s first shot is of a youth who pushes a floating calabash across still, pure water; the boy returns in the final shot to offer the calabash to a pair of hands reaching in from offscreen (Cissé would have his audience drink from this sacred source). Before the credits of both *Yeelen* and *Waati*, Cissé proposes geometric ideograms that are elements of an obscure cultic system meant to orient the episodes that follow, directing and sustaining heroic action, and representing in both cases an Africa in touch with a precolonial past and prepared for a postcolonial future. Consider *Yeelen*'s famous conclusion, where father and son at last stand to confront each other with all the powers they have mustered: here Cissé elevates his discourse from fiction to utter "fabulation." Again, a preadolescent boy unrelated to the film's plot brings an offering, this time a young goat. A powerful bull then lopes in from nowhere and approaches the camera in slow motion; a lion and an elephant are superimposed on the combatants until a flash of light annihilates the scene. Atop the completely desolate landscape, and across dunes of sand that have covered whatever was left of the past, runs a young boy, the hero's son born after his death. He digs two ostrich eggs from the sand (DNA, the perfect "body without organs," the virtual spirits of the impious father and the righteous son). He carries one back to his mother, who drapes his father's mantle on his shoulder. Under the confident pounding of a drum they mount another dune into some future.[44] And open land it is, sand moving underfoot that no colonizer will claim again. It belongs only to those who belong to it—to nomads who refuse to leave it, who live with it, and who locate its secret sources of energy, and release them.

Nomadic and free, *Yeelen* nevertheless recounts a patently tribal tale in which a son stands up to and destroys his father to make room, in turn, for his son and the growth of the family tree. On his journey to the Bandiagara cliffs, the womb of Malian culture, the son is urged on by the sudden appearance of a hyena's form in an enormous tree; the fabulous shape of this tree houses the spirits of his ancestors in this otherwise deserted and featureless landscape. Only an incalculable network of roots can sustain such a tree. In the sahel, raked by the harmattan winds that blow sand across the present, one gravitates to a tree like this or retreats to its shade as one does to history: it is made of memory. It stands as a living marker of the debt the present owes the past. The nomad may live creatively on open terrain—but he or she would quickly expire without heeding the admonitions and accepting the aid of the past. Indeed, this and other such African films should serve to caution those who find in Deleuze's vision of the nomad a completely untethered force. Already in 1972, he and Guattari took account of the organization of primitive societies, describing their complex and strict filiations and alliances, distinguishing them from the Oedipal organization that is the fate of those raised under capitalism.[45] On the one hand, Deleuze and Guattari argue that "one does not encounter in primitive societies any of the mechanisms or any of the attitudes that make it [the Oedipus complex] a reality in our society. No superego, no guilt. No identification of a specific ego with global persons." But they stipulate, on the other hand, that the primitive subject (the nomad) is nevertheless bound and located by "group identifications that are always partial."[46] What else are tattoos, scarring, circumcisions, excisions, and initiations if not marks of identity and belonging? If nomadic affiliations are ultimately "healthy," though, this is because they are fully external, always partial, and dispersed among series of ancestors or fragmented among cousins and comrades.[47] Hence, the struggle of father and son in *Yeelen* is neither personal nor psychological; it is cosmic. As Deleuze would have it, mother earth once served as the motor that organized "the flux," including especially the bodies and labor of social groups. But when the power of mother earth was replaced by that of the despot (the father, in the case of *Yeelen*), the flux was coded in an increasingly abstract manner. Son annihilates father to return the earth to its primordial, uncoded state in which humans again carry out its needs rather than strive to dominate it.

Nianancora, the son, may be a hero, but he is not in any important sense an individual; nor is *Yeelen* a bildungsroman. Nianancora holds a position by birth that puts him in the way of forces operating all around him. He accumulates resources and relays powers outside himself, focusing them wherever needed. Enormous energy, enough to remake the earth, passes through him, provided that he aligns himself properly. He may shift ground as a nomad, but only so as to maintain or improve alignment. All this requires specific knowledges: knowledge of fire, initiation to the seven grades of the Komo society, knowledge accorded by herbs and by animals, powers gained in an alliance with the Peuls, and most important the secret of the fetish stones in the Wing of Kore. Such esoteric knowledge can conjure and consolidate within humans various powers in the earth. When these powers are privatized or squandered (as in the case of Soma, the father), stagnation and misery follow; when, instead, they are nurtured and released by human groups, a general bounty accrues, resulting in an age of plenty (the Malian empire of the thirteenth and fourteenth centuries, for instance).

Thus, nomads are not rebellious individualists; rather, they are diligent students of the earth, which they serve and to which in a real sense they belong. The markings on their bodies (affiliating them with a certain group, allying them with a specific animal, signaling their state and occupation) do not so much reify them as make them available for action (and nomads exist only to act). In concert with others (with an assemblage), they become more than their bodies, as their identities dissolve into the "becoming" of some act for which specific bodies with specially marked functions are required. In a sense, "Nianancora as individual" was annihilated from the outset, well before his confrontation with his father, whereas "Nianancora as marked man" was essential to the cosmic drama for which he was selected.

Deleuze and Guattari point forward to Nianancora when, in *Anti-Oedipus*, they list the two primary characteristics of the hunter (the nomad), that "great paranoiac of the brush or the forest: real displacement with the flows and direct filiation with god."[48] Indeed, these are the founding characteristics of Gaston Kaboré's *Wend*

Kuuni. A quiet film made the same year as *Finyé* (1982), it too goes in search of indigenous African values in the precolonial era. In its easygoing style and music, and in its occasional voice-over narration, *Wend Kuuni* sounds like a communal performance of a village legend. The film opens with a young boy lost in the brush who is given the name Wend Kuuni, "Gift of God," by those who discover him. His wandering will henceforth be spiritual, for, mute and amnesiac, he is determined, under the benevolent care of his adoptive family, to recover his past and his speech. Marie-Magdalene Chirol has argued that, in discovering his identity (that is, mother and father), Wend Kuuni effectively discovers "ma" and "da, " the primary phonemic elements that permit articulate speech.[49] This *Nachträglichkeit* occurs one dark evening when he leaves the village to look for a knife he has left under a baobab tree. What Wend Kuuni discovers, instead, is that from one of the branches of the baobab an outcast of the village has hanged himself. Suddenly, he is shocked into a "rememory": memories of Wend Kuuni and his mother being expelled from their village overcome him, and finally he recollects how she died, from sickness and starvation, under a baobab tree. Confronting the corpse, Wend Kuuni is released from his ignorance; he returns able to speak to his new family and to greet a welcoming village that has patiently awaited his recovery.

Adoption here (and in Cissé's 1996 *Waati*) suggests that social relations transcend biology and that the baobab tree of Africa is so vast as to interrelate distant branches and roots. Nevertheless, identity and heritage are at the top of those specifically African values that Cissé believes an indigenous cinema must express. This is unmistakably the case in *Keita*, whose original title, "From Mouth to Ear," announces its connection to the oral tradition. A triumph at the 1995 Pan-African Film Festival (FESPACO), *Keita*, like *Wend Kuuni* and *Yeelen*, recounts a recovery through memory of the lost power of ancestors, but this time memory and narration are more than the *means* to recovery; they have taken center stage as the *recovery itself*. The boys of the earlier films wander alone into the wilderness to seek their destiny in the past, but young Mabo Keita never leaves the bustle of Ouagadougou, where his parents and teachers bring him up in a style proper to our times. And yet, the young Mabo, urged on by Djeliba, the griot, embarks on his own life-changing journey against the wishes of his parents and teachers, whose language and values he comes to question. One day, when the boy is reading aloud from a French science book, he is interrupted by Djeliba, who is shocked to hear Mabo recite that humans descend from gorillas. Henceforth, Djeliba determines to tell Mabo of his genuine ancestors so as to help him establish his name and place.

To halt the smooth slide of education from family to state modernism, the griot plants a vertical obstacle in the way, a tree of memory one must avoid or whose roots and branches one must explore. The film would be such an obstacle for its spectators, who for a time (ninety-six minutes in this case) are diverted from their habitual paths and onto another plane of experience, a parallel one of fabulation. The deliberate construction of a world, fabulation sets *Keita* going with the chant of origins that accompanies the opening credits. The camera pans along the body of Djeliba, sleeping in his hammock, slowing closing in on his face; as we enter his mental space, where images of lava and larvae intermix, his voice recounts the birth of the world from chaos. How long has the griot slept? Centuries perhaps, for he comes from another time, as the hunter will tell Mabo in the final sequence. Now, however, Djeliba is awakened by an antique hunter and rises to intervene in our time. He gathers his lanky form and lopes across the lyrical landscape, bringing his story and his truth into a city full of motorbikes and merchants. He will relate to Mabo the great epic of Soundjata, the king who consolidated the Malian empire in the fourteenth century; indeed, it is an epic whose first incident features the hunter who awakened him in the first place. Thus, we travel along the film as on a Möbius strip, for the hunter has tweaked the memory of the griot, who sings a tale of this very hunter. Moreover, centuries ago the hunter predicted for the king of the Mande the actions that would make him the legendary king whose dynasty has trickled down through history to this boy—the same boy listening fascinated to the legend of his origin. The film's climax lies not in the legend, since Djeliba stops with Soundjiata's exile rather than with his triumph, but rather in Mabo's life, when, incurring the anger of his parents and teachers, he determines to accept the quest to bring his heritage to life.[50] Djeliba abandons him by a baobab near his house (the same tree in which he sat, relaying to his friends the griot's sacred knowledge). In the final shot, Mabo circles its immense trunk, promising to locate other griots to help him explore the roots of his past and to project the branches of the future of his people. A sacred bird circles above, auguring success . . .

And succeed he does, for the boy (or rather a boy, Dani Kouyate) grew up to make this very film. The griot, Djeliba, is played by a genuine griot—the director's father, Sotigui Kouyate, a familiar voice and face to those in West Africa. Thus the son "in real life," as we say, having heard his father's tales, did indeed go in search of his larger past, taking a doctorate in ethnology in Paris and earning a certificate in filmmaking so as to sing this tale to a new generation, in a new (visual) register.

In the very form of its narration, *Keita* passes down not only Djeliba's parting words to Mabo that "the present always emerges from the past," but also the implication that the past is controlled by those in power. For Djeliba has also asserted, and the film has directly shown, that "there are several sorts of truth," several "in compossible worlds," to use the term Deleuze borrows from Leibniz. The griot, rather like Deleuze in the realm of philosophy, borrows, reworks, and re-cites from a tradition so as to bring something new into existence. In countering the French teacher, Djeliba recites an adage apt for the film as a whole: "Do you know why in stories, the hunters always kill the lion? It's because they are the ones who tell the stories. If lions told stories, they would win from time to time." *Keita* is a tale told by a lion. The animal and the vegetal, like the past, hover about the present and can be called upon—called up—through a certain use of speech. Deleuze terms such speech "fabulation," and more and more African movies are made of it. The baobab is, thus, a "fabulous" tree that encourages transit among worlds.[51]

The attractive conceit of cineast as griot, explicit in *Djeli, Keita, Jom, Waati, Po di Sangui,* and *Guimba,* implicit in *Yeelen, Wend Kuuni, Sababu,* and dozens more, empowers an otherwise impoverished African cinema by neutralizing the demands of realism on the one hand and of spectacle on the other. Med Hondo proclaimed this hierarchy in the final moments of his *Sarraounia* (1985), the epic of a historical warrior woman who stood up to colonization just before the turn of the century. Victorious first over her local rivals, then holding out bravely against French invaders, Sarraounia marches triumphantly back into her palace at the head of an assortment of African peoples whom she will rule with a strong yet liberal hand. Her magnificent speech proclaiming a new era of fraternity and tolerance would seem to be the film's last word, but Med Hondo reserves that for himself, or rather for his forefather, the griot in the film who sings: "what good are glorious deeds without the griot to call them up? When all is dust, only the griot's words will be left."

But the griot's role as "fabulator"—one who brings past and possible worlds into coexistence with a present whose "reality" is greatly reduced—must be disciplined by his more primary function as "relay." True, the griot may liberally adapt lore and traditional wisdom to the concerns of the moment; but he must never forget the past, which is both a tree of knowledge to which he is bound (literally indebted) and a family tree to which he is simply bound by fortune of birth. In this he shares more with the devoted historian that Paul Ricoeur celebrates[52] than with the wild inventor that Deleuze has in mind. The griot may conjure the past to liberate his people from the yoke of Islam (*Ceddo*) or from French colonialism (*Jom*), but the past he calls upon exacts its own demands and is as inescapable as fate. The griot gathers his group beneath the revered baobab, where he reassures them once again of their identity, both collective and individual ("Do you know what your name means, Keita?") in the face of colonial armies and global businesses that would parcel out the land in abstract "coordinates." The tree may very well root the culture to terrain; outside its shade, however, one dies of exposure.[53]

In his "nomadology," Deleuze writes not of griots, but of smiths who follow veins of ore, liquefying metal in an alchemical transformation. The griot's ore must be the incontrovertible lessons of the past, the wisdom and legends he transforms into tools and weapons that can be used today. He passes down what might be termed familial, tribal, or racial heritage. The griot searches the flat expanse of the African sahel for evidence of history, for traces of ancestors and animals, knowledge that is essential to nourish the village, to keep it from blowing away in the harmattan winds of change. A nomad of the spirit, the griot locates catch basins of holy water where the past collects in subterranean wells. For many years now, a wonderful line of African filmmakers have, again and again, dipped their buckets into those wells so as to turn this land into something sustaining.

THE IDENTITY OF NOMADS AND GRIOTS

Walter Benjamin distinguished storytelling as a literary and political act, as opposed to the novel, which he argued had degenerated into a false and vain object, a fetish.[54] The storyteller's public ethos mocks the privacy of the novelist, who, late at night, alone in a study, concocts the intimate psychological states of characters. Bent on invention, the novelist fixes words to a page, pages in a book, and books in the institution of the library so as to solidify this airy practice. The griot, by contrast, relays a common heritage. He shapes traditional tales with wit and savvy to fit the moment of their performance; he names landmarks in a complex genealogy that he accesses by moving in time up and down the trunk of the great tree. In *Keita*, for instance, Djeliba brags to the French instructor that he knows the meaning of the names of all but a few animals. To name is to call up the power of an animal or a spirit in a tree. Storytelling amounts to a grand gesture of naming, a supremely political act that reanimates the community that listens. No wonder so many African filmmakers have claimed, perhaps prematurely, the mantle of the griot: they would address with vivid images a local community to whom those images starkly apply.

Nevertheless, filmmakers fix their tales indelibly on celluloid, and they send them off as commodities in a system of cultural and entertainment exchange. Few African films muscle their way into the local distribution system, where they might speak to the groups they aim to both challenge and reassure; for distribution is dominated in the cities by a single global company (Sopacia) and in the rural areas by Lebanese entrepreneurs who tender mainly Hindu movies.[55] *Guelwaar*, perhaps the most discussed African film of the decade, waited years to get a booking in Sembène's home city of Dakar. In Africa the film could be seen at FESPACO, as well as at other festivals; Sembène literally followed it around the world. Indeed, although African filmmakers might well prefer the image of the nomad, many seem destined to live like migrants, moving from festival to festival, campus to campus, to present their work.[56] On these travels they conjure up future projects with others in the caravan, or they attach themselves to the sources of money and technology that they come across: a distribution promise from a European TV network, a grant for post-production in a Parisian editing house, an alliance with an Afro-pop composer encountered at a festival cocktail party.

On the one hand, then, African filmmakers keep from foundering on the hazards of a haphazard existence by projecting images of a rooted past, an ancestral tree that secures an identity they can proudly proclaim. On the other hand, by so adamantly announcing who they are, these filmmakers may yet limit what they can become. At least, this is the warning that Deleuze and Guattari sound at the outset of *A Thousand Plateaus* when they flatly rail against social, cultural, and philosophical systems that depend on models of trees or roots. Instead, they propose the rhizome or rat's maze, where intricate paths are dispersed and interconnected without trunk or center. The nomad, the smith, and (by extension) the griot are meant to exemplify the unpredictable movement and wildcat production patterns associated with rhizomatic multiplicity. But Deleuze's search for a deterritorialized cinema, a cinema of images without representation,[57] a desiring machine functioning on a smooth surface without the responsibilities and reassurances of "identity," runs into the submerged wells and roots that so aptly characterize African art. Needless to say, griots and the traditions that they relay promote the stability of family, tethering people to land. They pass on the past as parents pass on genes to their children. Heritage, paternity, and territory compose the content and the form of orality, an indispensable cultural function for groups living in fragile ecological zones such as the West African sahel. Thus, *Keita* attains its self-confidence (enough to boldly challenge Western science, history, and cinema) only by retreating to tradition in a manner seemingly at odds with Deleuze's expansive conception of the nomadic. *Keita*, and above all *Yeelen*, proclaim the victory of a new Africa over suffocating oppression, but they do so by venerating the laws of lineage and of repetition, rather than those of freedom and dispersal that Deleuze associates with the nomad.

Can African filmmakers make themselves and their peoples feel secure *about* their roots without securing them *to* those roots? This is the explicit project of *Keita*, because Mabo is determined not only to learn the repressed traditional knowledge of his group, but also to attend French school and perhaps one day to study ethnography in Paris. The future of Mabo's city, Ouagadougou, will likewise need to draw from a varied past and varied languages. The griot teaches Mabo to revere, explore, and call upon the tree of heritage, particularly in times of need; presumably, once nourished and rested, once secure about his value, Mabo (suggesting Africa) will go out from the shade of the tree into the sahel at large to encounter the new in a perpetual act of becoming a people. In this way heritage can be taken as a stage, a state of accumulated power, a "plateau" on the way to becoming something else. Identity serves as a stake or "marker" in Africa's gamble with modernity. Rather than "winner take all," this game rewards compromise and negotiation as Africa develops an appropriate stance in unpredictable conditions.

For African filmmakers, negotiation takes place at European festivals where "difference" is prized. Precolonial tales and tales depicting village life, especially when these involve animist practices, have been welcomed because they are so prominently marked and so readily *identifiable*. They have also been patronized as "calabash" films, that is, as endearing but unsophisticated pictures. Some Western connoisseurs and critics, raised in the auteurist spirit of the New Wave, scout each year's small crop of films for "naive" masterpieces with fresh cinematic syntax and technique. The warm European reception accorded Idrissa Ouedraogo, for instance, stems surely from the picturesque village scenes and practices he portrays without apology (the "Pagnol of the sahel," he has been dubbed). In 1972, Djibril Diop-Mabety surprised the West with *Touki-Bouki,* whose inventive verve was favorably compared to *Pierrot le fou* and *Easy Rider*. After a hiatus of twenty years, Diop-Mambety again startled the critics with his ingenuity, even though *Hyenas,* his new film, was adapted from a canonical European play (Friedrich Dürrenmatt's *The Visit*). *Hyenas* constituted a "discovery" because its exotic locales, brash colors, and unabashed theatricality produce an allegory of African desperation—a desperation perhaps underscored by the story's Swiss origin. In sum, the bold assertion of (ethnic) identity and difference, so important in the works I have grouped as griot films, plays well in the auteurist ambiance of film festivals.

The central tenet of auteurism, that a cinematic style exhibit a consistent and distinct worldview, prepares Western viewers to welcome African films that veer from known patterns, particularly when they do so in a deliberate (exotic) manner. Conceived, marketed, and viewed as "authored" works, the griot films that have drawn attention since 1980, perhaps despite themselves, contribute to a modernist idea of cinema in the West, and this initiates a familiar hermeneutic. The Western spectator, confronting an image issuing from a very different world, struggles to understand that world not so as to adopt it but so as to comprehend his or her own world from an expanded perspective. Paul Ricoeur provides the terms of this hermeneutic, which can be deduced from his theory of metaphor as productive insertion of the foreign into discourse. In Ricoeur's hermeneutics, human beings and entire nations stand open to change and interchange when their own worlds become vulnerable to complete rediscription through the shocking and exciting application of an image or perspective that comes from some other human or nation.[58] Identity, including national or ethnic identity, exhibits the stability of a text; although one can interpret, criticize, or supplement it, its coherence is presumed, if only to be modified in history. Modern cinema, auteurist and textual, invites and rewards such a hermeneutic. Insofar as African films present themselves as texts or are treated as texts harboring a different vision of the world, they assert an identity, and they do so identifiably.

In a book tellingly titled *Soi-même comme un autre* (*Oneself as*

Another), Ricoeur treads a middle way or, more precisely, weaves a network of paths between the extremes of the indubitable Cartesian ego on the one side and the shattered a-subject of Nietzsche and Deleuze on the other. These paths, he argues, are narratives perpetually on the way toward identity. Whether an individual human, a social group, or an entire nation is at issue, "identity" is projected by narratives whose temporal form permits an image of a coordinated "body" to emerge.[59] Because narratives depict a character (or self) in the making, they constitute a privileged means of exploring, doubting, and experimenting with identity.

The nation or social group is a relatively stable collection of subjects whose habits and features have sedimented into an "identifiable" people (117–21). Of course, habit is just what Deleuze is out to destroy; after all, he exhorts a "repetition becoming difference" that would effectively unhinge life from its habitus, from its certainty. But habit can be, as it is for Ricoeur, an affirmation of constancy in the face of change, including the change of the body that houses (maintains) the habit. Ricoeur does not argue for an immutable ego, still less for a substantial self. His distinction between "idem" and "ipse" is meant to nuance what Deleuze paints as a stark opposition between flux and fixity (2–4). "Idem" refers to the selfsame entity; when time is factored in, it implies organic growth. Ricoeur resorts to a familiar metaphor to distinguish "idem" in narratives and in history, the metaphor of the acorn inevitably becoming the oak. "Ipse," on the other hand, refers to the agent of narrative or of history who is a source not just of growth but of self-questioning and even of radical change. "Ipse" may undergo changes, but it does not disperse into Deleuze's "being of becoming"; that is to say, "ipse" acknowledges today promises made in the past, even against the mutations that meanwhile have occurred not just in the world but in the self. Ricoeur applies his terms to the nation as well as to the individual: as "idem," the nation is taken to be a set of immutable traits (this is the "racial" position of fascism), but as "ipse" it is a changing, historical entity that nevertheless maintains its alliances, treaties—in short, its promises—both to its people and to other nations (123). The nation as "ipse" acts and speaks not out of immutable traits but out of a past it faithfully attests to as its heritage, even though it may seek a different future.

Originally, it was the protean character of storytelling that led me to the griot films of Africa as the most promising sites (or engines) of Deleuzian nomad thought. But the textual integrity of *Wend Kuuni*,

Yeelen, *Keita*, and the others, particularly because they attest to a distinct tradition represented by a sacred tree, urges instead that they be treated as solid beings with which spectators and critics engage in dialogue and critique. This standard hermeneutic enterprise amounts to a more familiar and a tamer politics than that implied by Deleuze's nomadology. Perhaps anticipating this recuperation, insisting on the deeply revolutionary aspirations of the strongest strain of African cinema and determined to ally this strain with Deleuze's radical project, D. N. Rodowick has fastened on African "fabulation" to dissolve identity altogether. His task is delicate, for he applauds films that shatter identity into fragments that can recombine in a movement of "becoming-other" while he simultaneously ratifies the political goal of African filmmakers to provide "an image that will summon a people into existence as identity becoming-other."[60] This double action of *shattering* while *summoning* identity liberates the force of cohesion that lies behind what was once termed "subjectivity" and "nation." In the millennium Deleuze longs for, this force would thus stand available for untold mutations and combinations. The enemy of the "force" is the "reactionary" philosopher (Aristotle or Descartes, one might imagine) who "would bolster the Ego against change, exhausting life by freezing identity." "Ego = Ego is replaced with *I is an other*," writes Rodowick, and "[t]o become-other is not to identify or to identify with and so to-become-the-same-as. Rather ... it is to affirm the ever-recurring possibility for change" (150–51).

Ricoeur's hermeneutics likewise outruns foundational philosophy and paves the way for profound change—but change that occurs incrementally to established entities. When Deleuze asks the rhetorical question, "Which is your will to power? To become-the-same-as or to become-other?" he could very well have Ricoeur in mind. Deleuze insists on pressing the subject beyond its presumed "self" and into affiliations and conjunctions (such as, perhaps, the incipient nation) that it does not control. The cinema, conventionally deemed the premiere medium of imitation, finds its true and compelling mission, according to Deleuze, in producing a "discourse [that establishes] the potentiality for the enunciation of the collective will" (152). Ricoeur, by contrast, would retain Deleuze's insistence on "becoming" without relinquishing the historical remnants, the roots, of what the entity has already become. Ricoeur understands continuity of development to yield unpredictable outcomes in history, the result of encounters between an ultimately unknowable other with a predicating (and to that extent "predictable") self. The griots of *Djeli*,

Jom, *Keita*, and *Po di Sangui* (especially the latter two) confidently predicate the heritage that makes them what and who they are. And exactly what are they? They are texts addressing a people; they are textual bodies addressing and addressed by us.

EPILOGUE: SURVIVAL, GOING WITH THE FLOWS

Deleuze's cinema machine outruns the anthropomorphism of textual bodies, including the griot films that stand out so deliberately as texts in the art-cinema tradition. However, it should run directly into a more recent strain of images spewing from the nascent urbanism across the African continent. In Ouagadougou (*Haramuya*), in Yaounde (*Quartier Mozart*), and in Kinshasa (*Macadam Tribu*), unauthorized communities can be glimpsed taking shape beneath the repressive official life of the cities into which they have burrowed. Diverse religions, moralities, pasts, and pursuits tangle and intertwine haphazardly in a kind of Afro-pop cinema, as these films take on a rhythm and tone that give them, and the groups they treat, a powerful momentum toward an open future. In *Macadam Tribu*, whose title makes this very point, the characters survive by outwitting authorities, making accommodations to one another, and fashioning communal projects (notably a theater) that begin to provide definition and cohesiveness. Among the several characters whose plot lines are juggled in all three films, one finds a griot figure speaking the wisdom of the village past. But the authority of tradition for which they stand ends up contributing to, rather than dominating, the life of the urban village in the making. An underground economy serves nontraditional family organizations: pleasure, money, and education somehow emerge in a swirl of movement accelerated by the pace of urban sounds and transportation. People who do not count—who literally are unaccounted for by the state—concoct ingenious tactics to survive and sometimes to thrive on the side streets and in the ghetto maze of alleys and shanties. Whether they bring it with them from the brush or whether it blossoms in this chaotic environment, a musical pulse lends character and raw hope in even the worst of situations.

Where *Keita* and *Yeelen* stand firm as trees in the sahel reaching down with their roots to the pure water of heritage, *Macadam Tribu*, *Quartier Mozart*, and *Haramuya* sing the hybrid sounds of Afro-pop, skimming across the streets of mushrooming cities, picking up instruments and new rhythms as they move along. The protean quality of the many characters in these films, their need to adapt to constantly changing conditions so as to exploit the slightest opportunity, corresponds to the equally protean quality of the social groups they come to compose. All three films celebrate the persistence of an indomitable spirit by bringing to bear their own irrepressible vitality. The result of ad hoc financial and production "hustling," each of these films has projected itself into existence by dint of an entirely fabricated (fabulated) momentum. Afro-pop films cannot fall back on some bedrock of tradition, for in an urban environment any form of "identity" must factor in differences in religion, language, and morality. Yet confident they are, as their characters trump up ingenious solutions and contrive unlikely combinations to survive against insurmountable economic obstacles and outright injustice. Tracing rhizomatic patterns now that the roots back to their villages have been severed, these characters—these urban nomads—invent themselves as groups or groupings. Such invention is suffused with an exuberant rhythm that it would be unthinkable to stop (unthinkable, for movement is, effectively, what is thought).

In the final sequences of *Macadam Tribu*, for instance, a community enterprise transforms a boxing ring into a theater and prepares its first production. While actors rehearse a play onstage about popular rebellion, television and radio broadcast reports of the country's dictator toppling; artistic invention and the social imaginary seem to project an actual political future that is equally ad hoc, equally in the making. In a wonderful gesture of irony, this local theater must, in order to survive economically, alternate its repertoire with Bruce Lee movies. Indeed, the film's last line of dialogue cites Bruce Lee, an international hero for the downtrodden as well as a media star. And why not? Purity has never been the aim of Afro-pop. Many sounds are needed, many different tempos, whose interplay, if the musicians are skillful and confident enough, will produce from this cacophony a new rhythm altogether, giving a provisional shape to separate lines and forces. "Identity" in these three Afro-pop films is nothing other than persistence and survival. Identity is on the move in African cities, for in such places identity *is* movement ... exciting, unpredictable, and rhizomatic movement.

One final astonishing development attests to the "health" of African cinema despite all the factors that combine to strangle it. Today in Nigeria and Ghana entrepreneurs shoot videos with camcorders in Igbo, Hausa, and especially Yoruba languages for the direct-to-video market.[61] A completely decentered system of production, video films largely bypass centers of exhibition as well. These images are never projected at festivals and are scarcely exported. Indeed, they are not made for movie theaters (which, dangerous to attend in Lagos and other cities, are being transformed into churches one by one). Nevertheless, their success in these densely populated countries and their minuscule budgets have made these video films the first commercially successful motion-picture movement in Africa. Whereas throughout its history Nigeria had produced fewer than two hundred features in thirty-five millimeter, more than five hundred video films were made from 1993 to 1997.[62] Speculators in Ghana, a country without any feature film heritage, turned out more than fifty of these video films in a single year.[63]

Such wildcat production boomed once distributors realized that they could easily sell tapes in the city markets in addition to renting halls with video projectors for a paying audience. They find a huge public through billboard advertising of newborn stars, through radio and television spots, and through word of mouth (still the strongest source of information in Africa). A traditional system of debts and favors has kept costs low, for actors appear in films for free, just to pay off an earlier reciprocal favor. Such alliances and filiations in production, as well as the exploitation of open (or black) markets, and of ancient trading routes in distribution (especially to Yoruba villages), make video films an unbelievably disorganized yet energetic enterprise. Of course, what appears disorganized to the state, which still manages to exact a censorship fee in most cases, or to any centralized view of culture suggests a kind of "self-governing" economy of which Deleuze would, I think, approve. These images seem to come up through cracks in the culture; mostly uncataloged and unlisted, they spread and multiply wherever they find room. Western critics may never know or care to know what they look like. Effectively self-generating and unauthored, they should be classified as events rather than texts. They do not solicit scholars like Deleuze, but circulate in apparent randomness in West Africa. They do not stand up for themselves like baobab films; nor do they reach an international audience like the Afro-pop movies. So far they have succeeded in bypassing us altogether. These are "movies-that-are-missing," movies that circulate outside our discourse; they are significant by virtue of being insignificant to us—or, better yet, by virtue of frustrating our critical radar. Ultimately, the vitality, rather than the wisdom or beauty, of these images attests to a force before which philosophy and criticism stand hopelessly in awe.

NOTES

1. Gilles Deleuze, "Letter to Serge Daney: Optimism, Pessimism, and Travel," in *Negotiations, 1972–1990,* trans. Martin Joughin (New York: Columbia University Press, 1995), 77.
2. Gilles Deleuze, *The Movement-Image,* trans. Hugh Tomlinson and Barbara Habberjam (Minneapolis: University of Minnesota Press, 1988), 206.
3. Deleuze seems to have encountered the cinema precisely during the insurgency of auteurism, when he was a young intellectual of the postwar era. Although he elaborates the "time-image" in relation to auteurs, it is a concept whose logic would seem to transcend this period and attitude of the cinema.
4. Fredric Jameson develops the three stages of classicism, modernism, and postmodernism in "The Existence of Italy," in *Signatures of the Visible* (New York: Routledge, 1991).
5. Timothy Corrigan, *A Cinema without Walls* (New Brunswick, N.J.: Rutgers University Press, 1993).
6. Gayatri Spivak, "Can the Subaltern Speak?" in *Marxism and the Interpretation of Culture,* ed. Cary Nelson and Lawrence Grossberg (Champaign: University of Illinois Press, 1988), 271–318 (especially 275).
7. Ibid., 280.
8. Gilles Deleuze and Félix Guattari, *A Thousand Plateaus: Capitalism and Schizophrenia,* trans. Brian Massumi, (Minneapolis: University of Minnesota Press, 1987), 53.
9. Paul Ricoeur, *La Métaphore vive* (Paris: Éditions du Seuil, 1975), especially 379.
10. Deleuze and Guattari, *A Thousand Plateaus,* 367.
11. In Gilles Deleuze, *The Movement-Image* and *The Time-Image,* trans. Hugh Tomlinson and Robert Galeta (Minneapolis: University of Minnesota Press, 1988), see especially the latter, 222–23; in D. N. Rodowick, *Gilles Deleuze's Time Machine* (Durham, N.C.: Duke University Press, 1997), 156–59.
12. Laura Marks has embarked on this project, though employing the notion of "hybrid" rather than "nomadic" cinema. See her "A Deleuzian Politics of Hybrid Cinema," *Screen* 35:3 (autumn 1994).
13. Deleuze, *The Movement-Image,* 1–3.
14. André Bazin, "Defense of Rossellini," in *What Is Cinema?,* vol. 2, trans. Hugh Gray (Berkeley: University of California Press, 1970).
15. This curious and unconscious echo of Bazin one finds in Deleuze and Guattari's *A Thousand Plateaus* (369) in a section whose topic is precisely bridge building! Deleuze and Guattari also mock "stonecutting . . . by means of *templates,*" which comes from "Royal Science" (365), and promote "ambulent sciences that consist in following a flow in a vectoral field across which singularities are scattered like so many 'accidents'" (372).
16. "[Life] is a pure process that always operates in the middle, *au milieu,*" writes Daniel Smith in his introduction to Gilles Deleuze, *Essays Critical and Clinical,* trans. Daniel W. Smith and Michael A. Greco (Minneapolis: University of Minnesota Press, 1997), liii.
17. Deleuze and Guattari, *A Thousand Plateaus,* 374.
18. See my "Praying Mantis: Enchantment and Violence in French Cinema of the Exotic," in *Visions of the East,* ed. Matthew Bernstein and Gaylyn Studlar (New Brunswick, N.J.: Rutgers University Press, 1997), 233–41. Poirier himself had just contributed to this genre with *Caïn,* a 1929 "ethnographic fiction" involving the peoples of Madagascar, to be sure, and filmed largely on location, but whose star, it turns out, though Malagasy by birth, had been raised in luxury in Paris and spoke without an accent. Poirier's personal itinerary from filming the pygmies of Central Africa to photographing a beautiful Parisian citizen who signified "Africanness" measures the shift toward the highly coded images of the classical period.

19. I take this distinction between tactics and strategy from Michel de Certeau, *The Practice of Everyday Life*, trans. Steven Rendall (Berkeley: University of California Press, 1984).
20. Dana Benelli, "Jungles and National Landscapes: Documentary and the Hollywood Cinema in the 1930s," unpublished Ph.D. thesis, University of Iowa, 1992.
21. Arthur Calder-Marshall, *The Innocent Eye* (Baltimore: Pelican Books, 1970), 77.
22. Deleuze, *The Movement-Image*, 143.
23. The best source of information on this film comes from Pat Mullen, *Man of Aran* (Boston: MIT Press, 1935), 99–112.
24. Calder-Marshall, *The Innocent Eye*, 213.
25. André Bazin, *What Is Cinema?*, vol. 1, trans. Hugh Gray (Berkeley: University of California Press, 1967), 50–51.
26. Deleuze and Guattari give four laws of the "nomad or minor science." The first law insists that fluidity rather than solidity is the primary state of physical being, while the second insists that "the model in question is one of becoming and heterogeneity, as opposed to the stable, the eternal, the identical, the constant. It is a 'paradox' to make becoming itself a model" (*A Thousand Plateaus*, 361).
27. See especially Deleuze and Guattari: "the mercenary or mobile military instructor, and the technocrat or transhuman analyst, the CIA and IBM" (ibid., 403).
28. Fernando Solanas and Octavio Getino, "Toward a Third Cinema," in *New Latin American Cinema*, vol. 1, ed. Michael T. Martin (Detroit: Wayne State University Press, 1997); Julio García Espinosa, "For an Imperfect Cinema," originally published in *Cine-Cubana* (1970), translated in *Jumpcut* (May 1979).
29. The term *oral cinema* has become common since the essay by Manthia Diawara, "Oral Literature and African Film: Narratology in *Wend Kuuni*," in *Questions of Third Cinema*, ed. Paul Willemen (London: BFI, 1987), 199–211.
30. In fact, Flaherty was Irish by ancestry and is remembered as a legendary storyteller himself.
31. Yeats actually used the term *nomad* in characterizing Irish literature.
32. Yeats, however, was hardly a promoter of uprooted existence. His "Prayer for My Daughter" was that she be "rooted in one dear perpetual place." This comforting image of the "spreading laurel tree" of tradition corresponds to that of the African baobab tree celebrated in the films under discussion here.
33. Julie Dash, "Interview with bel hooks," in *Daughters of the Dust* (New York: New Press, 1992), 32.
34. Paul Stoller, *The Cinematic Griot* (Chicago: University of Chicago Press, 1992).
35. This is the title of Manthia Diawara's 1997 film on Jean Rouch, from which I have taken a great deal.
36. Albert Cervoni, "Une confrontation historique en 1965 entre Jean Rouch et Sembène Ousmane: 'Tu nous regardes comme des insectes,'" *CinémAction*, no. 81 ("Jean Rouch ou le ciné-plaisir," 1996): 104–6. See also Ibrahimi Signaté, *Med Hondo, un cinéaste rebelle* (Paris: Présence Africaine, 1994), 40.
37. Deleuze, *The Time-Image*, 223.
38. Deleuze and Guattari, *A Thousand Plateaus*, 380.
39. The French split the Tuareg people into four separate "countries" (Mali, Niger, Algeria, and Mauritania), the better to control them. But the Tuaregs have never been good citizens and, on many occasions, have not only ignored borders but have actively struck back from their shifting desert positions.
40. André Gardies, *Cinéma d'Afrique noire francophone: l'Espace miroir* (Paris: L'Harmattan, 1989), 7–8; my translation.
41. Dudley Andrew, "The Falaise in the Sahel," *iris* 18 (spring 1995): 113–24.
42. Souleymane Cissé, *Magazine Littéraire* (May 1983): 44; my translation. Cissé goes on to say, "Even if I take it [colonialism] into account, I don't consider it

fundamental in the emergence of certain values. By neglecting our own values we remain alienated, controlled by the values of others."

43. Samuel Lelievre, doctoral thesis on *Finyé* (University of Strasbourg, 1999).
44. See Susan McRae's essay on this film, "*Yeelen*: A Political Fable of a *Komo* Blacksmith," *Research in African Literatures* 26:3 (fall 1995): 57–68. See also my own essay, "The Falaise in the Sahel," and that of Philip Gentile, "In the Midst of Secrets: Souleymane Cissé's *Yeelen*," *iris* 18 (1995): 125–36.
45. Deleuze and Guattari address the family links of tribal societies in section 3 of *Anti-Oedipus: Capitalism and Schizophrenia*, trans. Robert Hurley, Mark Seem, and Helen R. Lane (Minneapolis: University of Minnesota Press, 1983).
46. Ibid., 143.
47. In his Introduction to Deleuze's *Essays Critical and Clinical*, Daniel Smith emphasizes that Deleuze substitutes the value of "the healthy" for the traditional value of "the good" in recentering philosophy on life and on the earth rather than on man and society (xv).
48. Deleuze and Guattari, *Anti-Oedipus*, 148.
49. Marie-Magdalene Chirol, "The Missing Narrative in *Wend Kuuni*," *Research in African Literatures* 26:3 (fall 1995): 53.
50. A survey of an indigenous audience after screenings of the film in Burkina Faso found spectators frustrated and disappointed that the famous legend was cut short ("Fespaco 1995 Critique cinématographique," ed. Jean-Claude Traoré Biny [dactylograph, Bobo-Doulasso, February 17, 1995], 15–24).
51. Among a host of films featuring fabulous trees, let me single out Safi Faye's *Mossane* (Senegal, 1995) and especially Flora Gomez's *Po di Sangui* (Guinea-Bissau, 1996). The latter, told by a female griot, is based on the premise that in villages of Guinea-Bissau a tree is planted at the birth of each child. The tree invariably outlives the person, for whom it is a metonymy; indeed, the spirit of the person passes into the tree at death. The drama turns on the destruction of a forest of such trees by those modernizing the country.
52. Paul Ricoeur, *Time and Narrative III*, trans. Kathleen McLaughlin and David Pellauer (Chicago: University of Chicago Press, 1988), 177. Ricoeur likens the novelist's fidelity to the fidelity the historian shows vis-à-vis the past.
53. Olivier Barlet takes a somewhat different view from mine in his extensive discussion of the cinematic griot: "The cineast is the modern griot . . . but his discourse is new. The confrontation of ancestral speech and imported modern values forces a new kind of discourse in which contemporary man (by means of a melange of cultures, and whether considered African or not) can recognize himself," *Les Cinémas d'Afrique noire: le regard en question* ([Paris: L'Harmattan, 1996] 168–69; my translation). Barlet writes of the *griot engagé*: "If the filmmaker sets the griot up as a model, it is to turn it around: his goal is not the cohesion of the group so much as its evolution" (179). That evolution now includes hybridity, the acceptance of certain Western influences, impurity, whereas I emphasize the griot as the one who aims first at the cohesion of the group through its heritage.
54. Walter Benjamin, "The Storyteller," in *Illuminations*, ed. Hannah Arendt, trans. Harry Zohn (New York: Schocken Books, 1969), 87 and 99.
55. Some filmmakers have taken their films on the road in their own country, showing them in village after village for a pittance (Christophe Bottéon, "Cinéma d'Afrique noire ou le talent sans moyens," *Cinéma*, no. 590 ([September 1997]: 15–17).
56. A few hours from where I write of them, a number of African filmmakers have appeared four times this very month, April 1998 (Creteil, Perpignan, Lyons, Milan).
57. See Spivak, "Can the Subaltern Speak?" 273–75. Since the composition of this essay, Christopher Miller has published *Nationalists and Nomads* (Chicago:

University of Chicago Press, 1998), which densely documents several key moments wherein France and French intellectuals have made use of an image of Africa. The final chapter, "Beyond Identity," is particularly apt, devoted as it is to a critique of Deleuze's concept of the "nomad."

58. Relevant here is Deleuze's (not quite parallel) concept of "the minor," where a foreign language or literature arises within a dominant one. See Gilles Deleuze and Félix Guattari, *Kafka: Toward a Minor Literature*, trans. Dana Polan (Minneapolis: University of Minnesota Press, 1986).
59. Paul Ricoeur, *Oneself As Another* (Toronto: University of Toronto Press, 1995), 142 and 147.
60. Rodowick, *Gilles Deleuze's Time Machine*, 141.
61. Most of my information regarding Nigerian video films comes from Onookome Okome, who has published several papers on the topic and lectured on it at the University of Iowa in April 1997. See especially his coauthored contribution to *Nigerian Video Films*, ed. Jonathan Haynes (Ibadan: Kraft Books, 1997).
62. These statistics can be found in Afolabi Adesanya, "From Film to Video," in Haynes, *Nigerian Video Films*.
63. Esi Sutherland-Addy, "The Ghanaian Feature Video Phenomenon," unpublished paper, Accra, 1996.

Thinking Images

Chapter 9

Cinema and the Outside

Gregg Lambert

The Fourth Dimension?! Einstein? Mysticism? Or a Joke?

—Sergei Eisenstein

CINEMA AND THE "FOURTH DIMENSION": EISENSTEIN'S THEORY OF INTELLECTUAL MONTAGE

One of the most important consequences of the direction taken by Gilles Deleuze in his two cinema books is not only to have raised the often neglected status of the cinematographic image as fundamental to any modern philosophy of time, but also to have situated the study of the image as crucial for discerning the link between the subject and thought that has evolved in the modern period around the problem of ideology. As a result of Deleuze's inquiry into the cinematographic "movement-image" as basis for understanding the nature of this link, we are again compelled to consider the relationship between cinema and thought. In other words, what kind of image is to be deduced from thought and how can thinking be determined by an image? How does the image first acquire its power over thought in order to provoke the event called "thinking" to happen within a subject?

Taking up these questions as early as 1929, Eisenstein wrote a brief review in the journal *Kino* in which he announced the discovery of a "fourth dimension" of cinematographic duration—spatially inexpressible, "time added to three-dimensional space"—the appearance of which is the result of "overtonal conflicts" between visual and sound images.[1] For Eisenstein, with the advent of the montage process, the fact that new arrangements of aural and visual signals cannot be determined spatially underlines the significance of the cinematic apparatus for registering a sensation of movement that is impossible for "natural perception." This is because visual and aural overtones are *"a totally physiological sensation"* and, consequently, "they are *of one and the same kind*, outside the sound and visual categories that serve as guides" (70; emphasis in original), but rather function as "conductors" that introduce new effects within the spectator's perception-consciousness system and engender the possibility of newer and ever finer affective capabilities on the part of the mass audience. This discovery concerns what Eisenstein (and later Deleuze) would discuss almost in terms of a new synthesis of the sensible, the "being" of the sensible, a body that exists before discourses, before words, clichés, and made-to-order representations—the "I FEEL" of the cinematographic subject.[2]

> For the musical overtone (a throb) it is not strictly fitting to say: "I hear."
> Nor for the visual overtone: "I see."
> For both a new uniform formula must enter our vocabulary: "I feel."[3]

Underlining the radical significance of this discovery, as well as the singular relationship of this dimension to the industrial art of cinema, Eisenstein writes: "Possessing such an excellent instrument of perception as cinema—even on its primitive level—for the sensation of movement, we should soon learn a concrete orientation in this four-dimensional space-time continuum, and feel as much at home in it as our own house-slippers. And soon we'll be posing the question of a fifth dimension" (70).

As in all the public lectures and theoretical statements written during this period, Eisenstein is most concerned with the development of the future of cinematic narration and the culture of montage in the advent of the sound film. This concern bears on two distinct tasks for "intellectual cinema": first, to continue to purify cinema of, on the one hand, the conventions of theatrical representation and, on the other, of literary conventions; second, to prevent the arrival of sound and speech as new elements of the cinematic ensemble from becoming dominant or determinant of the "whole." Just as Eisenstein sought to overcome the resistance of the shot, that "minimally pliable unit of cinema," by opening it to the infinite possibilities of montage, so he wants to ensure the freedom of the movement-image from its subordination and possible enslavement to the vulgar "naturalism" of the talkie—that is, the "illusion" of talking people and of audible objects. This is nowhere more evident than in the statement of 1928 in which Eisenstein, Pudovkin, and Alexandrov underline the potential impasses that may occur after the "fading of the virginity and purity of the perception of new technical possibilities" of the initial period (*Film Form*, 258). The statement further cautions that the period that will follow risks being one in which the naturalism of the sound film may give way to an epoch of its "automatic utilization for 'highly cultured dramas' and other photographed performances of the theatrical sort"; "to use sound in this way will destroy the culture of montage, for every ADHESION of sound to a visual montage piece increases its inertia" (ibid.). On the contrary, the three directors argue that the sound and visual images should not be perceived as accompanying one another, reasserting here the principle later theorized by Foucault that "talking is not seeing" ("parler ce n'est pas voir"), but rather must discover new arrangements between the visible and the audible by a refinement of the contrapuntal method. Therefore, "THE FIRST EXPERIMENTAL WORK WITH SOUND MUST BE DIRECTED ALONG THE LINE OF ITS DISTINCT NON-SYNCHRONIZATION WITH THE VISUAL IMAGES" (ibid.; emphasis in original).

Eisenstein contrasts this technique with the function of "orthodox montage" in cinema, which operates by means of the "dominant" (a leading indicator or guiding shot). For example, taking the following sequence of montage images—

(a) a gray old man
(b) a gray old woman
(c) a white horse
(d) a snow-covered roof

—the meaning of the sequence will be determined, in orthodox montage, by the guiding shot, which "'christens' the *whole* sequence in one direction or another" (65). For example, we might add, preferably earlier on in the series, the whiteness of cataracts in a pupil, thereby producing the *feeling* of the hardening of old age, or a rhume of saliva forming at the corner of the mouth expressing its concomitant regression, or "becoming-child"; perhaps even a wide-angle shot of a winter field in which all distinguishable boundaries are erased by snowdrifts, producing the impression of the fading of memory and the approach of death. These elements come together to produce the illusory effect of cinematic duration much in the same manner that analytic philosophy might construct the following formula to account for the "illusion" of conscious duration: a red light is followed by a green light, producing in the spectator's consciousness the "illusion" of continuous movement, or "red becoming green."

This illusion, baptized as such by the presence of a subject who determines the separate components as synthetically real, is precisely the shadow traced by the movement-image across an interval made up of overtonal associations and undertonal depths; that is, "the *central* stimulus . . . is attended always by a *whole complex* of secondary stimuli" that are spatially inexpressible and compose a dimension that is exterior to the image, but from which the image draws its components for expressing a feeling of lived duration, a duration that closely resembles "intuition," although this must be understood as overflowing a purely psychological determination (69).

For Eisenstein, the earlier lesson of the Kabuki offered a highly artificial and stylized set of conventions for the production of cinematographic representation while avoiding the trappings of "naturalism" or "vulgar realism." Its contrapuntal method provides the example of an extreme formalism with regard to the possibilities of construction and, at the same time, an extremely free and indeterminate range of possible combinations with regard to the elements of expression. Consequently, there is a certain freedom sought in the ensemble of the elements of the spectacle, although this does not presuppose that they are uncoordinated. Rather, their assemblage bears the collective unity of a team toward a common goal—"Kabuki is soccer"—and the "goal" is precisely the event that is defined above as the "*total provocation* of the brain" (21). In fact, the "goal" in soccer is a perfect illustration of the nature of the cinematographic event. Although the various components and elements come together as its condition (the ball, the players, the grid or field of play, the rules of the game, etc.), they do not take the form of a direct causality, because the scoring shot is an "effect" that surpasses the former even though it presupposes their free and indeterminate coordination. Without this freedom and "play" between the various components, scoring a goal would simply be a matter of following a predetermined order or causal sequence like a physical process or a mathematical equation. Thus, it is by a strict adherence to technique that film becomes a *process* that can break open the already established forms of perception and thought and discover a fresh syntax before words, before images.

In his 1935 speech "Film Form: New Problems," Eisenstein applies many of these principles to his discussion of the syntax of "inner speech," which forms an example of his theory concerning the forms of sensual thought processes (or "earlier forms of thinking") that underlie "the formal laws governing the construction of the form and composition of art-works"—and not only of cinema, but also of painting, theater, and literature:

> Inner speech is precisely at the stage of image-sensual structure, not yet having attained that logical formulation with which speech clothes itself before stepping out into the open. It is noteworthy that, just as logic obeys a whole series of laws in its constructions, so inner speech, this sensual thinking, is subject to no less clear-cut laws and structural peculiarities. These are known and, in light of the considerations here set out, represent the inexhaustible storehouse, as it were, of laws for the construction of form, the study and analysis of which have immense importance in the task of mastering the "mysteries" of the technique of form. (130)

The example that Eisenstein gives this process is from *Potemkin*, the shot of the "pince-nez" of the drowned surgeon, which transcends simple *pars pro toto*, but even supplants the necessity of representing the bloated corpse of the surgeon himself, and "does so with a sensual-emotional increase in the intensity of the impression":

> As you perceive, for the purposes of a sensual artistic impression, we have used, as a compositional method, one of those early laws of early thinking which, at appropriate stages, appear as the norms and practices of everyday behavior. We made use of a construction of a sensual thinking type, and instead of a "logico-informative" effect, we receive from the construction actually an emotional-sensual effect. We do not simply register the fact that the surgeon has drowned, we emotionally react to the fact through a definite compositional presentation of this fact. (133)

This is the "goal" of montage process. The shock produced by the spectator's own "realization" that the surgeon has drowned bears a greater intensity—the emotional-sensual effect of a "fact" that is physically experienced—than if it was either represented or reported. What this exemplifies is the goal of "thought montage," which breaks with preestablished forms of visibility and sense in order *to restore the immanence between thought and the body*: to give thought a sensible form, one of shock, which yields an emotional intelligence (one of conviction, or belief), and which, in turn, lays claim to the *reality* of what is perceived.

But why would the physiological effect of shock brought about by this new form of montage be the "goal" of Eisenstein's theory of intellectual cinema? Taking up Deleuze's response to this question, the image first acquires this power over thought because the industrial art of cinema already "makes movement the immediate given of the image" and it is only a small step between movement and thought inasmuch as "[*a*]*utomatic movement* gives rise to a *spiritual automaton* in us, which reacts in turn on movement."[4] In other words, cinema achieves by direct means what was only indirectly present (or even demanded) by the other arts, where it is spirit (or mind) that causes movement to occur: for example, the eyes to trace the words across the page, to follow the curvature of the lines in painting or sculpture, or to apprehend the composition of bodies in dance or theater, or the ears to discern the melody across a surface of notes. Within cinematic duration, on the contrary, "[i]t is the image which itself moves in itself" (i.e., automatic movement), no longer dependent "on a moving body or an object which realizes it, nor on a spirit which reconstitutes it."[5] The movement-image is primary and now occupies the position of the *subject-that-moves* or that causes movement; the mind must react or respond to the movement that is immediately given and this response is organically part of the image itself, marking an event that Deleuze will define by the concept of "nooshock." The cause of thinking and perceiving is no longer on the side of the subject, and so thinking is no longer a logical possibility that one can either take up or not, but rather becomes a physiological imperative, a "total provocation of the brain." The mind of the spectator is forced to respond, to react, to think; and this, in turn, changes the shape and the sensibility of thought, which appears from a shadowy region that is outside the subject's own powers of autoaffection—as if in this moment reception is structured by a command.[6]

We might take these remarks concerning Eisenstein's theory of intellectual montage as preliminary to a more general discussion of the relationship between cinema and thought so long as we keep in mind that a battle is being waged over the territory of the human brain that appears here both as the "spiritual automaton," the dummy of natural consciousness, and as its double, "the cinematographic I THINK." If the threat of "naturalism" is what Deleuze calls a certain "spiritual automaton" that exists within each one of us, the principal lesson that Eisenstein derives from the Kabuki solves this problem by the artificial creation of another automaton that enters into conflict with the first by causing it to react. "Shock," therefore, is simply the effect of an *opposition* between two "spiritual automatons" that is mediated by the dialectic of intellectual montage. Deleuze describes this dialectic as follows:

> [Intellectual] [m]ontage is in thought "the intellectual process" itself, or that which, under the shock, thinks the shock. Whether it is visual or of sound, the image already has harmonics which accompany the perceived dominant image, and enter in their own ways into supra-sensory relations . . . : this is the shock wave or the nervous vibration, which means that we can no longer say "I see, I hear," but I FEEL, "totally physiological sensation," And it is the set of harmonics acting on the cortex which gives rise to thought, the cinematographic I THINK: the whole as subject.[7]

Thus, as "the most notable of arts," the industrial art of cinema assumes the pinnacle of the progression that Hegel had earlier established for philosophy; Eisenstein himself had described the potential for cinema to replace philosophy as the true and authentic expression of dialectical materialism. If the "dialectic" can be understood as the movement-image that causes thinking to occur in the subject, even as the unfolding of thought itself in its relationship to perception and to language, then the movement-image in cinema has a more direct means of causing movement to occur and to make language and perception the material of a thinking brain; therefore, "[t]he form of montage is a restoration of the laws of the process of thought, which in turn restores moving reality in process of unrolling."[8] If Deleuze shares in this optimism, however, the experience has been modified by the direction of cinema and philosophy in the modern, postwar period. If the event of thought itself, which has been named by both Heidegger and Artaud, is the moment that we understand that we are not yet thinking (an event of *impouvoir*), then cinema shares in this event by establishing as its highest goal that moment when we "comprehend" that we are not yet perceiving or hearing the world *as it is*. Yet it is around this goal, as we will see, that Deleuze still holds out for the potential of modern intellectual cinema.

CINEMA AND THE SUBLIME: THE DYNAMIC PRINCIPLE OF "NOOSHOCK"

In *The Time-Image*, Deleuze takes up Eisenstein's earlier argument that what is directly realized in cinema, the movement-image, is only indirectly present in the other arts. "Because the cinematographic image itself 'makes' movement, because it makes what the other arts are restricted to demanding (or to saying), it brings together what is essential in the other arts."[9] The weakness of the shock (the montage effect) such as it occurs in theater, according to Eisenstein, precisely describes the architectural parameters of theatrical space itself, which limits the possibilities proper to montage. The visual and aural image cannot accede to new arrangements; the visual image is limited to the confines of the stage, and the aural image to the speech of actors, or to the noise of props. Moreover, theatrical construction is limited by bodies, highly artificial conventions that have historically determined the possibilities of perception, for example, the "role" of the actor in relationship to the audience as well as to the action itself. The "outside" is reduced to a small opening in theatrical space by means of a referent (the world, reality) and the action-image appears as an oblique (or indirect) angle of reflection "on everyday happenings," as Brecht said. As a consequence of its indirect relationship with the whole, the "shock" effect becomes overly didactic, in that its power is mediated by a command structure that is often identified with the expression of political will. We should recall Benjamin's argument concerning the strategic and political effect of "shock" on the audience in Brecht's epic theater, although in this case "alienation effect" (or *Verfremdungseffekt*) becomes the dominant affect of theatrical montage. Here, "the truly important thing is to discover the conditions of life. (One might say just as well: to alienate [*verfremden*] them.) This discovery (alienation) of conditions takes place through the interruption of happenings."[10]

A fundamental principle that one can find at work in both Brecht's epic theater and Artaud's "theater of cruelty" is therefore the destruction (or "fissuring") of theatrical space itself (or at least its classical automatons), where the effect of "alienation" entails the "suppression of all protective barriers" and strikes against the mental automatons of artificial and exterior mimicry "that cast the mind [not only of the spectators, but also the actors and creators as well] into an attitude distinct from force but addicted to exaltation."[11] The "goal" would be a spectacle acting as a force rather than as a reflection on external happenings; for Artaud, as for Brecht, this would position the spectator in the center with the spectacle surrounding, the distance from the spectacle no longer abstracted from the totality of the sensory milieu. Yet, as in Brecht's "gestic" theater, this cannot truly occur where thinking is presented (or rather, represented) by the demand for movement that is still virtual and not yet actualized in the image, because the image remains external to the movement, is still *over there* (representation), and has not yet touched the very cortex of the spectator. As Deleuze writes, "It is only when movement becomes automatic that the artistic essence of the image is realized: *producing a shock to thought, communicating vibrations to the cortex, touching the nervous and cerebral system directly.*"[12] Here we find the dynamic principle of "nooshock." The cinematographic discovery of a higher faculty of "emotion," the figure of desire that is represented by the "I feel" of the movement-image, is that which causes movement of the "spiritual automaton" within the spectator; in other words, it causes the already constituted and partial subject to be surpassed in favor of another subject that is capable (or incapable, as it were) of thinking, desiring, or willing the whole. This "whole," Deleuze argues, is perhaps the "subject" of modern cinema; "[t]he cinematographic image must have a shock effect on thought, and force thought to think itself as much as thinking the whole. This is the very definition of the sublime."[13]

But why does Deleuze compare here the effect of shock on the nervous system of the spectator to the concept of the sublime? This is a very subtle comparison, but one that radically reenvisages the Kantian sublime from the modern perspective of the brain in its confrontation with chaos. Deleuze's interpretation of the Kantian sublime concerns the infamous violence experienced by the faculty of the imagination when confronted by a formless and/or deformed immense power and, as a result, is thrown back on itself as upon its own limit (or in an important phrase that echoes the original Kantian description, utilized prominently in *Anti-Oedipus* and elsewhere, "se rabat sur," that is, "falls back" or "recoils upon itself"). This phrase represents the uniqueness of Deleuze's intuition around the function of the imagination in the Kantian analysis, which he reconfigures by resolving the impasse of the imagination no longer in terms of a principle of representation (as Kant did) but in terms of the Bergsonian definition of the brain as a pure interval (or "gap"), opening onto a "virtual whole" that is actualized according to divergent lines that "*do not* form a whole on their own account and *do not* resemble what they actualize," because the "whole is never 'given.'"[14] This comparison returns in the closing chapter of *What Is Philosophy?* where the original Kantian faculties are reconfigured under the three sources of representation: science, art, and philosophy. "In short, chaos has three daughters, depending on the plane that cuts through it—art, science, and philosophy—as forms of thought or creation.... *The brain is the junction*—not the unity—*of the three planes.*"[15] In the

Critique of Judgment, however, it is reason that appears in the role of power and the figure of formlessness is itself the direct presentation of failure of the imagination "to unite the immensity of the sensible world into *a Whole*."[16] The figure of formlessness or deformation is, in fact, the sensible manifestation (let us say "embodiment") of the relationship between reason and imagination which is experienced as contradiction (or *conflict*), as dissension, as pain. Yet, it is only within this very conflict that a relationship first emerges, and it is only on the basis of this feeling of pain that pleasure first becomes possible. "When imagination is confronted by its limit with something which goes beyond it in all respects it goes beyond its own limit itself, admittedly in a negative fashion, by representing to itself the inaccessibility of the rational Idea [of the Whole] and by making this very inaccessibility something which is present in sensible nature" (ibid.; emphasis added).

For Kant, therefore, the feeling of the sublime opens a "gap" (*écart*) in experience through which the idea of "subject as Whole" is engendered (literally given birth) as "something which is present in sensible nature." The faculty of desire is given an object, even though this object is immediately inaccessible, and a destination, even though this destination is "suprasensible," because "the suprasensible destination of the faculties appears as *that to which a moral being is predestined*" (52; emphasis in original). Therefore, as Deleuze writes, "in the sublime there is a sensory-motor unity of nature and human, which means that nature must be named *the non-indifferent*," because it is apparently nature itself that issues the demand for unification of the whole within the interiority of a subject and it is by reacting to this demand *"that we discover that which is fundamental to our destiny"* (ibid.; emphasis added). Art in the West—at least from the baroque period onward—can be said to be founded on this demand inasmuch as through it the faculty of desire gives birth to the presentation of a "higher finality," which is symbolized by the unity of the artwork.[17] The effect of "alienation" (*Verfremdungseffekt*) and the different conceptions of "shock" that we have been analyzing can therefore be understood as figures of the "discordant-accord" (Deleuze) between finite, a posteriori imagination and a spontaneous, a priori power that belongs to the idea of the whole. Thus, the feeling of "alienation," the aesthetic principle of modern political representation, can itself be understood to reproduce a central tension that belongs to the sublime inasmuch as the feeling of suffering that it immediately engenders in an audience of spectators also gives birth to the suprasensible idea of itself as another nature, that of a spontaneous collective subject, or "a people." However, hemmed in and confined by the limit of theatrical space—a limit that *fuses* with and partially institutes the concrete and historical limits of the imagination itself—such a "suprasensible idea" must first appear as a negative or critical *force* that breaks open the frames of classical representation and spills over to link together thought and action, causing the base-brain or "spiritual automaton" of a mass to undergo a change of quality.[18]

Whether this force takes the form, as in Brecht, of an "interruption" of sympathetic identification (estrangement) or, as in Artaud, of "cruelty" and even "absolute sadism," it marks the ferocity of desire for a higher finality that belongs to the nature of modern political theater, and of certain experimental traditions of modern art in general. To inflict a symbolic violence in perception, language, opinion, character, mood; to destroy common sense and wage a war against all forms of cliché internal and external; to bathe the prose of the world in the syntax of dreams; to wash the image in the grain of light or to evacuate it in favor of a pure "blankness" that lies underneath—these are the hallmarks of modern art. We might understand these as figures of the "negative apprehension" of an idea of the whole that the artwork bears within itself like a seed, which marks both the temporal nature of its duration and the manic desire for total achievement that characterizes every finite attempt to express this nature in one formal unity. Within the contemporaneousness of the present that defines the current stage of its achievement, however, the idea of this nature is expressed as an internal dehiscence or bears the aspect of "danger" (Artaud) like the violent frenzy of a wounded animal. Consequently, in the sensible appearance of this ferocious and violent nature, we might also see a mise-en-scène of the sublime itself. First, the perfection of the work of art represents the overpowering nature of a demand for the "subject as whole" and reproduces this demand within the intercerebral interval between stimulus and response, between image and reaction, or, as Kant defined this interval in classical terms, between *apprehensio* and *comprehensio* (that is, between the presentation of the artwork and the comprehension of the spectator). Second, inasmuch as the whole of this interval extends beyond its own powers to actualize within a complete circuit that would run between image and brain (what Deleuze calls a "sensory-motor unity"), a certain figure of "formlessness" appears that comes to symbolize this unity in a negative manner and also to characterize the appearance of the artwork generally.

It is this moment of "failure" that also characterizes a certain cyclical movement (the "cyclone," or spiral) through which modern art "recoils" from manifesto to cliché, then from a state of inertia (or fossilization) to its renewal in the next movement, the next manifesto, the next style, each promising to discover the means of restoring the vital connection between nature and human. In other words, the cerebral interval becomes a deep "gap" or "void" that it cannot fill, an immense distance or abyss that it cannot cross, emerging instead as the crack or fissure that creases its body and constitutes an "outside" that it cannot express in language or present in the image: "deeper than any interiority, further than any exteriority" (a formula that Deleuze adapts from Foucault), the outside describes that mute and formless region that appears at the center of the modern work of art and becomes the principle cause of its "deformation" and even appears as its defect, its symptom, or its neurosis. This characteristic quality of "deformation" or "formlessness," however, cannot be understood simply as an aspect of the *style* of the modern artwork, but rather belongs to the "total physiological sensation" (or "I FEEL") that defines the experience of modern experimental art, in particular, and is caused by the failure to attain the "action-image" it posited as its higher finality.[19] That is to say, the sensation or "feeling of formlessness" gives us an indirect representation of the whole that, although it can propose an image only in a negative manner, remains outside the powers of art to realize. As Kant wrote nearly two centuries earlier concerning a kind of "knowing" (thinking, apprehending) that is specific to the experience of art, one that breaks with the conditions of a knowledge that is immediately connected to a mental image of "action" (as in the cases of science and handicraft): "Only that which a human, even if he *knows* it completely, may not therefore have the skill to accomplish belongs to art."[20]

But how does the emergence of cinema change this state of affairs? Let us recall that, for Eisenstein, the movement-image promises "the subject as whole" (i.e., to represent the synthesis of image and thought in a sensory-motor unity). How is this subject different from that of art? As an industrial art form, the cinematographic subject of knowledge is distinct from that of the fine arts (or from the kind of *knowing* that belongs to art as Kant defined it above) in that it composes, at least potentially, a synthesis of science, handicraft (skill), and art. Therefore, in its confrontation and struggle with chaos (i.e., "formlessness"), cinema behaves like a science when it knows how to slow down and place limits on this chaos by providing it a reference, the *"open,"* by which it makes the whole appear indirectly as the object of the movement-image; at the same time, cinema behaves like an art when it allies itself with the force of chaos in order to forge new visions and new sensations, which it uses in its struggles against the preestablished clichés and ready-made linkages of image and thought (including those clichés, as we have seen, that belong to field of art itself). Under this second aspect, what formerly appeared as chaos here becomes a "fourth dimension" that cinema discovers through its knowledge of the process of montage as "the inexhaustible storehouse, as it were, of laws for the construction of form, the study and analysis of which have immense importance in the task of *mastering* the 'mysteries' of the technique of form" (to cite again a passage from Eisenstein's 1935 speech).[21] As a synthesis of these two aspects of knowledge, therefore, Eisenstein's *theory* of cinema appears both, like science or handicraft, as a set of "functives" (or axioms) that compose a machinic assemblage for the construction of cinematographic form and, like art, as a "monument" of sensation, or "compound of percepts and affects."[22] Recalling the Kantian statement above, contrary to the other arts, *cinema both posits or thinks the whole and, at the same time, it is capable of—or at least posits for itself—the knowledge and technical skill of realizing it.*

If the "realization of the whole" becomes the highest task of classical cinema, this is because in a certain sense it is already *completely given.* "The material universe, the plane of immanence, is [itself only] a *machine assemblage of movement-images,"* as Deleuze writes earlier in *The Movement-Image.*[23] A question only remains concerning whether this realization will be accomplished by the primacy of montage or by the technical perfection of the movement-image itself. By situating this achievement within the region of the sublime, Deleuze is also suggesting the emergence of a new subject that categorizes space-time: a purely cinematic subject, or I THINK, which is interposed between the brain and the world, or between the brain of a supra-intelligence and the *"open"* through which the whole itself undergoes a dialectical "conflagration."[24] However, because this subject necessarily bears the character of an *absolute knowledge,* we might discern here the portrait of what Deleuze calls a "cinematographic Hegel" in Eisenstein's theory of cinema as the dialectical automaton in the service of social realism. If, according to Hegel, "Spirit [or mind] is alienated" and must pass through the stages of the dialectic in order to become reunited with its own form of expression, then for Eisenstein, this passage is accomplished by the cinematographic technique of montage, which breaks open the historically "alienated" forms of perception, language, and character in order to reconnect thought to its primordial immediacy and immanence for the subject. As Deleuze writes,

> [a] circuit which includes simultaneously the author, the film and the viewer is elaborated. The complete circuit thus includes the sensory shock which raises us from the images to conscious thought, then the thinking in figures which takes us back to the images and gives us an affective shock again. Making the two coexist, joining the highest degree of consciousness to the deepest level of the unconscious: this is the dialectical automaton. The whole is constantly *open* [the spiral], but so that it can internalize the sequence of images [within the subject], as well as becoming externalized in this sequence [as total object, or world]. *The whole forms a knowledge, in the Hegelian fashion, which brings together the image and the concept as two movements each of which goes towards the other.*[25]

It is only by technically achieving this dual movement between the most unconscious region of the image and the most abstract region of thought that cinema will construct a knowledge of the whole as the condition of montage and will gradually become equal to the task of realizing the true promise of the dialectic that Hegel had earlier defined for philosophy as *spirit thinking itself as subject*. It does this by gradually mastering the dialectical progression between image and concept, or, using Eisenstein's terminology, between "pre-logical, sensual thinking" and the highest forms of symbolic logic, thus surpassing both forms and uniting instinct and reason in an image of thought that at the same time discovers at the "deepest level of the unconscious" the conditions of action for the historical subject (thereby becoming "action-thought," or what Eisenstein refers to elsewhere as the "'habit logic' of the future").[26] This constitutes the highest goal of the culture of montage, according to Eisenstein, namely to present within the vivid immediacy of the movement-image the unity of the "subject as whole," that is, to individuate the perceptions of the masses so that the consciousness of the spectator no longer appears isolated, but rather as the collective subject of his or her own reaction, or even as an objective force of nature itself. Nature appears on the side of the subject of cinema (becoming "the non-indifferent"); cinema appears on the side of the masses (becoming spirit or "I feel" of a people to come). This is why Deleuze refers to Eisenstein's theory as essentially monist. "*Action-thought simultaneously posits the unity of nature and man, of the individual and the mass: cinema as art of the masses.*"[27]

CINEMA AND IDEOLOGY 1: EISENSTEIN'S WAGER—BETWEEN TWO BRAINS, EXCEPTIONAL ART OR ORDINARY FASCISM

Cinema, art of the masses! If this slogan sounds a bit hollow, like a modern advertising jingle, it is because something has happened in the interval that has made us extremely skeptical of all such beliefs concerning art. It is around the nature of *belief* that Deleuze's teleology of modern cinema diverges significantly from that of Eisenstein, and he must resort to Artaud and to Blanchot in order to situate the relationship between thought and cinema in its modern period, after the belief in a pure or revolutionary cinema has gone unrealized; or, much worse, after the discovery of cinema's potential to attach itself to the cortex and to touch the cerebral system directly has been perverted and "has degenerated into state propaganda and manipulation, into a kind of fascism which brought together Hitler and Hollywood, Hollywood and Hitler" (*The Time-Image*, 164).

> Hence the idea that the cinema, as art of the masses, could be the supreme revolutionary or democratic art, which makes the masses a true subject. But a great many factors were to compromise this belief: the rise of Hitler, which gave cinema as its object not the masses become subject but the masses subjected; Stalinism, which replaced the unanimism of peoples with the tyrannical unity of a party; the break-up of the American people, who could no longer believe themselves to be either the melting-pot of peoples past or the seed of a people to come. (216)

This does not come about because cinema fails to accomplish everything that Eisenstein dreamed it would, but rather it is that the dynamic principle on which it was founded, the movement-image, succeeds in the worst manners.

Consequently, the optimism with which Eisenstein originally held the muscular syntax of inner speech and the forms of "sensual, pre-logical thinking" as primary sources for montage and of a "habit logic of the future" also harbored the possibility of fascism, manipulation, and the infinite alienation of the masses. Thus, rather than breaking through to achieve a form of thinking that would give birth to the idea of "a people" as a collective and international subject, the cinema revealed a dead and mummified "sensualism" and an archaic and familial unconscious as its wellspring. (Like both Artaud and Bataille before him, Deleuze rejects the surrealist and modernist definitions of the unconscious and the dream as sources of liberation.) The dream, as it turns out, was a false source of profundity; and the unconscious, rather than constituting a true depth and wellspring for the creation of forms, was a basement filled with junk. Even worse, when these are attached to an apparatus of mass projection they give birth to a world filled with mummies, ghouls, and vampires. Thus, the ideological force that finds its privilege in the cinema of the modern period can be seen as the "return of these archaic norms and laws of conduct" (the murderous impulses that belong to racism, genocide, and nationalism), which are provided newer and more effective eidectic combinations through the cinematographic inventions that surround the development of the movement-image in the first and second waves of cinema. The state finds in the dominant principle of classical cinema (the action-image) the very means of breaking into the "storehouse of primitive or sensual thinking" and new techniques for establishing these patterns of habitual thought or normative laws toward the achievement of its own desire for finality (totality, absolutism, immanence). Hitler becomes the "spiritual automaton" who gives birth to the German people in the Nazi period, "the subject as Whole."

Eisenstein himself had also perceived this danger in what he called "psychological retrogression," where cinema becomes subordinated to the automaton of "sensual, pre-logical thinking," which can suddenly become a "dominant" even in the most complex of social constructions, because the margins between the higher phases of intellectual order and the primitive and baser instincts are extremely mobile, volatile, and often undergo sudden shifts at each stage of development:

> This continual sliding from level to level, backwards and forwards, now to the higher forms of an intellectual order, now to the earlier forms of sensual thinking, occurs at . . . each phase in development. . . . The margin between the types is mobile and it suffices a not even extraordinarily sharp affective impulse to cause an extremely, it may be, logically deliberative person suddenly to react in obedience to the never dormant inner armory of sensual thinking and the norms of behavior deriving thence. (*Film Form*, 143)

The common example he gives for the above is that of a girl who tears the photo of her beloved into fragments "in anger," thus destroying her "wicked betrayer" by destroying his image in an act of magical thinking (based on the early identification of image and object) (ibid.). In other words, development does not proceed in a straight line, on the level of either the individual or the whole social construction: for example, "the regress of spiritual super-structures under the heel of national-socialism" (145). However, rather than recoiling in fear and thereby avoiding further research into these early forms that compose the basis of any possible action-image (or "habit logic"), Eisenstein sees in the cinematic apparatus the potential for a dialectical progression that maintains the pursuit of highly complex intellectual forms and processes and, at the same time, the "analysis" of the early forms of sensual thinking.[28]

This represents Eisenstein's wager: to invent not merely a rhetorical cinema, but an analytic cinema, a cinematographic science of thinking. Cinema must achieve by means of technical montage and the contrapuntal method what Engels had earlier defined as "the third stage" in the construction of thinking through which humanity must pass: neither the primitive and diffuse complex of sensual thinking of the first stage, nor the formal-logical stage, which negates the former (perhaps even "forecloses" it in the psychoanalytic sense), but rather the "dynamic perception of phenomena," which dialectically absorbs the first two "in photographic detail" (i.e., social realism). It is for this reason that Eisenstein's theory of cinema is founded on a dynamic principle of conflict with these two other automatons. It must avoid becoming too sensual, on the one hand, and too formal and abstract, on the other, always seeking as the principle of its development a certain *balance* (in a Whiteheadian sense). Here, the total process achieves the figure of a dialectical circle or a "spiral," as Deleuze calls it, following a "dual unity" in which the highest form of art has as its correlate the deepest form of subconscious:

> The effectiveness of a work of art is built upon the fact that there takes place within it a dual process: an impetuous progressive rise along the lines of the highest explicit steps of consciousness and a simultaneous penetration by means of the structure of the form into the layers of profoundest sensual thinking. The polar separation of these two lines of flow creates that remarkable tension of unity of form and content characteristic of true art-works. Apart from this there are no true art-works.[29]

Of course, we do not need to demonstrate that Eisenstein lost his wager for a cinema that maintained a certain balance that could ensure both a higher form of satisfaction (intellectual complexity) and, at the same time, a higher form of "feeling" (passionate sensibility), the achievement of which would repair the broken accord between conscious perception and thoughtful action. The unfolding of history and the development of the cinematographic art in the modern period gives us ample evidence to forgo a demonstration, and I have already underlined the major points of this evidence. Such a balance could only describe an ideal cinema, that is, one that grew from the seeds that were planted in the soil of another world and would require for its actualization an entirely different nature than that of the masses, that is, a wholly "other" brain. These, moreover, would have to be prerequisites or initial conditions of the cinema that Eisenstein describes, rather than its "products" or even its "revolutionary effects."

Concerning the existence of such an ideal cinema, Artaud probably said it best: "The imbecile world of images caught as if by glue in millions of retinas will never perfect the image that has been made of it. The poetry which can emerge from it all is only a possible poetry, the poetry of what might be, and it is not from cinema that we should expect . . ."[30] The primary reasons Deleuze gives for this failure are quantitative mediocrity of products and fascist principles of production; these are generalized as the shortcomings of author and audience.[31] Again, "Hollywood and Hitler." "Popular cinema" and "nationalist cinema." In the former, we find a figurative cinema based on the automaton of vulgar sensualism (clichés of sex and violence); in the latter, we find a cinema based on the automaton of the state (clichés of history and action). Here again, in Eisenstein's defense, we should recall the earlier discussion of the "fourth dimension" of intellectual cinema and the contrapuntal method in the approach of the sound film, because both were conceived as preventative measures to avoid precisely the above state of affairs from determining the future of the cinematographic form. First, by linking the montage process to an "outside" that could not be determined by simple visual or sound images, Eisenstein hoped to avoid the situation where the "focus" of the visual image would be trapped on the surface of already composed and defined bodies (whether of objects, persons, already divided sexes, or even peoples). Second, by means of the contrapuntal method, he hoped to liberate the sound image from a situation where its "sense" would be determined monolinguistically, or bound too closely to the literary and dramatic conventions that might define a single national character or cultural imagination. These aspirations underlie a truly international cinematographic vision (an aspect often overlooked, even willfully ignored, in Deleuze's reading of Eisenstein), although it is a vision, perhaps even an "inner monologue," that is often hidden or obscured in the official rhetoric of the speeches and lectures that had to pass under the gaze of the Soviet censors and, in general, had to be concealed from the race of impudent masters Eisenstein's films were to serve. In fact, Eisenstein came under direct criticism of the Stalinists several times, particularly around the improperly dramatic treatment of the action-image in the heroic portrayal of *Alexander Nevsky*, which was judged as being too "Hamletian" in proportion and not an adequate vehicle for collective sentiment of the Soviet people.[32]

But then, this underscores a third reason—the most obvious one, perhaps—which even conditions the first two in the sense that the art of industrial cinema depends for its existence less on genius than on the *interest* of modern institutions and their systems of majority, in the form either of the state or of a culture industry. This distinguishes the cinema from the other arts (with the exception of architecture) and even predisposes it to assume an overtly ideological shape in its classical period or, in the modern period, frequently causes it to confront the limit of its internal presupposition, that is, *money*. "The film is movement," Deleuze writes, "but the film within the film is money, is time":

> The crystal-image thus receives the principle which is its foundation [what causes it to exist in the first place]: endlessly relaunching exchange which is dissymmetrical, unequal and without equivalence, giving image for money, giving time for images, converting time, the transparent side, and money, the opaque side, like a spinning top on its end. And the film will be finished when there is no more money left . . .[33]

Especially in the current period, one not encountered by Eisenstein, capital assumes the force of the whole, as that power which is equal to the *being* of the whole; at the same time, it apportions the limit to this representation precisely at that moment when the money runs out, which is also when the forms of desire (or interest) and imagination encounter their own internal limits. This final reason marks the "no exit" of modern industrial cinema, which can become *pure and dis-interested* only at a price, which can be tangibly measured and even calculated in advance as a condition of its production; however, the only place where it is really free (that is, from the pressures of these institutions) is that place, or those places, where it does not exist.[34] A cinema of pure possibility, or "of pure poetry," as Artaud said, *but one we should not expect*—not an art of the impossible, simply an impossible art.

CINEMA AND IDEOLOGY 2: ARTAUD'S PROBLEM, AND OURS—"BELIEF IN THE WORLD AS IT IS"

Deleuze argues that two dominant responses to loss of the idea of a just world in the West have been the creation of two spiritual ideals. The first is the revolutionary (or critical) ideal, which responds to the loss of the true world by an active engagement of science, politics, and art in the destruction of the previous world and the "fabrication" of a new world that will replace it. This amounts to the belief in a principle of creation (or negativity) that would be able to intervene between human and nature in order to set right, rectify, or even radically transform this relation. The other ideal Deleuze calls "catholic," which amounts to spiritualizing the human in the hope of a transformation (through an act of conversion or mysticism) into another nature. (Here, we might perceive an implicit kinship between Catholicism and Buddhism.) The former can be illustrated by Eisenstein's image of revolutionary cinema to intervene into the very brain of the human and thereby to transform its nature, which is the nature of its perception-consciousness system (or the spiritual automaton within us). Although Deleuze underlines a deficiency in Eisenstein's "monism," as well as in his tendency to express the conflict between these two spiritual automatons in terms of *opposition*, in actual fact there is less difference between their theories of cinema than one might expect. Their "goal" is identical: *a total provocation of the human brain*. Where is the point of divergence to be located? On the first level, it can be located in simple chronology. Eisenstein conceived of the possibilities of cinematic art in its earliest stages, and his experience belongs to the first and second periods of the "old cinema." On the other hand, Deleuze defines his earliest experiences with cinema in the period that runs immediately before and after World War II. As already outlined, his experience occupies a moment of transition not encountered by Eisenstein, when something happens that robs cinema of this total provocation (or "nooshock") as the dynamic principle of the achievement of cinematographic art as an *art of the masses*, something that causes the belief in the revolutionary nature of cinema to now appear as an overly naive and even fantastic premise, worthy of a museum filled with the lost aspirations of the golden age of art in the West.

On the second level, intimately bound up with the first, the point of divergence can be located in the "image of thought" that defines as its goal the total provocation of the brain (i.e., the principle of "nooshock"). Simply put, the difference is between thought identified as a power that would be placed in a circuit with the automatic image to effect a change in the whole, and a thought that appears deprived of this power a priori and, in fact, reveals a subject that is haunted by the automatic character of movement that animates it as well as by the source of images it is given to think. A qualitatively new monster emerges in the world at about the same time that it becomes a frequent character of modern cinema (particularly science fiction): an alien who latches on to the human face, smothering its victim without letting it die, and who lays eggs inside the victim's mouth. These eggs are the physical, optical, and auditory clichés—the "little organs" of the reproductive imagination—to which the spiritual automaton of modern ideology gives birth.

> Nothing but clichés, clichés everywhere.... They are these floating images, these anonymous clichés which circulate in the external world, but which also penetrate each one of us and constitute his internal world, so that everyone possesses only psychic clichés by which he thinks and feels, is thought and is felt, being himself a cliché among the others in the world which surrounds him. Physical, optical and auditory clichés and psychic clichés mutually feed on each other. In order for people to be able to bear themselves and the world, misery has to reach the inside of consciousness and the inside has to be like the outside.... *How can one not believe in a powerful concerted organisation*, a great and powerful plot, which has found the way to make clichés circulate, from outside to inside, from inside to outside?[35]

Here we can discern the figure of crisis that interrupts the achievement of the movement-image, an eventuality already foregrounded in this passage from the conclusion to *The Movement-Image*. Therefore, instead of opening to the birth of thought, the achievement of the movement-image in cinema not only hastens its own death but opens the subject to the moment when the possibility of thought itself can be "stolen away" by force, and this only deepens the subject's passivity before this possibility that appears like a "powerful concerted organisation" installed at the deepest point of its interiority. Ultimately, this crisis will lead to an absolute break in which modern cinema *recoils* from its desire for higher finality, understood in terms of the "action-image," and even renounces its power to give birth to "the subject as Whole," understood in terms of the movement-image. As Deleuze writes, "[t]his is the first aspect of the new cinema" that follows, which is "the break in the sensory-motor link (action-image), and more profoundly in the link between man and the world (great organic composition)."[36]

The reflections above on the inner mechanism of the movement-image offer us the occasion to understand more clearly the direct relationship between modern cinema and ideology. If we find an implicit analogy here between the crisis of the movement-image and the crisis of the imagination in the encounter with the sublime, it is because Deleuze uses this analogy to figure the relationship between the failure of classical cinema and the deformation that the power of reason suffers in the advent of the modern notion of ideology. Consequently, there has never been the possibility of a nonideological cinema and it is not simply by chance that modern critiques of ideology have found in the appearance of film one of the principal culprits in the reproduction of political, class, and racial ideologies. However, many of these critiques pursue a false distinction, believing that the subject of ideology is qualitatively distinct from the movement-image and appears "behind it" or "speaks through it" like a homunculus (reinforcing a classical mind–body dualism), rather than forming the material basis of the image and the laws of association peculiar to "sensual thinking," as Eisenstein discovered. Likewise, such critiques must propose an "inside" of conscious perception that is also qualitatively different from the "inside" of the image, as if there were first a subject whose perceptions were clear and distinct and then the transparent waters of consciousness were muddied over by false projections, illusions, lies, and clichés. In other words, they must *believe* in a subject that is not already composed of a tissue of clichés ("the veil of Maya"); such a subject must appear as composed of another nature, whether as an original nature like that of God, or pure cogito, or as the final nature of a transformed human (whose apotheosis becomes the shared goal of science, art, and politics in the West). On a historical level of the concept of knowledge, this situation addresses the problem faced by post-Enlightenment philosophies generally in which the idea of Reason, rather than guaranteeing to the subject of knowledge the certainty of its link with world, becomes deformed and reappears in the guise of opinion (*doxa*), even as transcendental opinion (or *Urdoxa*). However, in the life of the conscious subject, this feeling of disbelief points to what Deleuze calls a "real psychic situation" that both ideology (as the modern concept of truth) and cinema (as the modern concept of art) share as a formal condition of representation; the suspension of any verifiable link with the "true" world happens at the same time that the human appears as the subject of purely optical and sound situations. As Deleuze writes, "The modern fact is that we no longer believe in this world. We do not even believe in the events which happen to us, love, death, as if they only half concerned us" (*The Time-Image*, 171). And if the "real" subject cannot believe in the world that is presented, it is because the world has become nothing but bad cinema, and the subject has become a pure voyeur who regards his own being, as well as the being of others, as in an episode of *The Jerry Springer Show*, as "stock characters" in a psychic drama that unfolds from the hidden perspective of a *real* that, although external to the subject, is somehow internal (or necessary) to the world *as it is*:

> The sensory-motor break makes man a seer who finds himself struck by something intolerable in the world, and confronted by something unthinkable in thought. Between the two, thought undergoes a strange fossilization, which is as it were its powerlessness to function, to be, its dispossession of itself and the world. For it is not in the name of a better or truer world that thought captures the intolerable in the world, but, on the contrary, it is because this world is intolerable that it can no longer think a world or think itself. (169–70)

The figure of Artaud occupies the moment of this break where the "image of thought," rather than becoming identified with the power of the Whole, that is, the power of a subject capable of externalizing itself in a series of images by which the Whole undergoes change, becomes fissured and more receptive to a fundamental powerlessness that testifies to "the impossibility of thinking that is thought" (Artaud). "It is indeed a matter, as Artaud puts it, 'of bringing cinema together with the innermost reality of the brain,' but this innermost reality is not the Whole [as it was for Eisenstein], but on the contrary a fissure, a crack" (167).[37] Here, thought does not accede to a form that belongs to a model of knowledge, or fall to the conditions of an action; rather, thought exposes its own image to an "outside" that hollows it out and returns it to an element of "formlessness." We might conceive of this event in terms of the notion of formlessness that we explicated earlier in relation to modern art or literature, or even in terms of Eisenstein's discovery of the "fourth dimension" (although here, separated from its "dialectical automaton"), except that in this instance the relationship to the whole is not even given a negative expression, but rather undergoes an absolute break, which in the subject takes the form of a permanent and irreparable state of disbelief. Thus, the problem of ideology received its most authentic expression from Artaud when he cried: "my body was stolen away from me before birth"; "my brain has been used by an Other who thinks in my place." Artaud experienced and gave expression to this problem in its most extreme form, as if suffering from the memory of a physical, mental, and spiritual rape—that is, the cry of schizophrenic man. However, "rape" is not being employed here as a simple metaphor, but rather as the most direct translation of Artaud's complaint; it reveals the nature of "the total physiological sensation" of the automaton who enters to violate the subject even before birth.[38] In response to this intolerable situation, our question must then become how it is possible to distinguish between all the images that compose the subject's existence in order to choose the right one, or how to extract thought from all its various clichés in order to set it up against them. According to Deleuze, Artaud experienced this question as the problematic of thinking itself, which can be summarized as follows: the impossibility of not thinking, the impossibility of thinking, the impossibility of thinking differently.[39] Commenting on the first part of this triad, "the impossibility of not thinking," in relation to the subject of cinema concerns the automatic character of thought, which it shares with the movement-image, for even my refusal to think only signals that place where another thinks in my place. Not thinking, therefore, appears to Artaud as impossible a priori. Likewise, the second and third parts concern thinking as a power or quality that belongs to the subject and are impossible a priori—the first in the sense that all thinking is composed of clichés, the second in sense that thought itself (or "what is called thinking," represented either as a common notion, an opinion, or a kind of dominant image) must ultimately be determined a transcendental cliché, or an *Urdoxa*.

And it was only because the automatic character of thought already found a resemblance with the automatic character of the movement-image that cinema discovered the dynamic principle by means of which it could emerge as the *force* that causes the subject to think. The dominant image of thought appears in this resemblance as a power in accordance with the power of nature, or with the order of *technē*, by which knowledge intervenes to disturb, "work over," and fundamentally transform the interval nature-culture. According to this dynamic representation, *thinking is a power* that has as its beginning a point of projection (a subject) and as its end a transformed nature or a fabricated object (a world); between these two points there is a certain directionality or orientation by which thought is translated spatially from subject to object, from culture to nature, and back again; and temporally from idea of whole to the whole transfigured. Therefore, it is because of this *mere resemblance* that the movement-image acquires a certain power to determine the whole, and the appearance of this power is then consolidated as a specialized technical knowledge, that, finally, the whole problem of the resemblance between the movement-image in cinema and the ideological images deployed by the apparatus of the state ensues. And it is only on the basis of this resemblance that Paul Virilio's thesis is correct, namely, that there has been no diversion of the movement-image to ideological ends, but rather the "movement-image was from the beginning linked to the organization of war, state propaganda, ordinary fascism, historically and essentially."[40] However, this resemblance in fact only implies that the problem of ideology was already implicit in the "image of thought," that is, it was already latent in the subject and was simply awaiting its final birth: the automatic character of thought as a power, as either a "habitual" or a transformative force, one that could internalize the whole within a subject, and externalize the subject as a whole (a world, a state, a national conscience).

Should the failure of a classical cinema founded on the movement-image, as its goals and aspirations were formulated by Eisenstein, not be inferred from an image of thought that was still attached to this problematic resemblance? Did this resemblance not condition Eisenstein's belief that cinema will eventually achieve, by perfecting its knowledge of the movement-image, the means to repair the broken interval that appears as the cause of the subject's collective fragmentation? To unify the subject by crossing in both directions the gap between instinct and intelligence, and between thinking and action—both would amount to absorbing the interval into the synthesis of the movement-image. Because this perfection was understood primarily in terms of the action-image, conceived as the solution to art's neurosis and to collective fragmentation suffered by "a people who is missing" (both conceived as figures of "negative apprehension"), it is ironic to see that it was precisely this conception of the action-image itself that was the cause of this neurosis. All movement through space is constructed by clichés, and the "action-image" was itself a cliché of a special type; to evoke the "revolutionary" potential of the new cinema seems contradictory because it constitutes a cliché of the highest order, an *Urdoxa*, which posits either the total transformation of the whole or the "subject as Whole." It was, in fact, a false solution that only furthered the break between the human being and the world, even realizing this impasse as an absolute and giving it an objectified form of the purely optical and sound situations in which thought appears to be trapped. As a result of these situations, as Deleuze writes, "[t]he spiritual automaton is in the psychic situation of the seer, who sees better and further than he can react, that is, think" (*The Time-Image*, 170). Deleuze's thesis is that this is precisely the "no exit" on which the new cinema founds itself. Nihilism, therefore, is not a spirit that is restricted to philosophy alone. At the same time, he suggests, there may still be hope and the example of Artaud's relationship to cinema offers a way of "thinking through cinema by means of cinema."

Beginning from this situation, and even affirming it as the fundamental condition of the modern subject, the desire to make the interval appear directly is the solution that Artaud offers: to attach thought not to a motor image that would extinguish it in action, or absorb it in knowledge, but directly to the interval itself so that thought would find its cause no longer in the image, but rather would find what within the image refuses to be thought. In other words, if the whole problem of thought was that it was attached to an image that represented it, then Artaud turns this problem around to reveal its true experience for the subject. What this experience reveals is precisely the automatic, habitual, and instinctual character of the thought that thinks me, interpolates me, and determines me as a subject. One might still define this experience as "total provocation" or "nooshock"; yet, the nature of this experience with the cause of thinking has undergone a radical change. Under its previous image, shock, the neuronal messenger, simply travels along the same path that was opened, according to Artaud's cry, by a more fundamental power, thus referring the shock effect that appears as the basis of the projects of art and ideology to an event that occurs before my birth. But this implies that the cause of thinking remains unconscious *in principle,* because it can never really emerge as a motive of conscious understanding or become the condition of deliberative action. Instead, thought leaps over the interval to become *in principle* the conditions of an action that remains fundamentally unthought, like an involuntary reaction, habitual response, or nerve impulse. Under its new image, this dynamic representation of thinking as a force is no longer "the goal," and the problem is no longer in attaining an "image of thought" that would be equal to the force of the whole (i.e., the perfection of "the action-image"), but rather, according to Artaud, *it is this "image" of thought as a force or a power that itself is suddenly revealed as the problem of thinking.* It reveals precisely the shock that "I am not yet thinking" or that "what is called thinking" is a power that belongs to a subject who "I am not." The effect of this awareness bears a certain "dissociative force" that pries thought from its image, at the same time as it cuts the image off from the world, and exposes it to what Deleuze calls its "reverse proof," *"the fact that we are not yet thinking"* (167; emphasis in original).[41]

Both cinema and ideology are expressions of the same broken interval between the human and the world, an interval that has reduced the link to only what one hears or sees; both have participated in the transformation of the world into an object of belief—even if this belief should prove illusory. It is precisely because everything that I see and hear is capable of being false, the expressions of deceit or trickery, of false oaths and betrayal, that only my belief is capable of reconnecting me with what I see and hear. The situation I have been outlining as the basis of both the cinematic mechanism and the mechanism of ideology amounts to an extreme Cartesianism—however, one without any recourse to the principle of God, who provides the subject of the cogito with fundamental certainty of knowledge. This is because, under the axiom of I = the Other, the subject I feel myself to be in perceiving, willing, desiring can always be an "Other." As Deleuze writes, "It was already a great turning-point in philosophy, from Pascal to Nietzsche: to replace the model of knowledge with belief" (*The Time-Image,* 172). Likewise, modern cinema, by reducing the world to the image, can only intervene into the fold that runs between the human and the world; it is by changing the signs and affects of perception and consciousness that it is alone capable of provoking a change in the nature of consciousness itself. After all, what is a human being but the accumulation of conscious perceptions, affective qualities, and memory signs? The loss of the direct relation to the body, as Artaud experienced it, is only the ultimate expression of a universal predicament. Thought is full of clichés, memory is not to be trusted, and perception is made to order. It is ironic, then, that the only means we have of restoring a connection that has been broken or damaged is by the very means that has caused our separation, by means of perception-images, memory-images, sounds, and statements. This is why modern cinema, in particular, will be concerned with rendering an experience or connection between the body and the world, with creating new visual and sound images that might "give back" the body's relationship to the world, which has been lost in a chaos of clichés. Therefore, as Deleuze argues, cinema cannot intervene directly into the world, or cause this world to be transformed into another, but it may be one of the only means we have of restoring our belief—a strange optimism that can be formulated as follows: to continue to believe in cinema, despite everything, despite even the repeated "failures" of cinema itself, is to believe in the actualization of the world *as it is*.

Now, Eisenstein's belief in the power of "revolutionary cinema" is well known and we have underlined many of its principles. In Artaud, however, we have the figure of a "true believer" in the cinema who had to suffer through the stages of renouncing a too simple faith in cinema in order to discover a more profound reason to believe. "The nature of the cinematographic illusion has often been considered," Deleuze writes. "Restoring our belief in the world—this is the power of modern cinema (when it stops being bad). Whether we are Christians or atheists, in our universal schizophrenia, *we need reasons to believe in this world*" (ibid.; emphasis in original). The situation we face today only expresses this fact to an extreme degree, which underlies the radical uncertainty when the appeal to earlier models of knowledge and reason is exposed to the accusations of "bad faith." Nevertheless, the affirmative principle expressed by Nietszche (but also by Kierkegaard before him) can be understood as being the most sobering response to this predicament: to believe in the world *as it is*, neither in a transformed world nor in another world, and to provide an image of thought that thoroughly belongs to this world which is ruled by the powers of the false; moreover, to raise falsehood to a positive principle in the service of those who choose to live in this world and not in another. In either case, what we have been calling the "modern subject," for lack of a better name, is faced with a terrible choice: either continue to live in such a way that he or she can no longer believe anything he or she sees or hears (resulting in the loss of any connection to the world), or actively cultivate the reasons to believe in a world populated by fools, confidence men, and tricksters. Restoring our connection to the world, but also assuming a constant vigilance over clichés and ready-made linkages—these are the tasks of the cinema that emerges today from this new situation of thought.

CINEMA AND THE BRAIN: "WHAT IS INTELLECTUAL CINEMA?"

In the beginning of this essay, I posed the following questions: "What kind of image is to be deduced from thought and how can thinking be determined by an image? How does the image first acquire its power over thought in order to provoke the event called 'thinking' to happen within a subject?" In attempting to respond to these questions about the relationship between modern cinema and thought, I have followed Deleuze several times around a vague and nebulous interval where thinking is attached to an image, only in turn to go astray and lose its way back through "the image" to the actualization of the interval itself. Thinking gets bogged down in the images that represent it; either it gets trapped in its resemblance to a habitual automatic movement or it gets "stolen away" by its resemblance to a force that opens it to the idea of another nature, whether this *other nature* appears quantitatively in the idea of the whole, or dynamically in the terrible grimace of the sublime that is caricatured, in different ways, by art and politics in the modern period (the former, by its insane demand for the "whole as perfection," the latter by its insane demand for the "whole as immanence"). Moreover, as Deleuze argues, in the early "goals" of modern cinema we have a certain synthesis of the first two in the nature of the movement-image and in the insane demand for realization of the "whole as subject." Benjamin had clearly perceived the dangers of this third synthesis when he stated that the synthesis of the goals of art with the goals of politics could produce nothing more than the very conditions for the emergence of fascism. The fact that this may be a simplistic assessment, and has been surpassed by more difficult and finer analyses of the problems of mass art and mass politics in "an age of mechanical reproduction," does not make this statement any less accurate or thought-provoking today.

If, as Deleuze argues, with the emergence of cinema the material universe, the plane of immanence, can be conceived as a *machinic assemblage of movement-images*, then modern cinema has botched in its handling of this plane several times, just as modern philosophy and modern science have in their own manner and on their own respective planes. Perhaps this could not be helped, given the ways the problems were stated.[42] We have already discussed the other solutions Deleuze pointed to under the abbreviated signs of "Hollywood and Hitler," both of which abandoned the much more tortuous path that Eisenstein's dialectical cinema demanded and instead sought to provide an immediate satisfaction. But then, after all, perhaps this is what the subject wanted: a little bit of pleasure, a little peace of mind, a little belief, a little bit of identity, a little bit of death for others as well as for itself; "to shuffle off its mortal coils, perchance to sleep, to dream" (Shakespeare, *Hamlet*). But instead of seeing these demands that stem from a demented mind or the vulgar brain, could we not understand them as reactions to the same intolerable situation we have described around the figure of Artaud—the impossibility of not thinking, the impossibility of thinking, the impossibility of thinking differently? According to Deleuze's account, all of these impasses and false solutions finally led to a state of affairs where the plane of immanence was lost entirely, and wherein thinking becomes dispossessed of itself and the world. At this point, he offers Artaud's solution to the problem of cinema as well as to the problem of thought: that by directing its antennae toward what is invisible, toward what lies *outside* the image and no longer toward the image of the whole, cinema could survive its own death and could await its own rebirth by discovering a new image of thought that Deleuze addresses under the concept of the time-image. However, we must recognize that even here the solution that Deleuze offers is itself another wager that offers no guarantee that the new cinema will not develop differently than he imagines. Deleuze's wager, like Eisenstein's before him, remains a little more than a hope, and a little less than a conviction; as we stated, it takes the form of a will to believe in the powers that are proper to cinema and art, which he calls the powers of the false.[43]

Therefore, if Deleuze shares with Eisenstein a certain guarded optimism for intellectual cinema, he descends to discover its true principle, freedom, and its true subject, the brain. But freedom of what or freedom from what? Deleuze's response is quite simple: freedom from the motor-unity coordination of the movement-image and from the teleological unity of action-image. All of the different solutions to the problem of the image that cinema offers are paths leading to the brain, in the sense that all paths lead to the brain, although the images that these paths actualize never resemble the brain. *The brain is not an image, even though all the images actualize a certain aspect (or lobe) of the brain.* In a 1986 interview, Deleuze directly addresses the relationship between cinema and thought in terms of the brain:

> The brain is unity. The brain is the screen. I don't believe that linguistics and psychoanalysis offer a great deal to the cinema. On the contrary, the biology of the brain—molecular biology—does. Thought is molecular. Molecular speeds make up the slow beings that we are. As Michaux said, "*Man is a slow being, who is only made possible thanks to fantastic speeds.*" The circuits and linkages of the brain don't preexist the stimuli, corpuscles, and particles [*grains*] that trace them. Cinema isn't theater; rather, it makes bodies out of grains. The linkages are often paradoxical and on all sides overflow simple associations of images. Cinema, precisely because it puts the image in motion, or rather endows the image with self-motion [*auto-mouvement*], never stops tracing the circuits of the brain. This characteristic can be manifested either positively or negatively. The screen, that is to say ourselves, can be the deficient brain of an idiot as easily as a creative brain [of a thinker].[44]

The brain is the "goal." Of course, it was the goal all along, as we have seen with Eisenstein's remarks on the Kabuki. However, instead of conceiving of the brain as an organ, where thought is essentially a muscular contraction between stimulus and response, we might instead conceive it as the sensible screen (a membrane) that is interposed between the human and the world (the chaos of clichés) as the quality of a creative emotion that is capable of revitalizing the link between the human and the world. That is to say, with the discovery of what Deleuze calls "the time-image," cinema achieves a freedom from the sensory-motor schema, the spatial coordinates of the action-image and the movement-image. A third kind of image appears in the interval between perception and reaction, "emotion," understood as the "I feel" of the cinematographic subject, which occupies the interval without "filling it up." In this aspect, it shares a certain attribute with the image of the brain, which is simultaneously outside movement, before movement, and the cause of movement. As Deleuze writes, "the interval is set free, the interstice becomes irreducible and stands on its own" (*The Time-Image*, 277).

At the same time, we might ask what has happened that has made the brain appear as the object of the new cinema, something that Deleuze finds explicitly in the films of Resnais (e.g., *Mon Oncle d'Amérique*), where the brain itself becomes subject, where characters become the shadows of the living reality of mental theater, and where feelings become "the true figures in a 'cerebral game' which is very concrete" (125). *This is because, to a great degree, modern memory is already cinematographic, and the brain of the world (the past) is made from cinema.* According to Deleuze, this is what happens when the image becomes time-image: "The world has become memory, brain, superimposition of ages or lobes, but the brain itself has become consciousness, continuation of ages, creation or growth of ever new lobes, re-creation of matter" (ibid.). The matter of cinema thus shares a material aspect of memory by which it descends into the interval to create memory and to actualize the past—whether this past is one of a people or culture (monumental past) or of a person (private associations). As the character Frank Volterra states in Delillo's *The Names*, "the whole world is on film."[15] In other words, to echo a similar statement by Heidegger, *the world worlds cinematographically.* This recalls a moment that occurs earlier in *Bergsonism* when Deleuze first posits a fictive and fabulous faculty, or "storytelling function," which appears in the interval between intelligence and society. And, according to the argument, it is by means of this "storytelling function" that society makes itself obeyed. This "[v]irtual instinct [is a] creator of Gods, inventor of religions, that is, of fictitious representations 'which will stand up to the representation of the real and which will succeed, by the intermediary of intelligence itself, in thwarting intellectual work'" (108). Can we not perceive the movement-image as the modern avatar of this mythmaking function that appears as the ground of society? Moreover, does this passage not recapitulate the problematic alliance we have discovered between the movement-image and a certain social intelligence of modern ideologies that, as the intermediaries of intelligence itself, prevent the possibility of thought? At the same time, as Bergson had earlier argued, it is also within the very same interval that something appears without "filling it up" or causing it to contract into instinct. This "something that appears," according to Deleuze, is *emotion*, because "only emotion differs in nature from both intelligence and instinct, from both intelligent individual egoism and instinctive social pressures" (110). It is around the nature of this emotion that Deleuze resorts to the solution that Bergson used to characterize the interval between perception and response as the "gap" that allows the human being to become open to a duration that remains "outside" its own plane, to transform the limited and "closed" present of habit or instinctive reaction into the openness of creative intuition.

But we must ask why emotion is here described as primarily an expression of the brain. In response, we must recall the situation we described earlier in which belief was the only thing capable of restoring our connection to the world. Thus, in the statement "I FEEL," we do not have an image, but rather a mode that expresses a degree of openness that only then is filled by an image (joy, sadness, pain, conflict, etc.). Here, we must see belief (or disbelief) as a fundamental expression of emotion. Therefore, if the human being finds itself in the situation in which its only connection to the world is by what she or he sees or hears, then that belief determines the strength or weakness of this connection, as well as characterizes a certain quality of intensity that defines this connection. We could say the same of disbelief. For example, in the statements we often hear ourselves and others pronounce—"I can't believe what I'm seeing" or "I can't believe what I'm hearing"—there is a certain quality that characterizes the connection to our perception or understanding. At what level do we separate thought from this emotional quality? Is not thinking itself a manner of developing perceptions and statements under the signs of belief or disbelief, in such a way that what we describe as real or true are simply the objective signs of belief that thinking has created? In other words, reality itself is composed of signs that produce a lesser or greater degree of belief, and these signs in turn are qualities that one finds in the world and that are bound up with the qualities of conscious perception, subjective memory, or the qualities of objects themselves. It is for this reason that Bergson characterized thought or creative memory as *in principle* an emotional being, because thinking operates on the objective signs and traces of belief and disbelief that compose the material connections that make up a world. Thinking operates on these signs either by giving them fresh, new perceptions and reestablishing their connection, or by destroying them and working them over in favor of new connections. As Deleuze writes concerning the creative principle by which thinking operates: "The principle that works in this way does so through a notion of 'detonating the past': a virtual or fabulous instinct in the human is super-added to the animal instinct, producing the capability of 'destroying' previous relations between perception-images and recollection-images, thereby creating the path toward new linkages and associations" (105).

This could be called the primal work of intelligence. We can find this principle at work in the dream. Even in their dreams, human beings are constantly "working over" and preparing matter by destroying previous relations (the residual traces of the day's experiences) and creating a complex assemblage of new linkages. However, when the form of the dream itself is mistaken for this principle, as it was in the solution offered by surrealism, making the form of the dream represent the power of this principle, then we lose the principle by enclosing it within the image of the dream—that is, by subordinating the principle under its image, or representation. A similar state of affairs was already discussed concerning the relationship of cinema and thought, which was enclosed in the form of the movement-image and its resemblance to the automatic character of thought. As a result, thought was enclosed in this resemblance and lost touch with the principle of thinking. This is the principle of memory that plunges into the interval between perception and consciousness, which expands or scrambles the residues of perception and prepares them for new combinations and rearrangements by conscious recollection. Here, the "past itself" cannot be determined outside this possibility of being scrambled and entering into new combinations with the present, with any present whatever: thus, memory conditions the principle of freedom whereby life frees itself from determination—from the whole of the "past and its 'it was.'" "Freedom has precisely this physical sense: 'to detonate' an explosive, to use it for more and more powerful movements" (107).

How does this come about? According to Deleuze, it is possible because the brain actually constitutes a special type of matter that is more supple and less "closed." In other words, "nothing here goes beyond the physico-chemical properties of a particularly complicated type of matter" (ibid.). Contrary to a kind of matter that is "determined," the matter of the brain is capable of becoming "determining determination" (*naturing nature*). This is why, in *What Is Philosophy?*, Deleuze and Guattari identify the brain (*le cerveau*) as nothing less than spirit itself (*l'esprit*); and in Deleuze's *Bergsonism*, the concept of élan vital represents the positive "discovery" of the privilege of the brain, by which life "makes use" of the matter of the brain (that is, the matter of memory) in order to "get through," to leap from the closed circle of an already determined and "closed" nature. This would appear to be a problematic moment, because Deleuze is here affirming that the form of man "*is* the purpose of the entire process of evolution" (106). In other words, he would appear to be saying that the nature of human being is the highest duration, and occupies the pinnacle of the teleology of all of nature, as if all of nature is not only determined by the nature of the human, but even has as its only goal to *become human*. However, this would not be an accurate conclusion, which is why Deleuze and Guattari return to the same argument in *What Is Philosophy?* If the nature of human is (*quid facti?*) the naturing nature of the brain, then the question becomes "What is human?" With this question, the priority is reversed and the duration occupied by the human is subordinated to the principal creation of memory (of the brain). Although this might appear to be circular reasoning, it is actually the difference and repetition inserted between brain and subject: "Will the turning point not be elsewhere, in the place where the brain is 'subject,' where it becomes subject? It is the brain that thinks and not man—the latter being only a cerebral crystallization. We will speak of the brain as Cézanne spoke of the landscape: man absent from, but completely within the brain."[46] In other words, "nature" does not find its end with the form of man, because this form is closed, alienated from itself, and must be overcome, and the brain is the machine that is capable of making this happen.[47]

Concluding with these observations from *Bergsonism* on the importance of the brain in Bergsonian philosophy may help to clarify why Bergson returns as a central figure in the cinema books. Using Bergson's distinction, there is only a quantitative difference in degree between the human brain (as "spiritual automaton," or determined determination) and the cinematographic automaton, although there is equally for both a qualitative difference, or difference in kind, when we speak of the brain *in principle*; that is, when we speak of cinema as a process (as both Eisenstein and Deleuze speak of it), the quantitative differences between the two brains are dissolved into a single dynamic principle of creation and order—when we speak of the cinematic brain as a "*subject-superject*" (Whitehead). This might also clarify the relation of thought that Deleuze argues for the cinema, as well as his arguments concerning the "cinematographic subject" (I THINK), which precedes a people and causes its creation, even fabulously; therefore, the subject of such a cinema would necessarily have to be outside language, national culture (or story); that is, it would have to be a "people" that was created by cinema itself, and could not depend on politics for its creation, because politics actually "creates" nothing but only makes use of the creations of philosophy, art, and science. In an original manner, therefore, it was Eisenstein who discovered in the "machine" of cinema a means of transcending the mechanisms of perception, opinion (common ideas, or views), and cliché in order to invent newer and finer articulations of the linkages between the human and the world, what Deleuze would later call the creation of "percepts and affects." Cinema does this precisely by making use of the conventions and determinations "to pass though the net of determinations that have spread out" into a world (determinations of perception, opinion, character, etc.) and, as a result, it fashions its own conventions, which become *doxa* as well—and there is always a danger that these forms will become rigid and dominant. There is also the danger of cinema in the service of an already-existing national character, a kind of monumental cinema that represents the propagandistic function of both Soviet cinema and American popular cinema.[48] Applying the statements above to the brain constructed by cinema, we might recognize in the "goal" of intellectual cinema the desire to build a better brain, "to leap from the circle of closed societies"; moreover, cinema "makes use" of the matter of the brain (that is, the matter of memory) in order to "get through," to leap from the closed circle of natured nature, "to make a machine to triumph over mechanism," "to use the determination of nature to pass through the meshes of the net which this very determination has spread."[49]

Does this not imply a doubling of an earlier solution that Bergson found in the élan vital? That is, if the brain was invented to surpass a closed plane of nature, does the human in turn invent cinema in order to surpass the closed duration of man? Here, the whole question of the relationship between cinema and thought resides, and it all depends on what kind of brain we want—the deficient brain of an idiot, or the creative brain of a thinker.

NOTES

1. Sergei Eisenstein, "The Filmic Fourth Dimension," in *Film Form*, trans. Jay Leyda (New York: Harcourt Brace Jovanovich, 1949), 64–71. This notion of "overtonal conflict" recalls Eisenstein's early reflections on the Kabuki around the event of "physiological shock," defined as the "total provocation of the human brain" (20). The principle that Eisenstein witnessed in the Kabuki is the function of a pure montage in which each element is viewed from the perspective of the total effect produced by the complete theater: "In the Kabuki ... the Japanese regards each theatrical element, not as an incommensurable unit among various categories of affect (on the various sense organs), but as a single unit of theater.... Directing himself to the various organs of sensation, he builds his summation [of individual "pieces"] to a grand *total* provocation of the human brain, without taking any notice *which* of these several paths he is following" (64; emphasis in original). "Thus," he writes, "the Japanese have shown us another extremely interesting form of ensemble: *the monastic ensemble* where sound/movement/space/voice do not accompany each other, *but function as elements of equal significance*"(20; emphasis in original). The emphasis on a free, indeterminate accord of the elements of expression, with no one determining the significance of the others, recalls a fundamental principle that belonged to Artaud's Theater of Cruelty, which I will discuss later.

2. See also Gilles Deleuze, *Difference and Repetition*, trans. Paul Patton (New York: Columbia University Press, 1994), especially chapter 5, "Asymmetrical Synthesis of the Sensible."
3. Eisenstein, "The Filmic Fourth Dimension," 71.
4. Gilles Deleuze, *The Time-Image*, trans. Hugh Tomlinson and Robert Galeta (Minneapolis: University of Minnesota Press, 1989), 156.
5. Ibid.
6. Rainer Maria Rilke, "The Archaic Bust of Apollo," in *Collected Poems*, trans. Stephen Mitchell (New York: Pantheon Books, 1983). This command structure is something that Rilke attempted to capture in terms of the poetic image with the headless bust of Apollo, signifying a radical deformation, followed by the command: "You must change your life."
7. Deleuze, *The Time-Image*, 158.
8. Sergei Eisenstein, cited in ibid., 211.
9. Deleuze, *The Time-Image*, 156.
10. Walter Benjamin, "What Is Epic Theater?" in *Illuminations*, ed. Hannah Arendt, trans. Harry Zohn (New York: Schocken Books, 1969), 150.
11. Antonin Artaud, *The Theater and Its Double*, trans. Mary Caroline Richards (New York: Grove Press, 1958), 10. Cf. also Derrida's exposition of this principle in "The Theater of Cruelty," in *Writing and Difference*, trans. Alan Bass (Chicago: University of Chicago Press, 1978), 232–50.
12. Deleuze, *The Time-Image*, 156.
13. Ibid., 158. It is interesting to note that the argument that Deleuze makes for the cinematographic image here is exactly the same argument for the function of the drug in the section "Becoming Molecular" from *A Thousand Plateaus: Capitalism and Schizophrenia*, trans. Brian Massumi (Minneapolis: University of Minnesota Press, 1987). Consequently, there is an implicit connection between a dynamic representation of the sublime (i.e., the principle of "nooshock"), the experience of the drug, and what happens within the brain (and body) of the cinematic spectator. Eisenstein himself had first commented on this relationship in "Film Form: New Problems," which he identifies with the forms of prelogical, sensual thinking: "That is, that art is nothing but an artificial retrogression in the field of psychology toward the earlier thought-processes, i.e., a phenomenon identical with any given form of drug, alcohol, shamanism, religion, etc." (*Film Form*, 144).
14. Gilles Deleuze, *Bergsonism*, trans. Hugh Tomlinson and Barbara Habberjam (New York: Zone Books, 1988), 104–5.
15. Gilles Deleuze and Félix Guattari, *What Is Philosophy?*, trans. Hugh Tomlinson and Graham Burchell (New York: Columbia University Press, 1995), 208. In fact, the manner in which chaos is figured will depend on how it is "cut up" by the three planes (a process resembling montage), each of which engages it from its own distinct procedures and problems, which causes chaos to appear differently within each plane. Cf. part 2, "Philosophy, Science, Logic, and Art," 117–218.
16. Gilles Deleuze, *Kant's Critical Philosophy: The Doctrine of the Faculties*, trans. Hugh Tomlinson and Barbara Habberjam (Minneapolis: University of Minnesota Press, 1984), 51; emphasis added.
17. This underscores the significance of the baroque for Deleuze and the importance it bears for establishing the direction and the problem of artistic and political representation in the modern period. See especially Gilles Deleuze, *The Fold: Leibniz and the Baroque*, trans. Tom Conley (Minneapolis: University of Minnesota Press, 1993).
18. As I will discuss later, however, the direct realization of this force also addresses a problematic relationship that Benjamin discovers at the basis of fascism. See especially Walter Benjamin, "The Work of Art in the Mechanical Age of Reproduction," in *Illuminations*, 217–51.
19. The event of this repeated failure whereby art comes to a limit and recoils upon

itself can be understood to lie behind two principal tensions that can be found in the movement of art. First, the sense of "recoil" can be expressed as the *schism* between the "culture" of the artist and creator and a mass or popular cultural subject, underlying the tendency of modern art to withdraw and to enclose itself in an aristocratic social form. This "schism" characterizes the relationship between the "spiritual automaton" of modern art and the major-brain or mass subject that is mediated by the forms of conflict, opposition, and even disgust; at the same time, it expresses the quantitative degree of its failure in the sense that its power (or "nooshock") is capable of affecting only the minor-brain of an elite or aristocratic class composed mostly of artists themselves. The second sense of the "recoil" of modern art can be figured as its *obsession* over the idea of self-achievement and of conceiving the *work* of art as a total movement that passes historically through uneven stages of development in order to reach an absolute expression (e.g., Mallarmé's "Absolute Poem") or to restore it to an immanent relationship with the movement of life itself (e.g., Artaud's "theater of cruelty"). The duration occupied by each art form must be conceived from the perspective of this idea of the whole in such a way that each successive "failure" also represents the possibility of teleological renewal in its progress toward achieving a final "goal." Eisenstein's dialectical theory of the artwork, which finds its penultimate expression in the emergence of modern cinema, participates in this teleological image of the modern artwork.

20. Deleuze, *Kant's Critical Philosophy*, 146.
21. Deleuze defines this distinction in the following manner: "Art takes a bit of chaos in a frame in order to form a composed chaos [or 'chaosmos'] that becomes sensory, or from which it extracts a chaoid sensation as variety; but science takes a bit of chaos in a system of coordinates and forms a referenced chaos that becomes Nature, and from which it extracts an aleatory function and chaoid variables" (*What Is Philosophy?*, 206). I am arguing that both aspects are present in cinema as Eisenstein conceived it in its earliest stages, and this becomes explicit in Deleuze's critique of what he calls Eisenstein's "monism," which he develops in the final sections of *The Time-Image*.
22. Deleuze and Guattari, *What Is Philosophy?*, 164.
23. Gilles Deleuze, *The Movement-Image*, trans. Hugh Tomlinson and Barbara Habberjam (Minneapolis: University of Minnesota Press, 1986), 59.
24. Deleuze, *The Time-Image*, 159ff.
25. Ibid., 161; emphasis added.
26. Eisenstein writes: "The point is that the forms of sensual, pre-logical thinking, which are preserved in the shape of inner speech among the peoples who have reached an adequate level of social and cultural development, at the same time also represent in mankind at the dawn of cultural development norms of conduct in general, i.e., laws according to which flow the processes of sensual thought are equivalent for them to a 'habit logic' of the future" (*Film Form*, 131).
27. Deleuze, *The Time-Image*, 162; emphasis added.
28. Here, contrary to Deleuze's assertion, Eisenstein's "goal" appears less Hegelian and more Whiteheadian in his aspiration to draw up more primitive states of satisfaction and emotion into higher orders of intellectual satisfaction and complexity, the aesthetic or artistic dimension of the cinematographic process figured in this process as the achievement of "balance" between the two forms. See Alfred North Whitehead, *Process and Reality*, ed. David Ray Griffin and Donald W. Sherburne (New York: Free Press, 1978), especially "The Higher Phases of Experience," 256–80.
29. Eisenstein, *Film Form*, 145.
30. Antonin Artaud, cited in Deleuze, *The Time-Image*, 165.
31. Ibid., 164.
32. This criticism is the subtext of Eisenstein's 1935 speech "Film Form: New Problems" (*Film Form*, 122–49).

33. Deleuze, *The Time-Image*, 78.
34. Given this state of affairs, it is odd that contemporary intellectual cinema has not resolved this problem in a manner similar to the solution of postmodern architecture by creating a genre of films that will never be produced and that exist only virtually in the forms of scripts, picture boards, and designs.
35. Deleuze, *The Movement-Image*, 208–9; emphasis added.
36. Deleuze, *The Time-Image*, 173.
37. On the nature of this "crack" or caesura in thought, see Peter Canning's important discussion of this Deleuzian topic in "The Crack in Time and the Ideal Game," in *Gilles Deleuze and the Theater of Philosophy*, ed. Constantin Boundas and Dorothea E. Olkowski (New York: Columbia University Press, 1993), 73–98.
38. I could apply this event to two different discursive regions of modern knowledge in order to validate the statement that Artaud's expression of spiritual rape is integral to the problem of ideology. The first region is that of psychoanalysis, where, in the Freudian concept of the primal scene, this event, although not explicitly attached to the notion of ideological automaton, takes on the character of something that occurs outside or before conscious life and the temporal form of a "trace" (like the shadow of an earlier force) that returns to disturb and even to *deform* perception and thought. The second region would be contemporary forms of ideology critique where the figure of rape, this time as "metaphor," is frequently used—particularly by feminism (e.g., Pratt, Mohantry, Suleri) and postcolonial theory (e.g., Fanon)—to represent the nature of psychic violence that is suffered by the subject, and to signal the affective disturbances of memory and thought (feelings of disconnection, splitting or "dual consciousness" [Fanon], parodistic or hybrid forms of socializing this crack or splitting of the subject, even as prescriptions for resistance [Bhabha]). My argument (which represents a reading of Deleuze around this point) is that Artaud's expression clarifies the affective image of powerlessness that appears as the problem of thought in the modern critiques of ideology, even perhaps addressing a "universal" condition of the modern subject—that, indeed, Artaud's problem is also ours. On this last point, it is interesting to note that most criticism around the subject of Artaud has concerned precisely, if not exclusively, whether his experience represents either an "exemplary" or simply an "exceptional" case. On this point, see particularly Derrida's "La parole soufflée," in *Writing and Difference*, 169–95.
39. This is a formula I have adapted from Kafka, and it represents a problem that modern literature has discovered as well, which can be proposed in terms of movement. As both Kafka and Beckett testify, any movement is infinitely treacherous and is filled with hallucinations of motor coordination and the false hopes of arriving somewhere. As Beckett asked, "Where now, who now?"—that is, "Where would I go if I could go, who would I be if I get there?" On the one hand, as Kafka proposed with the character of Gregor Samsa, it is better not to move at all, "to lie on my back with a thousand tiny hands waving desperately in front of me"; however, Gregor discovered that this solution was too unbearable, if not already impossible, because he was already moving in his nature and this "metamorphosis" was a movement that he could neither remember willing nor something that he could control. On the other hand, this is Beckett's proposal in the characters of Molly, Malone, and the Unnameable: he could achieve another means of movement; thus, if he could not walk, he could crawl, if not that, he might roll, if not that, then what? Likewise, this solution became impossible; even when he found himself without arms or legs, just a floating head in a barrel, he was tortured by the organs of thought that moved within him.
40. Deleuze, *The Time-Image*, 165.
41. Deleuze borrows this formulation from Heidegger's famous statement that occurs in *What Is Called Thinking?*: "the most thought-provoking thing that we are

given today to think is the fact that we are not yet thinking" (Martin Heidegger, *What Is Called Thinking?* [New York: Harper and Row, 1952], 4).

42. For example, earlier we saw how Eisenstein originally had the intuition of this interval as a "fourth dimension" of cinematographic space-time, and in the discovery of a new subject, the "cinematographic I FEEL," but then botched his original intuition when he attached it to a motor image of thought (the dialectical automaton); that is, he imagined a teleological duration through which cinema would unfold, attaching the primitive emotions and instinctual forms of thought to the higher phases of abstraction and symbolic processes, to finally achieve an image of thought that itself took the form of montage, which would restore the laws of the process of thought, which in turn would restore moving reality in the process of unfolding.
43. I discuss this concept in "On the Powers of the False: How the True World Finally Became a Fable," in *Chaos Theory and the Textures of Time*, ed. Paul Harris (forthcoming).
44. Gilles Deleuze, "The Brain Is the Screen" (included as chapter 13 in this collection). Originally published in *Cahiers du cinéma* 380 (February 1986): 26.
45. Don Delillo, *The Names* (New York: Vintage Books, 1982), 200. Delillo's novel, in fact, corresponds to the situation we have been describing, the break between the human and the world, and even exhausts all the semiotic modes for repairing this break (psychology, anthropology, science, literature, film, probability statistics, and so on). The alphabet itself is reduced, on the one hand, to pure silence and exteriority (as in the meaningless talk of the personal that takes place between James, the main character, and his estranged wife and son), and, on the other hand, to pure violence and absolutely interiority in the series of cult murders whose only objective is to return death to the plane of immanence and to destroy any image and any external surface of recording.
46. Deleuze and Guattari, *What Is Philosophy?*, 210.
47. The conclusion of *What Is Philosophy?* ends with the discussion of the brain (*le cerveau*), which is ironic because the brain is itself the origin of all duration(s). It constitutes the absolute beginning; without the brain, there would be nothing. In fact, there would not even be nothing, because nothing is already the negative limit, which cannot be extracted from the possibility of consciousness, and therefore already presupposes the brain as its a priori condition.
48. Again, this is why Eisenstein was particularly concerned with the "artificial construction" of montage that would not be immediately naturalized by perception, by the aural image that would not be subordinated to national language or character, and by "feeling" (the fourth dimension) that would be immediately simply understood as emotion, the psychological representation of a subjective affection. If, according to our earlier examples, the sound-image is bound too closely to a particular language, a certain literary tradition or folk culture, then its capacity will be drastically reduced. Likewise, the visual image bound to the conventions of a "highly cultured drama" or national theater also reproduces the dramatic types that underlie certain national characteristics or regional stereotypes. Therefore, Eisenstein's earlier call for an "international cinema" must now be understood as the subject of cinema as "subject-*superject*." A combination of Spinoza and Whitehead: for every image, there is also a subject. Yet this subject comes from the outside, as do the creation of some images; it strikes the automaton and raises the possibility of a new subject who has never before existed on the earth. This explains why Deleuze's project on cinema focuses on the very means by which cinema makes use of determinations of perception, emotion, character, and cliché in order to surpass them by the creation of crystalline narration, perceptions, and affects of a subject that "is missing and still to come."
49. Deleuze, *Bergsonism*, 107.

Chapter 10

Midday, Midnight

The Emergence of Cine-Thinking

Éric Alliez

Translated by Patricia Dailey

> *We seek to determine an impersonal and pre-individual transcendental field, which does not resemble the corresponding empirical fields, and which nevertheless is not confused with an undifferentiated depth.*
>
> —Gilles Deleuze, *The Logic of Sense*[1]

> *[T]he essence of cinema—which is not the majority of films—has thought as its higher purpose, nothing but thought and its functioning.*
>
> —Gilles Deleuze, *The Time-Image*[2]

1

The two volumes that constitute Deleuze's inquiry into the cinematic image, *The Movement-Image* and *The Time-Image*, are like two facets of an inquiry that, together, form one remarkable book of philosophy—a book situated in the very middle [*au milieu*] of Deleuze's philosophy. This milieu, in which the essence of a thing appears, is likewise the milieu of a *cinema-thinking* that rescinds any phenomenological privilege from natural perception in order to lay itself open to the "materialist programme"[3] of a Bergsonian world. In this world, the identity of the real and of the image (i.e., that which appears) results in the affirmation of an ontological indifference between Image, Movement (irreducible to any "pose"), Matter (the "in-itself" of the image), and Light. Propelled by the cinematographic postulate of a world become image, this amounts to the affirmation of a plane of immanence in which consciousness is no longer consciousness *of* something; rather, consciousness *is* something, an eye in things grasped by a camera-consciousness, the eye in matter undergoing universal modulation such that all images vary in relation to one another, a machinic consciousness open unto duration as a whole.[4] Hence, rather than a unified theater of phenomenological representation, we have a metacinema of ontological thought that enables us "to reach 'another' perception, which is also the *genetic element* of all perception."[5] From this genetic and differential element of pure optical and auditory perceptions, one can then *deduce* human perception proper in terms of its actualization in determinate space-times, and then *re-produce* the anchoring of the "I" and the horizon of the world in a central and privileged "special image"—an image that includes their sensory-motor linkage that allows for the imperceptible shift from perception of things to action on things. This cinematographic milieu is that of Deleuze's thought in its double movement of ascent and descent along lines of differentiation; and here, once it is only a difference of degrees between the "matter-image" (the real) and the "image-matter" (cinema), ontology then presents itself as a *material heterogenesis, a truly transcendental genesis.*[6]

In his second commentary on Bergson, which takes up the "brilliant first chapter of *Matter and Memory*,"[7] Deleuze explains that because cinema suppresses the anchoring of the subject in the horizon of the world, it allows us to "go back up towards the acentred state of things,"[8] toward a state of pure molecular vibrations, which now require transformation, and not translation. Philosophy may only be able to access this state of "pure uninterrupted becoming" once it has given up the project of tracing out the transcendental from the empirical, unlike Kant and Husserl (who continued this tracing and thereby created the "rational or rationalized caricature of true genesis").[9] As such, "the universe becomes a cinema in itself, a metacinema, which implies a completely different view of the cinema than the one Bergson proposed in his explicit critique."[10] In other words, it implies a deterritorialized vision that is able to *undo* the system (the objects) of perception-action (of the subject), starting from the point in between the two, the interval that is punctuated by the "the coincidence of the subject and the object in a pure quality"[11] and is abstracted from spatiotemporal coordinates, a pure impersonal—though highly singular—expression.

It follows that Deleuze defines the affect, or the autonomy of the affect, in terms of the nonactualizable part of an event. The importance given to affect—which can be seen in the three chapters at the very heart of *The Movement-Image* (if we count its continuation into the impulse-image), chapters that are situated *between* the perception-image and the action-image—is owing to the fact that the affect reflects the image in terms of power [*puissance*] and expresses the power of heterogeneity in the image itself. We can thus understand *why* the virtuality of the affection-image haunts the organic representation of the action-image in an immanent fashion, by cutting perception off from its motive continuation; and *how*, from within, it sets the stage for its historical undermining [*mise-en-crise*], which gives rise (with the emergence of pure optical and sound situations, at first in Italian neorealism) to a new way of thinking of the image, to a time-image in which the initial condition is the indiscernibility or coalescence of subjective and objective, real and imaginary, physical and mental, actual and virtual poles. Under the aegis of a renewal of philosophy, a new image of thought emerges that is inseparable from an aesthetics of force.[12] Thus, an infinite force field between philosophy and art appears, the exploration of which calls for "an experimental affective physics."[13]

These two books on cinema are therefore at the very heart of Deleuze's thought because of their antiphenomenological dimension and their Bergsonian horizon, considering that "[t]he opposition between Bergson and phenomenology is . . . a radical one."[14] But, at the same time, these two books suggest a kind of heterogenesis in Deleuzianism, in that Deleuzianism immediately presents itself here as a *Bergsonism beyond Bergson*. (Note that there is no such thing as a Bergsonian aesthetics proper, even though its "pedagogical" necessity may be incarnated by those "men whose *very* purpose it is to see and to make us see that which *we do not perceive naturally*. Those men are artists.")[15]

2

The fourth and final chapter of Bergson 's *Creative Evolution* bears the title "The Cinematographic Mechanism of Thought and the Mechanistic Illusion." Under the heading "Mechanism and Conceptualism," Bergson links the mechanism of conceptual thought to the cinematographic artifice. He writes:

> We take snapshots, as it were, of the passing reality, and, as these are characteristic of the reality, we have only to string them on a becoming, abstract, uniform, and invisible, situated at the back of the apparatus of knowledge, in order to imitate what there is that is characteristic in this becoming itself. Perception, intellection, language so proceed in general. Whether we would think becoming, or express it, or even perceive it, we

> hardly do anything else than set going a kind of cinematograph inside us. We may therefore sum up what we have been saying in the conclusion that the *mechanism of our ordinary knowledge is of a cinematographical kind.*[16]

When cinema is taken as a mechanism *adequate to* that of natural perception, à la Xeno, it partakes in the illusion par excellence that consists in grasping a movement produced over a uniform time through immobile cuts and in reproducing the mobility of the real through arrested images [*images arrêtées*].[17] Thus, movement in action [*se faisant*], *effecting a change in concrete duration,* is replaced by the ready-made [*tout fait*] immobile scheme of the movement covered, in which we can count as many instantaneous views as we like, in an abstract time over space. This static conception of the real forces itself on our intelligence through our senses and through language, as used as intelligence is to thinking of the moving via the intermediary of the immobile. This characteristic trait of the natural metaphysics of human intelligence is incarnated in the *concept* by a *cinematographic method* and obeys the general conditions of the sign, meaning that it records a fixed aspect of reality in an arrested form; it does not, however, take into account the *life of the real,* which would in turn require a true metaphysics of intuition—a metaphysics that, in certain respects, still participates in a *philosophy of presence.* But wasn't this the price one had to pay for *inverting* the classical order of the subordination of the image to the concept, meaning to the Idea that grounds the transcendence of the image?

One commentator neatly summed up the difficulty and the "discomfort" of Bergson's position in the following way: "'to go beyond,' we are told, concepts which we are told elsewhere that we cannot do without, and 'to free' ourselves from them when we cannot dispense with them."[18] Pursuant to these preliminary remarks, I myself had hoped to show that the Bergson/Deleuze relationship could be thought of as a chiasmatic structure in which Bergson's non-conceptualization of his own conceptual practice—in a concept of the concept that goes beyond that of its identity with general, abstract, and *arrested* ideas, and so on—is differentiated and counterposed by Deleuze in a conceptology that only exists and functions by integrating the whole set of Bergson's intuitions in the concept itself.[19] This results in a kind of *second-level* reading of Bergson that *systematizes* these themes starting from the concept of a concept, which, *for Deleuze,* stands for that virtual center, that "single point" mentioned by Bergson, so extraordinarily simple in its original intuition, but so complex in the abstractions that in turn translate it, that "the philosopher was never able to say it himself."[20] But Deleuze nevertheless knows that, *for Bergson*, what determines this impossible expression is the *incommensurability of the intuition to the concept*, as it is given in the present in *attention* and as it speculatively renews itself in *contemplation*. Thus, this major decentering is what involves the meaning of Bergson's oeuvre *for* the production and genesis of Deleuze's philosophy, in its innermost movement of affirming the vitalism of the concept. By this, I mean to stress Bergson's unique place in Deleuze's oeuvre, keeping in mind that there is never any *Bergson-case*—to use a phrase of Badiou's while marking our differences—because Bergsonism is never a *case of the concept*; rather, Bergsonism is the *paradoxical cause of the Deleuzian concept, and of his concept of the concept, in the free indirect discourse* that only retains from the history of philosophy's "cases of the concept"[21] the absolutely univocal concept of Being and Thinking, against everything that makes up the world of reflection of subject and object. Bergson, then, but a Bergsonism projected beyond the caesura between the metaphysical intuition of life and the philosophy of the concept, cleansed of any spiritualism of presence (presence, as Deleuze says, "is too pious"). Deleuze, then, at the point of an expression of a metaphysics of life qua philosophy of the concept. In other words, the full experience *of* the concept in its vital self-motion (or in its biophilosophical self-motion, as it is expressed in *What Is Philosophy?*). And the Bergsonism *of* Deleuze, who celebrated in Bergson "one of the first cases of the self-motion of thought." But which can the other ones be, if the "[m]otion was brought into concepts at precisely the same time it was brought into images"?[22] For, "cinema does not give us an image to which movement is added, it immediately gives us a movement-image"[23]—that "extraordinary invention of the first chapter of *Matter and Memory*,"[24] which Bergson seems to have "forgotten" ten years later in *Creative Evolution* when he refers to the cinema.

We should just briefly note here that cinema will only truly become "Bergsonian" (an idea brought up several times in both *The Movement-Image* and *The Time-Image*) once it has *first* become Deleuzian with regard to the "cinematization" [*la mise-en-cinéma*] of the concept. By this I mean that the thesis according to which cinema is composed of mobile cuts could easily seem to be "precariously supported" and "undoubtedly weak"[25] if it is not tied to the intraphilosophical plane that bolsters it up, *oltre Bergson, via Nietzsche* between intuition and concept. Or, in other words, Bergson's coming up against the question of the concept (as it immediately relates to cinema), contrasts with Deleuze's thinking of the image/Deleuze's image of thinking, which is affirmed at the very end of *The Time-Image,* when he states that "there is always a time, midday-midnight, when we must no longer ask ourselves, 'What is cinema?' but 'What is philosophy?'"[26]

(We could also say, along with Jean-Luc Nancy, that this question lies at the *core* of Deleuze's philosophy insofar as it can be thought of as a *cine-thinking*: "in the sense of having its own order and screen, a singular plane of presentation and construction, of displacement and dramatization of concepts.")[27]

3

The chronological divide between the two volumes points to the resonance of this time, midday-midnight, as being resolutely modern, *inasmuch as it relates thinking to a perception that no longer passes into action.* Rather than forming a sensory-motor whole, perception is infiltrated by a pure optical image that does not allow for any object presupposed, other than the one given via this image's falsifying, multiplied description.[28] (In the midst of this process—a process Deleuze primitively explores within a Humean framework in terms of the world as a fiction of the imagination, a theme that will quickly become tied to Bergson's "fabulation" and then hybridized with Nietzsche's critique of the will to truth—the perception = hallucination relation must be posited. Whence the parallel with the Impressionist revolution and the ubiquitous references to Cézanne.)[29] Deleuze's way of proceeding once again cannot stop until it grasps the genetic element of this new "thinking image." Here the genetic element is the crystal-image, "when the actual optical image crystallizes with *its own* virtual image, on the small[est] internal circuit."[30] It is nonchronological time grasped in its constitutive bifurcation into the actual image of the passing present and the virtual image of the past that is preserved *in itself,* the fleeting limit between perception and memory, the contemporaneity of the present with the past and what will come. It is the "affection of self by self"[31] as an *ontological* definition of time, the mirror-image of time; a direct time-image (from which movement derives, a movement that is necessarily aberrant), and not an indirect one (that flows from the movement of the montage), which makes us pass from the affect (suspending and "puncturing" chronological time) to a purely chronic time. It is a time that is internal to the event, which "is no longer confused with the space which serves as its place, nor with the actual present which is passing."[32]

Dispossessed from itself and from the world, this new "subjectivity" of time—oh so much more inspired by Nietzsche than by Bergson . . .[33]—makes man a *seer*. It inscribes our contemporaneity in the very rupture between man and the world; thus the being-outside-the-world finds his or her only manner/matter for thought in this powerlessness. The only thing left to do is to invest the interval, or, more precisely, the interstice[34] between two images of a "world which looks to us like a bad film."[35] And it is here that everything overturns. For the constitution and the linkage of things now only *objectively* depend on the differential and in-between-images, that make us *believe in this world, in this image here*, in the identity of thinking and life in relation to the new *genetic value* of a "so-called irrational cut." As it neither belongs to the preceding image nor to the following image, this "irrational cut" determines noncommensurable relations between images, which in turn cause an *Outside* to emerge out of "an unchained depth," an *Outside* that shows itself to be the *differentiating force* of time as becoming and the very *constitutive virtuality* of thought. In its chronogenetic irreducibility to the dimensions of space, the "irrational cut" becomes a value in itself, through its in-actuality, by positing the identity of the seeing body, of the acentered brain, and of the unchained world, into a living image in which its singularity will fully come forth.[36] As an event on the edge of the sensible and the visible, this cut "accumulates a fantastic potential energy which it detonates by dissipating itself." A pure image then, nothing but an image, "as it maintains itself in the void outside space, away from words, stories, and memories,"[37] in its returning to the plane of immanence in its ultimate belonging to time.[38]

As the potentiality of the powers of the image, and in this sense primary,[39] the visual-thinking time-image thus becomes "*archaeological, stratigraphic, tectonic*":[40] it becomes virtual-thinking, for it signals the turning around of the Image to show its reverse side, "like the first dimension of an image that never stops increasing in its dimensions." [41] It introduces a new disjunctive aesthetics of the image. In its incommensurability to all representation, it implies a dissociation of the visual and the auditory ("but with an 'irrational' relation which connects them to each other, without forming a whole, without offering the least whole").[42] In defining the new cerebral image as resistance to any kind of integration into a whole as self-consciousness (the organic representation of the subject in the hodological space of lived experience), it then becomes inseparable from a *false movement* (the relinkage of independent images) that initiates a series of audiovisual powers cut off from the external world (the functional association of objects represented in Euclidean space), the variations of which are part and parcel of a new affective constitution of bodies (bodies without organs). "This is why," Deleuze concludes, "thought, as a power which has not always existed, is born from an outside more distant than any external world, and, as power which does not yet exist, confronts an inside, an unthinkable or unthought, deeper than any internal world."[43] That this absolute outside and absolute inside are topologically and vitally in touch with each other *in* the brain thus allows us, in one and the same stroke, to define thought as the only object-subject of modern cinema *and cinema as the most contemporaneous image of modern thought.*

It follows, then, that in his more "cinematographic" commentaries in *The Time-Image*, Deleuze puts forth a genuinely machinic archaeology of the present. In Deleuze's audiovisual pedagogy, it is the present itself that comes forth: the *direct* presentation of the present as such.[44]

NOTES

1. Gilles Deleuze, *The Logic of Sense*, trans. Mark Lester with Charles Stivale, ed. Constantin Boundas (New York: Columbia University Press, 1990), 102.
2. Gilles Deleuze, *The Time-Image*, trans. Hugh Tomlinson and Robert Galeta (Minneapolis: University of Minnesota Press, 1989), 168.
3. Gilles Deleuze, *The Movement-Image*, trans. Hugh Tomlinson and Barbara Habberjam (Minneapolis: University of Minnesota Press, 1986), 81.
4. The best "formula" is given by Raymond Ruyer, in his critique of phenomenological intentionality from the viewpoint of a philosophy of genesis. Ruyer specifies that primary consciousness is neither the consciousness *of* a perceiving Spirit-subject, nor the consciousness *of* an ideal or a real Object. Consciousness *is* all active forming in its absolute activity, and likewise, all forming *is* consciousness (*La genèse des formes vivantes* [Paris: Flammarion, 1958], chapter 12, "A Philosophy of Morphogenesis"). Or, to speak like Whitehead, using a term that the reader finds in *The Movement-Image*, all *prehension* anticipates psychic life in some fashion.
5. Deleuze, *The Movement-Image*, 85; emphasis added.
6. As Maurizio Grande writes, "In other words, we can say that matter is the movement-image's plane of immanence *minus cinema*, and that cinema is the movement-image *minus matter*; thus it is one of the degrees of reality and not simply an 'illusion' that is supposed to replace the real." He concludes, "We see that what is at stake in the idea of a movement-image is the concept of the real, *according to cinema*." ("Les images non-dérivées," in *Der Film bei Deleuze/Le cinéma selon Deleuze*, ed. Oliver Fahl and Lorenz Engell [Berlin and Paris: Verlag der Bauhaus-Universität Weimar/Presses de la Sorbonne Nouvelle, 1997], 286).
7. Deleuze, *The Movement-Image*, 58

8. Ibid.
9. Deleuze, *The Logic of Sense*, 97–98.
10. I have translated this passage myself from the original French. The passage can be found in the English edition of *The Movement-Image*, 59.—Trans.
11. Ibid., 65.
12. Raymond Bellour notes this *affective* development of Deleuze's thought, stating: "This vibration of pure affection and its interval become precisely that which the time-image frees in itself, meaning the *aberration* which is and will become the aberration of the concept itself as a 'center of vibration'" (in *What Is Philosophy?*). See Raymond Bellour, "Penser, raconter. Le cinéma de Gilles Deleuze," in *Der Film bei Deleuze/Le cinéma selon Deleuze*, 39.
13. Using Ronald Bogue's expression, from his fine article "Gilles Deleuze: The Aesthetics of Force," in *Deleuze: A Critical Reader*, ed. Paul Patton (Oxford: Blackwell, 1996), 267.
14. Deleuze, *The Movement-Image*, 61.
15. Henri Bergson, "The Perception of Change," in *Mélanges* (Paris: Presses Universitaires de France, 1972), 893. In fact, it turns out that, "[r]ather than being constituted by the gradual association of simple elements, our cognition is the effect of a sudden dissociation. In the *infinitely* vast realm of our virtual cognition, we have gathered all that pertains to our actions on things in order to turn this into actual cognition; we ignored the rest. The brain seems to have been created with this work of selection in mind" (895). For Deleuze's critique of Bergson's brain, see *The Time-Image*, 209–11.
16. Henri Bergson, *Creative Evolution*, trans. Arthur Mitchell (New York: Henry Holt and Company, 1911), 306.
17. An "arrested" image implies an image of a movement that has been "caught," "stopped," or "arrested" in its mobile trajectory.—Trans.
18. Alain de Lattre, *Bergson: Une ontologie de la complexité* (Paris: Presse Universitaires de France, 1990), 284.
19. See my essay "Sur le bergsonisme de Gilles Deleuze," in *Gilles Deleuze: une vie philosophique*, ed. Éric Alliez (Luisant: Synthélabo, 1998), 243–64.
20. Henri Bergson, *La pensée et le mouvant*, in *Œuvres* (Paris: Presses Universitaires de France, 1959), 1346–47.
21. See Alain Badiou, *Deleuze: "La clameur de l'être"* (Paris: Hachette, 1996), 25. See *Futur Antérieur*, no. 43 (1998), for more on the impossible "dialogue" between Badiou and Deleuze, as it is sketched out in the first chapter of *The Movement-Image*: "The whole and the 'wholes' must not be confused with *sets*. Sets are closed, and everything which is closed is artificially closed.... But a whole is not closed, it is open" (10).
22. Gilles Deleuze, *Negotiations, 1972–1990*, trans. Martin Joughin (New York: Columbia University Press, 1995), 122.
23. Deleuze, *The Movement-Image*, 2.
24. Ibid.
25. See G. Fihman, "Deleuze, Bergson, Zénon d'Elée et le cinéma," in *Der Film bei Deleuze/Le cinéma selon Deleuze*, 69; and D. N. Rodowick, *Gilles Deleuze's Time Machine* (Durham, N.C.: Duke University Press, 1997), 22: "Deleuze's reasoning [about this identification of movement and image] is certainly weak here."
26. Deleuze, *The Time-Image*, 280.
27. Jean-Luc Nancy, "The Deleuzian Fold of Thought," in *Deleuze: A Critical Reader*, 110. Originally published in French as "Pli deleuzien de la pensée," in *Gilles Deleuze: une vie philosophique*, 119.
28. See the beginning of chapter 6 in *The Time-Image*: "It is now the description itself which constitutes the sole decomposed and multiplied object" (126).—Trans.

29. One should keep in mind that, in a certain way, Deleuze's book *Francis Bacon: Logique de la sensation* (1981) prepares the ground for the work on cinema. Together they form a series that cannot simply be reduced to their shared "aesthetic" framework. Deleuze actually poses the question of how cinematographic affection "explodes" in the neorealism–New Wave periods, by means of the pictorial sensation that emerges from the Cézanne–Bacon lineage.
30. Deleuze, *The Time-Image*, 69.
31. Ibid., 83.
32. Ibid., 100.
33. See Constantin Boundas's article "Deleuze on Time and Memory," *Antithesis* 8:2 (1997): especially 22–24, concerning Deleuze's divergence from Bergson's notion of duration *stricto sensu*. Here we find the question of presence (left open above) posed once again. On the Nietzschean dimension of the direct image of time and its determining relation to the "power of the false," see Rodowick's suggestive analysis in *Gilles Deleuze's Time Machine*, chapter 5.
34. See Tom Conley's essay in this volume in which he duly stresses that the interstice is the "event" that "exhausts" the space recast by the interval, or at least in the way that it is framed in sensory-motor cinema.
35. Deleuze, *The Time-Image*, 171.
36. The fact that Deleuze followed *The Time-Image* (1985) with *Foucault* (1986)—in which a number of themes such as "the thinking of the outside"and the "inside of thinking"are taken up from a biopolitical point of view—emphasizes, if need be, the essentially *political* dimension maintained throughout *The Time-Image*.
37. Gilles Deleuze, "*L'épuisé*," afterword to Samuel Beckett's *Quad et autres pièces pour la télévision* (Paris: Éditions de Minuit, 1992), 76. In this text, Deleuze develops the idea of a third level of language, called *Language III*, which refers to "immanent limits that are constantly moving, hiatus, holes, or tears" in composing an Image. And he concludes that "What counts in the Image is not the meager content, but the mad energy that is tapped into, and is ready to explode. This causes images to last for only a short while."
38. In *The Time-Image*, the interstice is understood to be "a spacing which means that each image is plucked from the void and falls back into it" (179).
39. Using Alain Ménil's formulation, "it is not so much that the time-image is located 'beyond' the movement-image, as much as it maintains itself 'on the threshold' [*en-deçà*] of its own power" (Alain Ménil, "L'Image-temps: une figure de l'immanence," *iris* 23 [1997]: 171).
40. Deleuze, *The Time-Image*, 243.
41. Or, according to Christine Buci-Glucksman, "We could even say that thought is *a virtual to the image* and not just the virtual of the image" ("Les cristaux de l'art: une esthétique du virtuel," *Rue Descartes*, no. 20, *Gilles Deleuze: Immanence et vie*, ed. Éric Alliez, Daniele Cohen-Lévinas, Françoise Proust, Lucien Viciguerra (1998): 106–7.
42. Deleuze, *The Time-Image*, 256.
43. Ibid., 278.
44. Which is probably why the *philosophical* quality of the work that concentrates on Deleuze's two books on cinema is so exceptional. Quoting them was thus not simply a way of expressing respect for their authors. It was also a way of acknowledging the actuality of Deleuze's thought as an ontology of the present.

Chapter 11

The Film Event

From Interval to Interstice

TOM CONLEY

Modern French philosophy would do well to stake a claim to its origins in the *Essais* of Montaigne. Descartes and Spinoza count among the first readers and inheritors of his style of thinking, and Gilles Deleuze among the most recent and powerful avatars. Indeed, something uncanny ties the event of Deleuze's death at the beginning of November 1995 to the demise that Montaigne imagined for himself in the beginnings of his self-portraiture. Distorting the lexicon of the Pléiade poets who were forever dying "a thousand deaths" in their many distortions of Petrarch, Montaigne expires and returns to life to assure himself an immortality in the crypt of his personal essay. Deleuze, we can recall with grim and stoic admiration, took death in his own hands when he made a final affirmation of life by jumping from his apartment window overlooking the Avenue de Niel in Paris. Plummeting the distance of seventeen floors, his frail body was crushed by a molar surface of asphalt that quickly welcomed him.

> La mort a des formes plus aisées les unes que les autres, et prend diverses qualitez selon la fantasie de chacun. Entre les naturelles, celle qui vient d'affoiblissment et appesantissement me semble molle et douce. Entre les violentes, j'imagine plus mal aiséement un precipice qu'une ruine qui m'accable et un coup tranchant d'une espée qu'une harquebousade; et eusse plustost beu le breuvage de Socrates que de me fraper comme Caton. Et, quoy que ce soit un, si sent mon imagination difference comme de la mort à la vie, à me jetter dans une fournaise ardente ou dans le canal d'une platte riviere.[1]

> [Death assumes some forms easier than others, and acquires diverse qualities according to each and every fantasy. Among the natural ones, what comes from weakening and weighing seems soft and sweet.

> Among the violent, I have more difficulty imagining a precipice than a ruin that crushes me and a swath of a sword than a harquebus blow; and I'd rather have imbibed Socrates' elixir than impaled myself as Cato. And since it's all the same, my imagination feels the difference as if from death to life in tossing myself into a burning blaze or into the canal of a flat river.]

Montaigne preferred to go softly into the night where indeed Deleuze, in full day, jumped with hard and firm resolve. One created an event of death through the anticipative imagination, the other realized it in when he unplugged the tubes that kept his body throbbing, went to his window, and let himself drop.

The difference between Montaigne's speculation over a fall into death, here described in "De la vanité," and Deleuze's affirmative leap should not lead us to believe that the bodily style of one philosopher is so remote from that of the other. Both think as physical beings, and both make their immanence an event of their writings. Although Montaigne hardly ever appears in Deleuze's work—not a shard of a reference to Montaigne figures in *Difference and Repetition* or either volume of *Capitalism and Schizophrenia*—Deleuze mulls over the event with respect to its function and figuration at the crux of his philosophy of cinema in *The Movement-Image* and *The Time-Image*.[2] The novelty of the personal essay inspires reflection about the nature of events and of their relation to the perception of the world; close to the experience of film, the essay reports what might also be the realization that "point of view" is not a sensation of our relative position in the world when we sit in the dark of a multiplex theater in a reclining seat whose fuzzy cushions smack of stale vegetable oil and popcorn. It is, rather, the state in which we apprehend a variation, "the condition in which the truth of a variation appears" to us.[3] The shift from a discernment of relativity to that of a site of a variation is an event that "takes place"—such as the spot of Montaigne's fall or, as Paul Klee would have it, as a "site of cosmogenesis."[4]

Thus, the task of these pages is double. First, how can we discern a sense of the term *event* in its philosophical, somatic, and cinematographic dimensions? Second, how can we contemplate the event from its articulation in Montaigne up to its salience in cinema and the media? The approach will take the form of an itinerary moving from the *Essais* up to the end of *The Time-Image*. It will be marked by two points of reference, the first centering on Deleuze's reflections on the concept and actualization of events in the dialogues he maintains with Samuel Beckett, and the second on the central chapter in *The Fold*, titled "Qu'est-ce qu'un événement?" ("What Is an Event?"). From there we will follow a comparison of the event to the coupling of the notions of interval and interstice in *The Movement-Image* and *The Time-Image*.

AN EXEMPLARY CASE

At the beginning of "De l'exercitation" ("Of Practice"), the chapter of the *Essais* (II, vi) that heralds the project of the writing of his self-portraiture, Montaigne tells the tale of a "slight" (*legier*) but paradoxically exemplary accident that befell him. At the time of the Wars of Religion, in the midst of the second or third wave of conflict—he avows that he cannot remember which; his memory is, he attests, murky and liable to error—the author ventured out to get some fresh air by taking a ride on horseback. Struck by a "powerful warhorse" assaulting his smaller horse from behind, the author is suddenly unsaddled. He falls, strikes the ground, and swoons. Taken for dead, paralyzed, unable to make the slightest sign to the people huddled around him, he is carried home by his companions. He later awakens in a somnolent state of bliss. Witnessing his own rebirth, the author undergoes excruciating pain in the return to life. The softness of the narcotic sleep in which he had been bathing slowly disappears. After having regained consciousness "par les menus et par un si long traict de temps" (in bits and after a long lapse of time)—his "premiers sentimens estoient beaucoup plus approchans de la mort que de la vie" (first feelings seemed much closer to death than to life)[5]—he sums up the famous moment that will soon become the project of self-portraiture:

> Mais long temps apres, et le lendemain, quand ma memoire vint à s'entr'ouvrir et me representer l'estat où je m'estoy trouvé en l'instant que j'avoy aperçeu ce cheval fondant sur moy (car je l'avoy veu à mes talons et me tins pour mort, mais ce pensement avoit esté si soudain que la peur n'eut pas loisir de s'y engendrer), il me sembla que c'estoit un esclair qui me frapoit l'ame de secousse et que je revenoy de l'autre monde. *Ce conte d'un évenement si legier est assez vain*, n'estoit l'instruction que j'en ay tirée pour moy; car à la verité, pour s'aprivoiser à la mort, je trouve qu'il n'y a que de s'en avoisiner. (Ibid., 357; emphasis added).

> [But for a long time afterward, and the following day, when my memory happened to jar open and represent to me the state in which I had found

> myself at the instant when I had glimpsed this horse barreling down upon me (for I had seen it on my heels and took myself for dead, but this thought had been so sudden that fear never had leisure enough to be generated), it seemed to me that it was a bolt of lightning that struck my soul with a shock that I was returning from the other world. *This tale of so slight an event is rather vain*, weren't it for the lesson I have drawn from it for myself; for in truth, to practice death I find that we only need to brush up against it.]

He then begins to fathom what in the following sentences he calls an "espineuse entreprinse, et plus qu'il ne semble, de suyvre une alleure si vagabonde que celle de nostre esprit; de penetrer les profondeurs opaques de ses replis internes; de choisir et arrester tant de menus airs de ses agitations. Et est un amusement nouveau et extraordinaire, qui nous retire des occupations communes du monde . . ." (ibid., 358) (thorny business, greater than it may appear, of following an allure as vagabond as that of our mind; to penetrate the opaque depths of its inner folds; to choose and arrest so many of its slightest vibrations. And it's a new and extraordinary pleasure that draws us away from the common dealings with the world . . .). Montaigne's hagiographers often witness in this moment of the *Essais* a dramatic staging of the topos that the author develops in an aridly rhetorical style earlier, in the first volume, in "Que philosopher, c'est apprendre à mourir" (That to philosophize is to learn to die).[6] In "De l'exercitation" Montaigne thus somatizes the project of philosophy. In refashioning or returning to the theme in the second book, a given topos explodes into an event. At issue is an accident, one that not only inaugurates and mobilizes a movement of style, but also another, enveloped in an overall project whose outcome is unknown, that draws the line of a trajectory of meditation connecting Montaigne and Deleuze.

The episode told in "De l'exercitation" is created by virtue of its style.[7] The resurgent memories of the accident are neither below nor beyond the words and letters before our eyes. The past is evoked, we might say, as it goes, *chemin faisant*, in the folds and creases of an errant and vagabond writing. Yet it is a sudden fall that inaugurates the first great autobiographical *event* of the *Essais*. The mode of presentation marks the beginnings of a philosophical project, the creation of countless events, that the essays will seek at once to capture and to release over and again. Here the tale of Montaigne's equestrian promenade, his "exercitation," is set in epigraph in order to discern the sense of an event in a context embracing philosophy and film theory. Not that the story Montaigne recounts suits rewriting in the shape of a screenplay, even if it would be easy to compare it to the aims of many classical films;[8] but what celebrates the birth of a philosophical subject brings forward the broader lines of what Deleuze calls *événement* in his work on cinema. Even the most cavalier reading of his writings shows that the word cutting through his works resembles the trace of a vanishing line with "thousands of traits." It recoups not only the studies on Antonioni, Beckett, and Melville, but also concepts such as the spiritual automaton, spaces of "any-kind-whatsoever," and the ritornello.

Multiform and variable, the event serves the purpose of calling into question the frame of the history that contains *The Movement-Image* and *The Time-Image*.[9] Where the bodily or "sensory-motor" movement that informs classical cinema gives way to film as thinking (*film-pensée*), the *événement* returns as a dividing line, as does the Vinteuil sonata in Deleuze's reading of *Un amour de Swann*.[10] The event, a point that had been central, decisive, even unique in the régime of the movement-image, suddenly "multiplies" and "proliferates" in the new world of the time-image. All of a sudden, in the time of the crisis of the "action-image," cinema "ne pouvait transcrire des événements déjà faits, mais se devait nécessairement d'attendre à l'événement en train de se faire"[11] (was not able to transcribe events that had already happened, but had to attain the event as it was happening). How and why? In what ways are the inflections due to cinema and its own transformations? Where does it originate and how does it figure in the work in general?[12] Without begging answers, the reading that follows seeks to broaden the field of inquiry.

BECKETT: THE FALL OF THE EVENT

In "L'épuisé," a study of Samuel Beckett's multimedia plays that make use of television monitors, tape recorders, and video machines, Deleuze remarks that the theatrical event is defined by the abolition of imaginary space, a space that would have formerly carried the guarantee of preestablished presence. "Dieu, c'est l'originaire, ou l'ensemble de toute possibilité. Le possible ne se réalise que dans le dérivé, dans la fatigue, tandis qu'on est épuisé avant de naître, avant de se réaliser ou de réaliser quoi que ce soit ('j'ai renoncé avant de naître')"[13] (God is the originary or the sum of all possibility. What is possible is realized only by derivation, in fatigue, while we are exhausted before being born, before being realized or realizing anything at all [I refused before coming to life]). An event is coextensive with a state of extenuation, a condition of being beyond oneself. It is far from being—as Montaigne seduced his reader into believing—the labor of a creation drawn through an itinerary of self-circumscription. Here, by contrast, nothing is contained in an event. "D'un événement, il suffit largement de dire qu'il est possible, puisqu'il n'arrive pas sans se confondre avec rien et abolir le réel auquel il prétend" ("L'épuisé," 59) (Of an event it is generally enough to say that it is possible since it does not occur without being confused with nothing and abolishing the real to which makes claim). An event is a space-time in and by which the possible is pulverized. It causes a destruction of mimetic process, recovery, or even memorialization. "Quand on épuise le possible avec des mots, on taille et on hache des atomes, et, quand on épuise les mots mêmes, on tarit les flux. C'est ce problème, d'en finir maintenant avec les mots ..." (66) (When the possible is exhausted by way of words, atoms are cut and chopped, and, when words themselves are exhausted, all flowage dries up. That's the question, how now to be done with words ...)

The transformation of "subjectivity" is at issue less in movement in space than in an *invention of an erasure of space.* We might say, by way of a neologism, that between *invention* and *event* is the echo of an *evention,* the event being at once what creates and pummels space. It is perceptible in "L'épuisé," in which the idiom that Deleuze calls Beckett's "third language" would be composed of statements that no longer refer to "des voix émettrices, mais à des limites immanentes qui ne cessent de se déplacer, hiatus, trous ou déchirures dont on ne se rendrait pas compte" (69–70)[14] (voices that emit, but to immanent limits that are endlessly moving, hiatuses, shreddings of which we are unaware). Deleuze gives the name *image* to the movement of these immanent limits. This mobile site is always drawn between the limit of what can be thought—the "thinkable"—and the nameable. Even though it remains impossible to hold in memory, the "pure" image is nonetheless folded "within language, in names and voices" ("L'épuisé," 73), and makes itself felt in all of Beckett's telecinematographic work.

No sooner than Deleuze describes what an image is—no sooner than he perceives it as a force that begins to plot the outside of language—he distinguishes its extensive qualities.

> Ce dehors du langage n'est pas seulement l'image, mais la "vastitude," l'espace. Cette langue III ne procède pas seulement avec des images, mais avec des espaces. Et, de même que l'image doit accéder à l'indéfini, tout en étant complètement déterminée, l'espace doit toujours être un espace quelconque, désaffecté, inaffecté, bien qu'il soit géométriquement déterminé tout entier ... L'espace quelconque est peuplé, parcouru, c'est même lui que nous peuplons et parcourons, mais il s'oppose à toutes nos étendues pseudo-qualifiées, et se définit "sans ici ni ailleurs où jamais n'approcheront ni l'éloigneront de rien tous les pas de la terre." (Ibid., 74–75)
>
> [This outside of language is not only the image but also the "vastitude" of space. This third language comes not only from images, but also from space. And, just as the image has to accede to what is indefinite, all the while being completely determinate, space must always be a space of any-kind-whatsoever, disaffected, unaffected, although it may be entirely geometrically plotted ... Space of any-kind-whatsoever is inhabited, crisscrossed, it even is what inhabits and crisscrosses us, it is opposed to all our pseudoqualified extensions and is defined "without here or elsewhere where all the footsteps of the earth ever will approach or move away from anything."]

In the performance, we see that the person walking on stage or in the film becomes the one who "épuise les potentialités d'un espace quelconque" (76) (exhausts the possibilities of a space of any-kind-whatsoever). The event would be the exhaustion, too, of the potentiality of spatiotemporal articulations of language.[15] The explication of the image in Beckett's televisual theater betrays an apparently voluntary confusion that makes the construction of the image tantamount to what Deleuze soon calls an event:

> L'espace jouit de potentialités pour autant qu'il rend possible la réalisation d'événements; il précède donc la réalisation, et la potentialité appartient elle-même au possible. Mais n'était-ce pas également le cas de l'image, qui proposait déjà une manière spécifique d'épuiser le possible? On dirait cette fois qu'une image, telle qu'elle se tient dans le vide hors espace, mais aussi à l'écart des mots, des histoires et des souvenirs, emmagasine une fantastique énergie potentielle qu'elle fait détoner en se dissipant. Ce qui compte dans l'image, ce n'est pas le pauvre contenu, mais la folle énergie captée prête à éclater, qui fait que les images ne durent jamais longtemps. ("L'épuisé," 76)

> [Space is enraptured with potentialities for as long as it makes possible the realization of events: it thus precedes the realization, and the potentiality itself belongs to the possible. But wasn't this also the case of the image that was already proposing a specific way of exhausting the possible? This time we might say that such as it is held in the void outside of space, but also away from words, stories, and memories, an image piles up a fabulous potential energy that it causes to detonate in being dissipated. What counts in the image is not the impoverished content but the crazed energy captured, ready to explode, which means that images never last for very long.]

Following the same line of reasoning, at an ultimate point events "se confondent avec la détonation, la combustion, la dissipation de leur énergie condensée. Comme d'ultimes particules [ils] ne durent jamais longtemps" (ibid.) (are confused with detonation, combustion, the dissipation of their condensed energy. Like ultimate particles that never last for long). An event atomizes and evacuates the space in which it has just "taken" place. The process is achieved through an explosion of lexical material within and by way of its virtue as an image.

Here a "language of images and of spaces" cuts holes into lived material and will immediately "exhaust space" (81). With respect to *Quad*, Deleuze explains that the sublimation of both extension and time is accomplished within the frame of a square, where "la possibilité qu'un événement lui-même possible se réalise dans l'espace considéré" (82) (the possibility that an event in itself possible is realized in the given space). The only possible event inside of the place may be the collision of ambulant bodies that meet at the center. The space is exhausted when its potentialities are expended, when the walking figures cause us to foresee a meeting that forever takes a tangential course. We might say that a *depotentialization of space* is constitutive of the event before and in place of the meeting that would be at the center of the given frame or stage.

It is seen in "ce léger décrochage central, ce déhanchement, cet écart, ce [*sic*] hiatus, cette ponctuation, cette syncope" (83) (this slight central unhinging, this dislocation, this aside, this hiatus, this punctuation, this syncope) of figures in movement. About *Trio du fantôme* Deleuze notes that the confusion of the image and the event possesses a different allure. First, a camera enumerates in close-up what the voice-over (but out of theatrical frame) is concurrently naming. Objects are "des parties grises rectangulaires homogènes homologues d'un même espace, distinguées seulement par les nuances de gris" (85) (rectangular gray homogeneous parts homologous to a single space, distinguished only by nuances of gray). These objects floating in space are paradoxically identical to what the camera has just framed. Deleuze thus calls it "un espace quelconque à fragmentation, par gros plans" (86) (a space of any-kind-whatsoever in fragmentation through close-ups). The perception inspires his recollection of the cinematographic style of Robert Bresson, for whom "la fragmentation est le premier pas d'une dépotentialisation de l'espace, par voie locale" (86) (fragmentation is the first step in the direction of a spatial depotentialization along a local path), and then Michael Snow. In *Wavelength*, he recalls, a zoom that lasts for three-quarters of an hour "explore un espace rectangulaire quelconque, et rejette les événements à mesure de sa progression en les dotant seulement d'une existence fantomatique" (87) (explores some kind of a rectangular space and rejects events as it progresses by endowing them with nothing more than phantom-like existence). Thus, by exhausting the possibility "d'un événement comme possible, qui n'a même plus à se réaliser dans un corps ou un objet" (93) (of an event as a possible, that no longer needs to be realized in a body or an object), the "event" of *Trio du fantôme* brings about the disappearance of the space of any-kind-whatsoever that would have conferred it with a potentiality.

From the essay appended to *Quad* it is easy to deduce that Deleuze conceives "space of any-kind-whatsoever" as the site or point of view of an event that becomes one before it happens. In the lexicon of Godard it is a sort of *prénom*, taking place before its name intervenes. It is exhausted by means of the image that happens in its own vanishment or explosion. In other words, "l'image est ce qui s'éteint, se consume, une chute" (97) (the image is what is extinguished, is consumed, a fall). The sense of an eventual "cadence" might be discerned in the history of the word, but what Deleuze is suggesting cannot be readily culled from etymology; for if "event" derives from *evenire*, from the verb meaning "to happen," the inflection of vanishment or destruction of potential stands at a far remove from proper acceptions. If, too, in view of the remarks on style that crank into motion the machinery of *Essays Critical and Clinical*, where Deleuze notes that interferences of idioms constitute a pertinent trait of modern literature (the writer, such as Beckett, inserting and inventing other languages in what is given), *événement* would be marked by its own molecular "air" or *vent*. *Tête à l'évent* ("airhead" or "space cadet") Deleuze would see in the concept a gamut of molecular, gaseous, vaporous, atmospheric agitation, a trembling by which objects and spaces are diffused and dissipated by dint of being pulverized or atomized.

FOLDS OF THE EVENT

In *The Fold: Leibniz and the Baroque,* Deleuze approaches events from the angle of words atomized in spaces they both create and vaporize. He remembers the fans of Madame Mallarmé that swirl the atmosphere in disseminating particles of words and images in her husband's lines of circumstance. Mentioned, too, is the earth dispersed in whirlwinds under the galloping hoofs of horses speeding across the steppes in the novels of Thomas De Quincey ("the gentle morning breeze had a little freshened, the dusty vapour had developed itself far and wide into the appearance of huge aerial draperies, hanging in mighty volumes from the sky to the earth; and at particular points, where the eddies of the breeze acted upon the pendulous skirts of these aerial curtains, rents were perceived . . .").[16] With Leibniz Deleuze follows the phantasm of blocks of marble striated not with elastic undulations but with "poissons qui [l']habitent comme plis organiques"[17] (fish that inhabit them like organic folds). He wants to discern in Leibniz a philosophy that might concretize the "baroque" as a lasting cultural phenomenon, perpetually developing from its initial manifestations in the historical frame of the seventeenth century. Deleuze addresses the topic by dealing with space amplified and folded from inside over its own outer edges. In the central chapter of *Le Pli,* an axis toward which the book seems to be written, and away from which its itineraries diverge, he poses the question that haunts the work in its entirety: "What is an event?"[18]

The tentative answer becomes the event itself. The definition that Alfred North Whitehead advances in *The Concept of Nature* is turned upon the implicit qualities given in Leibniz. An event is not what takes place or is framed by a cause, an effect, or what would have the appearance of a datum (Deleuze taking as an example "a man is crushed").[19] It is rather what is endowed with duration. "La grande pyramide est un événement, et sa durée pendant 1 heure, 30 minutes, 5 minutes. . . , un passage de la Nature, ou un passage de Dieu, une vue de Dieu"[20] (The Great Pyramid is an event, and its duration for a period of one hour, thirty minutes, five minutes. . . , a passage of Nature, of God, or a view of God). Events are discerned thanks to a pliable screen placed over the chaos of the world, the latter described as "un universel étourdissement, l'ensemble de toutes les perceptions possibles comme autant d'infinitésimales ou d'infiniment petits" (*Le Pli*, 104) (a universal giddiness, the sum of all possible perceptions being infinitesimal or infinitely minute [*The Fold*, 76]). The screen (an elastic membrane, an electromagnetic field, or a receptacle of the *Timaeus*) is used to extract from this chaos "différentielles capables de s'intégrer dans des perceptions réglées" (ibid.) (differentials that can be integrated in ordered perceptions).

From this continuum, seen extending from Plato to the *Theodicy*, Whitehead extracts three distinguishing features. First of all, an event has *extension* perceptible insofar as one element is connected to those that follow, forming an infinite series "qui n'a pas de dernier terme ni de limite" (105) (that contains neither a final term nor a limit). The seriality of the event transposes it into a "vibration, avec une infinité d'harmoniques ou de multiples, telle une onde sonore, une onde lumineuse, ou même une partie d'espace de plus en plus petite pendant une durée de plus en plus petite" (ibid.) (vibration with an infinity of harmonics or submultiples, such as an audible wave, a luminous wave, or even an increasingly smaller part of space over the course of an increasingly shorter duration [*The Fold*, 77]). In the context of Beckett's theater that uses multimedia installations, the progressive reduction of spatiotemporal quanta implies that the seriality defined by the order of shrinkage resembles, once again, the exhaustion of the possible.

"Les coordonnées abstraites de toute les séries" (ibid.) (the abstract coordinates of all series [*The Fold*, 77]), space and time constitute the signs of extensive series bearing "intensive" properties, that is, *intensities* or *degrees*. This second component of the event, perceived through vectors tracing itineraries of force mapped according to grids of duration and extension, breaks all lines of demarcation between an inside and an outside or between private and public worlds. The relation of extension to intension leads Whitehead to note that the third component of the event is the *individual*. It remains that the individual is a "concrescence of elements" (ibid.), and that *prehension* becomes its grounding unity:

> Toute chose préhende ses antécédents et ses concomitants et, de proche en proche, préhende un monde. L'œil est une préhension de la lumière. Les vivants préhendent l'eau, la terre, le carbone et les sels. La pyramide à tel moment préhende les soldats de Bonaparte (quarante siècles vous contemplent), et réciproquement. On peu dire que "les échos, reflets,

> traces, déformations prismatiques, perspectives, seuils, plis" sont les préhensions qui anticipent en quelque manière la vie psychique. (106)
>
> [Everything prehends its antecedents and its concomitants and, by degrees, prehends a world. The eye is a prehension of light. Living beings prehend water, soil, carbon, and salts. At a given moment the pyramid prehends Napoleon's soldiers (forty centuries are contemplating us), and inversely. We can say that "echoes, reflections, traces, prismatic deformations, perspective, thresholds, folds" are prehensions that somehow anticipate psychic life. (The Fold, 78)]

In this universe, the datum or the prehended is what itself becomes individuated, "une préhension préexistante ou coexistante, si bien que toute préhension est préhension de préhension, et l'événement, 'nexus de préhensions'" (ibid.) (a preexisting or coexisting prehension, such that all prehension is a prehension of prehension, and the event thus a "nexus of prehensions" [*The Fold*, 78]). In this nexus, the subject who is given to prehend is the one who "actualizes a potential" by virtue of spontaneity or perception, an "active expression" that seeks *self-enjoyment* (in English in Deleuze's text) of its own becoming. The movement of the individual goes toward what is new and is thus defined by its creativity.

Summing up Whitehead and Leibniz in the same passage, Deleuze remarks that the final component of the event is *movement*. Extensions and intensions are endlessly displaced and alternated:

> Les événements sont des flux. Qu'est-ce qui nous permet de dire, dès lors: "c'est le même fleuve, c'est la même chose ou la même occasion... ? C'est la grande pyramide.... Il faut qu'une permanence s'incarne dans le flux, qu'elle soit saisie dans la préhension. La grande pyramide signifie deux choses, un passage de la Nature ou un flux, qui perd et gagne des molécules à chaque moment, mais aussi un objet éternel qui demeure le même à travers les moments." (108)
>
> [Events are fluvia. From then on what allows us to ask, "Is it the same flow, the same thing or the same occasion... ? It's the Great Pyramid.... A permanence has to be born in flux, and must be grasped in prehension. The Great Pyramid signifies two things: a passage of Nature or a flux constantly gaining and losing molecules, but also an eternal object that remains the same over the succession of moments." (The Fold, 79)]

So-called eternal objects happen, as the author announced at the beginning of "L'épuisé," to be possibilities or evidence of God. But here they are "realized in flux" (109)[21] in that they are the sign of an event when their inner prehension is perceived, or when the individual perceives that he or she lives in a network of prehenders prehended.

The end of the chapter on the event takes a different turn. The expressive unit of the individual is the proof of the force and flux of events forever interprehending each other. For Leibniz, the perception of the four components takes place in a *closed* world that the monad might share with other monads, sometimes in a direct relation, at other times unbeknownst to this surrounding infinity. By contrast, for Whitehead, "c'est une condition d'ouverture qui fait que toute préhension est déjà préhension d'une autre préhension, soit pour la capter, soit pour l'exclure: la préhension est par nature ouverte, ouverte sur le monde, sans avoir à passer par une fenêtre" (110) (a condition of opening causes all prehension to be already the prehension of another prehension, either to control it or to exclude it. Prehension is naturally open, open onto the world, without having to pass through a window [*The Fold*, 81]).

The world becomes a pre- and post-Joycean "chaosmos" or process in an *open* world, a world in which events—bifurcations, divergences, discords that belong to a single and same "motley" continuum—are no longer found in individuals or in expressive unities. As a result, all being is splayed or held open, figuring in a world "de captures plutôt de clôtures" (111) (of captures instead of closures [*The Fold*, 81]). Deleuze concludes that baroque thinking, such as it is inaugurated by Leibniz and revived by Whitehead, marks a transition in the history of modern mentalities. There is sufficient reason for the reader to believe that the "baroque event" introduces divergences, discords, and flows of meaning into classical reason all the while it is sought to be reconstituted. We witness a broadening of the chromatic scale of sensation or an "émancipation de la dissonance ou d'accords non résolus, non rapportés à une tonalité" (112) (emancipation of dissonance or of unresolved accords, accords not brought back to a tonality [*The Fold*, 82]) ruled by reason. The event that takes place inside the inside-outside is opened and causes perception to scatter—and even to exhaust—itself.

FROM FOLD TO FILM

In these difficult and polyvocal pages—pages that move to and from architectural, narrative, and musical terms—are found some figures that tie the event to cinema. In a most schematic way, the event becomes the fold of *The Fold*. It is a cartographic component, drawn in the middle of the essay, put forward to distinguish three styles of thinking (roughly categorized as distinctions of classic, baroque, and modern). A crisis of perception becomes visible in the alteration of the word's defining traits. The event becomes the sign of a break that goes from the closed world where different things are "compossible" to what will destroy all perceptive or prehensive potential. In miniature we see the diagram for the project taken up in the two volumes on cinema. Where *The Movement-Image* might pertain to the "closed" world of Leibniz, *The Time-Image* bears comparison to the openings and captures of that of Whitehead.

In anticipating and betraying the "conclusions" to this essay (that would otherwise be better put to remain open and unlinked in order to belong to the régime of the event), we might say that in *The Movement-Image* the formulation of the concept of the "perception-image" (chapter 5) queues the staging of the event in the monadic and expressive régime of what Deleuze calls "sensory-motor" cinema (based on its appeal to affect the motor régime of the body in the rhetoric of movement). The perception-image carries the possibility and potentiality of a "space-event" that the spectator has the leisure of studying and exploring. The space-event is located in intervals opened by the differences of the sound and image tracks or the visible and lexical registers of the film. The viewer moves from an act of perception to an act of intensive speculation that becomes an event. In other words, the viewer moves from the position where he or she is a receiver of images to that where, in relation to the film, others, not forcibly enclosed in the film, are created. It is up to the spectator to engage the risky operation of exploding or dissipating time and space, the two components that in classical cinema remain the guarantee of the possibility of meaning.

Thus the study of the event that Deleuze takes up in "L'épuisé" and in the central pages of *The Fold* is developed otherwise in the context of film, but in a way no less multiform or protean. The event irrupts in the middle of the chapter on the perception-image, returns in the remarks that explain the meanings of "any-space-whatever" (*l'espace quelconque*) in Italian neorealism at the end of *The Movement-Image*, and then resonates in the opening pages of *The Time-Image*. Once again—a telling sign—it is by way of Beckett's *Film* that the film event is explained. Beckett's short subject thresholds Deleuze's substitution of the classic categories of the *shot* with a terminology of his own wit. The "perception-image" supersedes the long shot, the "action-image" the medium shot, and the "affect-image" the close-up.[22] In the "acentric purity" of Beckett's unique cinematic creation Deleuze discovers "la matrice de l'image-mouvement telle qu'elle est en soi"[23] (the matrix of the movement-image such as it is in itself). "'*Esse est percipi*,' être c'est être perçu, déclare Beckett. . . ; mais comment échapper aux 'bonheurs du percipere et du percipi,' une fois dit qu'une perception au moins subsistera tant que nous vivrons, la plus redoutable, celle de soi par soi?"[24] ("*Esse est percipi*," to be is to be perceived, declares Beckett. . . ; but how can we escape the "delights of the percipere and the percipi," given that a perception will at least subsist as long as we live, the most formidable, that of the self by itself?). Over and again, Deleuze maps out a project that turns perception into an image, akin to an event, as we witnessed in the work on Beckett's theater that exhausts the space and time of its being.

AN EXEMPLARY EVENT

The chapter ends with the explication of the three kinds of images that complicate the received definitions of the close-up, the medium shot, and the long shot. The perception-image is seen as the vehicle of the event insofar as the birth of visibility takes place within the cadre of deep focus and a great depth of field. But somehow the supportive example does not appear to be chosen with equal rigor. At this point the text suddenly collapses, it extenuates, falling from the crest line of its own formulation—but in such a way that its own difference with respect to itself becomes an event. We could say that when Deleuze marshals his "example" to "illustrate" the concept of the perception-image, he thinks of the exemplum in its strongest philosophical and historical sense as a "clearing in the woods," an opening that constitutes an aporia or an opening in an otherwise indifferently conceived logical surface.[25] A gap is opened when he demarcates a memory-space in a parenthesis that follows his telling remarks about the western being a genre that deals with both the birth of vision and the narration of epic action.

> Le western ne présente pas seulement des images-action, mais aussi bien une image-perception presque pure: c'est un drame du visible et de l'invisible autant qu'une épopée d'action; le héros n'agit que parce qu'il voit le premier, et ne triomphe que parce qu'il impose à l'action *l'intervalle* ou la seconde de retard qui lui permet de tout voir. (*Winchester 73*, d'Anthony Mann)[26]

> [The western offers not only action-images but also an almost pure perception-image: it is a drama of the visible and the invisible as much as it is an epic of action; the hero acts only because he is the first to see and triumphs only because he imposed on the action the *interval* or the delay of a second that allows him to see everything. (*Winchester 73* by Anthony Mann)]

In the guise of a good materialist, Deleuze materializes what he means by interval in the very form, literally, of the interval given in the parenthetic example. The reader of the original text is jolted when a purely "American" reference falls into the drift of the French. "Winchester" (do we hear "vinchezstère" in glossing the title?), a proper name that has no pregiven grammatical place in whatever locution in which it is placed, precedes "73," a numeric sign ostensibly more mathematical than lexical in its graphic traits and in its referential potential ("soixante-treize" would refer to the originary "copy" of the gun around which Anthony Mann's film of 1951 is constructed, a famous "year" in American history that contrasts the French "93" or "Quatre-vingt-treize" of Victor Hugo . . . or is it merely a singularity in a series 68-69-70-71-72-73-74, etc.?). Is 73 the differential sign of an event? Is there a "capture" of a multiplicity at work in the relation of the concept to the parenthetic example?

The response to the question can only be in the affirmative. A reader strains to recall what it is that makes *Winchester 73* a fitting example of a film in which the hero wins because, imposing an interval in a continuum of action, he gains a vital advantage of visibility. We would nod in approval by recalling how Will McAdam (James Stewart) pursues his enemy brother, who goes by the alias of "Dutch Henry Brown" (Steve McNally) up the rocky escarpments standing over the horizon of a western mesa seen at the end the film. The two engage in gunfire, the one shooting at the other from the crannies and accidental crenelations of rocks and crags in the harsh landscape. After Dutch Henry expends a tubeful of bullets ("I'm gonna smoke you out," he has shouted to the hero from on high), he begins to reload ammunition into the cylinder of the carbine from his bandoleer strapped about his waist—an action that allows McAdam time enough to peer over a rock and see the entirety of the landscape, in effect, to *see* the entire world of the film in which he plays a commanding role.[27]

Such would be the fantasy we might supply to plug the gap opened by the laconic reference to Mann's film. But when we recall

McAdam's pursuit of Brown across the desert from Tascosa up and by the outlaw's hideout, the hero gallops across an inhuman space—what would be in the tradition of the western the "any-space-whatever" of a nondescript desert outside of the inhabited world—studded with cacti. They become icons or signposts that are natural equivalents of the form of the "Winchester 73," vegetal correlatives of the object of everyone's crazed desire in the film. Pushed into the ground like rifles that display their triggers as branches, the cacti literally *multiply* the fetishes of desire in the film, all the more so as the hero rides among them, in the thick of a "forest of symbols," with an obliviousness that as spectators only we are able to perceive. *Esse est percipi*, except that here what Deleuze calls an "interval" is also a frenzied multiplication or what he calls a *fourmillement* of sensation in his work on the rhizomatics of desire in *A Thousand Plateaus*.[28]

The swarming of "a thousand little cacti" in the film might indeed be the point where the interval in fact no longer pertains to *Winchester 73* in the opaque depths of Deleuze's choice of example. The event of the instance of Mann's film betrays what he says of the perception-image better than what he would designate through elaboration of the concept of the interval. The interval that commands the "conscious" register of the text is traduced by the "unconscious" event of the multiplication of points of desire in the memory-images of Mann's film. In this sense, the "event" that befalls the quotation of *Winchester 73* is also one that runs contrary to most of the classically Freudian interpretations of the film, in which the repeating rifle is reduced to a phallic object to serve the Lacanian purpose of being a signifier in symbolic circulation. Deleuze's reference implies an event folded into the difference between the concept of the perception-image and the interval.

The reader of chapter 4 of *The Movement-Image* invariably notes that the interval constitutes the frame of an event insofar as it is experienced in the sensory-motor régime. By contrast, in the world of *The Time-Image* the interval gives way to the *interstice*. In other words, the instant in which a psychogenesis of the image takes place—as seen in two different sequences in *Winchester 73*—a birth of the labors of the visible and the invisible comes into view. It is exactly what Montaigne described in the tale of his fall from the horse in "De l'exercitation," and here it becomes the staging of filmic events. The interstice is the interval turned into something infraliminary in a continuum in which an event can no longer be awarded the stability of a "place" in the space of the image. The interstice becomes what *exhausts*—and thereby creates—whatever space remains of the image in the sensory-motor tradition. It supersedes the interval and, by doing so, multiplies the happenings of events. With respect to Godard, Deleuze notes that

> une image étant donnée, il s'agit de choisir une autre image qui induira une interstice *entre* les deux. Ce n'est pas une opération d'association mais de différentiation, comme disent les mathématiciens, ou de disparition, comme disent les physiciens: un potentiel étant donné, il faut en choisir un autre, non pas quelconque, mais de telle manière qu'une différence de potentiel s'établisse entre les deux, qui soit producteur d'un troisième ou de quelque chose de nouveau.[29]
>
> [one image being given, another image has to be chosen that will induce an interstice *between* the two. It is not an operation of association but of differentiation, as mathematicians are wont to say, or of vanishment, as physicists might put it: one potential being given, another must be chosen, but not any one whatever, but in such a way that a difference of potential is established between the two, that will be productive of a third or of something new.]

From one image another: cinematic events are tantamount to the chance and to the risks run in the construction of an *image juste* (or else, by way of Godard's usual chiastics, *juste une image*). Rossellini stated that he organized his films around a single—fleeting and fugacious—image seen and stolen away within the narration, the unfortunately necessary alibi that makes the film a marketable commodity. The event is just this image. It is also what is multiplied in the régime of the time-image.

Here the reader attests to what Deleuze implies by the proliferation of events as an indication of the advent of the time-image.[30] There exists a sempiternal process of differentiation and of vanishment that empties perception, that puts it to death. This operation, Deleuze later explains, hardly carries within itself the production of empty spaces or voids either between or within image-shots. At stake, rather, is the notation of an incommensurability of the image in view of what it is supposed to represent. In this sense, the difference dissipates the sensory-motor tradition of the movement-image. "La coupure, ou l'interstice entre deux séries d'images ... c'est l'équivalent d'une coupure irrationnelle, qui détermine les rapports non-commensurables entre images" (278) (the cut, or the interstice between two series of images ... is the equivalent of an irrational cut that determines the noncommensurable relations between images). Thus there are no more closures to cross either twenty-four times per second or in the passage from one shot to another.

The world is reinvented in each shot or in each interstice. "A la limite" (At the limit), at the beginning of his sentence, Deleuze clearly underscores the aspect of the interstice that approximates it to an event. The apparently neutral formula is laden with the charge of a *limit-experience*—"il n'y a plus de coupures rationnelles, mais seulement irrationnelles" (279) (there are no more rational cuts, but only irrational cuts). If we can speak of concatenations, they would take place *between* given images, they would be articulated in *unlinked* ways, as "open captures" in the way that Whitehead had described, that characterize the hazardous enterprise of seeing and thinking. "Au lieu d'une image après l'autre, il y a une image *plus* une autre, et chaque plan est décadré par rapport au cadrage du plan suivant" (299) (instead of one image succeeding another, there is one image *plus* another, and each shot is unframed with respect to the framing of the previous shot). In this régime of pure parataxis, the world is invented by simultaneous actions of addition and subtraction.[31]

In this respect, cinema places thinking "en rapport avec un impensé, l'inévocable, l'inexplicable, l'indécidable, l'incommensurable" (*L'image-temps*, 279) (in relation with something outside of thought, the inevocable, the inexplicable, the undecidable, the incommensurable). Such is the cinematographic event in its maximal degree, what Deleuze calls "une mort cérébrale agitée" (an agitated cerebral death) or "un nouveau cerveau qui serait à la fois l'écran, la pellicule et la caméra" (280) (a new brain that would be at once the screen, the film, and the camera). The fold, what would have been a space or an interval in the baroque world, is now transformed into a *pellicule* or a membrane between the inside and the outside, life and nonlife, or the brain and the cosmos.

In the gap between *The Movement-Image* and *The Time-Image*, the interval gives way to the interstice; the latter exhausts the former. Whence the exemplary event that falls at the conclusion. The concept returns on the last page of the second volume, but on this occasion it is mantled in a discussion bearing on the utility of books of film theory (365). Godard, Deleuze reminds us, observed how in the "good old days" of *Cahiers du cinéma*, the writers and editors—all of whom were future auteurs of the New Wave—were working "in the interstices" between criticism, theory, and cinematographic writings. Practitioners of a *caméra-stylo*, they wrote of an always theoretical or virtual cinema. Deleuze adds that film theory, like philosophy, engages a practice of concepts that must be judged as a function of "des autres pratiques avec lesquelles elle interfère" (ibid.) (the other practices with which it interferes). To fancy how cinema "thinks" leads to a swarm of events confirming this "agitated cerebral death." Here, at the end of an itinerary begun with Montaigne's fall from his horse, an inaugural moment of modern philosophy, and at the very end of *The Time-Image*, the film event takes place, always at its own limit.

NOTES

The essay that follows is crafted from two studies, originally in French, that appeared in *Der Film bei Deleuze/Le cinéma selon Deleuze*, ed. Oliver Fahl and Lorenz Engell (Weimar and Paris: Verlag der Bauhaus-Universität Weimar/Presses de la Sorbonne Nouvelle, 1997), 325–49, and "Événement-cinéma," in David N. Rodowick's special issue of *iris* (titled "Deleuze, Philosopher of Cinema") 23 (1997): 75–86. I express gratitude to the editors for their generosity in allowing me to build the text of this essay from the work begun in these studies.

1. Montaigne *Essais* (III, ix, "De la vanité"), in *Oeuvres complètes*, ed. Albert Thibaudet and Maurice Rat (Paris: Gallimard/Pléiade, 1962), 962. Subsequent reference to the *Essais* will be made to this edition and followed by my own translation into English.
2. Also titled *Cinema 1* and *Cinema 2*, respectively, and published in Paris by the Éditions de Minuit in 1983 and 1985. All translations from Deleuze and other French sources are mine. Reference will be made to the French editions of Deleuze's writings.
3. Gilles Deleuze, *The Fold: Leibniz and the Baroque*, trans. by Tom Conley (Minneapolis: University of Minnesota Press, 1993), 20.
4. As quoted in ibid., 15.
5. Montaigne, *Essais* (II, vi), 353.
6. In Pierre Villey, *Les sources et l'évolution des "Essais"* (Paris: Hachette, 1908; New York: Burt Franklin Reprints, 1968); Donald M. Frame, *Montaigne's Discovery of Man: The Humanization of a Humanist* (New York: Columbia University Press, 1955). "Que philosopher, c'est apprendre à mourir" appears in the *Essais* (I, xx).
7. Georges Van Den Abbeele argues for the envelopment of the paternal instance in the episode in a meticulous reading of the chapter in *Travel As Metaphor: From Montaigne to Rousseau* (Minneapolis: University of Minnesota Press, 1992), 19–32. I have taken up the scattering effect of the representation of the same "event" in *The Graphic Unconscious in Early Modern French Writing* (Cambridge: Cambridge University Press, 1992), chapter 5.
8. The film essay on the death of the agent creating the images is the topic of Robert Enrico's *An Occurrence at Owl Creek Bridge* (1964), but also the incomparable form of Rudolph Maté's *D.O.A.* (1949). The essay could be conceived as a specifically filmic project in which lap-dissolves would superimpose horses, stableboys, and other riders; dream sequences use fade-outs in black or jump cuts; special effects conveying the violence of the fall and the point of view of the victim, who sees woozy images of the accidental landscape over the shores of Dordogne.
9. A study of the term in the critical field reaches back to the projects of the *Annalistes*, for whom history was no longer involved in defining the great moments of

chronicle or of crisis events that constitute memory. Pierre Nora recalls that from the time of the advent of mass media, the historical event is at once very close at hand but also indicible. From the beginning of the era of radio and television, the auditor or spectator *attends* the event, all the while being sheltered from its effects. "Press, radio, and images act not only as means for which events would be relatively independent entities, but as the very condition of their existence" (Pierre Nora, "Le retour de l'événement," in *Faire de l'histoire I: Nouveaux problèmes*, ed. Jacques Le Goff and Pierra Nora [Paris: Gallimard/Folio, 1974], 288). The historian notes that the event might become a commodity that the media imposes on the public. Paul Virilio shares the same hypothesis in *Logistique de la perception: guerre et cinéma* (Paris: Gallimard/Cahiers du cinéma, 1982), when he notes that perception becomes the object of what strategic forces (affiliated with the capitalist economy) would wish to program. Deleuze joins Virilio with respect to the concept of the spiritual automaton, a topic that would have been inaugurated by fascist powers. Deleuze follows a similar line of reflection in *L'image-temps* (203–5). In its strong sense, the event becomes the very pursuit of Deleuze's philosophy, at least according to François Zourabichvili, in *Deleuze: une philosophie de l'événement* (Paris: Presses Universitaires de France, 1994), who observes that the term is inflected by "a constancy of the virtual, an exteriority of relations, a final identity of the outside, of meaning, and of time" (127). Film is an integral part of this rich and lucid labor.

10. In Gilles Deleuze, *Proust et les signes* (Paris: Presses Universitaires de France, 1964/1979), signs are events insofar as they bear "a primordial complication, a veritable eternity, an original and absolute time" (60) that can go by the name of *style*, "not man, but essence itself" (62), that "individualizes and determines the material in which it is made incarnate, such as the objects that it encloses in the rings of style, such as the radiantly red septuor and the white sonate of Vinteuil" (62).
11. Deleuze, *L'image-mouvement*, 277–78.
12. We can recall that in his obituary commemorating Deleuze's death in *Le Figaro* (Tuesday, November 6, 1995), Jacques Derrida calls the author of *Difference and Repetition* the sublime and supreme philosopher of the *event*.
13. "L'épuisé," afterword to Samuel Beckett, *Quad et autres pièces pour la télévision* (Paris: Éditions de Minuit, 1992), 58; in crisp English translation in Gilles Deleuze, *Essays Critical and Clinical*, trans. Daniel W. Smith and Michael A. Greco (Minneapolis: University of Minnesota Press, 1997), 152–74.
14. Here the "third language" is endowed with what Christian Metz called "weakened deixis," by which subject positions of interlocutors become difficult to discern. In other words, at the moment of its projection, speech mobilizes the possible position of the speaker and receiver. See Christian Metz, *L'énonciation impersonnelle ou le site du film* (Paris: Méridiens Klincksieck, 1991), chapter 1.
15. It is worth recalling that Deleuze's "L'épuisé" is in intimate dialogue with a trailer-title of another of Beckett's works, *D'un ouvrage abandonné*, that falls below *Têtes-mortes*: "d'un ouvrage abandonné—assez—imagination morte imaginez—bing—sans" (Paris: Éditions de Minuit, 1972 [expanded edition]). The new edition of *Têtes-mortes* plays, of course, on "more text" within the frame of "death's heads," but with the effect that "from an abandoned work" something is reprinted. In this light "L'épuisé" would carry the connotation of a labor or "work" *out of print* in a graphic and material sense. It is almost impossible for an English translation to convey this dimension of the term, an event that is given within itself, evanescent in Deleuze's title.
16. Deleuze, *The Fold*, 94.
17. *Le Pli: Leibniz et le baroque* (Paris: Éditions de Minuit, 1988), 14 (*The Fold*, 9). Here and elsewhere, all English translations are taken from the edition cited in note 3.

18. Deleuze, *Le Pli*, 76. In *The Time-Image*, Deleuze takes to task construction composed in terms of centers, be they novels or plays following an Aristotelian template (toward a turning point or a trophy) or of a painting whose form is ruled by the application of Albertian perspective. Nonetheless, a theory of stylistic and compositional intensity forces recall of Blanchot, for whom, even if it is fragmentary, even written in "lopins" (the word is affiliated with Montaigne) or shards, a book always seeks, consciously or unconsciously, a series of centers. See the epigraph to Maurice Blanchot, *L'espace littéraire* (Paris: Gallimard, 1955); in English as *The Space of Literature*, trans. Ann Smock (Lincoln: University of Nebraska Press, 1982): np.
19. Philosophers are *causeurs*. Such is the name that Montaigne attributes to adepts of causality. "Je vois ordinairement que les hommes, aux faicts qu'on leur propose, s'amusent plus volontiers à en cercher la raison qu'à cercher la verité: ils laissent là les choses, et s'amusent à traiter les causes. Plaisans causeurs . . ." (III, xi, 1003) (I ordinarily see men who, before the facts put in front of them, are more willingly amused by seeking for them than seeking truth: there they leave things and are amused with treating causes. Pleasant gossips [*causeurs* . . .]). It would be tempting to say that the example anticipates Deleuze's last act of affirmation in the choice and accomplishment of his suicide.
20. Deleuze, *Le Pli*, 103. Notably, the pyramids looked to Montaigne the same way: "Touctes choses y branlent sans cesse: la terre, les rochers du Caucase, les pyramides d'Aegypte, et du branle public et du leur" (782) (All things waver ceaselessly: the earth, the Caucasus Mountains, the pyramids of Egypt, both of public toss and of their own). They also mark the landscape of all of Deleuze's writings. See Jean-Louis Leutrat, "L'horloge et la momie," in Fahle and Engell, *Der Film bei Deleuze/Le cinéma selon Deleuze*, 406–19, especially 409.
21. In the original French, Deleuze writes that such possibilities "se réalisent dans les flux."
22. D. N. Rodowick offers a clear and extended discussion of the categories in *Gilles Deleuze's Time Machine* (Durham, N.C.: Duke University Press, 1997), 36–37 and elsewhere, that fills out what is sketched here.
23. Deleuze, "L'épuisé," 97.
24. Ibid.
25. For the history of the "example," see John Lyons, *Exemplum: The Rhetoric of Example in Early Modern France and Italy* (Princeton, N.J.: Princeton University Press, 1989). Lyons begins by quoting "De l'experience" of the *Essais* (III, xiii) of Montaigne: "Tout exemple cloche" (every example limps—or, literally, is a bell chiming out of tune). Exempla are illustrative because they do *not* suffice to carry or to represent the concepts that are supposed to precede them. Deleuze's frequent references to films that "illustrate" his taxonomies are exemplary in the cockeyed way indicated by Montaigne's remark about the ideology of exempla and instantiation.
26. Deleuze, *L'image-mouvement*, 102; emphasis added.
27. The memory of the classic battle in the film thus confirms Jean-Pierre Esquenazi's terse and telling remark about cinematic subjectivity in Deleuze: "If we designate by image-movement a signficant unit of cinema, an event of film, it must be added that this unit is the correlation of two movements, a *world-movement* and a *subject-movement*. The former makes manifest the sum of singularities that compose the actuality of the world of the film; it also expresses the event that constitutes the totality of the film. The latter embodies the perspective in which the world-movement is glimpsed. It also figures the image-of-the-subject produced by the film. The formation of meaning proceeds from the correlation of these two images" ("Film et sujets," *iris* 23 [1997]: 137; my translation).

28. "A multiplicity of pores, black spot, little scars, or webbings. Tits, babies, and bars. A multiplicity of bees, football players, and touaregs. A multiplicity of wolves, of jackals. . . . None of that can be reduced, but only refers us to a certain status of the formations of the unconscious," or the very desert of Freudian dreams, note Deleuze and Félix Guattari, *Mille plateaux* ([Paris: Éditions de Minuit, 1980], 42).
29. Gilles Deleuze, *Cinéma 2: L'image-temps* (Paris: Éditions de Minuit, 1985), 234. In this passage we can observe that on two occasions Deleuze mentions—in the filigree of the style of his argument—qualities or quantities "étant données" (being given). In the imaginary dimension of the formula is encrusted an interrogation of the limits of visibility and desire in the homonymous title of Marcel Duchamp's famous painting *Étant donnés* (1946–66), which lurks in the shadows of the discourse. As Dalia Judovitz has shown, the painting is an "infrathin" *event* insofar as the spectator "rediscovers only that which is already given as looked for" (*Marcel Duchamp: Art in Transit* [Berkeley: University of California Press, 1995], 200).
30. See *L'image-temps*, 279.
31. By way of comparison, in the work of Jean-François Lyotard, parataxis constitutes the cadre of the event: "En somme, il y a des événements: quelque chose arrive qui n'est pas tautologique avec ce qui est arrivé. Nommez-vous ce qui arrive *le cas*?—Le cas, *der Fall*, serait qu'il arrive quelque chose, *quod*, plutôt que ce qui arrive, *quid*.—Diriez-vous que 'le monde est tout ce qui est le cas . . .'" (In short, events exist: something happens that is not in a tautology with what happened. Do you name what happens *the case*?—The case, *der Fall*, would be that something might happen, *quod*, rather than what happens, *quid*.—Would you say that "the world is everything that is the case . . .") (*Le différend* [Paris: Éditions de Minuit, 1983], 120–21).

Chapter 12

The Imagination of Immanence

An Ethics of Cinema

PETER CANNING

CINEMA, MORALITY, REPRESENTATION

The most uncanny image in cinema must be the sudden apparition of Simon Srebnik in *Shoah* returning from the dead, accompanied by Claude Lanzmann's film crew. To the Polish villagers who heard him sing for his life more than thirty years before and who assumed he had finally died with the rest of the Jews, the victim of an SS bullet, Srebnik's reappearance proved so strange that they hastened to frame him with their bodies, to voice over his tale with their own "song of the Holocaust."[1] For every occurrence, no matter how weird, the human sensory-motor mechanism generates a narrative of "recognition," a story telling how things came to be this way and why. In fact, it was this very fabulative mechanism that put "the Jews" in the impossible position of being called to account for the disruptions of "modernization" they were held to represent. The Holocaust was justified by an account made to the German people of their victimization at the hands of the international Jewish-Communist-Banking-etc. conspiracy controlling the world, just as it was again being justified thirty years after the fact by pious villagers whose story of victimage was far more "original"—drawn straight from their New Testament source of all sense-making narratives. It is the narrative structure of representation, together with its generative matrix in the sensory-motor schema, that has broken down, "shattered from within"[2] in modern life and cinema, and *for good reason.* This reason is primarily ethical.

The key to morality is this: if there is pain and suffering in the world, it must be because of the presence of evil or transgression. Therefore, because the human community has committed a fault, this crime must be expiated by punishment of the guilty party or its expulsion from the group. But if it is the entire group that is guilty by its very nature, it must sacrifice an innocent victim, which represents the group, in order to pacify the wrath of the angry god who otherwise will punish the entire community (with plague, scourge, war, famine . . .). Morality and representation go hand in hand. Their combination (in its many variations, including pagan sacrifice itself) is designed to enable the community to act when its sensory-motor mechanism is at a loss as to what to do to remedy the situation. Whenever the human schema is about to break down before the inevitable fact of illness, accident, storm, drought, death, and suffering . . . the moral vision comes like a sudden revelation of Truth to save the sensory-motor apparatus from anxiety and despair, and to restore its function by supplying a *moral meaning* and a *scapegoat responsible to god and representing the community*. This is the "hidden narrative" of literature and cinema.

Take the Christian subjects Lanzmann interviewed: for them, the murder of the Jews was a live morality play whose explanation made perfect sense. The Jews had long ago promised themselves and their children to this sacrifice as penalty for the murder of Christ: "Let his blood be on our head and on our children." The Christ-Lord is the signifier of exceptionality: a scapegoat for a despotic signifying régime, as crucified God-Man he takes on the fault of humanity that disobeyed God and fell from grace, and redeems all who believe in him. His self-division and separation reveal the secret of the signifier, namely, that the power that condemns is also the one that pardons and saves—the power of Judgment. It is this libidinal condition (to learn to love each other by bonding against evil) that constitutes the basis of the spatiotemporal form of cinematic totalization studied in *The Movement-Image*. The cinema of health and wholeness—like the society it mirrors—is formally constructed on the basis of this moral contest. Hatred gives a focus to vague fear and anxiety and an object to unfocused aggressivity, enabling formation of a united community. But in our time, hero and villain tend to become indiscernible, and the Signifier has ceased to represent the Good.

The moral relay of the action schema has ritually collapsed in Christian and European civilization, reflecting the "arbitrary" victimization of the Jews.[3] The Allies had shared with the Nazis a fundamental heroic-victim narrative linking episodes of persecution with reaction against injustice and eventual triumph over the adversary, an endopsychic myth (mental automatism) informing and inspiring their sensory-motory mechanism: our community is threatened by a satanic enemy that must be destroyed to save civilization (or "race"). Each simply put the other in the place of evil. Now the Allies, the Good, had triumphed over Evil Hitler; so what is the matter, what happened to the action schematism?

The problem begins with dysfunction in the most crucial phase of the action, the process of *recognition* that sets the sensory-motor mechanism in motion by resolving the question: what am I perceiving? It is not that the Holocaust was unrecognizable. As Lanzmann says, it was *"unique but not aberrant* ... the expression of the most fundamental tendencies of Western civilization," that is, "to agree to kill those *for whom there [is] no place.*"[4] And it is not as if the Americans and their allies who won the war had not practiced precisely this kind of eradication, removal, and (if necessary) extermination of those who are occupying a place to which they have no title, to make way for civilization (the "clearing" of the West of "Redskins" for white emigration, the "subduing" of "savage races" the world over, etc.). Why, then, the crisis and breakdown in the post-1945 era? In one sense, or in the mainstream, there has been no interruption of the action schema, either in movies or in the "real life" that reenacts or exteriorizes the endopsychic moral narratives of war and peace, anarchy and community, good and evil. All of this continued even into Vietnam and beyond, the Gulf War, "getting tough on drugs," cleaning up the streets, and so on. It seems that two events have nonetheless provoked a psychomoral crisis. The first is that no commonsense explanation for the Holocaust has been found that could be agreed upon by educated men and women to serve as moral lesson: the thing just refuses to fit into any intelligible category. The mass extermination of a "race" that was serving a useful economic function just does not make *economic* sense—the only kind of sense that democratic capitalist morality is equipped to recognize. Taking Jews off war-production assembly lines (where there were shortages of workers, and when the war machine was desperate for supplies) and feeding them into incinerators is evidence of economic self-destruction, of insanity. What could this mean for the problem of determining responsibility, for the problem of moral judgment in general?[5]

In the meantime, a second event was preparing itself: decolonization, especially the exposure and condemnation of white racism. Here, as with the Holocaust, there was a crucial shift in "enunciation." The victims (former scapegoats) of racist imperialism and colonization began to speak for themselves and to denounce their former masters as evil hypocrites. Scapegoat consciousness, as self-consciousness of negative exceptionality, became transvalued into victim identity, consciousness of the injustice of the Other. The casualties of history understandably wanted to turn the tables and condemn their oppressors, and so the moral signifying régime thereby remained intact. But no matter how resilient moral automatism is—and it always snaps back into place because it is the libidinal-aggressive basis of the collective ego, of narcissistic community, which takes over from nature the body-brain apparatus of individuals and reconstructs it for social function—something has been lost, some fundamental confidence in the "man of action" and his world, and in community constituted by the legend of his heroic struggle and triumph over evil. It is getting ever more difficult to deny, misrecognize, and censor the truth about this "warrior theater"[6] that has led to the continuing disaster of our age, "racial hygiene" and extermination camps, the ongoing hunt for "aliens among us," once communists, now carriers of infectious disease or spreaders of "immoral filth," and so on.

"The intolerable is no longer a major injustice but the permanent condition of an everyday banality," explains Deleuze. "Man is not himself a world different from the one in which he experiences the intolerable and feels himself cornered."[7] In the general shock and disillusionment following the war we have lost our belief in *our own place* on earth, and in the *connection* between humans and the world they are devastating.[8] The refrain of *The Time-Image*, "Eros is sick," bewails the predicament of liberal self-consciousness. Is it sick because the conditions of love and bonding are unhealthy, or does it remain healthy, or at least "sane"—no matter how atrocious its conditioning—as long as it can keep from becoming conscious of itself? For that is its dilemma, to go on performing its sensory-motor functions no matter how intolerable their psychic condition, or to become aware of the frightful structure of its libido, thereby to face and realize its constitutional sickness and risk breaking down and becoming unable to go on living and acting as before. In this respect, the situation of a thinking cinema is no different from that of writing (for example, Beckett). The sensory-motor narrative of both, their story-matrix of love, betrayal, revenge, and salvation (new love), has always oriented itself unconsciously on the ground of a libidinal conditioning that Freud first enunciated, warning that *it is always possible to bind a group together with love, as long as there are some left over on whom to vent its aggression.*[9]

That is to say, it is possible as long as a moral narrative can be constructed to justify this foundation. Three centuries have passed since Spinoza innocently and profoundly denounced ideas of "good and evil" for what they are, human fictions, delusions of moral judgment. But we live in a different age, in which we have discovered with shame (Primo Levi said his experience of the camps made him ashamed to be human: how can we go on living and thinking?) that those fabulations are real and effective institutional creations: *evil consists in the morality that invented it and lives on it, by campaigning for and practicing its eradication*. Evil is the fundamental perversion that is moral law,[10] the essential structure of signifying subjectivity.

It is enough to make one sick with shame, this all-too-human *form of erotic-aggressive temporality* providing the *link between images* in a totalizing narrative of good versus evil and light versus darkness, as all the old stories and heroic clichés and phantoms continue to be revived from the dead and reappear on-screen and in life, to reinforce the signifying fantasy structure that is the sorry basis of human passion; they promptly produce new scapegoats as the condition of harmonious community; and the film industry cynically feeds these moving images to the "people"—to channel their psychic hunger for "passion," their neural receptors' thirst for erotic-aggressive transmitters—in exchange for money to feed back into reproduction. It is a convenient arrangement for the very capital that is organizing and spreading worldwide the misery of cynical psychosis (egotism, paranoia, and distrust) to be itself the purveyor of images of harmony and unanimity following the apocalyptic cleansing action of the latest *Top Gun*. The system that undid the communal bond internalized its scapegoat structure in its guilty-conscious (liberal) subject. But moral conscience itself begins to implode when it realizes that the moral law creates the evil it prosecutes both within the subject and without. This self-destruction opens the political-aesthetic field to interminable reruns of the psychomoral heroic automaton. As the stricken conscience of the masters turns them into disabled liberals, their "schematism" begins to crack and crumble. Do they not become confused and disoriented, perhaps susceptible to reindoctrination by the avatars of bourgeois ideologies, buying into the virtues of "clean living" (and its capitalist conditions), suddenly discovering themselves repulsed by "filth" and endorsing the "law and order" that promises to wipe the country clean for new development? An architecture of terror. And even when they refuse to repress or simplify the truth, does their commitment to lucidity about the moral basis of heroic action not condemn them precisely to ineffectualness against the confident ignorance of new breeds of masters (in several varieties) that are eager to take their place at the controls?[11]

The moral law is a signifying chain empowered with the force of compulsion and aggression. It represents human subjects and commands their behavior, directing their feeling and thinking toward obedience and enforcement, but also (postsignifying) trickery and escape, (pre- and countersignifying) perversion, subversion, transgression, revolt, and revenge—the relentless cycle of "revolutions."[12] It is this moral structure that relays the sensory-motor schema of human action and grounds it transcendentally from within its purified form (the moral law). Deleuzian ethical philosophy is directed toward destroying the moral human form whose good consists in persecuting evil and toward reconstructing an ethics of the human body and brain, affect, action, thinking, capable of affirming our good fortune in living through the death of moral god and moral man, to become reborn as animal, vegetable, and mineral experimenting in molecular relations.

But human beings are addicted to morality, clinging to their self-enslavement and self-torment, as Baudelaire said, "like a beggar nursing his fleas." The reasons for this are manifold and complex, but the crux of the matter is that we want regularity and predictability in our metaphysics. We are afraid of freedom as if it were death itself. Freedom is a kind of chaos, an uncontrolled complexity, like a wave or a high wire on which one is precariously balanced. And furthermore, the very nature of language confronts us with its "power of the false," the freedom to lie, to delude others and ourselves, to bear false witness, to spread slander—to which morality opposes its power of judgment, its claim to represent the cause of truth and demand for confession or truth telling, its tendency to treat existence as a case at trial.

The real power of language is to *create* truth—to invent social reality—under the guise of representing it as god-given. Triggering a production of images, ideas, and affects, language by its epistemic categories mediates a feedback loop between the brain and the perceptual world. And, by its moral categories and their psychic representatives (e.g., memory-images of parents, authorities), it induces and programs behavior and suggests moral and immoral reactions. Psychotics who experience this endopsychic cinema of words and images complain of an "influencing machine" implanting thoughts and feelings, making them see things, and controlling their movements.[13] Language does not represent a referent or an abstract truth, it produces a complex intensity (or affect) in the central nervous system; but the régime of moral judgment needs to represent its significations and its "references" as absolute and universal, authorized and handed down from god or Substance. That claim to universal truth is the Lie that grounds the signifying system controlling the sensory-motor apparatus, determining its perceptions, feelings, and movements according to categories of understanding and purposive behavior diagrammed in neural networks and scored into the nervous system. That this system of perception and judgment is grounded in transcendent truth is the fundamental delusion or perversion it requires its subjects to believe or enforce and enact, in return promising them a share of the *jouissance* it generates in the name of Right.[14]

Indeed, signifying community first creates and performs itself by posing two limits to participation, an upper limit (represented by the master signifier surrounded by a cadre of priests and bureaucrats interpreting its "truth") and a lower limit, scapegoat or alien, criminal, madman.... This lower or outer limit of belonging is indispensable to the formation of an interior and group of insiders. The group is marked by the trait of membership, while outsiders are judged and scored for exile, execution, sacrifice, or redemption, correction, rehabilitation (discipline, the "gentle way in punishment").[15] Social order is performed on the overlapping or intersecting planes of expression and content, chains of signs and images, chains of bodies, actions and passions strung out on a time line and threaded with libido and aggression. The sign-image chain is an internalized theater of intensities produced by semiotic elements arranged to perform social structures. Those who are fitted for connection in the chains are the subjects. Subjects are "guilty" (a priori), that is, indebted and responsible. Their dual status (the split self-judging subject) conditions them for self-regulation and punishment by guilty conscience; the internal agent of self-control is a "superego" that represents the moral law, judges responsibility, and executes the sentence on the ego. Guilt, as the psychic court says, "is never to be doubted" (Kafka). It is a kind of "moral thread which duplicates the thread of time" (the "form of the determinable") and *determines* the subject.[16] Guilt is the judgmental power of the internalized signifier, derived from the structure of debt, which is a fundamental moral force operating as a *differential* signifying element determining the *content*—in action, feeling, thinking, and "behavior"—of the human form of time (the determinable body-brain-affect system).

Moral community spans the range of behavioral determinations, from traditional religious membership excluding "heathens," to racial and national borderlines excluding aliens, to capitalist-democratic society excluding only those who are not "responsible" for their actions (namely, their debts), such as the mad, those beyond rehabilitation. Membership in a moral universe is not optional, it is categorical and "universal." The signifier does not give you the option of living outside the law. Nevertheless, the moral law does not represent anything except the form of determination and obedience to the differential signifier—and when its system of judgment becomes conscious of its hollow core (the absent substance), it risks infection with a kind of nihilistic or cynical malaise, a moral disease distinguished from the "sane illusions" of naive morality by this self-consciousness. Moral delusion threatened with becoming aware of itself has three existential choices for avoiding demoralization and disillusionment. It can foreclose awareness, thereby becoming psychotic (cf. religious radicalism, racism, etc.); it can "disavow" reality by officially enforcing the perversions of institutional bigotry and ignorance while imagining itself to be a freethinker without illusions; or it can hang on to illusion by repressing the truth (awareness of its false condition) and sustaining a disciplinary-subjective position torn between fantasies of transgression, with occasional peccadilloes, and its own bad conscience (the "normal neurotic" position represented by the "Name of the Father"). Is the ultimate function and purpose of moral judgment not to evade awareness of itself, to foreclose, condemn, deny, and censor the movement of self-exposure? Is this not the significance of the primal and originary repression that "grounds" the sensory-motor schema and keeps it "healthy" by protecting it from consciousness of its own false pretense (the "work ethic" only translates moral law into its empty form)? Then what happens to the search for truth in such an all-too-human predicament? Finally, is it consciousness of falsehood and delusion that makes us sick, or is the moral vision of the world already sick of its own lies, while not yet aware of it?

All of Deleuze's work, like Spinoza's and Nietzsche's, constitutes an ethics that presupposes the rejection of morality with its procedures of representation, a categorical refusal of judgment according to ideas of good and evil. One must turn the tables against the moral vision of the world in which, as Spinoza said, men struggle for their slavery as if it were freedom. Like his two great ethical teachers, Deleuze makes a continuing call for liberation from moral servitude. In a way, he goes further even than Spinoza, who still believed in physical, natural necessity and law—the "divine substance" of which all existing things are modes and functions. With Nietzsche and Deleuze, the substance begins to "turn about the modes," thereby liberating itself even from the necessity that governs the scientific vision of the world.[17] Indeed, Deleuze strives and struggles, plays and experiments to discover how to destroy morality and its signifiers, whose cost in ignorance, abomination, and stupidity—with its systematic delusion and foreclosure of the real, its formally perverse-psychotic superego implant—is only now beginning to be reckoned. Although it is in the subject's self-interest not to experience the falsehood of its metaphysical position, many signs do indicate a change of consciousness and perhaps the sliver of an opportunity for a "deregulation of the senses" and liberation of humanity.[18]

The "first lie" (*proton pseudos*) is that there is a preexisting universal truth to be represented. The metaphysical foundation of morality is the belief in an immutable reality that can be matched with knowledge (as represented in language) to determine the truth. *Veritas* as *adequatio intellectus et rei*. But, as Deleuze learned from Nietzsche, the "thing," the real, is not representable because it does not preexist its emergence or production, its becoming. It is this process of emergence that is the only truth, the truth of creativity, which cannot be justified and does not have to be—even if "[c]reative chaos is illegality itself."[19] Of course, the régimes of power (including scientific metaphysics) have an interest in representing "the" truth as a kind of eternal divinity and repressing consciousness of creative emergence, and so Deleuze affirms the power of becoming, of time and of the simulacrum, the image as pure difference against the false assertion of fixed truth.

According to the system of representation, an image is what "should not" be here, both in the absolute sense of the impossibility of understanding (the real of existence), and in the Judeo-Platonic moral sense of what usurps the place of the real (or ideal) thing. Whence its prohibition by Jewish, Muslim, and Platonic law (as by Christian iconoclasm). There can be no image *of* . . . because the thing is just what it is; just as there can be no name of the thing that is ("I am that I am"). But isn't it possible that the thing itself, which has no name or image, no representative of any sort (verbal, iconic), might just *be* an image, the differential time-image it makes not of itself but *as* itself becoming? This image does not represent anything, nor can it be represented, nor is it true (or false). Furthermore, although it has no pronounceable name, the thing just might be in itself a name or "expression" (not expression *of* . . . but combination, *chiffre*). The elucubrations of cabalists and other magi came to such a conclusion: what allows no image of itself and cannot have a name is in itself an image *and* a name or cipher. However, this strange, uncanny inference, which allows the divine miracle of existence to be both name and image, though it has no name or image, does not allow for any relation of representation to subsist between these two aspects of the thing. The thing would be a kind of transcendental immanence consisting both in a self-constituting image and in a self-pronouncing word, but not in any relation between them.

This seems to be the conclusion both of modern cinema (Straub-Huillet, Duras, Syberberg . . . beginning with the "unevocable" of Welles) and of modern thought (Kant: the prohibition against positive representation of the divine Good; Heidegger: the event of withdrawal and disjunction of being from beings; Blanchot, Foucault: saying is not seeing, and we never can say what we see—but seeing is not saying either, and "this is not a pipe"). *Shoah* drives home this impossibility—the negative of the "ensemble of all possibility" that defines classical divinity—but by inverting the terms of prohibition: it is not God or Good that must not be seen or represented (by word or image), it is Simon Srebnik, the Survivor, who cannot be imagined or conceived, or represented, although he must be seen and must be heard.

CINEMATIC COSMOLOGY

An uncanny image cannot be understood or acted on, only witnessed. A pure optic-sonic *sign,* it should not be there according to sensory-moral reason. The world, the very existence of "something rather than nothing," is a kind of uncanny simulacrum: very strange, when we begin to think about it. Yet all kinds of reasons are given why the world-image can or must be here; most of these reasons begin and end in God or "universal law." Even still, the most determined physicist tends to ask, Why is there something and not rather nothing? "What is it that breathes fire into the equations and makes a universe for them to describe?"[20] The Gnostics wondered why existence has come to disturb the serenity and purity of nonbeing, thereby preparing the essential moral question. Indeed, the idea of life as debt that has to be made good by death (or destruction) is the moral basis of the principle of sufficient reason.[21] On the other hand, if the universe grounds and causes its own existence, to whom does it owe any debt or death? It presupposes a kind of transcendental memory of itself, and this autohypothesis is its raison d'être and ultimate "symmetry principle."[22] If "energy (matter, substance) can neither be created nor destroyed," this implies eternal self-creation or becoming. The Image (world) is neither excess nor lack, neither a debt to be repaid nor something missing its own ideal truth. It is a fractal labyrinth of "self-consistency," a baroque zoological garden of infinite variety. Galaxies are self-reproducing factories creating elements whose adventure is mutual catalysis, the "hospitality" of life. An image is not the distinction of being from nonbeing, nor of a being from being; it is an "eternally self-replicating fractal inflationary universe."[23] Eternity is pure spontaneity "grounded" only in the cipher of its self-affection—an autocatalytic "replicant."

A self-grounding process is indiscernible from groundlessness, and has no need of any ground once liberated from the moral-representational metaphysics of being.[24] The image emerges without ground, because it *emerges through the opening of ground*. As Bergson-Deleuze said, being is the past (memory) but becoming is the opening of being. The present opens the past, the living present emerges—through (or as) "zones of indetermination"—by opening past time to an unexpected, unforeseeable future. It is not a matter of creating new energy; it is a question of something new coming into the world by transformation of existing energy. This power of metamorphosis or "evolution" is called Eros or libido—not energy but desire, creativity that irresistibly and irreducibly informs matter from within and makes it live. The totality of time is neither closed nor given; "duration signifies invention, creation of forms, continuous elaboration of the absolutely new"[25]—something no equation, no memory-function can determine in advance.

The existence of a self-made universe, continuing to become itself, is surprising. "Self" is a simulacrum, differing from itself by the force of preexistence and becoming, a differential image, not a debt (or lack). The apparition of *any* image is uncanny, like the emergence of a world out of chaos.[26] In cinema, the world "becomes its own image," becomes uncanny to itself, mechanically conscious of itself. It becomes a conscious simulacrum or simulacrum of consciousness, an Apparition ("difference in itself") enjoying "repetition for itself."[27] A living simulacrum is not "self-determined," because only a fixed (dead) mechanism is determined and life is the discovery and invention of the indeterminate, "complexity." True self-determination could only mean determination of the present by the future reflecting itself in a memory it is continually re-creating. This future is not determined by a purpose (concept or image causing or guiding its own production) but reflected in a "purposiveness without purpose" that allows reason and understanding to resonate with imagination, in harmony or dissonance. Reason is represented by the idea of totality; imagination synthesizes absolute becoming without cause or reason. Their "conflict of powers" is the wave or wire on which freedom (creativity) balances as we "advance" from one world-image to the next across an "irrational" abyss or interval.

The world is a simulacrum, a double-sided image traversing a difference of potential. This difference is a *plane of immanence* that cannot be conceived or represented but can (and must) be thought and "drawn" (like a diagram). It is a kind of modulating sieve (*crible*) that strains or filters cosmos out of chaos, or thought out of unthought; a "chaosmos" of immanence between chaos and order, by which the chaos of disappearing apparitions affects itself with becoming-cosmos, as unthought or the unconscious affects itself with thought and perhaps consciousness. The self-affection of chaos means *mutual affection* of those apparitions by which they *bring each other into being* as forces and particles capable of evolving together as a universal community. There is not a subject who faces chaos, there is a *crible* from which chaos is "inseparable"[28] and which is like a germ (or crystal) of becoming that draws on chaos for its forces. Simulating randomness, it is a game of chance or "selection" in which the power of growth and becoming is always implicit or virtual. Sometimes the filter is imagined as a membrane that weaves itself, or as a physical field that distributes potentials. But it is always a threshold between the "unthinkable origin" and the space-time-matter evolution in which we find ourselves and try to take our bearings.

The *crible* is chaos imagining itself—making an image of itself, expressing itself—but this self-image comes out as cosmos. Chaos cannot be imagined, but this is because imagination creates and synthesizes order.

The becoming of time can be read or deciphered in a germinating "crystal."[29] The cinematic image is a modulating crystal that is in the process of reflecting itself and becoming aware of itself. An image is *like* an idea, as Plato complained—they are indiscernible, and time is not a "moving image of eternity," the eternal idea is a frozen image of becoming, a static crystal synthesis of the movement-image. The cinematic crystal effects a distinction, thereby overturning Leibniz's principle of indiscernibles: it is not indiscernibility that proves identity, it is becoming that distinguishes the indiscernible, future-past. Order in the future, chaos in the past; chaos in the future, order in the past. Germination, crystallization, autocatalysis (or rather, mutual catalysis of fluctuations becoming particles or "elements," signs); fluctuation, perturbation, amplification of chaotic fluctuation, uncontrollable descent into an unknown future. Existence, difference, the simulacrum, is not an exception, it is immanence. Without the pretense of universal law there are only singularities linking (or relinking) with other singularities in series that proceed from one turning point (zone of indetermination or neighborhood of singularity) to another. Singularities (not subjects) communicate by emission of signs and images across a difference of potential that is their plane of immanence.

The "first" or primary image the world makes is just itself creating itself; the "second" is an image it makes of the primary image. And the relation (or connection) between these two instances of imaging would be a "third"—no longer an image, perhaps, yet somehow linking, binding, or relating images together in community. These three moments (or avatars) of the image engender the triad of the sign, according to Peirce. First, there is the *power* to imagine, to make an image, "something that goes back [or refers] only to itself, quality or power, pure possibility," which is thus an *icon in and of itself*. Second, there is the *actuality* of something "that goes back [or refers] to itself only by way of something else, existence," which is the *index of the other*. Third, "something that refers [returns] to itself only by relating one thing to another, relation, law," necessity: the *symbolic sign*.[30] The three moments or movements of the sign correspond to the three Kantian categories of modality, three ways or modes in which a thing (image) can be related to time.

A thinking of immanence cannot accept the primacy of possibility as represented by the metaphysical tradition. Bergson's skepticism concerning the reality and significance of possibility must be adopted together with the categories of *Matter and Memory*, perception (the actual) and memory (the virtual). In lieu of the priority of possibility—the transcendental element, the a priori "necessity of a possibility"—there is *actuality of perception*, a "zeroity" in the order of the deduction of signs and images. It signals a kind of *body without organs* (or plane of immanence) of the sign or image. However, this priority too is provisional; for what is prior and absolute—"before" zeroity—is movement, the *consistency* of the image-movement in itself, distinguished from chaos by an indiscernible membrane (*crible*). A crystal, crystallization, through which chaos *becomes* (genesis). Whence the emergence of a crucial insight: the symbolic sign (signifier) should consist in the relation of actuality to possibility, but prior to (or instead of) that deduction, we find perception, which is the prehension or capture of one image by another, and a pure movement, which is that of chaos or the absolute conditioning itself. The absolute is inseparable from its own genesis and self-ordering. We can call this genetic element a crystal, or call it memory. Memory is the power of chaos to "retain" itself, to suspend or delay the disappearance of an apparition, a self-image that emerges from chaos to extend for the duration of a universe.

Memory, crystal, membrane (*crible*)—all refer to a power to exist and endure. Memory is affect, the power of the virtual. But perception, actuality, invents itself, emerges of itself. "The thing and the perception of the thing are one and the same thing, one and the same image, but related to one or the other of two systems of reference. The thing is the image as it is in itself, such that it relates to all the other images [with which it interacts]. But the perception of the thing is the same image related to another, special image, which frames it" and selects those traits of the image to which it is sensitive, by which it is capable of being affected.[31] This selection capability is the cosmogenetic filtering process, a kind of spontaneous receptivity or affectivity of the self-emergent *crible*-membrane. In other words, perception (which Bergson had wanted to distinguish from memory, as actual from virtual) is already memory, already virtual, or implies as immanent within it a virtuality or power circuit. The virtual is an *intensive ordinate* that explores and invents possibilities opened up by chance or creativity in the extensive order of space-time.[32] It is not memory but the invention of memory, not possibility but the creation of possibility, not the horizontal time-succession linking phases of the event into a chain but its vertical and diagonal becoming, an "interstice" that breaks the linkage of the moral chain and opens it out. For the outside is the unknown future, but also the power to "fold" the future inside ourselves—not to know or to determine it, but to experiment, to improvise, to experience something beyond understanding, a membrane, topological "co-presence of an inside deeper than any interior milieu, and an outside further away that any exterior environment."[33]

Secondarity (actuality) implies primacy (possibility, power). But actuality is perception, which goes immediately back to zeroity or the unmediated interaction of each image with all others ("it submits to the totality of their action and reacts to them immediately").[34] The idea of immediacy is deceptive: it means the absence of a medium, of relation, of a law governing the interval—in the sense of a suspension ("interval of movement"). The interval is likened (by Bergson and Deleuze) to a brain, memory, and affect. The brain is a complex interval, interstice, a movement of thought relating one thing to another. Its operation is determined by the third state of the sign, symbolic relation. Thus perception implies an interval that frames and selects, but the power to frame, the power of the interval between movements, implies relation or the tertiarity of the sign. These semiotic, imaging processes are inextricable. What is certain is that the quasi chaos of spontaneous and absolute image-movement, which is inseparable from the interval-membrane that spontaneously emerges to filter and perceive it, is thereby also inseparable from the relation that is implied by the interval of perception.

Perception means *prehension* (Whitehead's term for the process of one image capturing or "taking" another), and the mutual interaction of all images (chaos) is a kind of com-prehension or spontaneous mutual synthesis, immanent physical imagination. There is no chaos, or chaos is inseparable from the *crible* or crystal of its self-perception. To perceive is never to perceive chaos; and chaos does not exist to the extent that *there is* perception in and of itself. This self-perception of the imperceptible (chaos) is the power of seeing the future, the virtual outside, and folding or reflecting it inside oneself.

The philosophy of absolute immanence transforms phenomenology and enhances its possible consistency: it is no longer the subject that transcends itself toward objects, but immanence that is a *transcendental field* or plane of virtual consciousness, "pure current of a-subjective consciousness ... absolute consciousness ... immediate consciousness without object or ego." Hence subject and object—images—can only be "out-of-field" (*hors champ*) and transcendent.[35] The transcendental plane or field of immanence is likened to a *cinematic stream* of images. But it is not the image, or symbolic sign, that realizes the "current" of transcendental immanence. Images or their sensible matter ("the element of sensation") are not the differential element of immanence or "transcendental empiricism" that is Deleuze's philosophical creation. Sensation makes a "cut in the current of absolute consciousness," as does intelligence, or the element of the intelligible (idea). Objects, subjects, sensations, ideas, images are local syntheses of this unlocalizable "movement without beginning or end," this "passage" or becoming.[36] It is this passage or movement, this virtual consciousness (*conscience en droit*), that might rightly be called a *virtual cinema* that *forces thought to think*, even before it is "capable." Although thinking has no object or subject, it is now possessed of something else, a force that carries it along, a passage, a becoming, before-and-after image.

If the image is not immanent in cinema, what is? It is *movement*, or the passage from one image to another. But what is this movement? It is not the matter-movement-image, which can only be "transcendent" to the movement of immanence. It is by the current of immanence that Deleuze defines *affect* as *transition* from affection to affection, from sensation to sensation or image to image.[37] Affect is the movement of immanence, a virtual movement or becoming-time. What makes this transition happen? This is the question Deleuze addresses in his work on cinema (as nowhere else). And yet, there is something missing from the story as told there, which is partially supplied in the title of Deleuze's final essay: "L'immanence: une vie . . ."

What makes the image on-screen move? It is not the same as what makes the image move on-screen. What makes the image move on-screen is a motor, a projector. Another motor, a movie camera, "captured" the life-movement of the image. It is "energy" that makes or actualizes virtual (immanent) movement. But what makes the image itself move, what *makes the image move itself*? It is no longer (or not yet) the actuality of energy but a "a life," a virtual life, that makes the image move, in itself, of itself. What makes life move?

What moves is the libido of time—not movement-time (time determined as a function of periodic movement) but life-time, the event of immanence, the feeling or intuition of being alive. Spinoza called it power "the essence of substance"—not energy, spontaneous activity, but something in energy that tends to form such combinations of molecules as are capable of sustaining their alliance and thereby coming alive. Libido or Eros is the life force of energy, immanence—a life. Yet Eros or desire is not itself an image, nor can it be presented as such, however it may be that everything, even the "inorganic" life of things, is self-made by its power. It is not an intelligible form or subject nor a sensible object. It is not an image, then, but *the indiscernible passage between images,* not affection or sensation but *the transition from one sensation to another,* affect through which one affection changes to another. Libido is an affect through which *one life becomes another.*[38] Is time libido, then, or is there a libidinal form of time? Or is time, as is more often said or imagined, the oeuvre of death and slow (or sudden) passage to the outside of life?

The human form of Eros is the social link that binds humans in relations—communal relations, sexual relations, image-relations. The fundamental purpose of morality, then, is to gain control of the social bond and determine all relations by a signifying chain to (re)direct the flows of movement, of bodies, and of images. It is this bond(age) that, even indiscernible, transversal to the lives it orders, the movements it arranges, the emotional configurations it induces, binds the traits of image together with each other into one whole by shutting out (or in) evil, and makes a linkage between images seeking and affecting one another, interacting, loving, and hating (narcissism, erotomania)—all under the Name of the Father. A new order of time begins when the signifier of the father, theoretically foreclosed by science but remaining as transcendental category, structure of understanding, is removed by an act of Deleuzian–Spinozist philosophy, and the real "absence of link"[39] emerges in and for itself *without representation,* an opening in time, becoming outside, future, launching a process of another nature, and calling for creation of a new kind of love, an immanent libido without ego or object or subject. For it was finally the transcendental-erotic subject-form that chained the ego to its object in love and hate, that chained the social images and movements to one another in delusional consensus, and that thirsted for salvation and transcendence to another world beyond the world.

Nothing is more crucial to ethical-aesthetic thinking (the "turn" beyond ontology) than the problem of relation. Relations among humans, between human and animal, between animals ... among elementary particles. An ethics of particles, a physics of human relations. In cinema, the composition of the image (shot) and the passage between images reflect the logic of the whole—the open whole of intelligible sensory-motor time; or the outside-time reflected in the nonrelation between images, visual and sound. Libido is the stuff of relation, Eros making the linkage between images, between inside-brain and outside-world, between humans, humans and animals, with earth. If we have "lost the world," as Deleuze says, if

Eros is sick, it is because relations (sexual, social, affective, epistemo-phenomenological) mediated by the signifier that keeps us unconscious of their erotic-aggressive condition have broken down and only money-power differentials link one "character" to another, one movement or gesture to another, in a chain of erotic-aggressive attitudes. In the modern world, the time differential assumes the universal form of money. Money preoccupies and rationalizes the superego, thus purifying the moral law of any residual traditional content, extracting human body movement from inherited constraints, and abstracting a "universal human subject" exposed to determination by a differential signifier commanding its behavior. The human can thus be ordered to perform any desired action—ordered like a movie, a pizza, or a war. The only "categorical imperative" of capital (replacing the quaint and obsolete moral law of Kant) is *always pay your debts in a timely fashion*. Aside from that, anything goes (as was learned recently, the Swiss banking system was happy to fence gold extracted from the teeth of Jewish victims, because business is business; money tends to erase its own history). Money, the diffuse conspiracy of capital, is the *immanent symptom* of our "universal schizophrenia."[40]

Relations are internal or external to the terms in which, or between which, they are effective. If internal, then the behavior of elements or particles is determined, the terms are signs in a semiotic system (or language form) whose relations program their future interactions. From this perspective of internal relations, physical systems are like communities of signs being-together in physical consistency: an Image-World-Monad. If all relations were "internal"—coded into the terms or elements that play and act them out—there would be no problem of morality, for there would be no free play in the behavior of the human automaton. But life is the invention of relations, experiment in combinations, chance encounters between molecular complexes that try out syntheses and interactions with each other. Life is this molecular adventure whose future cannot be programmed: external improvisations becoming internalized as affects, powers of affection.

The affects of life are linked together in a sensory-motor ensemble, a molecular assemblage that perceives, feels, reacts, lives, reproduces. Morality consists in an effort to program human behavior and social, sexual relations and to represent this program of conformity as if it were the natural, organic, genetically coded behavior of the sensory-motor schema it relays and supplants; it is the operation of naturalizing human culture. Morality, consisting in the formulas and automatisms of consensus community, treats all relations as internal, encoded, and predetermined. But ethics experiments in external relations, in encounters, events, and processes whose outcome is not determined in advance but invented during the actualization of a virtual event, the realization of a possible event. Experimentation in affect, mutual affections of living beings, the affects or powers of plants and minerals, means experiencing the inorganic life of things, the immanent animation of all matter-energy. It is inseparable from aesthetic experiment in feeling, in creating new affects and powers of perception, percepts, monuments of sensation that make us see and feel in a different way, that invite us to enter another universe. Ethics means discovery, rediscovery of the virtual; invention, reinvention of the possible.

Both morality and ethics depend for their existence on the emergence of surprise, the unforeseeable, unpredictable advent of a living "zone of indetermination" (Bergson). But whereas creative ethics affirms this indetermination and plays with the unexpected harmonies and dissonances, sympathies and antipathies that result from encounters with something outside—outside body and soul with their technical extensions (in an unforeseeable future, meetings with an "other," *autrui* expressing other possible worlds)—morality hastens to determine the zone, to determine the future of encounters by reducing them to cases of law and social code, permitted or forbidden categories, and degrees of deviation from, or conformity to, the norms of conceiving, imagining, and behaving or misbehaving that constitute consensus and community.

Ethics consists in discovering and inventing external relations capable of internalization. In that sense, "evolution" is entirely ethical. But it is entirely an ethics of power, whose outcome is determined by the "law of natural selection," of survival and reproduction (the gene-determined affect-action that enables the being to survive and reproduce is "good" and will be internalized in the genome). And it is an ethics of sensory-motor action determined by purpose, by goals set in the future and the present programmed to realize that future. Whereas the dream of morality is to effect a closure of the ethical sensory-motor apparatus by fixating it upon a moral goal or purpose and programming it to realize that purpose (it is like an orchestration of all perception, thought, feeling, movement, a minute choreography, a symphony of human affect and behavior), the dream of ethics is to open up the sensory-motor apparatus and hold it open to an unknown future outside the moral program, open to possible relations with others, to capturing their affections or being captured, to composing new affects, to experiencing other worlds. The ethical universe is a chaosmos of improvisation, inseparable from the aesthetic creation of percepts and affects, and thus ready for cinema . . .

COSMOLOGICAL CINEMA: TOWARD ABSOLUTE CINEMANCE

The age of symbolic-signifying morality may now be ending, or it may be coming back. In either case, the morality that is now evolving or returning will not be the same as it was before the age of discipline and control began. In reality, the methods of instruction and training, techniques of conditioning body and soul, have always been layered geologically in time, integrated genealogically, and dispersed and zoned geographically.

Capital, with its differential signifier, is the dynamic temporal form of the "conspiracy of unequal exchange" that coerces and controls the affect and movement of bodies, signs, and images. It is an influencing machine that produces in its subject the vaguely conscious sensation of a *diffuse world conspiracy that is organizing the misery.*[41] It is a technocratic Apocalypse executing the fantasy program of Western metaphysics by realizing an immanent morality of the differential signifier of debt determining the future.

The virus of Control is not language (as Burroughs said) but the moral signifier of capital in the age of information, taking over from discipline the function of conditioning obedience. Kubrick's *A Clockwork Orange* (1971) shows the transition in progress, as Alex, a "vicious hoodlum" addicted to "ultraviolence" (and inspired by Beethoven's Ninth), who is immune to either paternal law or maternal correction, is handed over to a new breed of doctor-therapists for moral treatment according to the medical model. He is eventually cured of immorality by injection of nausea-inducing chemicals taken in conjunction with moving images of sex and violence (viewed strapped down with his eyes pinned open), until the very thought of aggression makes him sick and want to puke. Everyone is a victim, everyone a torturer, in this world of universal sadomasochistic psychomoralistic conditioning.

Signifying morality sustained itself through the "self-critique of reason" by representing unrepresentability as a transcendental moral signifier determining the subject in its freedom. It has converted the symbolic law of "thirdness" into a law of "castration" or "negativity" disallowing positive representation of what is to be done, while reconverting the "external reflection" of this negativity into an immanent negativity of reflection (Hegel) or an immanent but void positivity of a formal law without content determining the subject to obey itself, a "self-legislating categorical imperative" (Kant). The ethics of the future will not accept this "morality of freedom," this pseudoethics of pseudofreedom consisting in the supposed self-determination of relations, because it is not at all an ethics of "free will"—nor even an exaltation and glorification of will (as Adorno thought)—but a *determination of the will* (the differential element or dynamic multiplicity of self-immanence) *by the Signifier*, by the Other. This solution to the problem of relation is invalidated a priori by the only true law of representation—the Truth of the Other—which is to cancel itself by reason of the Other's unrepresentability. No one knows what the Other wants by virtue of the fact that the Other is other.

Universal democracy constitutes itself on the basis of a consensus, the will of the majority. However, it must represent—*even to itself*—the principle of collective will as being universally valid, otherwise it is "every man for himself," and universalism becomes suspended, supplanted by an improvisational aesthetic-sensual ethics of experimenting in the invention of possible communities or sociosexual relations. To avoid this libidinal-economic anarchy of ethical creativity, when a community agrees on a system of laws, of "right and wrong," it must convince itself that its values are god-given or universal.[42] In Kant and Sade the Enlightenment produced its culmination and its subversion: the Good, good behavior in itself, cannot be represented (Kant). Sade merely reinforced this disillusionment by demonstrating (writing in flesh) that it is always possible *not* to agree on what is good to do and what is bad. But Sade inadvertently betrays the perversion at the heart of the entire system of morality: its obsession with "universal law," the Law of the Father-Signifier, law of the reproductive Mother, law of nature—all of which he took great pains to violate whenever possible by simply inverting the moral law,[43] thereby only reinforcing the viciousness and sadism of the superego, which enjoys pain but is tempered by the Law of the Father.

Spinoza began the devaluation of morality and the rebirth of ethics in the modern world by realizing that there is no moral universal (the moral universe is a confabulation) because there is no moral God. Nature is the direct revelation of god—but this includes humanity with its techniques and perversions, its self-enforced delusions of Good and Evil, right and wrong as given in themselves. These fictions—lies when represented as truths, ineffective if not—are the driving ideologies or *mots d'ordre* of history. Thus history, for Deleuze, is deadweight or the totality of almost negative conditions for an event to occur, for something new to come into the world. History is an endless search for justice, vindication, or vengeance, a chain of events or linkage of deeds and moral reasons.

Alluding to disaster, Yeats lamented that "the best lack all conviction while the worst are full of passionate intensity" ("The Second Coming"); contemplating the human holocaust from a philosophical distance, Spinoza alleged it is the very form of moral passion that enslaves human beings to self-made disaster. Today it is possible (and necessary) to think about these matters, and the events of our time, in such a way as to expose the form of moral reason and its passion to the consciousness of its self-destruction (in the best of cases), and to decipher in its formation and self-maintenance the rationale of the "worst," the "malady of Eros" that infects human "nature" or community in its good sense (purpose) and in its common sense (ground and consensus). In so doing, it is the structure of human reason that must reinvent itself even in the process of its self-destruction. It is this double eventuality of breakdown and recovery—not restoration but discovery that "begins the new harmony . . . the drafting of new humans and their go-ahead . . . the new love"[44] beyond narcissistic conditioning—that can be shown and told in cinema, as nowhere else; even writing cannot show and tell this story, which requires real bodies and real brains for its exposition in a living image.

Normally, it is the function of cinema in capitalist society to produce a constant supply of variations and repetitions of a few basic guilty-transgressive fantasies, as it is the function of immoralists and criminals to act them out, and of the law-abiding public to turn them in, of the police to catch them, juries to try and convict, judges to sentence, jailers to punish, and the man or woman on the street to offer an opinion about guilt or innocence. Cinema works effectively because it acts directly on the brain and central nervous system and does not depend on linguistic representation for its intelligibility.[45] However, the fundamental rule remains in force, universal subjection to the differential signifier of capital that orders the movements of bodies, images, and signs. Only when the system of control becomes sick to death of itself (as capitalist discipline nearly did in the period of "dialectical materialist revolutions" from 1850 to 1950) will a chance open up—in a future being dreamed, experimented, and invented perhaps more intensely now with the collapse of "communism"—for a creative ethics without metaphysical ground or reason, a gift of hospitality, perhaps, and love, an aesthetic anarchy in which beauty emerges through a game without rules, and sublime genesis confronts reason with an "excess of principles," as All-Possibility (eternity) becomes indiscernible from absolute becoming.[46]

The paradox of cinema is that the postwar collapse of the structure of classical narrative implies the breakdown of that "open" model of time, itself based on the sensory-motor schema of living beings guided in their actions by perception, affection, instinct, impulse, and the purposes of life; whereas the classical-baroque version of time as "closed vessel" (monad) is implied by the new informational schema based on the idea of the *program* or coded function determining the future according to the ad hoc purposes of "evolution" (i.e., the evolution of control-capital). However, it is precisely this model of the information machine or cybernetic automaton that has broken into the old sensory-motor schema animated only by its own spontaneity or élan vital (though already obscurely guided from within to seek goals "innate" in its functioning)—or rather, as Deleuze implies, the break-in and breakdown was already internal to the functioning of the "open" sensory-motor schema itself.

In the first place, the sensory-motor schema was not as open as it might have seemed, because its behavior was always regulated by the purposes of survival and reproduction, as relayed, enacted, and represented by the moral program. In the second place, did not the smooth functioning of the schema, and the "classical" narrative it generated, depend on the constant conjuring or exorcism of any threat to this function, whether originating as "dysfunction" from within or as "alien" or "enemy" from without? Was the form and action of classical narrative not directed ultimately by the purpose of failing to become conscious of its own internal conditions? For it is these conditions that become questionable—if not intolerable to contemplate—once the system becomes aware of its libidinal-aggressive constitution ("régime of signs").

For Deleuzian or neo-Spinozistic philosophy, this is the time of a true metamorphosis of morality (both paternalistic and perverse-maternal) into a radical ethics of multiplicity, by which the differential elements of force (power) find out what they are capable of doing with each other through a process of experimentation with affects, percepts, and relations. For cinema, this means affirming and exploring the ruination of the sensory-motor schema of the heroic-communal-relational action-image under the stress of "events that are just too much."[47] The indirect symbolic relation held open the sensory-motor apparatus long enough to complete the closure of a preordained harmonic community, or to reopen the "situation" for creative evolution. But today's postmodern automaton is no longer certain there is any possible opening, only a confrontation between two closed data systems, a hallucino-genetically programmed cerebro-nervous information network operating on the inside, and an outside to which it is exposed and which is represented on an interior (psychic) screen by images and symbols. The two worlds are in topological contact across a polarized membrane or *crible*, consciousness on one side, chaos, danger, and opportunity on the other. These worlds are not entirely closed to each other; it is possible to capture or be captured by the aliens on the other side of the screen, "door or window." Guided by its calculations and directed by a mysterious command program (the Other, Alien within), the replicants struggle to advance the cause of natural selection. There is no place in such a régime for symbolic mediation, much less radical ethical-aesthetic experimentation (hunting and capture involve strategy and tactics, not ethics). What power is capable of inventing a new social link that can connect and relate these cybernetic monads and give us a break from our breathless "galloping schizophrenia"?

The ethical movement of philosophy begins in a becoming-scapegoat (Socrates, Spinoza, Nietzsche) as a result of defying the moral law, not for the purpose of transgression but as an effect of making an escape—a Spinozist *voyage sur place*, mental voyage through the destruction of the signifier, into memory, time, and becoming. This is not a conscious choice, it is an effect of a prior transcendental-libidinal decision, made in eternity, for experience, experiment in affect and percept. It is easy to identify with masters (it is all we do, whether to love or hate), but to become an exile initiates another order of experience.

The scapegoat inevitably becomes a subject-victim complaining of misuse, accusing oneself and others (especially the "masters"). If this phase continues, the movement of becoming reaches stasis and sterility or drives itself insane with bitterness, resentment. But the divided subject has begun its movement outward and there is no turning back. Or rather, there is a third movement that is a circuit of return, formation of a "war machine" that turns back and strikes at the signifying-subject régime that condemned it. However, this is really an extension and intensification of the disciplinary subject-machine divided between self-abuse and rage against the Other. Its temptation is fascism, psychosis ("passional delusion"), perversion, and destruction. *The war against the delusionary signifier is a struggle for liberation, not for annihilation, even of an enemy.*

Deleuze has taught us to transvalue the movement of exile from symbolic structure in the following ways:

1. The "erratic movement" of the broken sensory-motor linkage turns into a *nomadic* movement of thought and feeling a way through labyrinths of world-memory. Chance, the adventure of immanence, becomes the "only guiding thread" of thought making way through a quasi chaos of budding images, ideas, and feelings.[48] The rules (categories) change with every move and synthesis, every apparition, connection, disjunction, and combination. Power is not the only rule or principle, there is harmony, dissonance, relations improvised between incompossible ensembles with lines shooting out from singularities, emitting "rafales de signes," gusts of intensities crossing potentials that stretch from being to being. These transitions or affects are *pointes de déterritorialisation* for departures and becomings.

   So although we are sentenced to death by the signifier, to inalterable identity, the limit of identity is transversely a line of escape into modulations and powers ("false" according to the moral logic of Truth).
2. Loose or absent links between images, persons, ideas, turn into a *positive connection through absence*, a body without organs, unlocalizable linkage with the future. Death becomes the zero-form of intensive connection between lives, the "real distinction" between beings becoming indiscernible. Every encounter with another life is an encounter with a "god," a *gift of hospitality* (which is the genesis of ethics within anarchy).[49] When we meet another being, we begin to experiment with our relations and *create possibilities* together. This creation of possibility is an

aesthetic act, an experiment in vibration, resonance, *composition of affects* (mutual synthesis of powers).[50]

3. The noetic and affective disorders of mass "popular" culture manifest themselves in a swarm of clichés and images flooding the brain from which they project outward into action and speech and are recycled inward through media. This endo-exo-psycho-cinematic feedback loop turns into a simulacrum that becomes *capable of thinking* and *becoming conscious of itself.* A simulacrum is a multiplicity that has internalized the conditions of its own reproduction, so that it makes no reference to any external cause or master signifier or model form, but subverts the conditions of judgment by consisting in informal self-improvisation (mutual affection of traits of multiplicity), continual syntheses of forms and relations. The plane of consistency (BwO) is the composition of simulacra, the consciousness of immanence is the "current" that feeds the world-brain loop. The self-conscious simulacrum is not "negativity" (neither "external" nor "self-reflective") but a *crible* that reflects itself as in "a city or a cell."[51]
4. Denunciation of the "plot," the money-image loop, the influencing machine, determination of image-movement, image-affect, and idea by capital, the superego mechanism of Control society (internalization of the temporal structure of debt—purified of traditional "content"—determining "behavior"). The ethics of experimental relations and hospitality is a practice or performance of anticapital, which Spinoza called "intellectual love of God," "not insofar as we imagine him as present" or "actual" in "a certain time and place," but insofar as we conceive the beings we encounter "under a species of eternity," that is, as they are "involved in the eternal and infinite essence of God" or divine nature.[52]
5. A cinema that sees and hears makes itself the virtual eyes and ears of an actuality becoming conscious of itself and engages "an event under way."[53] This "detour through the direct" confronts the cinema-brain (director, crew, spectator) with an *outside* that is not the "outside world" included in sensory-motor perception, but an *unknown* reflected—or pre-flected—in the unpredictable reactions of role players (scripted or not) in actuality to the presence of the camera crew and actors, the incalculable delayed effect of the image-montage, its eventual interpretation, an entire *virtual future* included, pre-flected in

the shooting of actuality. Filmmaking becomes a kind of counterconspiracy that forces open the Hollywood Monad—like Captain Mandrake in *Dr. Strangelove* cracking the code that will call back the planes from Armaggedon. We are living in an incompossible world of neo-baroque monads sealed off from communication with each other like Colonel Ripper's air force base (or the war room enclosed inside a hollow sphere illuminated with a "big board" projecting all possible and actual strategic world-positions, and connected via telephone hot line to the "Russians")—each world-reality accessible only by key code—each monad staring at a data screen representing possible outside futures threatening to break into its body without organs centered on command-and-control, a paranoid Brain preoccupied with alien invasion (to destroy or be destroyed). This universe of "capture" cannot be restored to "common sense," its delusion is already that of a paranoid consensus. What matters is not just to break the code that engages this body-brain circuit (fleets and armies as bodies or organs controlled by the brain) but to intervene within the money-image circuit that programs the fantasy reserve of the brain itself, its self-representation (e.g., "democracy"). Really, cinema can do no better than *reflect* this *incompossible ensemble* of apocalyptic monads by intervening in the circuit of its self-consciousness. But how do you get inside the consciousness of a population of sealed monads each glued to a video screen on which numbers represent the differential flows of money it captures and feeds on, and fears losing, while interspersed select erotic-aggressive "leisure" images recharge its perverse-paranoid fantasies?

Answer: Nomadic Cinema. In the "dispersive situation" of our "universal schizophrenia," what matters is to affirm the movement of *errance* and hospitality (sharing of essences)—the *force of the outside*—against the sedentary-paranoid disposition of consensual community, not only because the community form (both signifying and disciplinary) is sick, but because its control superego tends to *inhibit the possibility of thinking*. The force of thinking is to become capable of the *nonrelation* that enables (forces) thought to *come back from outside* like a war machine. This movement of return or "feedback" from outside, from the future to the present or past (memory), becomes the Markoff form or process of "reflection," *relinkage back across an irrational limit* or incommensurable interval between image-movements.

What is unthought is immanence, the coexistence of all spatio-temporal planes (Memory), the simultaneity of all presents, "presences" or images. Cinema captures these phantoms and projects them onto our brain, its screen, "contact independent of distance." Cinema, "a brain that blinks, and relinks or makes loops,"[54] feeding images back and forth: this is the operation of a *crible*, chaosmic membrane that extracts or crystallizes order out of chaos, feeding residual chaos back into order, stabilizing one, destabilizing the other. For cosmos makes an image of chaos, which in its delusion it figures as a rebellious "feminine" monster it imagines itself to have "conquered" once upon a time and dreams of binding forever or exterminating, not realizing that it is itself made of "chaos and horrible chance," shuttling back and forth and weaving feedback loops between indiscernibles.[55]

The power of modern cinema, as we learn from *The Time-Image*, is to project an image that is "body, brain, and thought," a time-image unregulated by the sensory-motor schema guiding the movements of classical narrative. That classicism showed, in all its variations, the power of the Name of the Father to determine the course of action, as well as the identities of things and beings, in the name of the moral law of the Other. The classic American duel is resolved by a pacifying force that constitutes community; the Soviet-cinematic class struggle is resolved by the completion of the historical dialectic; expressionist film persists with the recurring struggle between light and darkness and between organic and inorganic life-forms, between the sublime and infinite powers of imagination and reason. In a remarkable analysis, Deleuze shows the passage from the "spirit of evil" to "our share in the divine" through "the ultimate sacrifice" of our organic nature. This is exactly the genesis of the Name of the Father ("the spiritual relation in which we are alone with God as light"),[56] which connects German expressionism with the "rise of the Hitlerian automaton in the German soul."[57] Not that Hitler was a "father figure" (or even a big brother), but he was precisely the embodiment of the unmediated narcissistic "duel" or "dialectic" between "good and evil."

The true "function of the father" is to quell the violence of its own aggression and to pacify the anarchy of a universal "struggle for recognition." (This function cannot be taken over by the disciplinary "matrix" of symbolic maternity, the all-embracing total institution, which is one reason for the failure of schools and prisons to pacify their inmates.) Whatever its moral reason, however, the symbolic function of the Name of the Father is to represent the *whole* that cannot be presented, the relation that is indirectly represented by the affective interval of our sensory-motor apparatus (body, brain), and—in the psychocinematic narrative based on this schema—by the entire arrangement or montage of images, the moral logic determining the *linkage* of one image to the next. Montage is the God-Father or the symbolic Other of cinema, its "principal act," which "links one movement-image to another," thus "constitut[ing] the whole and giv[ing] us an image *of* time."[58] That is, the symbolic function guarantees a structure of differential time in which movement finds meaning in the form of an open totality interiorized in the subject as the structure of divided consciousness or moral conscience. Relation is thus established, a sociosexual tie guaranteeing that survival and sexual regeneration will continue, that the world will go on being recognizable as long as its dangerous opening to the future is represented by the symbolic Father.

The function of the symbolic father is to *make relation possible*, to make the movement-image possible, there where no further progress seems possible, where movement ends or grows infinite, where intensity disappears into nothingness or becomes absolute and consumes everything. It is this becoming-spirit that is guided and inspired by the Name of the Father, which is perfectly capable, as Kant showed ("with Sade"), of annihilating all of nature in order to "sublimate" body into soul; for, in the end, invoking the father's name does not save us from our own continuing "dialectic" with organic nature, the evolution of automatons, and their invasion of the psyche. And it is no longer a question of those quaint and "sinister" robot simulacra who make evil grimaces while they burn at the stake, like the robot witch in *Metropolis*; the new endopsychic automatons are indiscernible from the functions of the brain itself in their technoscientific "evolution." These operations are indistinguishable from the "outside world" and only cinema, perhaps, can show us this directly (Resnais, Kubrick). It is no longer a question of mothers and fathers, who are reproductive functions without ulterior significance (listen to Professor Laborit or Doctor Sci-Love); the cerebro-nervous complex is on its own now, pursuing a strange course of evolution . . .

The symbolic function mediates the sensory-motor movement beyond ego into death, regeneration, and tribe, the sublime passage beyond movement into spirit, beyond this world into the next, sublimation of all movement into the "whole of relation," or time. But the question concerning the present time is no longer a matter for movement, even spiritual, or relation, even sublime; it is now a question of nonrelation, yet at the same time, of belief, not in another world, but in this very world in its becoming, "before and after" movement, a feeling or *seeing before perception*, a *thinking after relation*.[59] That seeing-thinking has no object, its perception has become *hallucination*, its relation has become *delusion*.[60] But it now sets itself the task of intuiting or thinking the nonrelation of delusion and hallucination as they are in themselves, that is, in us; not the delusions of hallucinatory psychosis but the ordinary perceptual hallucinations of "good sense," of the sensory-motor schema; and the everyday "common sense" delusions that determine individuals, peoples, nations in their passage into action.

When symbolic function fails, this structure of psychosexual temporality breaks down and the social reality it guaranteed becomes unrecognizable—"it is not now the succession of representations that appears but representation itself."[61] The social identity of things is disinvested and they lose their names; the structure of reality collapses; the image appears "without metaphor" and "mental vision" becomes hallucination, "the thing in itself surging literally in its excess of horror or beauty"; a factory turns into a prison (Foucault as bourgeois housewife whose symbolic schema has broken: "I thought I saw survivors in reprieve running toward dark shelters").[62] When the symbolic relation breaks down, reality collapses and the real appears. Foucault *sees* a prison in school, in the factory; Freud *hears* a censorship at work inside our minds; Nietzsche *feels* eternity in repetition; Spinoza *senses* that God is nature naturing itself. This pure intuition of time becoming without category or metaphor emerges from the risk of disbelieving in the symbols of reality, as Descartes for a moment disbelieved in the world outside and the whole thing suddenly became a vision, a hallucination conjured by an evil demon manipulating his ideas. This demon (Control) operates at the core of language and consciousness.

The reality of an event is not exhausted by its actualization in a state of things; there is a part of the event that its incarnation does not realize, a real but virtual portion consisting in the sense (or nonsense) it makes, always before or after its actualization. This virtual past and future subsist in the form of fabulation and interpretation. One could say that fabulation prepares the actual event, interpretation makes sense of it after the fact. Both are included in its process, but as virtual or nonactual realities. In decoding and breaking down the traditional structures of ritual and narrative, the capitalist moral universal (differential signifier) has purged the virtual, fabulative-interpretive reality of its fictional or mythic background, thus (as Marx revealed) exhibiting the form of human slavery purified of illusion. Then why does humanity not yet rid itself of its master? Is it because we enjoy sadism and masochism and do not want to be liberated (this was Freud's thesis, the "death drive"), or are we resigned to determination by the money form, the purified superego of indebtedness, because we have witnessed the horrors of slave labor without capitalists in "Marxist-Communist" totalitarianism, in which bureaucratic knowledge directs the body and brain of the sensory-motor proletariat, and we feel confident that capital is less "stupid"? In any case, ethical creativity does not have to wait around for the human subject to come to consciousness and liberate itself from the morality of money (debt); it can invent a new social link based on hospitality[63] and cooperation.

To survive the end of mediation, we should learn to *think without Law*, without Father, to develop an *absolute ethics* that begins where symbolic-moral mediation leaves off and an aesthetic experience of nonrelation appears. It remains an ethical experiment, however, in that it is always a question of discovering and inventing new relations, new powers, without falling into nostalgia or perverse denial that never *seems* to tire of killing the father (in reality it lives and dies in despair)—but never risks a step beyond it.

NOTES

1. Is not the calling of cinema "to make heard a cry in visible things," and "to make a gleam of light shimmer in words"? It is in the endopsychic theater of the brain that *the phantoms come to meet us*. See Gilles Deleuze, *Foucault* (Paris: Éditions de Minuit, 1986), 124; in English, *Foucault*, trans. Seán Hand (Minneapolis: University of Minnesota Press, 1988), 116. Note that in the essay that follows, unless otherwise indicated, all passages from Deleuze are taken from the French (I have provided my own translations). However, in the Notes I have provided citations from both the French and the standard English translations of Deleuze's texts.
2. Gilles Deleuze, *L'image-temps* (Paris: Éditions de Minuit, 1985), 58; *The Time-Image*, trans. Hugh Tomlinson and Barbara Hebberjam (Minneapolis: University of Minnesota Press, 1989), 41.
3. For the Christian structuration of the Holocaust, see Jules Isaac, *Jésus et Israël* (Paris: Albin Michel, 1948), and Rosemary Ruether, *Faith and Fratricide: The Theological Roots of Anti-Semitism* (New York: Seabury Press, 1974).
4. Bernard Cuau, Michel Deguy, Rachel Ertel, Shoshana Felman, Elisabeth de Fontenay, Elisabeth Huppert, Gertrud Koch, Sami Näir, Marcel Ophuls, Anny Dayan-Rosenman, Pierre Vidal-Naquet, Abraham Brumberg, Neal Ascherson, Timothy

Garton Ash, Jacek Näir, Jacek Kuron, Jean-Charles Szurek, and Claude Lanzmann, *Au sujet de Shoah: le film de Claude Lanzmann* (Paris: 1990), 311–12.

5. Questions like these call for repression and denial . . . to *save* the moral community from self-consciousness of its own conditions. It is necessary to deny or fail to recognize an unconsciously perceived and enacted reality—the programming of the collective moral automaton. Another strategy was, of course, to deny German guilt and blame the Jews for their own "self-destruction." But this is merely a variation on the basic psychotic-perverse-neurotic structure of willful misrecognition.
6. Serge Daney, *La rampe: cahier critique, 1970–1982* (Paris: Gallimard, 1983), 172.
7. Deleuze, *L'image-temps*, 221; *The Time-Image*, 170. Many important postwar films have approached recognition of this moral crisis, from antiwar films such as Kubrick's to subtle and perverse postmorality tales like Lynch's *Blue Velvet* (1986) in which the evil Frank says to his quasi protégé, good Jeffrey, "you're like me." In Kubrick's *A Clockwork Orange* (1971), the force of evil aggression and the controlled experimental policy of treating it like a disease curable by endopsychic programming and neurochemical reconstruction turn into symbiotic political partners. Alex's behavioral modification is undone in the end ("I dreamed someone was messing with my brain") but, as we know, the research into a cure for unscheduled aggression continues.
8. The culmination of the system of Judgment is Apocalypse, the Christian fantasy program of the end, fabulation of world destruction, whose goal is "to disconnect us from the world and from ourselves." "What is individual is relation, it is the soul, not the ego. The ego has a tendency to identify itself with the world, but this is already death, whereas the soul stretches out the thread of its living 'sympathies' and 'antipathies.' Stop thinking like an ego, in order to live like a flux, an ensemble of flows, in relation with other fluxes, outside oneself and in oneself" (Gilles Deleuze, *Critique et clinique* [Paris: Éditions de Minuit, 1993], 56, 66, 68; *Essays Critical and Clinical*, trans. Daniel W. Smith and Michael A. Greco [Minneapolis: University of Minnesota Press, 1997], 41, 50, 52). This book is a dispersed, nomadic treatise in the aesthetics of ethical experimentation.
9. See Sigmund Freud, *Civilization and Its Discontents*, in *The Standard Edition of the Complete Psychological Works of Sigmund Freud* (*SE*), trans. James and Alex Strachey (London: Hogarth Press and the Institute of Psychoanalysis, 1953–74), vol. 21.
10. In Melville's *The Confidence Man* (New York: Norton, 1971), the Devil comes to earth as a riverboat con man of infinite disguises—preacher of Christian charity, beggar, borrower, swindler—but also as a dogmatist of self-reliance who never spoils friendship with charity or lending, and finally, consummately, as an Indian killer, a Christian militant whose sole passion is hatred of evil and whose mission is to exterminate every last red-skinned Satan.
11. Ridley Scott's *Blade Runner* (1982) epitomizes this "existential" predicament, but revitalizes it by making the replicants (who "just want to live" beyond their four-year deadline) and the bladerunners (who periodically hunt and destroy rebellious ones) morally indistinguishable; both are survivors and slaves, automatons without personal significance in the world of capital that produces them. The "promise" of genetic engineering and cyborgization makes death strangely unacceptable, intolerable to the new race of indiscernibles as machines develop victim consciousness (and even "immortal" androids will be afraid of accident and entropy).
12. See Gilles Deleuze and Félix Guattari, *A Thousand Plateaus: Capitalism and Schizophrenia*, trans. Brian Massumi (Minneapolis: University of Minnesota Press, 1987), chapters 4 and 5.
13. See Victor Tausk, "The Influencing Machine," *Incorporations* (New York: Urzone,

1993), 542–69. In his "Meditations," Descartes denounced the tradition (*vetus opinio*) as influencing machine preoccupying the psyche like a demon; Cervantes had already exhibited the hallucinatory perplexity of the endopsychic theater. In the age of Control, the influence becomes an informational "virus." See William S. Burroughs, *The Job* (New York: Grove Press, 1974). Lacan says the machine is a signifier that causes the "passion" of its human subjects (Jacques Lacan, *Le Séminaire, Livre 7: L'éthique de la psychanalyse, 1959–1960* (Paris: Éditions du Seuil, 1986).

14. *Jouissance* is a technical Lacanian term for participation in enforcement or violation of the moral law. The "*jouissance* of the Other" is the sadomasochistic enjoyment produced by this system for vicarious (social) consumption. See Gilles Deleuze and Félix Guattari, *L'anti-Œdipe* (Paris: Éditions de Minuit, 1972); *Anti-Oedipus: Capitalism and Schizophrenia*, trans. Robert Hurley, Mark Seem, and Helen R. Lane (Minneapolis: University of Minnesota Press, 1983). Also see Michel de Certeau, *Heterologies: Discourse of the Other*, trans. Brian Massumi (Minneapolis: University of Minnesota Press, 1986). If a subject becomes too conscious of this mechanism, he or she may become incapable of participating in the Other's *jouissance*, and may begin to experience it as a sinister and invasive (evil) power exercised by perverse demons and their humanoid automatons against innocent scapegoat-victims (i.e., oneself as unrecognized hero of resistance). See Willy Apollon, Danille Bergeron, and Lucie Cantin, *Traiter la psychose* (Québec: Gifric, Collection Nœud, 1990).
15. See Michel Foucault, *Histoire de la folie* (Paris: Librairie Plon, 1961); *Madness and Civilization*, trans. Richard Howard (New York: Vintage Books, 1988). Also see Michel Foucault, *Surveiller et punir* (Paris: Gallimard, 1975); *Discipline and Punish*, trans. Alan Sheridan (New York: Vintage Books, 1979). On the signifying group structure, formalized as totality bounded by "at least one" exception, see Jacques Lacan, *Encore* (Paris: Éditions du Seuil, 1975). There are two exceptions, or one double, contradictorily bound together in the *Urvater* who is originally both Leader and Scapegoat (criminal *père jouisseur*).
16. Gilles Deleuze, *Kant's Critical Philosophy: The Doctrine of the Faculties*, trans. Hugh Tomlinson and Barbara Habberjam (Minneapolis: University of Minnesota Press, 1984), viii-xi.
17. Gilles Deleuze, *Différence et répétition* (Paris: Presses Universitaires de France, 1968); *Difference and Repetition*, trans. Paul Patton (New York: Columbia University Press, 1994). When the idea of absolute chance invaded the foundations of physics, cosmologists such as de Witt and Wheeler began imagining a cosmos without physical law, or in which the laws change with every "big bang," each universe modulating its own structure ("mode") out of a chaotic sea of possibilities. See John Archibald Wheeler, *At Home in the Universe* (New York: American Institute of Physics, 1996); and articles by Martin Rees and Lee Smolin in *The Third Culture*, ed. John Brockman (New York: Simon and Schuster, 1995).
18. This is happening even as the capitalist signifier takes over determination and control of the human form, worldwide and without exception. For that immanent-transcendental signifier (money, debt as moral force or form without content) is all that stands now in the way of the de-moralization of the world.
19. Ilya Prigogine and Isabelle Stengers, Postface to Michel Serres, *Hermes* (Baltimore: Johns Hopkins University Press, 1982), 153.
20. Stephen Hawking, *A Brief History of Time: From the Big Bang to Black Holes* (New York: Bantam Books, 1988), 174. The *demonium meridiae* appears when things lose their shadows or insomniac Reason begins to hallucinate its world-image becoming a brain.
21. Genesis and destruction have the same source, "according to necessity; for they pay penalty and retribution to each other for mutual injustice according to

the assessment of time" (Anaximander). See G. S. Kirk and J. E. Raven, eds., *The Pre-Socratic Philosophers* (Cambridge: Cambridge University Press, 1957), 117.

22. See Murray Gell-Mann, *The Quark and the Jaguar: Adventures in the Simple and the Complex* (New York: W. H. Freeman, 1994).
23. See Andrei Linde, "The Self-Reproducing Inflationary Universe," *Scientific American* (November 1994): 48–55; and Lee Smolin, *The Life of the Cosmos* (New York: Oxford University Press, 1997).
24. As Heidegger showed in his seminar on Schelling's concept of freedom, any assertion of self-grounding reason has always been condemned by the metaphysical tradition as evil (Martin Heidegger, *Schelling's Treatise on the Essence of Human Freedom*, trans. Joan Stambaugh [Athens: Ohio University Press, 1985]).
25. Henri Bergson, *L'évolution créatrice* (Paris: Presses Universitaires de France, 1941 [1907]), 10–11; also see Deleuze's *Bergsonism*, trans. Hugh Tomlinson and Barbara Habberjam (New York: Zone Books, 1988).
26. In *Qu'est-ce que la philosophie?* Deleuze and Guattari adopt Prigogine's speculation that the universe is chaos in the process of self-crystallization. See *Qu'est-ce que la philosophie?* (Paris: Éditions de Minuit, 1991), 225 n. 1; *What Is Philosophy?*, trans. Hugh Tomlinson and Graham Burchell (New York: Columbia University Press, 1994). Also see Ilya Prigogine and Isabelle Stengers, *Entre le temps et l'éternité* (Paris: Fayard, 1988). Philosophy, in distinction from science, asks only "how to retain the infinite speeds [of chaos] while yet gaining consistency, while giving a proper consistency to the virtual [or: while giving—scil. to chaos—a consistency that is proper to the virtual]." This consistency is the work of a *crible*, or filtering membrane (plane of immanence), which "selects infinite movements of thought, and furnishes itself with formed concepts as well as consistent particles moving at the speed of thought [or: with concepts formed as particles moving as fast as thought]" (*Qu'est-ce que la philosophie?*, 112; *What Is Philosophy?*, 118). For some reason, Deleuze does not elaborate on the time-crystal—a concept he invented in *The Time-Image*—in his last collaboration with Guattari.
27. Gilles Deleuze, *L'image-mouvement* (Paris: Éditions de Minuit, 1983), 84; *The Movement-Image* (Minneapolis: University of Minnesota Press, 1986), 57. Also see *Différence et répétition*.
28. Gilles Deleuze, *Le Pli: Leibniz et le baroque* (Paris: Éditions de Minuit, 1988), 103; *The Fold: Leibniz and the Baroque*, trans. Tom Conley (Minneapolis: University of Minnesota Press, 1993), 76.
29. "The crystal is expression" (Deleuze, *L'image-temps*, 100; *The Time-Image*, 74). The crystal *shows* the power of expression indiscernible from the content it determines.
30. Ibid., 45 (French); 30 (English).
31. Deleuze, *L'image-mouvement*, 93; *The Movement-Image*, 63.
32. See Deleuze, *What Is Philosophy?*
33. Deleuze, *L'image-temps*, 275; *The Time-Image*, 212. Also see 234f. (179f. in the English) with respect to the interstice. "It is no longer a question of following a chain of images, even over the voids, but to get outside the chain or the association." "It is the method of the BETWEEN, between two images, that exorcizes all cinema of Oneness. It is the method of the AND, 'this and then that,' which exorcizes any cinema of Being = is."
34. Deleuze, *L'image-mouvement*, 93; *The Movement-Image*, 63.
35. Gilles Deleuze, "L'immanence: une vie…," *Philosophie* 47 (September 1, 1995): 3. *Hors champ*, out of field, means off-camera or offscreen, an invisible presence. Here it is the field that is a virtual and indiscernible current of space-time or immanence, *not identifiable* as "transcendental subject" or object.
36. Ibid.: "the passage from one [sensation] to another as becoming…"
37. See Gilles Deleuze, *Spinoza, philosophie pratique* (Paris: Éditions de Minuit, 1981);

Spinoza's Practical Philosophy, trans. Robert Hurley (San Francisco: City Lights Books, 1988).

38. In that sense it is also death, because it includes the immanence of death as a disjunctive passage from life to life. The transcendental plane of immanence is a current of intensity that runs at a diagonal, transversal to the transcendent field of subjects and objects, the plane of images or energy. This transversal can be conceived through "intensive ordinates" that transect the extensive abscissae of objective-energetic movement, space-time. See Deleuze and Guattari, *What Is Philosophy?*
39. Deleuze, *L'anti-Œdipe*, 369n; *Anti-Œdipus*, 309.
40. Deleuze, *L'image-temps*, 223; *The Time-Image*, 210. This is the thesis of *Anti-Oedipus*.
41. Deleuze, *L'image-mouvement*, 282; *The Movement-Image*, 210. Also see Deleuze, *L'image-temps*, 104; *The Time-Image*, 77.
42. The delusion (or perversion) of the Enlightenment consists in its claim to universal representation, whereas a law that is not universal must recognize exceptions—which makes it no longer enforceable as valid for everyone. This is the real dilemma that is currently being acted out in the controversy over "cultural relativism"—which means the "natural right" of people to preserve *and create* their own modes of life and thought, their own social reality.
43. Or rather, reversing its "value"—where Moses said "thou shalt not," Sade says "thou shalt"—Klossowski, Blanchot, Lacan, and Deleuze developed the modern theory of perversion, the key to which is *violation of moral law* (to which it is addicted). In David Lynch's *Blue Velvet* (1986), the transmission of perversion—from the sadist (Frank) to the ingénu (Jeffrey), from the masochist (Dorothy) to Jeffrey and through Jeffrey to his girlfriend—all occurs under the nose of the girl's father, whose watchful eye sees nothing because he has no imagination for perverse *jouissance* (his daughter has a keener eye, catching glimmers and desiring more of what she half suspects in Jeffrey: "I don't know if you're a detective or a pervert") and no conception of the truth about the Law he represents (that it stimulates and provokes perverts like his partner). His paternal function is to maintain blindness or unconsciousness about the phantasms he enjoys indirectly through his daughter's desire, while the movie seems to play at awakening (through Jeffrey) to the transmission of moral "disease" (Dorothy says to her "secret lover" Jeffrey, "you put your disease in me"—that is, he infected her with his inherited paternal normalcy while she was scratching him with her masochism) through cinematic phantasms, while somnambulating through a real nightmare, not incest-crazy Frank but the oedipal capitalist libidinal economy that displays his effigy to frighten the public into reinforcing reproductive clichés and moral sentiments. The movies teach us that perversion is a spicy daydream, while warning us not to stray too far from the signifier in our acts.
44. Arthur Rimbaud, "À une raison."
45. Deleuze, *L'image-temps*, 341; *The Time-Image*, 262. As cinema "brings to light an intelligible matter," a "spiritual automaton" that forms the substance of what language presupposes to be sayable, it neither reproduces natural perception nor works indirectly by forming a chain of ideas, but affects the human nervous system directly with *involuntary* percepts, thoughts, and feelings that consciousness cannot resist. Kubrick's *A Clockwork Orange* parodies this situation, but you do not have to tie the audience down and pin open its eyelids to insert an unconscious program into its nervous system; the cinematic automaton operates regardless of the awareness or intention of either producer or consumer. Cinema shows why humans cannot think, are not yet capable of thinking, or even confronting the incapacity of thinking that forces one to think.
46. Some recent films do show signs of being sick of reproducing fantasies to feed the

hunger for transgression and the rage for vengeance (the *jouissance* of the Other). Altman's *The Player* (1992), for example, exposes the predatory movie-production system and implicates the audience, in that we are paying to watch a film inspired by the assassination of a scriptwriter and vampirization of his woman to feed the industry and its consumers. *Man Bites Dog* (1991) crudely shoves the audience into position as director, right behind the camera filming a professional murderer explaining his business in documentary-style interviews intercalated with live demonstrations of his craft, a regular Sadean mise-en-scène. (See Deleuze's appreciation and critique of Altman's "pessimistic romanticism" in *L'image-mouvement*, 279–84; *The Movement-Image*, 207–10.)

47. Louis-Ferdinand Céline, *Guignol's Band*, trans. Bernard Freshtman and Jack T. Nile (New York: New Directions, 1954), 13E. "It's my reason tottering ... under the shocks of the circumstances!" The situation is the evacuation of Paris during a German air attack.
48. Deleuze, *L'image-mouvement*, 279; *The Movement-Image*, 207. The five present transformations follow (approximately) the course of the "crisis" disclosed at the end of *The Movement-Image*.
49. The trilogy of Klossowksi (*Les lois de l'hospitalité* [1965]) inclines toward a general manifesto of the ethics of aristocracy and anarchy, resonant with the etymology of Indo-European insitutions presented by Benveniste, *Vocabulaire des institutions indo-européennes* (1969).
50. See Deleuze, *Qu'est-ce que la philosophie?* (*What Is Philosophy?*), chapter 7; *A Thousand Plateaus*, chapters 10, 11.
51. Earlier the crible was likened to a kind of virtual, living crystal. An actual crystal, however, can be isolated in a state of equilibrium, "but the city and the cell, cut off from their environment, quickly die; they are an integrating part [simulacrum] of the world that nourishes them, they consitute a sort of local and singular incarnation of the flows they ceaselessly transform" (Ilya Prigogine and Isabelle Stengers, *La Nouvelle Alliance: métamorphose de la science* [Paris: Gallimard, 1979] 142–43).
52. Baruch Spinoza, *A Spinoza Reader: "The Ethics" and Other Works*, V P32, P29 Schol., trans. Edwin Curley (Princeton, N.J.: Princeton University Press, 1994) 258, 259.
53. Deleuze, *L'image-mouvement*, 277–78; *The Movement-Image*, 205–6.
54. Deleuze, *L'image-temps*, 281, 280; *The Time-Image*, 215, 216.
55. "Chaos and horrible chance": Friedrich Nietzsche, *Thus Spoke Zarathustra*; the shuttle: *Qu'est-ce que la philosophie?*; on the cosmological narrative of mastery, see Jean-Pierre Vernant, *Les origines* (Paris: Presses Universitaires de France, 1962).
56. Deleuze, *L'image-mouvement*, 80 (and the presentation of expressionist sublime, 69–82); *The Movement-Image*, 53 (40–55).
57. Deleuze, *L'image-temps*, 344; *The Time-Image*, 264.
58. Ibid., 51; 35 (English).
59. Ibid., 50; 34 (English).
60. "All perception is hallucinatory, because perception has no object" (Deleuze, *Le Pli*, 125; *The Fold*, 95).
61. Hölderlin in Philippe Lacoue-Labarthe, *Heidegger, Art and Politics: The Fiction of the Political* (Oxford; Blackwell, 1990), 41.
62. Deleuze, *L'image-temps*, 32, 65; *The Time-Image*, 20, 46.
63. In the sense of Klossowski's laws of hospitality, hospitality means experimentation in ethical and sexual relations, Deleuzian"nomadism" of thought and affect.

After-Image

Chapter 13

The Brain Is the Screen

An Interview with Gilles Deleuze

Translated by Marie Therese Guirgis

With the publication of *The Movement-Image* and *The Time-Image,* Gilles Deleuze was often asked to explain—or expand upon—his unique understanding of the cinema. One of the most wide-ranging, informative, and ultimately personal of these conversations took place with *Cahiers du cinéma* after Deleuze's second cinema volume appeared. Pascal Bonitzer and Jean Narboni had conducted a similar interview with Deleuze after the publication of *The Movement-Image;*[1] for this subsequent interview they were joined by A. Bergala, M. Chevrie, and S. Toubiana. The resulting text was, they explained, the "the fruit of a long conversation" and was subsequently "rearranged by him [Deleuze] in more of a synthesis and therefore rendered more dense."

FROM PHILOSOPHY TO CINEMA

How did the cinema enter your life, both as a spectator and, of course, as a philosopher? When did you begin to love cinema and when did you begin to consider it a domain worthy of philosophy?

I had a privileged experience because I enjoyed two separate phases of filmgoing. Before the war, as a child, I went to the cinema rather often: I think that there was a familial structure to the cinema because of subscription theaters like the Salle Pleyel. You could send children there by themselves. I didn't have the choice of program, sometimes it was Harold Lloyd or Buster Keaton, sometimes *Les Croix de bois* (The Wooden Crosses)—which upset me; they even showed *Fantômas,* again, which made me very scared.[2] It would be interesting to find out which theaters disappeared after the war in a given neighborhood. New theaters sprang up, but many disappeared.

And then, after the war, I returned to the cinema, but in another manner. I was a student of philosophy, and although I wasn't stupid enough to want to create a philosophy of cinema, one conjunction made an impression on me. I liked those authors who demanded that we introduce movement to thought, "real" movement (they denounced the Hegelian dialectic as abstract movement). How could I not discover the cinema, which introduces "real" movement into the image? I wasn't trying to *apply* philosophy to cinema, but I went straight from philosophy to cinema. The reverse was also true, one went right from cinema to philosophy. Something bizarre about the cinema struck me: its unexpected ability to show not only behavior, but spiritual life [*la vie spirituelle*] as well (at the same time as aberrant behavior). Spiritual life isn't dream or fantasy—which were always the cinema's dead ends—but rather the domain of cold decision, of absolute obstinacy, of the choice of existence. How is it that the cinema is so expert at excavating this spiritual life? This can lead to the worst, a cinematic catholicism or religious kitsch [*sulpicisme*][3] specific to the cinema, but also to the greatest: Dreyer, Sternberg, Bresson, Rosselini, and even Rohmer today. It's interesting how Rohmer assigns to cinema the study of the spheres of existence: aesthetic existence in *La Collectionneuse*, ethical existence in *Le Beau mariage*, religious existence in *Ma nuit chez Maud* (*My Night at Maud's*). One thinks of Kierkegaard, who, well before cinema, already felt the need to write in odd synopses.[4] Cinema not only puts movement in the image, it also puts movement in the mind. Spiritual life *is* the movement of the mind. One naturally goes from philosophy to cinema, but also from cinema to philosophy.

The brain is unity. The brain is the screen. I don't believe that linguistics and psychoanalysis offer a great deal to the cinema. On the contrary, the biology of the brain—molecular biology—does. Thought is molecular. Molecular speeds make up the slow beings that we are. As Michaux said, "*Man is a slow being, who is only made possible thanks to fantastic speeds.*" The circuits and linkages of the brain don't preexist the stimuli, corpuscles, and particles [*grains*] that trace them. Cinema isn't theater; rather, it makes bodies out of grains. The linkages are often paradoxical and on all sides overflow simple associations of images. Cinema, precisely because it puts the image in motion, or rather endows the image with self-motion [*auto-mouvement*], never stops tracing the circuits of the brain. This characteristic can be manifested either positively or negatively. The screen, that is to say ourselves, can be the deficient brain of an idiot as easily as a creative brain. Look at music videos: their power was in their novel speed, their new linkages and relinkages. Even before developing their strength, however, music videos had already collapsed in pitiful twitches and grimaces, as well as haphazard cuts. Bad cinema always travels through circuits created by the lower brain: violence and sexuality in what is represented—a mix of gratuitous cruelty and organized ineptitude. Real cinema achieves another violence, another sexuality, molecular rather than localized. The characters in Losey, for example, are like capsules [*des comprimés*] composed of static violence, all the more violent because they don't move. These stories of the speed of thought, precipitations or petrifications, are inseparable from the movement-image. Look at speed in Lubitsch, how he puts actual reasoning into the image, lights—the life of the spirit.

The encounter between two disciplines doesn't take place when one begins to reflect on the other, but when one discipline realizes that it has to resolve, for itself and by its own means, a problem similar to one confronted by the other. One can imagine that similar problems confront the sciences, painting, music, philosophy, literature, and cinema at different moments, on different occasions, and under different circumstances. The same tremors occur on totally different terrains. The only true criticism is comparative (and bad film criticism closes in on the cinema like its own ghetto) because any work in a field is itself imbricated within other fields. Godard confronts painting in *Passion* and music in *Prénom Carmen*, making a "serial cinema,"[5] but also a cinema of catastrophe, in the sense corresponding to the mathematical principle of René Thom. There is no work that doesn't have its beginning or end in other art forms. I was able to write about cinema, not because of some right of consideration, but because philosophical problems compelled me to look for answers in the cinema, even at the risk that those answers would suggest other problems. All work is inserted in a system of relays.

A PASSION FOR CLASSIFICATION

What strikes us in your two books on cinema is something that one already finds in your other books, but never to this extent, namely, taxonomy—the love of classification. Have you always had this tendency, or did it develop over time? Does classification have a particular connection to cinema?

Yes, there's nothing more fun than classifications or tables. They're like the outline of a book, or its vocabulary, its glossary. It's not the essential thing, which comes next, but it's an indispensable work of preparation. Nothing is more beautiful than the classifications of natural history. The work of Balzac is based on astonishing classifications.

Borges suggested a Chinese classification of animals that thrilled Foucault: belonging to the emperor, embalmed, domesticated, edible [*cochons de lait*], mermaids, and so on.[6] All classifications belong to this style; they are mobile, modifiable, retroactive, boundless, and their criteria vary from instance to instance. Some instances are full, others empty. A classification always involves bringing together things with very different appearances and separating those that are very similar. That is the beginning of the formation of concepts. We sometimes say that "classic," "romantic," or "*nouveau roman*"—even "neorealism"—are insufficient abstractions. I believe that they are in fact valid categories, provided that we trace them to singular symptoms or signs rather than general forms. A classification is always a symptomology. What we classify are signs in order to formulate a concept that presents itself as an event rather than an abstract essence. In this respect, the different disciplines are really signaletic materials [*des matières signalétiques*]. Classifications will vary in relation to the materials considered, but they will also coincide according to the variable affinities among materials. Cinema is at the same time a very uncommon material, because it moves and temporalizes the image, and one that possesses a great affinity with other materials: pictorial, musical, literary.... We must understand cinema not as language, but as signaletic material.

For example, I'm attempting a classification of light in the cinema. There is light as an impassive physical milieu whose composition creates white, a kind of Newtonian light that you find in American cinema and maybe in another way in Antonioni. Then there is the light of Goethe [*la lumière goethéenne*], which acts as an indivisible force that clashes with shadows and draws things out of it (one thinks of expressionism, but don't Ford and Welles belong to this tradition as well?). Yet another light stands out for its encounter with white, rather than with shadows, this time a white of principal opacity (that's another quality of Goethe that occurs in the films of von Sternberg). There is also a light that doesn't stand out for its composition or its kind of encounter but because of its alternation, by its production of lunar figures (this is the light of the prewar French school, notably Epstein and Grémillon, perhaps Rivette today; it's close to the concepts and practices of Delauney). The list shouldn't stop here because it's always possible to create new events of light; we see this, for example, in Godard's *Passion*. In the same way, one can create an open classification of cinematic space. One can distinguish organic or encompassing spaces (in the western, but also in

Kurosawa, who adds immense amplitude to the encompassing space); functional lines of the universe (the neowestern, but Mizoguchi above all); the flat spaces of Losey—banks, bluffs, plateaus that allowed him to discover Japanese space in his last two films; disconnected spaces with undetermined junctions, in the style of Bresson; empty spaces, as in Ozu or Antonioni; stratigraphic spaces that are defined by what they cover up, to the point that we "read" the space, as in the Straubs' work; the topological spaces of Resnais ... and so on. There are as many spaces as there are inventors. Light and spaces combine in very different ways. In all these instances, one sees that these classifications of light or space belong to the cinema yet nonetheless refer to other domains, such as science or art, Newton or Delauney—domains that will take them in another order, in other contexts and relations, and in other divisions.

THE NAME OF THE AUTHOR

There is a "crisis" regarding the concept of the cinematic auteur. Current discourse about the cinema might go as follows: "There are no more auteurs, everyone is an auteur, and all of them get on our nerves."

Right now many forces are trying to deny any distinction between the commercial and the creative. The more that we deny this distinction, the more we consider ourselves clever, understanding, and "in the know."[7] In fact, we are only betraying one of the demands of capitalism: rapid turnover. When advertisers explain that advertisements are the poetry of the modern world, they shamelessly forget that no real art tries to create or exhibit a product in order to correspond to the public's expectations. Advertising can shock or try to shock because it responds to an alleged expectation. The opposite of this is art produced from the unexpected, the unrecognized, the unrecognizable. There is no commercial art: that's nonsense. There are popular arts, of course. There are also art forms that require some amount of financial investment; there is a commerce of art, but no commercial art. What complicates everything is that the same form serves the creative and the commercial. We already see this in book publishing: the same material format is used for both Harlequins and Tolstoy. If you compare a great novel and a best-seller, the best-seller will always win in a market of quick turnover, or worse, the best-seller will aspire to the qualities of the great novel, holding it hostage. This is what happens in television, where aesthetic judgment becomes "that's tasty," like a snack, or "that's too bad," like a penalty in soccer. It's a promotion from the bottom, an alignment of all literature with mass consumption. "Auteur" is a function that refers to artwork (and under other circumstances, to crime). There are other just as respectable names for other types of producers, such as editor, programmer, director, producer ... Those who say that "there are no more auteurs today" suggest that they would have been able to recognize those of yesterday, at a time when they were still unknown. That's very arrogant. No art can thrive without the existence of a double sector, without the still relevant distinction between commercial and creative.

Cahiers did a great deal to establish this distinction in the cinema itself and to show what it means to be an auteur of films (even if the field also consists of producers, editors, publicity agents, etc.). Paini recently said some interesting things about all this.[8] Today, people think they are clever by denying the distinction between the commercial and the creative: that's because they have an interest in doing so. Every [truly creative piece of] work, even a short one, implies a significant undertaking or a long internal duration [*une longue durée interne*] (it's no great undertaking, for instance, to recount recollections of one's family). A work of art always entails the creation of new spaces and times (it's not a question of recounting a story in a well-determined space and time; rather, it is the rhythms, the lighting, and the space-times themselves that must become the true characters). A work should bring forth the problems and questions that concern us rather than provide answers. A work of art is a new syntax, one that is much more important than vocabulary and that excavates a foreign language in language. Syntax in cinema amounts to the linkages and relinkages of images, but also the relation between sound and the visual image. If one had to define culture, one could say that it doesn't consist in conquering a difficult or abstract discipline, but in perceiving that works of art are much more concrete, moving, and funny than commercial products. In creative works there is a multiplication of emotion, a liberation of emotion, and even the invention of new emotions. This distinguishes creative works from the prefabricated emotions of commerce. You see this, oddly, in Bresson and Dreyer, who are masters of a new kind of comedy. Of course, the question of auteur cinema assures the distribution of existing films, films that can't compete with the commercial cinema, because they require another kind of duration. But auteurism also makes the creation of new films possible. In this sense, maybe cinema isn't capitalist enough. There are financial circuits of very different lengths; the long term, the medium term, and the short term have to be distinguishable in cinematographic investment.[9] In science, capitalism has been able to acknowledge the importance of fundamental research now and then.

THIS IS NOT THE PRESENT

Your book contains a thesis that appears "scandalous," that opposes everything written about cinema and that precisely concerns the time-image. Cinematic analysis has always argued that in a film, despite the presence of flashbacks, dreams, memories, or even anticipatory scenes, no matter what time is evoked, movement is enacted before you in the present. But you assert that the cinematic image isn't in the present.

That's funny, because it seems obvious to me that the image is not in the present. What the image "represents" is in the present, but not the image itself. The image itself is an ensemble of time relations from the present which merely flows, either as a common multiple, or as the smallest divisor. Relations of time are never seen in ordinary perception, but they are seen in the image, as long as it is a creative one. The image renders time relations—relations that can't be reduced to the present—sensible and visible. For example, an image shows a man walking along a riverbank in a mountain region; in this image there are at least three coexistent "durations," three rhythms. The relation of time is the coexistence of durations in the image, which has nothing to do with the present, that is, what the image represents. In this sense, Tarkovsky challenges the distinction between edit and shot, because he defines cinema by the "pressure of time" in the shot. It's obvious if we consider examples: a still life in Ozu, a traveling shot in Visconti, and depth of field in Welles. On the level of the represented, it's an immobile bicycle, a car, or a man traveling in space. But from the point of view of the image, Ozu's still life is the form of time that doesn't change, even though everything changes within it (the relation of that which is in time with time). In the same way, Sandra's car in Visconti's film [*Sandra*] is embedded in the past, and we see it at the same time as she travels through space in the present. It has nothing to do with a flashback or with memory, because memory is only that which was once present, whereas the character in the image is literally embedded in the past, or emerges from the past. As a general rule, once a space ceases to be "Euclidean," once space is created—as in Ozu, Antonioni, and Bresson—space no longer contains those characteristics associated with previously accepted relations of time. Resnais is certainly one of the auteurs for whom the image is least in the present, because the image in Resnais's films depends entirely on the coexistence of heterogeneous durations. The variation of relations of time is the very subject of *Je t'aime, je t'aime,* independent of any flashbacks. What is false continuity, or the disjunction between speaking and seeing in the films of the Straubs or Marguerite Duras, or even the feathery [*plumeux*] screen of Resnais, or the black or white cuts of Garrell?[10] On each occasion, it's "a little time in its pure state," and not in the present. The cinema doesn't reproduce bodies, it produces them with grains that are the grains of time. When it is said that cinema is dead, it's especially stupid, because the cinema is at the very beginning of an exploration of audiovisual relations, which are relations of time and which completely renew its relationship with music. Television remains inferior because it clings to images in the present. Television renders everything in the present, except when it is directed by great cineasts. The concept of the image in the present only applies to mediocre or commercial images. It's a completely ready-made and false concept, a kind of fake evidence. To my knowledge, only Robbe-Grillet revitalizes it. But he does so precisely with diabolical malice. That is because he is one of the only auteurs to effectively produce images in the present, but thanks to very complex relations of time unique to him. He is the living proof that such images are difficult to create if one isn't content with that which is represented. The present is not at all a natural given of the image.

NOTES

This interview was originally published in *Cahiers du cinéma* 380 (February 1986): 25–32. The introduction to the interview read as follows: "One often hears it said, here and there, like the echo of a pessimistic leitmotif, that there will be no more theoretical advancements in cinema. The publication of the second volume by Gilles Deleuze, *The Time-Image,* is very much proof to the contrary. If the cinema, by means of genre, by narrative flow, or through the writing styles of singular auteurs, is the manifestation of a thought in motion, its encounter with philosophy was therefore inevitable. The important work accomplished by Gilles Deleuze shows that the relationship between thought and cinematographic art is rich in interactive shocks, vibrations, and influences—whether underground or visible—because a common necessity is at stake: the necessity to recount life itself. This second work, like the first, proves extraordinarily fertile for those who love the cinema and who attempt to reflect on and to ponder its history, its fractures, or its auteurs. Besides the specifically philosophical work, which consists of producing concepts that explain movement, this book also reveals Deleuze as a critic who delineates each auteur's place, his proper aesthetic configuration relative to key concepts: light, space, time, and signs. This interview is the fruit of a long conversation between *Cahiers du cinéma* and Gilles Deleuze, one that was rearranged by him in more of a synthesis and therefore rendered more dense."

1. See Gilles Deleuze, "On *The Movement-Image,*" in *Negotiations,* trans. Martin Joughin (New York: Columbia University Press, 1995), 46–56.—Trans.

2. An antiwar film set in the trenches during World War I, *Les Croix de bois* (1931) was one of the most influential (and expensive) French films of the interwar years. Much of the film was shot on historic World War I battle sites, relying on the French army for props and reenactment guidance (notably, all of the film's stars and supporting actors, as well as its director, Raymond Bernard, were veterans of the war). In 1936, Howard Hawks remade the film as *Paths of Glory*. Along with *Les Vampires* and *Judex*, *Fantômas* (1913–14) is one of the most important of numerous film series directed by Louis Feuillade. These films—*Fantômas* (1913), *Juve contre Fantômas* (1913), *Le Mort qui tue* (1913), *Fantômas contre Fantômas* (1914)—follow the bloody criminal antics of the menacing title character. Mixing realist Parisian location footage and melodramtic plot devices, the *Fantômas* films stand out in French film history for both their initial popular success and their later impact on the surrealists, who seized upon Feuillade's absurdism and his critique of the bourgeoisie.—Trans.
3. Deleuze seems to have coined this term to connote the gaudy aesthetic embodied in the cult of Saint Sulpice that abounded in the late nineteenth century. His term roughly derives from the word *sulpicien*, an adjective that often refers to the religious imagery sold in boutiques around Saint Sulpice Church during that time.—Trans.
4. Deleuze's somewhat ambiguous reference to Kierkegaard's "synopses" is partially clarified in a note to *The Movement-Image*, trans. Hugh Tomlinson and Barbara Habberjam (Minneapolis: University of Minnesota Press, 1986), 233. In note 17, Deleuze explains: "In the second half of the nineteenth century philosophy not only strove to renew its content, but to conquer new means and forms of expression, in very different thinkers, whose only common feature is that they feel themselves to be the first representatives of a philosophy of the future. This is clearly true of Kierkegaard." Specifically, Deleuze dwells on certain stories in Kierkegaard's *The Concept of Dread*, *Stages on Life's Way*, and *Fear and Trembling*, for "in each case it [the story] is already a kind of script, a veritable synopsis."—Trans.
5. "Serial" here refers to a technique of musical composition in which the components are arranged in an arbitrary order, which then serves as a basis for development.—Trans.
6. See, most notably, Michel Foucault, *The Order of Things: An Archaeology of the Human Sciences*, (New York: Random House, 1971), xv–xxiv.—Trans.
7. Translator's quotations.
8. [Dans un entretien des *Cahiers du cinéma*, no. 357 (March 1984).] This note was part of the original Deleuze interview that appeared in *Cahiers du cinéma*.—Trans.
9. Elsewhere Deleuze writes, "The only rejoinder to the harsh law of cinema—a minute of image which costs a day of collective work—is Fellini's: 'When there is no more money left, the film will be finished.' Money is the obverse of all the images that the cinema shows and sets in place, so that films about money are already, if implicitly, films within the film or about the film." (Gilles Deleuze, *The Time-Image*, trans. Hugh Tomlinson and Robert Galeta [Minneapolis: University of Minnesota Press, 1989], 77).—Trans.
10. In his book on Foucault, Deleuze addresses this issue: "There is a disjunction between speaking and seeing, between the visible and the articulable: 'what we see never lies in what we say,' and vice versa. The archive, the audiovisual is disjunctive. So it is not surprising that the most complete examples of the disjunction between seeing and speaking are to be found in the cinema. In the Straubs, in Syberberg, in Marguerite Duras, the voices emerge, on the one hand, like a story/history [*histoire*] without a place, while the visible element, on the other hand, presents an empty place without a story/history" (Gilles Deleuze, *Foucault*, trans. Seán Hand [Minneapolis: University of Minnesota Press, 1988], 64–65).—Trans.

Contributors

Éric Alliez is a professor at the Institut für Kultur Philosophie at the Akademie der Bildenden Künste in Vienna. His books include *Gilles Deleuze: une vie philosophique* and *Capital Times: Tales from the Conquest of Time* (Minnesota, 1996).

Dudley Andrew is professor of comparative literature and film studies at Yale University. He is the biographer of André Bazin and has written several books on film theory and aesthetics.

Peter Canning has taught comparative literature at the University of California, Berkeley and the University of Minnesota. He has published essays on literature, philosophy, psychoanalysis, and fabulation, and is completing a book on cosmology and a memoir.

Tom Conley is a professor of French at Harvard University. He is the translator of Gilles Deleuze's *The Fold: Leibniz and the Baroque* (Minnesota, 1993) and the author of several books, including *The Self-Made Map: Cartographic Writing in Early Modern France* (Minnesota, 1996).

Gregory Flaxman is a doctoral student in the Program in Comparative Literature and Literary Theory at the University of Pennsylvania. He has published articles on psychoanalysis, speech-act theory, and postmodernism.

András Bálint Kovács is associate professor of aesthetics at ELTE University, Budapest, Hungary. He is the author of *The Abstract Subjective Style in the French New Wave*, coauthor of *Les mondes d'Andrej Tarkovsky*, and he has translated Deleuze's *Cinema 1* and *Cinema 2* into Hungarian.

Gregg Lambert is assistant professor of English and textual studies at Syracuse University.

Laura U. Marks is the author of *The Skin of the Film: Intercultural Cinema, Embodiment, and the Senses*. Her essays have appeared in *Screen, Camera Obscura, Wide Angle, Afterimage, Parachute,* and *Framework*. She is assistant professor of film studies at Carleton University in Ottawa.

Jean-Clet Martin is program director of the Collège International de Philosophie in Paris. He is the author of six books, including *Variations, La Philosophie de Gilles Deleuze, Van Gogh, L'œil des choses,* and *L'âme du monde, Disponsibilité d'Aristote.*

Angelo Restivo has taught in the film studies program at the University of Iowa and is currently visiting assistant professor in the program in film/video, University of Michigan at Ann Arbor. His work has appeared in *Film Quarterly, Quarterly Review of Film and Video, Spectator,* and *The Road Movie Book*. His current project is to explore new theoretical paradigms for the cinema of the postwar period.

Martin Schwab teaches comparative literature and philosophy at the University of California, Irvine.

François Zourabichvili is program director at the Collège International de Philosophie. He is the author of *Deleuze: une philosophie de l'événement.*

Index

abstract relations, 212 n.16. *See also* thirdness; mental-image; relation-image
action-image, 5, 16–17, 21, 28, 35, 36, 37, 44, 94–95, 96, 98, 99–100, 101–2, 103, 113, 114, 116, 117, 118, 120, 123, 126, 131, 133, 144, 159, 174, 175, 180, 182, 260, 268, 269, 283, 294, 295, 317, 318, 328–29, 332, 333, 341, 346, 349, 350; crisis of, 6, 28–30, 43, 44, 95, 139 n.70, 160, 163, 164, 175, 183, 187–188, 189, 198, 200, 264, 274, 278, 279, 298, 307; in Hollywood, 28, 34, 174, 331, 354; large form, 164; and signification, 180. *See also* action-thought
action-thought, 266–67. *See also* action-image
actual, 20, 33, 67–68, 145, 149, 194, 197, 339–40, 341, 352, 353, 357; and space, 19, 30, 197; and time, 32, 194, 207, 284, 298, 299. *See also* actual and virtual
actual and virtual, 7, 31–32, 33, 61, 67–68, 194–95, 207, 295, 340–41. *See also* actual
actualization, 20, 32, 33, 72, 96, 157, 194–95, 197, 205, 210, 270, 291, 280, 281, 282–83, 294, 304, 314, 342, 345, 357; and the whole, 261, 263, 270
Adorno, T. W., 347
advertising, 189, 245, 267, 371
aesthetics, 129, 131, 189, 218, 262, 295, 299, 368, 371; and ethics, 11, 46, 47, 227, 344–46, 347, 349, 350, 352, 357; and history, 153, 158, 166, 215, 174; in Kant, 12–13, 189, 262; and nomadism, 224, 227; and ontology, 106, 109, 121, 124, 126, 127, 130
affect, 3, 4, 12–13, 28, 30, 35, 37, 38, 43–44, 47, 63, 68, 75, 82, 89, 92, 94, 116, 118, 122, 139 n.66, 197, 198, 200, 201, 254, 260, 265, 272, 279, 288, 289–90 n.19, 291 n.38, 292 n.48, 294–95, 298, 299, 301 n.12, 302 n.29, 316, 332, 333, 334, 340, 341, 342, 343, 344, 345, 346, 349, 350, 351, 352, 355, 362 n.45, 363 n.63. *See also* emotion; sensation; shock; vibration
affection-image, 17, 21, 30, 101, 113, 114, 115, 116, 117, 118, 120, 121, 126, 127, 128, 133, 139 n.76, 144, 156, 197, 198, 199, 200, 201, 208, 209, 210, 317, 352
affection of self by self (self-affection), 43–44, 47, 93, 104, 258, 298, 337, 338
affirmation; of constancy, 241; of change, 242, 336, 345, 350; of life, 303; of plane of immanence, 293; of thought, 278, 286, 294, 298; of the world as it is, 47, 280, 332, 354
African cinema, 228–45
Alexander Nevsky, 271
Alexandrov, Grigori, 254
alienation-effect. *See* defamiliarization
Alliez, Éric, 42–43, 293–302
Althusser, Louis, 7, 49 n.37
Altman, Robert, 55 n.171, 362 n.46
ambiguity, 30, 31, 181, 189; and voice, 177. *See also* indiscernibility
Andrew, Dudley, 34–35, 215–49
Angelopoulos, Theodorus 160
Anti-Oedipus, 26, 37, 47 n.6, 56 n.187, 131, 233, 261. *See also Capitalism and Schizophrenia*

Antonioni, Michelangelo, 5–6, 160, 165, 172, 175, 176, 307, 370, 371
any-instant-whatever, 18
any-point-whatever, 95, 97. *See also* perspective
any-space-whatever (*espace quelconque*) 5, 144, 161, 198, 309, 311, 316; in Beirut, 193–94. *See also* space
architecture, 62, 63–66, 73–74, 206, 225, 271; baroque, 16, 74; and image, 74; and interiority, 14, 73, 74; and philosophy, 73–74; of power, 39; and space, 73
archive, 25, 26, 194, 195, 209, 375 n.10
Aristotle, 5, 49 n.21, 81, 101, 242
Artaud, Antonin, 5, 41, 259, 260, 263, 267, 268, 270, 272, 275–76, 278, 279–80, 282, 291 n.38
art of the masses, 34, 40, 215, 267, 281. *See also* collective; people
ASA structure, 156
audible, 255, 313. *See also* sayable and seeable; sonsign; sound; speech-act
audiovisual culture, 166, 169, 300; and the archive, 25. *See also* digital culture; postmodernism
auteurism, 43, 164, 175, 215, 216, 219, 225, 239–40, 321, 371, 372, 373, 374. *See also* caméra-stylo
automatic movement (auto-movement), 19, 35, 258, 281, 283, 368. *See also* movement

Bacon, Francis, 14, 302 n.29
Badiou, Alain, 297
bal(l)lade, 31, 104, 175, 218
Balzac, Honoré de, 369
Bananas, 45
baroque, 16, 73, 262, 312, 315, 316, 321, 337, 349, 353
Barthes, Roland, 1
Bataille, Georges, 268
Baudelaire, Charles, 332
Bazin, André, 30, 31, 39, 105 n.8, 159, 167, 176, 215, 218, 219, 221, 223
Beckett, Samuel, 12, 96, 109, 291 n.39, 304, 307, 308, 313, 316
becoming, 19, 26, 43–44, 45, 46, 51 n.107, 104, 155, 165–66, 201, 294, 299, 335, 336, 337–39, 342–43, 349, 351–53, 356; in Bergson, 89, 90, 98, 100, 103, 295; in *Film*, 121, 120, 133; in *The Fold*, 314; and history, 24, 51 n.107, 172–73, 242–43; and literature, 18; and nomadism, 233; and painting, 75; of a people, 239, 241, 266; as system or process, 10; and the whole, 266. *See also* identity; time; time-image
becoming-child, 255
becoming-conscious, 334, 352
becoming-minor, 3
becoming-other, 197, 242
becoming-scapegoat, 351
becoming-spirit, 355
becoming-woman, 29
Bedroom in Arles, 74
being, 45, 70, 74, 184, 297, 315, 336, 337; of becoming, 45, 241; in Bergson, 98; in Eisenstein, 254; extrication of, 119, 120, 122, 123; of images, 110, 111, 112, 115, 120, 122, 125, 130; in Peirce, 128; as a perspective, 64; and thought, 76, 77, 79, 80, 81, 82, 83; and time, 45, 337; of the whole, 271
belief, 26, 46, 257, 267, 272–73, 279–81, 285, 350; in art, 267; loss of, 46, 97, 107 n.41, 165, 275–76, 285, 330; in minor cinema, 34; restoration of in cinema, 46–47, 280, 356
Bellour, Raymond, 301 n.12
Benjamin, Walter, 35, 53 n.140, 212 n.18, 225, 237, 260, 281, 289 n.18
Bentham, Jeremy, 25
Bergman, Ingmar, 160
Bergson, Henri, 2, 141, 287; and the cinematograph, 17, 87–90, 141, 157, 218, 295–96; and conceptualization, 296–98; and dualism, 90–92, 103; and duration, 18, 98, 154, 155; and élan vital, 287; and fabulation, 298; and identity, 62–62, 95–97, 100, 103; and images, 14–15, 16, 17, 23–24, 63–64, 70, 89, 92–95, 102, 110, 111–12, 113, 122, 124, 128, 141, 142–43, 144, 145, 146, 149, 293; and the interval, 22, 148, 261, 284, 341; and matter, 68, 70, 92, 112, 123, 143, 293; and memory, 32, 64, 66–68, 70, 83, 94, 285, 337, 341; and movement, 15, 17, 87, 88–90, 92–93, 95–96, 97, 98, 111–12, 113, 124, 143–44, 146, 149, 293, 297; and perception, 15, 19–20, 70, 88–90, 92, 94, 99–100, 102, 116–17, 122, 142, 143, 145–46, 196, 341;

and phenomenology, 105–6 n.11, 294, 295; and the sensory-motor schema, 16–17, 95–97, 99–100; and the virtual, 42–43, 50 n.60, 67–68, 161, 206–7, 296–97, 340, 341. *See also Creative Evolution; Matter and Memory*
Bergsonism, 16, 284, 286, 287
Berkeley, Bishop, 91, 122, 143
Bersani, Leo, 187
Blade Runner, 359 n.11
Blanchot, Maurice, 11, 267, 324 n.18, 336, 361 n.43
Blue Velvet, 358 n.7, 361 n.43
body: as any-space-whatever, 213; in Artaud, 276, 279–80; as center of indetermination, 20, 93; in dualism, 91, 92, 274; in Eisenstein, 254, 257, 289 n.13; as habitus, 241; as image, 63, 92, 94–95, 210, 241, 299, 354; and memory, 194, 195, 210; as moral-metaphysical mechanism, 330, 332, 334, 346, 354; in Peirce's semiotics, 30, 209; as the real, 181; and sensation in modern art, 264; in sensory-motor schema, 16, 94, 99, 316, 355, 357; in van Gogh, 75; and voice, 172, 184, 186, 188. *See also* body without organs
body without organs, 22, 38, 46, 104, 300, 340, 352, 353. *See also* plane of consistency; plane of immanence
Bohm, David, 194
Bonitzer, Pascal, 2, 185
Bordwell, David, 9, 49 n.37, 174
Borges, Jorge Luis, 2, 369
brain: in Atraud, 275–76, 282; in Bergson, 16–17, 92–93, 261, 285, 287, 301 n.15; in crystalline régime, 40, 83, 283–85, 287–88, 299–300, 348–49, 352, 353, 354; and deterritorialization, 29; and differentiation, 16–17, 20, 35, 92–93, 299; in Eisenstein, 256, 258, 259, 265, 272, 275, 287; ethics of, 332; as frame, 16, 19, 94; as interval, 16, 35, 94, 261, 283, 321, 341; and memory, 6, 195, 284, 287, 288; and morality, 333–34, 349, 353, 357; in natural philosophy, 14; and neuroscience, 40, 367; and the outside, 275–76, 282, 299–300, 321, 344, 353, 354; and sensory-motor schema, 16, 21, 35, 95, 103, 196, 263, 282–83, 355, 368–69; and shock, 35, 40–41, 103, 256, 258, 272–73, 288 n.1, 289 n.13, 289–90 n.19; and signs, 30, 196; as spirit (*l'esprit*), 286, 287; and the sublime, 261, 263; in van Gogh, 75–76, 78, 80, 83; in *What is Philosophy?*, 261, 292 n.47. *See also* gap; interval
Brecht, Bertold, 107 n.43, 260, 263
Bresson, Robert, 178, 311, 368, 371, 372, 373
Burroughs, William S., 11, 54 n.148, 346, 359 n.13

Cahiers du cinéma, 47 n.5, 321, 367, 372, 374
camera-consciousness, 14, 129, 293. *See also* consciousness
caméra-stylo, 321. *See also* auteurism
Canning, Peter, 45–46, 327–63
capital, 6, 55 n.173, 271, 344, 352, 372; as conspiracy of unequal exchange, 346. *See also* capitalism; industrial art; money
capitalism, 9, 178, 183, 219, 232, 322–23 n.9, 349, 360 n.18, 371, 373; and deterritorialization, 56 n.187; in *Il grido*, 177–78; and morality, 330, 331–32, 334, 349, 357; and postmodernism (neocapitalism), 178, 189; and time, 331. *See also* capital; industrial art; Marxism; money
Capitalism and Schizophrenia, 56 n.187, 304. *See also Anti-Oedipus; A Thousand Plateaus*
capture, 16, 275, 310, 315, 316, 318, 321, 340, 346, 353. *See also* prehension
Carroll, Noëll, 9, 49 n.37
Cassavetes, John, 46, 55 n.171
castration, 347
Cavell, Stanley, 131
Ceddo, 237
Celan, Paul, 205
center of indetermination, 20, 96, 115, 116, 117, 127, 131
Cézanne, Paul, 287, 302 n.29
Chabrol, Claude, 29, 179
chance, 12, 45, 47, 320, 338, 341, 345, 351, 354, 359–60 n.17
Chandler, Raymond, 184
chaos, 12, 13, 15, 40, 45, 47, 79, 92, 93–94, 97, 193, 261, 264–65, 312–13, 332, 338–39, 340, 341, 346, 350, 354; of clichés, 280, 283

chaosmos, 29, 315, 338, 354; and *crible*, 339, 340. *See also* chaos; *crible*

chiffre, 336

Chion, Michel, 172–73

Chirol, Marie-Magdalene, 234

Cissé, Souleymane, 234

Citizen Kane, 52 n. 115, 168, 219

city: Beirut, 193–94, 206, 208, 209–10; as site for perspective, 64, 65–67, 68–70; as site of production, 245

classical Hollywood cinema, 5, 8, 17, 158, 162, 173, 174, 215, 224, 225, 226, 353; crisis of, 29, 41; development of, 215, 220–21, 223; and ideology, 41, 101–2, 267, 270, 281; and montage, 27–28. *See also* classical narrative; movement-image; organic régime

classical narrative, 5, 21, 27, 104, 155–56, 158, 159, 162, 163, 164, 166, 171, 172, 174, 215, 246 n.18, 265, 271, 370; and capital, 55 n.173; crisis of, 29, 274, 277, 307, 349, 354; as habitus, 96, 218, 220; in the novel, 163–164; and realism, 182, 183; and sound, 173; and the state, 268; as system of judgment, 36–37, 38–39, 46, 349; and time, 6, 31, 32, 44, 155, 175, 316. *See also* classical Hollywood cinema, movement-image; organic régime

classical representation, 263, 315, 349; in painting, 74. *See also* representation

classification, 19–20, 23–25, 127, 154–55, 157–58, 159, 167–68, 369–70; in film studies, 7–8, 23, 36, 101, 159, 167–68, 194; in Peirce, 194–99

clichés, 9, 11, 38, 46, 193, 195, 199, 200, 209, 264, 265, 270, 278, 280, 331, 352; concerted organization of 9, 38; consciousness of 6,199, 273–76, 281; destruction of, 263, 283, 287–88

Clockwork Orange, A, 347, 358 n.7, 362 n.45

cogito, 2, 3, 12, 46, 241, 274, 279

cognitivism, 7, 9, 49 n.37, 96

collective, 40, 177, 256, 263, 267, 268, 271, 277, 330, 347, 358 n.5; enuniciation of, 237, 242. *See also* art of the masses; people

color: in *Dreams*, 75; of monism and multiplicity, 81–82; as percept and affect in painting, 4; in van Gogh, 76, 77, 78, 80, 81

Comolli, Jean-Louis, 105 n.8

complexity, 338; of the aggregate of images, 115; of the brain, 40; of freedom, 332

compossibility, 316. *See also* possible worlds

concepts: in Bergson, 295, 296; in classical philosophy, 11, 217, 296, 338; and classification, 23, 370; creation and constitution of, 3, 7, 9, 13 41, 73, 88, 296–98, 312, 322, 324 n.25; in crystalline régime, 166; in dialectical montage, 266; in film studies, 10, 157, 168, 322; in Leibniz, 71–72; and their milieu, 7, 11, 360 n.26. *See also* constructivism

Conley, Tom, 44–45, 303–25

consciousness: in Bergson, 93–94, 155; of the cinema, 6, 156, 161, 176, 338, 350, 352, 353; of clichés, 273; diffused, 81, 146, 293–94, 342; of duration 18, 83, 155, 255, 258, 284; limitations of, 76, 145; of the minor, 29, 34; and morality, 330, 334, 335, 348, 355, 357; as self-affection, 338; and sensory-motor schema, 71, 254, 272, 274, 285, 286; of the spectator, 266, 269, 279; of the whole, 299–300. *See also* camera-consciousness

constructivism, 3, 13, 53 n.143

control: as society, 11, 26, 54 n.148, 56 n.187, 189, 346, 349, 353, 357, 359 n.13

Cooper, Merian, 221

Corrigan, Tim, 216

countercinema, 107 n.43

Creative Evolution, 17, 18, 88, 89–91, 97–103, 157, 295, 297

Credits Included, 207–8

crible, 338, 339, 340, 341, 342, 350, 352, 354, 360 n.26, 362 n.51. *See also* chaosmos

Critique of Judgment, 12, 38, 261–62

Critique of Pure Reason, 4, 25, 87, 98, 102

crystal image, 70, 203, 207–8, 298, 339, 340, 358; and the brain, 287, 338. *See also* crystalline régime; indiscernibility

crystalline régime, 26–27, 30, 31–33, 42, 154, 156, 157, 158, 159, 163, 164–66, 169, 195 *See also* modern cinema; modernism; time-image

dadaism, 159
Daney, Serge, 2, 34, 189
Dash, Julie, 225–27
Daughters of the Dust, 225–27
death drive, 138 n.51, 357
de Certeau, Michel, 247 n.19
defamiliarization (*Verfremdungseffekt*), 107 n.43, 260, 262
deframing, 38–39, 44–45, 321. *See also* Markoff chain
Delauney, Robert, 370, 371
Delillo, Don, 284, 292 n.45
demark, 181
democracy: and representation, 347
Derrida, Jacques, 323 n.12
Descartes, René, 87, 91, 122, 242, 279, 303, 357, 359 n.13
De Sica, Vittorio, 160
desire, 217, 261, 263, 271, 319, 325 n.29, 343, 346, 361 n.43; faculty of (in Kant), 262 homosexual, 187; in Lacan, 179, 181, 183
despotic régime, 328
deterritorialization: and becoming, 43–44; and capitalism, 55 n.173, 56 n.187; of classical philosophy, 2, 3, 7, 294; of dogmatic image of thought, 12; failure of, 227, 229, 239; of gender, 29, 213 n.41; of habitus, 45, 46, 104; of memory, 194; as opposed to defamiliarization (countercinema), 107 n.43; and postcolonial cinema, 225; zones of, 104, 219
diagram, 39, 83, 316, 338
dialectic, 17, 105 n.2, 259, 266, 289–290 n.19, 355; in classical cinema, 5; in Deleuze, 123, 126, 265, 368
dialectical automaton, 265, 266, 276, 282, 292 n.42
dialectical materialism, 259, 349
dialectical montage, 27–28, 259, 269
dicisign, 197
Diderot, Denis, 126, 135 n.18, 136 n.27, 138 n.59
Difference and Repetition, 3, 13, 131, 304
differenciation, 20
differential image, 313, 318, 336, 338
differentiation: of the brain, 40; and camera-consciousness, 14; in an image, 148, 209, 320; of image types, 21–22, 109, 110–16, 118, 120, 122–25, 126, 127, 128–31, 133, 135 n.9, 136 n.23 and n.24; and the outside, 299; in painting, 77, 81; of perception, 23, 294
digital culture, 26, 166, 169, 173. *See also* audiovisual culture; postmodernism
Diop-Mabety, Djibril, 240
discipline: as society or *epistēmē*, 25, 346
disconnected space, 5, 371. *See also* any-space-whatever
disjunctive speech act, 26, 173, 178–79, 184–85, 204–5, 255, 270–71, 316, 344, 374, 375 n.10. *See also* sayable and seeable; sound; speech act
dividual, 19
Djeli, 228, 230, 236, 242
D.O.A., 322 n.8
documentary cinema, 30, 185, 193–211, 212 n.11, 219, 220, 221–24, 228
dream-image, 6, 32, 75, 161, 195, 202, 263, 268, 285–86, 328 n.8, 368
Dr. Strangelove, 353
Dreams, 75
Dreyer, Carl, 160, 368, 372
dualism, 61, 90–92, 95, 102, 127, 274; in classical art, 74
Duchamp, Marcel, 325 n.29
Duras, Marguerite, 26, 188, 336, 374
duration, 4, 6, 18, 98, 104, 142, 154, 155, 157, 175, 253, 255–56, 258, 263, 284, 286–87, 288, 289–90 n.19, 292 n.42, 292 n.47, 294, 296, 312, 313, 338, 340, 372, 373–74

early cinema, 20, 88, 97
Easy Rider, 240
écart. *See* gap, interval
Eisenstein, Sergei, 28, 40, 41, 148, 253–60, 264–70, 275–77, 280, 282–83, 287
élan vital, 43, 286, 288, 349. *See also* health; life
El Dorado, 101
electronic image, 183
emotion, 75–76, 77, 79, 257, 261, 284–85, 290 n.28, 292 n.42, 292 n.48, 334, 372. *See also* affect
Engels, Friedrich, 269
Enlightenment, the, 274–75, 347–48, 361 n.42
Enneads, 73
Epstein, Jean, 370
Espinosa, Julio García, 225

Essays Critical and Clinical, 18, 311, 358 n.8
ethics: in classical narrative, 101; in Deleuze, 332, 335, 334, 344–46, 347–53, 357; of documentary, 223; of the time-image, 45–47, 189–90, 205
ethnography; in cinema, 219–221, 225, 227–28, 231, 246 n.18
ethnology, 212 n.11
Europa '51, 39
event, 7, 30, 44–45, 65, 82–83, 133, 144, 159, 160, 161, 165, 166, 175, 188, 194, 196, 205, 207, 245, 253, 256, 258, 259, 275, 276, 278, 294, 298–99, 303–22, 325 n.31, 341, 343, 345, 348, 350, 353, 357, 370; in Peirce, 197, 198; of voice, 178, 189
evolution: of life, 16, 93–95, 115–18, 136 n.24, 286, 337–39, 346, 349–50
experimental cinema, 22–23, 107 n.43, 142, 143, 144, 211 n.2

fabulation, 242, 285, 287, 327, 331, 357; in African cinema, 231, 235, 236–237; and Bergson, 298; faculty of, 284. *See also* falsifying narration; powers of the false
faciality, 30, 201, 206. *See also* affection-image
faculty: in Bergson, 99–100; in determining judgment, 38; of desire, 262; in disaccord, 13; of emotion, 261; of fabulation, 284; of imagination, 261; of perception, 99; in reflective judgment, 38–39; regularity between, 11, 12; of understanding, 43
false continuity, 6, 22, 33, 44, 104, 147, 175, 374. *See also* irrational cuts; irrational linkages
false movement, 7, 300
falsifying narration, 36, 161, 202, 203, 208, 298. *See also* fabulation; powers of the false
Fanon, Frantz, 291 n.38
Fantômas, 367
Fellini, Federico, 32, 160, 164
Fergusson, Frances, 184
Fichte, J.G., 72
Film, 21, 96, 316; and criticism, 119–133
film noir, 174, 183
film studies, 1–2, 7–8, 9, 17, 23, 36, 47 n.6, 154, 166, 168, 216
film theory, 2, 7–8, 9, 48 n.10, 49 n.37, 105 n.8, 153, 168, 321–22
Finyé, 230, 231
firstness, 30, 196–97, 198, 199, 200, 204, 209, 212 n.11. *See also* icon
Fisher, Jaimey, 180
Flaherty, Robert, 201, 212 n.11, 221–24, 225
Flaxman, Gregory, 1–57, 87–108
Focillon, Henri, 73
Fold, The, 16, 31, 73–74, 304, 312, 316, 321
force: aesthetics of, 295; of auto-movement, 276–277; of becoming, 43, 241, 338, 342; of capitalism 322–23 n.9; of cinema, 226; of control, 26; as differential, 14, 299, 350; of emotion, 75, 79; field of, 8, 25, 33, 47, 173, 201, 233, 295, 313; as genetic, 14, 20; impersonal, 119; of impower, 279; of life, 42, 343; of light, 370; of modern art, 263; of morality, 334, 360 n.18; of nomadism, 232; of the outside, 309, 354; as reactive, 37; as virtual, 72, 342.
Foucault, Michel, 1, 3, 25–26, 39, 105 n.8. 173, 204, 217, 255, 264, 336, 356, 370
frame, 18, 19–20, 94, 118, 144, 148, 175, 176, 201, 263, 310–311, 340, 341. *See also* set
Francis Bacon: Logique de la sensation, 14, 18, 302 n.29
free indirect discourse, 43, 129–30, 297
Freud, Sigmund, 46, 138 n.51, 291 n.30, 325 n.28, 330, 356–57; in film studies, 8, 319

gap, 16, 44, 93, 94, 115, 116, 118, 131, 136 n.27, 163–64, 165, 172, 175, 184, 188, 261, 262, 264, 277, 284, 309, 310, 317, 318. *See also* interval
Gardies, André, 228
Garrell, Phillipe, 374
gender: in *Kiss* Me *Deadly*, 29, 52 n.117, 184–188, 213 n.41
German Expressionism, 159, 176, 355, 370
Germany Year Zero, 104, 180
Gettino, Octavio, 225
gnosticism, 337
God: in Christian narrative, 328, 332, 337, 355; in classical philosophy, 4, 274, 279, 284; in Leibniz, 5, 42, 53

n.138, 307, 312, 315; and nomadic affiliation, 233; and representation, 336; in Schreber, 180; in Spinoza, 348, 357; as substance and relation, 333, 352–53
Godard, Jean-Luc, 32–33, 36, 39, 46, 55 n.173, 100–101, 107 n.43, 167, 183, 199, 211 n.2, 311, 320, 321, 369, 370
Goethe, Johann Wolfgang von, 370
Grass, 221
Gravity's Rainbow, 53 n.142, 138 n.60
Green Berets, The, 41, 101
Grémillon, Jean, 370
Grierson, John 201
Griffith, D. W., 4, 176, 215
Grosseteste, Robert, 73
Guattari, Félix, 1, 3, 8, 10, 14, 17, 34, 37, 44, 232, 233, 286, 287
Guelwaar, 238
Guillaume, Gustave, 162
Guimba, 236

haecceity, 14
Haj-Ismail, Roula, 207
Haramuya, 243
Harmonia Praestabilita, 42. *See also* God; Leibniz, G, W.
health: and literature, 248 n.47; of nomadic affiliations, 232; non-organic, 42; organic, 41, 328, 330, 335. *See also* élan vital; life
Hegel, G. W. F., 3, 17, 24, 40, 81, 87, 94, 105 n.2, 107 n.39, 126, 138 n.54, 155, 259, 265, 266, 347, 368
Heidegger, Martin, 35, 42, 43, 53 n.139, 82, 133 n.1, 138 n.54, 190 n.19, 259, 284, 291–292 n.41, 336, 360 n.24
Herdsman of the Sun, 224
hermeneutics, 3, 240, 242. *See also* Ricoeur, Paul
Herzog, Werner, 224
Hiroshima, mon amour, 42
Hitchcock, Alfred, 2, 29–30, 139 n.76, 144, 159, 170 n.16, 172, 179, 181, 199
Hjelmslev, Louis, 24, 262
Holocaust, 41, 205, 327–30. *See also Shoah*
Hondo, Med, 228, 236
Huillet (Straub-Huillet), Danièlle, 336, 371, 374, 375 n.10
Husserl, Edmund, 105 n.11, 113, 294
Huxley, Aldous, 82
Hyenas, 240

icon, 110, 124, 135 n.13, 196, 319, 336, 339. *See also* firstness
ideas, 4, 11, 12, 17, 27, 53 n.138, 71–73, 76, 82, 91, 102, 109, 199, 262–63, 267, 268, 276, 281, 296, 338, 339, 342, 351, 352, 362 n.45
identification: in the cinema, 35, 96
identity: in African cinema, 226–45; alienation of, 263; of community, 46, 239–43, 327–35, 356; of concepts, 3, 296; deterritorialization of, 43–44, 45, 63, 97, 104, 233, 242, 302 n.36, 352–53, 354; of subjects, 29, 46, 103, 224, 231, 281; of victims, 329
ideology, 36, 40, 95, 101, 253, 273–76, 277, 278, 279, 331, 348. *See also* clichés; reterritorilization
Il grido, 29, 171, 174, 175, 178; and trauma, 177
image (noncinematic): in Bergson, 14–15, 63, 92–94, 110, 142–43; and the brain, 16, 35, 93–94; civilization of, 8–9; cosmological, 337–39; in Greek philosophy, 90; in Judeo-Platonic tradition, 336; and matter, 15, 23–24, 92–93, 110–12, 143, 340; and movement, 15, 17–18, 23, 92–94, 110–13, 340; on the plane of immanence, 7, 61, 81–82, 342; as sensible aggregate or sign, 12–13, 23–24, 94, 110, 194–95, 339–41; and thought, 7, 13, 6, 81–82, 302 n.37, 308–10; and the virtual (memory), 63–72, 74
image of thought, 2–3, 11–12, 13, 17, 36, 42, 46, 61, 68, 83, 153, 266, 273, 275, 277, 279, 280, 282, 191 n.42, 295
imagination, 104, 161, 271, 273, 274, 298, 304, 338, 339, 341, 354; in Kant, 13, 261–63
immanence: of affection-image, 295, 342; of any instant whatever, 18; and chance, 351; of chaos and order, 338; in the cinema, 342–43; and conceptualization, 73, 157; of Deleuze's philosophy, 42; and event, 304, 343; and film theory, 9, 157; in Hegel, 347; of image, 309, 336; and life, 342–43, 345, 361 n.38; of matter and memory, 66, 71, 81, 83, 340–41; and montage, 266; of movement and image, 93, 289–90 n.19, 342; and out-of-field, 361 n.35; of

perception and matter, 22–23, 73, 75, 257; of power, 96; of sign and image, 24; as simulacrum, 339; and third language, 302 n.37, 308; and time, 299, 342–43, 361 n.35; of transcendental field, 342; and unthought, 354; and the Whole, 268, 281. *See also* plane of consistency; plane of immanence
impower (*impouvoir*), 41, 259. *See also* outside, problem of thought, and unthought
impressionism, 28, 210, 298
impulse-image, 159, 294
incompossibility, 42, 165, 166, 207, 236, 351, 353. *See also* possible worlds
index, 197, 198, 208, 340. *See also* secondness
indiscernibility, 31, 32, 79, 81, 195, 207, 295, 337, 339, 340, 343, 349, 352, 354, 359 n.11, 360 n.29, 361 n.35. *See also* actual and virtual; crystal image
industrial art: of the cinema, 6, 19, 254, 264, 271–72, 331. *See also* capital; capitalism
inner speech, 257, 290 n.26
inorganic, 27, 42, 182, 343, 345, 354. *See also* crystal image; crystalline régime.
intellectual montage, 253–59
interstice, 44–45, 89, 283, 299, 302 n.38, 319–21, 341, 361 n.33
interval: in classical narrative cinema, 22, 44, 101, 318; as substance of thought or event, 16, 17, 35, 43–45, 93–94, 101, 115, 116, 118, 129 n.53, 131, 132, 136 n.23, 136 n.27, 199, 256, 261, 263–64, 277–78, 279, 281, 283, 284, 286, 292 n.42, 294, 299, 301 n.12, 316, 318, 319, 321, 338, 341, 354, 355; in van Gogh, 77, 78; in Vertov, 22, 147, 148. *See also* brain; gap
Into the West, 225
intuition: in Bergson, 71, 144, 284; and duration, 256, 284; in Kant and metaphysics, 4, 296–97; in Spinoza, 343, 357
Irish cinema, 225–26
irrational cuts, 43, 44, 210, 299, 320–21, 374. *See also* false continuity; irrational linkages
irrational linkages, 33, 204, 299, 338, 354. *See also* false continuity; irrational cuts
Italian neorealism. *See* neorealism
Ivens, Joris, 96
I Vitteloni, 159
I Wet My Hands Etched and Surveyed Vessels Approaching Marks Eyed Inside, 209

Jameson, Fredric, 37, 54 n.153, 180, 184, 216
Jancsó, Miklós, 160
Jarmusch, Jim, 160
Je t'aime, je t'aime, 374
Johnny Guitar, 41
Jom, 243
jouissance, 131, 189, 333, 359 n.14, 361 n.43, 362 n.46
judgment: aesthetic, 371; as arbitrary, 45; and capital, 311, 346, 352, 357, 360 n.18; determining, 3–4, 25–26, 36–37, 38–39, 103, 286, 287, 288, 333, 334, 346, 347, 355, 360 n.29; in documentary, 207; moral, 328–29, 331, 332–35, 347, 355, 358 n.8; and narrative, 37, 331; of oneself, 334, 347, 338; premature, 1; reflective, 38–39, 356–57; and the sensory-motor schema, 36–37, 54 n.144, 333, 335, 355; and the signifier, 54 n.144, 328, 333, 334, 344, 346, 347, 360 n.18; subversion of moral judgment, 292 n.48, 335, 352; and thirdness, 30, 198–99; and truth, 4, 332, 333; of the visible, 25–26, 105 n.8, 327

Kaboré, Gaston, 233
Kabuki, 256, 258, 283, 288 n.1
Kafka, Franz, 217, 291 n.39
Kafka: Towards a Minor Literature, 3, 34
Kant, Immanuel, 2, 4, 6, 12–13, 25, 36, 38, 43, 49 n.37, 53–54 n. 143, 72, 73, 87, 93, 98, 102, 103, 107 n.50, 118, 162, 189, 261–62, 263, 264, 265, 294, 336, 340, 344, 347–48, 355
Keaton, Buster, 119, 367
Keita, 234–36, 238, 239, 242, 243
Kierkegaard, Søren, 288, 368, 375 n.4
King Kong, 221
kino-eye (*kinoglaz*), 146
Kinshasa, 243
Kiss Me Deadly, 29, 172, 178, 183
Klee, Paul, 304
Kouyate, Dani, 235
Kovács, András Bálint, 27, 153–70

Kubrick, Stanley, 55 n.171, 346, 356, 358 n.7, 362 n.45
Kurosawa, Akira, 75, 371

Lacan, Jacques, 1, 29, 46, 52 n. 117, 54 n.144, 56 n.175, 138 n.51, 179, 180, 191 n.31, 319, 359 n.13, 359 n.14, 359 n.15, 361 n.43
La Collectionneuse, 368
La Croissière noire, 220
Lady from Shanghai, The, 176–77, 219
Lambert, Gregg, 40–41, 253–92
language: in Bergson, 100, 102–3, 295; in Beckett, 308–10, 311; cinematic effect upon, 258, 266, 362 n.45; cinematic evasion of, 259, 264, 287, 292 n.48, 349; as constraint on cinema, 100, 270–71, 296; and the future, 344–45; and minorization, 34, 249 n.58, 311, 372; and modern art, 263; in Peirce's semiotics, 195, 212 n.18; as power of the false, 332–33, 334, 357; as production of intensities, 180; as theory of cinema, 8, 23, 157, 162, 195, 283, 368, 370, 373. *See also* metaphor; sayable and seeable; signifier; speech act; third language
language III. *See* third language
Lanzmann, Claude, 205, 327, 328, 329
large form (big form), 44 n.21, 164. *See also* SAS' structure
Las Meninas, 74
Last Year in Marienbad, 42
L'avventura, 6, 175
Le Beau mariage, 368
Lee, Bruce, 244
legible, 38–39
legisign, 195, 198, 200
Leibniz, G. W., 2, 5, 16, 42, 53 n.138, 64, 71–72, 73, 83, 93, 194, 207, 236, 312, 314, 315, 316, 337, 339
Les Croix de bois, 367, 375n.2
Les Peiroulets Ravine, 83
Levi, Primo, 331
libido, 46, 333, 337–38, 343, 344, 345
life: and alienation, 260; appearance of, 16, 93, 113, 114–16, 136 n.27, 337; in crystalline régime, 27, 42, 104, 165, 286; deterritorialization of, 35, 45–46, 47, 55 n.173, 56 n.187; as élan vital, 43; and firstness, 196, 201; and health, 258 n.47; and literature, 18, 42; of movement or the real, 147, 148–49, 296, 297, 338, 342–43, 369, 289–90 n.19; in organic régime, 163–64, 349, 354; and painting, 75, 77, 78, 81; and prehension, 300 n.4, 314; regulation of, 21, 242; and transformation, 47, 246 n.16, 286, 299, 321, 343, 345, 352, 361 n.38.
light: in aggregate of images, 15, 93, 112–13, 293; and classification, 25, 370–71; creation of, 372; in the frame, 19, 146, 176, 197, 369, 370–71; prehension or perception of, 16, 116, 122, 145–46, 314; as the visible, 25, 145–46, 204, 358 n.1; in volumes, 73–74
lines of flight, 34, 61, 104, 217
Lloyd, Harold, 367
Logic of Sense, The, 181, 293
Losey, Joseph, 369, 371
Louisiana Story, 222
Lubitsch, Ernst, 369
Luhmann, Niklas, 131
Lukács, Georg, 54 n.153, 163–64, 167
Lulu, 197
Lumière, Louis, 88, 219
Luxemburg, Rosa, 8
Lynch, David, 358 n.7, 361 n.43
Lyotard, Jean-François, 172, 325 n.31

Macadam Tribu, 243–44
machinic assemblage, 22, 142, 146, 149, 265, 281. *See also* Vertov, Dziga
Magnificent Ambersons, The, 168
Malebranche, Nicolas, 4
Malraux, André, 21
Man Bites Dog, 362 n.46
Mandabe, 229
Man of Aran, 222
Ma nuit chez Maud, 368
Mann, Anthony, 317–19
Man with a Movie Camera, 96, 143–49
Markoff chain, 45, 354. *See also* deframing
Marks, Laura U., 30, 193–214
Martin, Jean-Clet, 14, 17, 61–85
Marx, Karl, 55 n.173, 113, 131, 138 n.57, 357. *See also* Marxism
Marx Brothers, 212 n.16
Marxism, 7, 49 n.37, 149, 357. *See also* capitalism; Mark, Karl
matter: and action, 94; and the actual, 67–68; and the brain, 83, 286, 288; and dualism, 91–92; and energy, 337, 338,

345; and image, 15, 16, 66, 92–93, 100, 111–12, 113, 136 n.24, 143, 146, 293, 294, 300 n.6, 337, 342; and interval, 16, 136 n.27, 147, 284; and memory, 66–69, 81, 83, 106–7 n.38, 284, 286, 288; and movement, 15–16, 92–93, 99, 111, 112, 131, 143, 293, 300 n.6, 339, 342; in natural philosophy, 14, 63; and nomadism, 218–19; and painting, 76, 77, 82; and perspective, 84, 93, 146, 293–94; and secondness, 198; and signs, 8, 23–24, 132, 135 n.13, 370; as site, 66–67, 69; and thought, 23, 41, 81, 286, 299; and time, 183

Matter and Memory, 14–16, 17, 62–63, 66–68, 69–70, 87, 89, 91–96, 97–98, 99, 100, 102, 103, 107 n.50, 141, 142 43, 157, 294, 297, 340

Melville, Herman, 307

memory: in African cinema, 232, 234, 235; and the body, 211; and the brain, 6, 83, 91, 284, 286, 287, 288, 341; and capitalism, 179; as cinematographic, 284; in crystalline régime, 6, 32, 91, 161, 168, 195, 207, 284, 285, 298, 340; and deterritorialization, 194, 206, 279–80, 299, 337–38, 354; and ethics, 351; and event, 308, 310, 318; as habitus, 63, 94, 232, 234, 235; and interval, 284, 286, 319, 341, 354; and matter, 64, 66–72, 74, 76, 81, 106 n.38, 168, 284, 286, 288; and minor cinema, 35; in Montaigne, 306; in organic régime, 32, 373; and the outside, 20, 195; and painting, 76, 81; in Resnais, 6, 42; in Rouch, 227; and sensory-motor schema, 94; in *Shoah*, 205; and signs, 285; and the time-image, 195, 298, 373; of the universe, 337, 340; and the virtual, 32, 68–72, 194–95, 340–41; and virtual perspective, 64, 66–72, 74, 207, 284; in Welles, 168. *See also* time-image; virtual

memory-images, 280, 319, 333. *See also* memory, time-image; virtual

Ménil, Alain, 156, 302 n.39

mental-image, 29–30, 75, 144, 156, 157, 163, 198, 199, 200, 201, 202, 206, 207, 209, 231, 264. *See also* relation; relation-image; thirdness

Merleau-Ponty, Maurice, 89, 105–6 n.11

Merrel, Floyd, 199

metacinema, 17, 47, 142, 145, 294

metaphor: of cinema in Bergson, 90; in Deleuze, 38, 39, 356, 357; of nomadism, 217–18; in Ricoeur, 240, 241

metaphysics, 3, 4, 36, 43, 87, 90, 111, 162, 296, 297, 332, 335–36, 337, 340, 346, 349, 360 n.24

Metropolis, 356

Metz, Christian, 23, 54 n.144, 154, 157, 195, 323 n.14

Michaux, Henri, 283, 368

minor cinema, 34. *See also* nomad cinema; nomadism

minor literature, 3, 34, 249 n.58

minor philosophy, 3, 50 n.72

Miraculous Beginnings, 200–201, 207

Missing Lebanese Wars, 209

Mizoguchi, Kenji, 371

Moana, 221

modern art, 263–64, 268, 276, 289–90 n.19. *See also* modern cinema; modernism

modern cinema, 7, 104, 160; and action, 159, 160–61, 163, 164, 174, 175, 274, 298; and auteurism, 215–16, 240; and belief, 280; and the brain, 40–41, 289–90 n.19, 296, 354; and capitalism, 178, 271–72; and clichés, 273, 280; as crystalline régime, 156, 159, 162–63, 165, 169; development of, 27–28, 156, 159–60, 169, 174, 267, 274; as disjunction between sayable and seeable, 38–39, 178, 336; and ethics, 46, 327; and history, 156–57, 158–59, 163, 165, 166, 169, 171, 172, 175, 179, 215–16; and interstice, 44–45, 164–65, 174, 264, 267, 281; and memory, 32, 178, 283; and narrative, 30–32, 33, 161–63, 164–65, 166; and ontology, 133–34 n.3, 138 n.54; precursors of, 159–60, 178; subject of, 261, 279, 280, 289–90 n.19; and the time-image, 32, 155, 156, 158, 161, 162, 283, 354; and the unthought (or outside), 189, 259, 300; and the virtual, 44–45, 161, 162–63. *See also* crystalline régime; modernism

modernism, 159–163, 165, 169, 170 n.16, 172, 215–216, 235. *See also* modern art; modern cinema

molar, 14, 15, 100, 303
molecular, 14, 15, 92, 100, 149, 283, 294, 311–12, 332, 345, 368, 369
monad, 71, 72, 74, 83, 93, 106 n.26, 315, 316, 344, 349, 350, 353
money, 54 n.153, 55 n.173, 55 n.187, 208, 238, 271, 331, 344, 352, 357, 360 n.18, 375 n.9; in *Psycho*, 180. *See also* capital; capitalism; Marxism
monism, 14, 127; in Eisenstein, 267, 272, 290 n.21. *See also Naturphilosophie*
montage: and architecture, 73; in Bazin, 218–19, 223; and capital, 55 n.173; in crystalline régime, 6, 44–45, 175–76, 353; in early cinema, 20, 88; in Eisenstein, 253, 254–55, 257–59, 260, 265, 267, 269, 270, 288 n.1, 292 n.42, 292 n.48; and narrative, 27, 355; in organic régime, 4–5, 19, 27–28, 44, 175, 265–66, 298, 355; and sound, 181; in Vertov, 22, 142, 143–44, 146, 147, 148. *See also* dialectical montage; intellectual montage
Montaigne, Michel de, 303–8, 319, 322
Monticelli, Adolphe, 77, 78, 79, 80
movement: aberrant, 31, 104, 175, 298, 351, 354; as affect, 342–343; and ancient philosophy, 17–18, 90, 98–99; blocks of, 4, 145; of the camera, 88, 96, 142; and capital, 271–72, 346, 349, 352; in cinematographic mechanism, 18–19, 90, 102, 142, 154, 253–54, 258, 283; and classification, 166; as cliché, 278; and concepts, 11; containment of, 35, 99, 118, 143, 144, 343, 346; in *Creative Evolution*, 17, 18, 88–89, 90, 98–100, 157, 297; deterritorialization of, 310; and duration, 18, 155, 255, 296; ecology of, 171; of the event, 314; false, 6, 23; in *Film*, 122, 124; and the freeze-frame, 148; and Hegel, 17, 24, 368; and interval, 94, 98, 148; and matter, 15, 23, 92–93, 99, 110–11, 112, 132, 143, 144, 145, 148, 293; in *Matter and Memory*, 14–15, 89, 92–93, 97, 157, 297; and memory, 206; and nomadism, 238, 351, 354; in painting, 18, 74, 80; and sensory-motor schema, 16, 94, 99, 174–75, 307, 316, 351, 354–55, 356; and signs, 132, 162; subordinated to space, 5–6, 18, 19, 90, 98, 296; and theater, 260–261; and thought, 13, 18–19, 153, 162, 165, 167, 210, 244, 253, 258, 276, 281, 286, 296, 341, 368; and time, 4–5, 18, 32, 113, 339, 365; and the universe, 63, 92, 97–98, 110–18, 122, 142, 149, 340; in Vertov, 22, 142, 144–49; and the virtual, 73, 342, 343. *See also* movement-image
movement-image: crisis of, 5–6, 26, 96, 131, 155, 159, 182, 189, 200, 204, 273–74, 282, 307, 320; as dialectical, 259; and fascism, 267–70, 277; in *Film*, 120, 122, 124, 125, 126; and Hitchcock, 179; as indirect image of time, 19, 134 n.7; and interval, 22, 94, 148, 256, 283, 341; as object (or thing in itself), 15, 116–17, 142, 145; machinic assemblage of, 22, 142, 149, 265, 281; and montage, 147, 146; as multiplicity, 144; and myth, 284; and organic régime, 5–6, 8, 20–21, 26, 28, 100, 155–56, 158–59, 173, 179, 182, 194, 215, 218, 258, 268, 274, 277, 316, 354; and rationality, 5; reality of, 195, 205; and relation, 199, 355; and sensory-motor schema, 5, 20–21, 28, 94, 99–101, 103, 131, 155, 274, 283, 316, 320; and signs, 30, 129, 132, 162, 196–99, 200, 210; and speed, 369; and the universe, 15, 20, 30, 92, 97–98, 110–13, 114–18, 132, 142, 149; varieties of, 100, 102, 113–18, 130, 142, 144, 148; and the whole, 19–20, 155, 156, 159, 261, 264–65, 266, 268, 273, 274, 277, 278, 281. *See also* movement; organic régime
multiplicity, 44, 71, 82, 144, 238, 318, 325 n.28, 347, 350, 352
Muqaddimah Li-Nihayat Jidal, 205
Muriel, 6, 42
music videos, 368–369
Musil, Robert, 47
My Darling Clementine, 28

Names, The, 284, 292 n.45
Nancy, Jean-Luc, 7, 298
Nanook of the North, 221–22
natural history, 24, 369
naturalism, 159. *See also* impulse-image
natural selection, 346, 351
nature: in Bergson, 14–15; and the brain, 286–87, 288; destruction of, 34, 355; in

dualism, 92; in Hegel, 107 n.39; in Leibniz, 312; in painting, 75, 76, 80–81, 82, 83; passage of, 312, 314; plane of, 61, 81, 82, 83, 288; power of, 277; in romanticism, 37; in Rousseau, 107 n.39; in Schelling, 14; and science, 290 n.21; and secondness, 212 n.11; in Spinoza, 14, 348, 352–53, 357; of subject and object, 36, 147; in the sublime, 262–64, 266–67, 272, 277, 281; in Whitehead, 312; and the whole, 281. *See also Naturphilosophie*

Naturphilosophie, 14, 61, 80–81. *See also* monism; nature

neorealism, 30, 32, 55 n.173, 104, 108 n.59, 159, 160, 165, 174, 175, 178, 219, 295, 302 n.29, 316, 370

new German cinema, 55 n.173

Newton, Sir Isaac, 371

New Wave, 55 n.173, 161, 240, 302 n.29, 321

Nichols, Bill, 201

Nietzsche, Friedrich, 1, 2, 4, 8, 12, 36, 47, 47 n.3, 69, 87, 96, 97, 103, 122–23, 125, 135 n.12, 138 n.52, 138 n.57, 161, 198, 201, 241, 280, 297, 298, 299, 335, 351, 357, 362 n.55

Night and Fog, 42

nomad cinema, 219, 224, 354

nomadism, 35, 53 n.138, 215, 216–18, 219, 221, 224–25, 226, 227–28, 232, 233, 237, 238–39, 241–42, 244, 247 n.26, 351, 363 n.63

nomad science, 218–19, 247 n.26

nonhuman, 15, 22, 23, 96, 145, 146, 147, 148. *See also* inorganic; preindividual

noology, 219

nooshock, 40, 258, 259, 272, 273, 278; and movement, 261. *See also* affect; shock; vibration

Occurrence at Owl Creek Bridge, An, 322n.8

ontology: beyond, 344; critique of, 127–31, 139 n.74; and *Film*, 119–27; of images, 13, 14–15, 21, 23, 24, 92–95, 98, 109–18, 133–34 n.3, 134 n.4, 136 n.27, 141, 293–94; and memory, 106–7 n.38; of nomadism, 225; and time, 134 n.7, 135 n.13, 135 n.20, 136 n.24, 138 n.54, 299. *See also* movement-image

opsign, 31, 43, 44, 161, 165, 175, 178, 210, 294, 295, 298, 337

optical-accoustical situation: in neorealism, 160–61

optical image. *See* opsign

oral cinema, 217, 225, 226, 228, 227, 234, 239

organic and crystalline, 26, 27, 33, 51–52 n.109, 158, 162, 165–66

organic régime, 24, 26–28, 33, 45–46, 101, 155–56, 158, 162, 164, 165–66, 176, 194, 258, 274, 295, 300, 345, 354–55, 370. *See also* classical Hollywood cinema; classical narrative

Ouedraogo, Idrissa, 240

out-of-field (*hors-champ*), 147, 342, 361 n.35

outside, 11, 12, 40–41, 43, 83, 147, 173, 194, 195, 199, 201, 211, 264, 270, 273, 276, 282, 284, 292 n.48, 299–300, 302 n.36, 308–10, 313, 315, 321, 322–23 n.9, 341, 343, 344, 345, 350, 353, 354, 358 n.8; and a people, 287; and sound, 172, 188; in theater, 260; and the whole, 19, 20, 176. *See also* impower; problem of thought; unthought

Ozu, Yasushiro, 371, 373

Parallax View, 41

paranoia, 37, 42, 46, 180, 183, 233, 331, 353, 354

Parmenides, 81

Pascal, Blaise, 279

Pasolini, Pier Paolo, 129, 176, 178

Passion, 369, 370

Passion of Joan of Arc, 197

peaks of present, 53 n.129, 202, 205

Peirce, C. S., 2, 23, 30, 51 n.95, 110, 128–29, 132, 134 n.4, 135 n.10, 139 n.66, 194, 195–98, 200, 202, 339

people: becoming of, 178, 239, 242, 266, 267–68, 284, 287, 331; as collective subject, 263, 266, 268; as nation, 241, 267; who are missing, 35, 202, 228, 229, 242, 278. *See also* art of the masses; collective; nomadism

percept, 3, 4, 43, 265, 288, 350. *See also* perception; perception-image

perception: acentering of, 15, 17, 21, 22–23, 63, 75–76, 79, 87–88, 92–93, 96–97, 105–6 n.11, 122, 138 n.63, 142, 143, 146–49, 294, 356; actuality of, 340,

341; of the artist, 295; centering of, 16–17, 20–21, 94–96, 97, 98–100, 116, 117–18, 143, 144, 146, 294, 373; cinematic effect upon, 7, 254, 256, 257–58, 259, 263, 265–66, 268, 272, 279, 287, 292 n.48, 298, 362 n.45; cinematic imitation of, 20–21, 88–89, 90, 96; in *Creative Evolution*, 17, 19, 88–89, 90, 97, 98–100, 102–3, 295–96; cut off from action, 31, 43, 156, 163–64, 210, 295, 298, 329, 356; ethics of, 54 n.148, 345; of the event, 312–13, 314, 315, 316–19, 320; in *Film*, 121–27, 133; and firstness, 196–97; gaseous, 211 n.2; genetic definition of, 145–46; in idealism, 91; and interval, 147, 148, 284–86, 294, 319, 341; in *Las Meninas*, 74; in materialism, 91; and matter, 15, 16, 23, 92, 99, 116, 146, 340; in *Matter and Memory*, 14–15, 63, 87–88, 92–95, 97; and movement, 15, 23, 92–94, 98–99, 113, 149, 254; and multiplicity, 71; objective and subjective, 117, 125–26; in phenomenology, 89, 105–6 n.11, 293; and prehension, 314–15, 341; and reality, 30; and representation, 100, 102; and secondness, 30, 197; and sensory-motor schema, 16, 20–21, 35, 95–97, 98, 101–2, 156, 174, 294, 333, 346, 349, 353; subjective and objective, 117, 196; as subtractive, 16, 35, 93–95, 99–100, 117, 122, 199, 340–41; and understanding, 285, 286; in van Gogh, 75–78, 79, 81; in Vertov, 144–45, 146–48, 211 n.2; and the virtual (memory), 64–65, 67, 68–71, 72–73, 143, 145, 340–41; and the whole, 19–20, 266. *See also* percept; perception-image

perception-image: derivation from movement image, 17, 94, 113–14, 115–16, 117, 145–46, 294–95; and the event, 316–19, 320; in *Film*, 120–21, 126; in *Miraculous Beginnings: Part I*, 200; and Peirce, 128–29, 132, 197; and restoration of belief, 280, 285; in sensory-motor schema, 17, 21, 101, 114, 117–18, 316–17; in Vertov, 144; in *Winchester '73*, 317–19. *See also* percept; perception

performative: nature of conceptualization, 13. *See also* fabulation, powers of the false; speech act

Perreault, Pierre, 202, 211 n.2

perspective: Albertian, 324 n.18; and the city, 64–66; molecular universe, 14, 93; as monad, 53 n.138; and montage, 143; nonhuman, 96–97; in régime of movement-image, 114; in van Gogh, 74, 81; as virtual position opened up by a site, 64–68, 69–71, 72. *See also* any-point-whatever

phenomenology, 3, 7, 89, 105–6 n.11, 293, 294, 295, 300, 342, 344

Phenomenology of Spirit, 87, 138 n.59

photographic image: in *Film*, 120; and historiography, 172–73; limits of, 184; in *Missing Lebanese Wars*, 209; as model of perception, 18, 93, 100, 117, 143, 145

Pierrot le fou, 240

Pisters, Patricia, 201

plane of consistency, 352. *See also* body without organs; immanence; plane of immanence

plane of immanence, 7, 11, 22, 47, 61, 93, 293, 300 n.6, 338–39, 361 n.38; as assemblage of movement-images, 15, 22, 30, 50 n.60, 103, 143, 265, 281; in Bergson, 16; as body without organs, 22, 104, 340, 352; and concepts, 7, 11; cooling down of, 15, 93, 115; failings of, 282; and the image of thought, 11; as light, 25, 112–113; in science, 360 n.26; and virtual, 7, 31, 360 n.26. *See also* body without organs; immanence; plane of consistency

Plato, 4, 8, 72, 73, 87, 90, 102, 313, 339

Player, The, 362 n.46

Plotinus, 73

Po di Sangui, 243

Poirier, Léon, 220, 246 n.18

pose, 17–18

possibility: and actuality, 340; and becoming, 349; category of, 149; conditions of, 7, 38; creation of, 237, 341, 345, 347, 351; in *Dr. Strangelove*, 353; and the event, 144, 309, 310, 345; exhaustion of, 308, 309, 310, 311, 313; and firstness, 196, 197, 200, 339; of perspective, 64–65, 67, 69, 81, 118; and plane of immanence, 7; primacy of, 340; and reality, 68, 310; sum of, 308–9, 313, 315; and the virtual, 31, 68, 341

possible worlds, 5, 42, 348. *See also* compossibility; incompossibility.
postcolonialism: and cinema, 178, 231. *See also* minor cinema
postmodernism, 45, 172, 181, 350; and architecture, 291 n.34; and cinema, 34, 62, 165–66, 169, 172, 216; and Hitchcock, 179–80. *See also* audiovisual culture; digital culture
Potemkin, 257
power: and affection, 57 n.193, 197, 198, 295, 340, 345, 352; and conspiracy, 37, 273; and control, 189; ethics of, 346, 350, 357; and field of forces, 25, 123, 218, 350; of firstness, 197, 339; and image of thought, 277; of imagination, 354; of judgment (language), 25, 54 n.144, 105 n.8, 328, 332, 333, 334; of life, 338, 343; and memory, 340; naturalization of, 36–37, 38, 332–33, 335–36; of nature, 277; and nomadism, 225; and the production of truth, 26, 332–33, 335–36; of reason, 262, 274, 354; revelation of, 38–39, 205; and secondness, 197–98, 341; and sensory-motor schema, 36–37, 49 n.37; and shock, 260–63; and the state, 218; and thirdness, 198; and thought, 41, 253, 258, 273, 276, 277, 279, 300; will to, 123, 135 n.12, 242; and the whole, 262–64, 266, 273–74, 275, 277. *See also* impower; powers of the false
powers of the false, 4, 33, 36, 45, 161, 202, 207, 280, 282, 300, 332, 336, 371. *See also* fabulation; falsifying narration
prehension, 16, 93, 314–15, 340, 341. *See also* capture
preindividual, 7, 22, 93, 293. *See also* inorganic; nonhuman
Prénom Carmen, 369
presence: of images, 354; philosophy of, 296, 297, 302 n.33; and the real, 65, 68; and sound, 185, 188; of space, 307
present, 31, 32–33, 42, 65, 168, 232, 236, 263, 286, 297, 298, 300, 337, 338, 364, 354, 356, 373–74
Prigogine, Ilya, 362 n.51
primal scene, 291 n.38
principle of sufficient reason, 337
problematic and theorematic, 199
problem of thought, 41, 53 n.139, 278, 282, 291 n.38. *See also* impower; outside
Proust, Marcel, 70
Proust and Signs, 13, 323 n.10
Psycho, 29, 172, 178, 179–83, 188
psychoanalysis, 1, 7, 47–48 n.6, 48 n.7, 49 n.37, 52 n.117, 54 n.144, 179, 186, 190 n.6, 269, 283, 291 n.38, 368. *See also* Freud, Sigmund; Lacan, Jacques
Pudovkin, V.I., 254
pure optical situation, 175. *See also* opsign
Pynchon, Thomas, 53 n.142, 138 n.60

Quad, 310, 311
qualisign, 196, 198, 199
Quartier Mozart, 243
quiet revolution, 172

Ra'ad, Walid, 200, 201, 207–9
Rain, 96
Rango, 221
rational connections, 5, 44, 45; breakdown of, 5, 31, 321. *See also* interval
real, 71, 74, 143, 193, 194, 195, 196, 198, 201, 211, 275, 284, 293, 294, 296, 308, 335–36; and imaginary, 30, 31–32, 33, 161, 163, 295; in Lacan, 181–82; and virtual, 7, 31, 65, 67–68, 72, 194, 207, 357. *See also* neorealism; realism
realism: aesthetic, 30–31, 182, 183, 236; philosophical, 15, 91–92; social, 266, 269; vulgar, 256. *See also* neorealism; real
real psychic situations, 275
reason, 13, 262, 266, 274–75, 315, 337, 338, 347, 348, 349, 354–55, 360 n.20, 360 n.24. *See also* principle of sufficient reason
récit, 32, 33
recollection-images, 32, 285. *See also* memory; memory-images
Reich, Theodore, 37
relation-image, 199, 203–4. *See also* Hitchcock, Alfred; thirdness
Renoir, Jean, 2, 28, 52 n.115, 96, 159, 218
repetition, 44, 163, 181, 241, 287, 338, 357
representation: appearance of, 356; in *Creative Evolution*, 100; critique of, 3, 4, 25, 36, 39, 54 n.144, 92, 204, 205, 278, 281, 286, 335–36, 343, 345, 347, 349, 361 n.42; death of, 56 n.175; and emotion,

254, 257, 292 n.48; and falsification, 202, 284; in *Film*, 123–24, 127; and incommensurability to image, 299, 320, 336; in Judeo-Platonic tradition, 336; and Kant, 261–62, 348; and materialism, 92; and morality, 327–28, 332–36, 345, 347, 349–50; and movement, 15, 17–18, 260–61; and nomadic cinema, 226, 238–39; and perception, 71; and phenomenology, 294; and plane of immanence, 338; in Plato, 72; and sensory-motor schema, 45, 54 n.144, 295, 349–50, 355; and sign, 194; and thought, 12, 162; and time, 32, 373–74; and time-image, 176–77, 299; violence of, 369; of the whole, 264, 355. *See also* classical representation
Republic, The, 87
Resnais, Alain, 6, 42, 167–68, 283, 371, 373–74
Restivo, Angelo, 28–29, 171–92
reterritorialization, 56 n.187, 206, 227–28
reume, 196
rhizome, 238
Ricoeur, Paul, 101, 217, 237, 240–41, 242
ritornello, 307
Rivette, Jacques, 370
Robbe-Grillet, 167–68, 374
Rodowick, D. N., 2, 24, 48 n.10, 153, 178, 190, 205, 217, 242
Rohmer, Eric, 29, 179, 368
romanticism, 37, 54 n.151
Rosenbaum, Jonathan, 48 n.11
Rossellini, Roberto, 104, 160, 218, 320
Rouch, Jean, 211 n.2, 227–28
Rousseau, Jean-Jacques, 107 n.39
Rules of the Game, 52 n.115, 219

Sababu, 236
Sade, Marquis de 347–38, 355, 361 n.43
Salloum, Jayce, 207–8
Sarraounia, 236
Sartre, Jean Paul, 105 n.11, 117
SAS structure, 156, 221. *See also* sensory-motor schema
SAS' structure, 48 n.21, 55 n.173, 221. *See also* large form; sensory-motor schema
Saussure, Ferdinand de, 195
sayable and seeable, 25, 26, 204–5, 275 n.10. *See also* audible; disjunctive speech act; sound; speech act; visible
Schefer, Jean-Louis, 2
Schelling, F. W. J. von, 14, 61, 81, 360 n.24
schemata: in Kant, 38, 103. *See also* sensory-motor schema
Schopenhauer, Arthur, 133 n.1
Schreber, Daniel Paul, 180
Schiller, Friedrich von, 27, 158
schizophrenia, 46, 56 n.187, 104, 108 n.59, 180, 206, 276, 280, 344, 350, 354
Schwab, Martin, 20–21, 109–39
science, 3, 10, 18, 23, 40, 61, 74, 81, 142–43, 154, 217, 239, 261, 264–65, 269, 272, 274, 282, 287, 335, 336, 356, 369, 371, 373
Scott, Ridley, 359 n.11
Searchers, The, 101
secondness, 30, 134 n.4, 196, 197–98, 200, 212 n.11, 212 n.16, 212–13 n.25, 341. *See also* index
self-affection. *See* affection of self by self.
Sembène, Ousmane, 228–30
semiotics: in film theory; 7, 49 n.37; in Metz, 54 n.144, 155, 195; in Peirce, 110, 128–29, 132, 195–99, 339–41; in Saussure, 195. *See also* signs; signaletic material
sensation, 12–13, 14, 15, 18, 23, 94, 174, 259, 264–65, 276, 288 n.1, 290 n.21, 304, 313, 315, 319, 342–43, 345; as firstness, 197, 198; and movement, 18, 253–54. *See also* affect; shock; vibration
sensible aggregate, 12, 32. *See also* signs
sensory-motor schema: and capitalism, 55 n.173, 357; and clichés, 35, 37, 38, 131, 199, 204, 356; and commercial success, 34; crisis of, 28, 30–31, 39, 41, 44, 96–97, 104, 156, 162–63, 175–76, 188, 274–75, 283, 319, 320, 327, 330, 337, 349, 350, 351, 353; development of, 17, 21, 22, 95, 99–100, 103, 294; and documentary, 199, 205; and ideology, 35–36; and interval, 44–45, 131, 132, 283, 319; and judgment, 36–37, 45–46; and memory, 31–32, 69; and morality, 54 n.144, 328, 331, 332, 335, 345–46, 349–50, 355; in organic régime, 5, 28, 32, 44, 101, 174, 307, 319, 331; and Peirce, 131–32, 196; and perception, 69, 71; and recognition, 327, 329; and time, 344; and truth, 26, 36–37, 328,

333; and video, 211 n.2. *See also* organic régime; sensory-motor unity
sensory-motor unity or whole, 262, 263, 264, 298, 345, 355. *See also* sensory-motor schema; subject as Whole; whole
serial, 217, 313, 369, 375 n.5
set (ensemble), 19, 94, 143, 155. *See also* frame
sheets of the past, 53 n.129, 168, 205
Shoah, 178, 205, 327, 336–37
shock, 19, 35, 40–41, 257–58, 259, 260–62, 266, 278–79. *See also* affect; nooshock; sensation; vibration
Shoedsack, Earnest, 221
shot, 19, 23, 93, 106 n.30, 142, 143, 144, 146, 148, 176, 182, 220, 254, 255, 256, 316–17, 320, 321, 344, 373
signaletic material (*matière signalétique*), 8, 23–24, 132, 370
signifier: and capital, 331, 346, 349, 357, 360 n.18, 361–62 n.43; and categories of representation, 45–46, 54 n.144; and esoteric word, 191 n.27; and the event, 319; of exceptionality, 46, 328, ; and fantasy, 331, 359 n.13; and film theory, 8, 47–48 n.6; foreclosure of, 46, 180, 343, 351; and ideological analysis, 36; and judgment or morality, 8, 332, 333–34, 335, 344, 346, 347, 351; law of, 348; master or transcendental, 182, 186, 333, 343, 347, 352; and possibility, 340; pure, 185; régime of, 328, 330, 351; and the sensory-motor schema, 54 n.144, 333, 344, 351, 354; sliding of, 184. *See also* language and speech act
sign-image chain, 46, 333
signs: and becoming, 351; and belief, 285; and the body, 94, 95, 107 n.41, 210–11, 333, 340, 346, 349; and capital, 346, 349; classification of, 23–26, 28, 154–55, 195–99, 370; conceptualization of, 7, 13, 103; in crystalline régime, 31, 32, 34, 38, 44, 195, 210–11, 279, 339; and events, 315, 316, 318; and falsification, 202–3; and history, 23–26, 157; and Hitchcock, 29–30; and morality, 332, 344, 350; and narration, 27, 32–33; in Peirce, 23, 30, 128–29, 131–32, 134 n.4, 138–39 n.4, 195–99, 200–1, 339–40, 341; production of, 14; and sensory-motor schema, 46, 95, 333; substance of, 8, 12, 23–24, 47, 94, 100, 138–39 n.64, 162, 194–95, 285, 296, 313, 323 n.10, 337–38, 370. *See also* sensible aggregate; signaletic material
Silverman, Kaja, 54 n.144, 186
simulacra, 36, 135 n.13, 185, 336, 337, 338, 339, 352, 356, 362 n.51
singularities, 7, 24, 39, 47, 50 n.55, 93, 218–219, 246 n.15, 299, 318, 324 n.27, 339, 351
sinsign, 197
situations, in crystalline régime, 28, 31, 38, 160–63, 164–65, 175–76, 275, 278, 285, 295, 354; in Eisenstein, 270; in Flaherty, 221–22; in Italian neorealism, 160, 178–79; as material, 63, 64, 65; in organic régime, 5, 28, 38, 44, 101–2, 164, 170 n.19, 203; in sensory-motor schema, 21, 35, 37, 44, 94, 350
Snow, Michael, 311
Soi-même comme un autre, 240
Solanas, Fernando, 225
sonsign, 31, 43, 44, 161, 165, 210, 292 n.48, 294, 295, 298, 337. *See also* sound; speech act; voice event
sound: in crystalline régime, 6, 173; as determinination of the visible, 26; disruption of in the time-image, 172, 173, 178, 183, 189, 190, 204–5, 255, 270–1, 280, 316, 344, 374; in Eisenstein, 254–55, 270; in *Il grido*, 177; introduction of Dolby, 172; in *I Wet My Hands Etched and Surveyed Vessels Approaching Marks Eyed Inside*, 209; in *Kiss Me Deadly*, 184–88; in *Miraculous Beginnings: Part I*, 200; in *Psycho*, 181, 182; and "quiet revolution," 172; and *Shoah*, 178, 205; in *The Time-Image*, 178; in *Wend Kuuni*, 234. *See also* audible; disjunctive speech act; sayable and seeable; sonsign; speech act
sound image. *See* sonsign
space: in the aggregate of images, 92–93, 112–13, 143, 146; in Beirut, 193; in *Creative Evolution*, 98–100; in the crystalline régime, 5–6, 33, 39, 160–62, 169, 176, 189, 298–300, 319–22, 373–74; deterritorialization of, 31, 219, 228; and the event, 30, 160–61, 307–22; exhaustion of, 19, 160, 204, 299,

319–22; in *Film*, 119–20; in *Il grido*, 175; in *Kiss Me Deadly*, 184; as measure of time, 4, 17–18, 98, 296; and memory (virtuality), 64–74; in the organic régime, 4–5, 19–20, 36–37, 44, 174, 176, 278, 318–19; private, 208–9; in *Psycho*, 181–82, 183; and secondness, 198; in societies of control, 26; territorialization of, 220–21; and theater, 260, 263, 307–12; and traditional classification, 167, 370–71. *See also* any-space-whatever
speech act, 25, 26, 38–39, 41, 45–46, 105 n.8, 173, 178, 188, 198, 199, 203, 204–5, 236, 241, 254, 260, 280, 285, 308, 323 n.14, 333–34, 352, 374. *See also* language; signifier; sonsign; voice events
Spinoza, Baruch, 7, 14, 37, 217, 292 n.48, 303, 335, 343, 348, 351, 352, 357
spiritual automaton, 19, 35, 162, 168, 258, 261, 263, 268, 272–73, 278, 287, 289–90 n.19, 307, 322–23 n.9, 362 n.45
Spivak, Gayatri, 217
Stagecoach, 44
Staiger, Janet, 174
statement. *See* language; signifier; speech act
State of Things, The, 6, 161, 163
Stendahl, 47 n.3
Stengers, Isabelle, 362n.51
Sternberg, Josef von, 368, 370
Story of a Love Affair, 159
Straub, Jean-Marie, 336, 371, 374, 375 n.10. *See also* Huillet, Danièlle
structuralism, 1, 7, 47–48 n.6, 49 n.7
subject as Whole, 40, 262, 263, 264, 266, 268, 274, 278. *See also* subjectivity and whole
subjectivity: in African cinema, 228; critique of, 8, 16, 36–37, 45–46, 103, 332–35, 344, 346–47, 355; in documentary, 201; in *Film*, 120–26; in film studies, 8; in Flaherty, 212 n.11, 221; images of, 6, 161; in Kant, 25, 43, 103; and movement-images, 16, 32, 90, 92–95, 98, 99–100, 114–15, 116–18, 131–33, 144, 146, 177, 253, 254, 256, 258–59, 261, 264–67, 292 n.42, 294, 297, 314, 324 n.27, 332–35, 346–47, 349; in *Naturphilosophie*, 14; in Peirce, 128–29, 196; in Ricoeur, 241, 242; loss or transformation of, 21–22, 23, 45–47, 75–76, 79, 81, 96–97, 103–4, 120–6, 138 n.51, 144, 147–49, 242, 273–80, 281, 283, 287, 291 n.38, 292 n.48, 295, 297, 299–300, 308, 339, 342–44, 351; and morality, 45–46, 332–35, 344, 346–47, 355. *See also* monad and sensory-motor schema.
sublime, 355, 356; in Eisenstein, 40, 259–65, 274, 281, 289 n.13; in French cinema, 28; in German cinema, 28; in Kant, 13, 189; in *Kiss Me Deadly*, 184
surrealism, 159, 228, 268, 285
Syberberg, Hans Jurgen, 26, 183, 336

Talaeen a Januub, 203
Tarkovsky, Andrei, 161, 373
Tarr, Bela, 160
taxonomy. *See* classification
technology, 9, 17, 55 n.73, 88, 90, 105 n.8, 146, 157, 167, 172, 185, 188, 189, 218, 222, 238, 247 n.27, 346, 356; as *technē*, 277
television, 9, 38, 183, 185, 189, 226, 322–23 n.9, 371, 374
theater, 3, 63, 220, 254, 255, 257, 258, 260–61, 263, 283, 288 n.1, 292 n.48, 307, 309, 310, 313, 317, 368
theorematic. *See* problematic and theorematic
They Caught the Ferry, 160
third cinema, 34, 225
third language, 302 n.37, 308–9; as image, 12. *See also* Beckett, Samuel
thirdness, 30, 110, 128, 134 n.4, 139 n.66, 196, 197, 198–99, 200, 212 n.11, 212 n.18, 212–13 n.25, 347. *See also* mental-image; relation-image
This Is Not Beirut, 208
Thom, René, 369
Thompson, Kristin, 174
thought. *See* affection; affection of self by self; impower; outside; problem of thought; unthought
Thousand Plateaus, A, 8, 44, 131, 142, 216, 217, 219, 238, 319. *See also Capitalism and Schizophrenia*
Timaeus, 73, 93, 313
time: and ancient philosophy, 4, 296, 339, 360 n.21; and becoming, 43, 336, 338–39, 343; and Bergson, 97, 98–99, 10

n.50, 206–7, 337; and cinema, 4–5, 7, 18, 316; classical philosophy, 4, 98, 349; and classification, 154, 165–69; and conceptualization, 153; and Eisenstein, 253–54; and Heidegger, 43; and history, 24, 184; idealization of, 72; and judgment, 36–37, 334, 355; Kant, 4, 43, 72, 98, 107 n.50, 162, 340; and Leibniz, 42, 72, 206; and money, 55 n.173, 208, 271, 344; and narrative, 27, 154, 189; and Nietzsche, 8; and Ricoeur, 241; as self-affection, 43, 298; and sets, 94; and signs, 24, 333; and succession, 18, 31, 98, 104, 298; and truth, 4, 206–7, 336; and the VCR, 216; and Whitehead, 313; and the whole, 20. *See also* becoming

time-image: as aberrance, 31, 175, 298, 301 n.12; and action, 28, 139 n.70, 159, 174–75, 179–80, 193, 210, 283, 295, 298, 307, 354; and becoming, 44, 342; and Bergson, 97; and the brain, 38; composition of, 113, 134–35 n.7, 135 n.20, 204, 302 n.39, 342–43; and crystalline image, 32, 52 n.120, 165, 176–77, 339, 360 n.26; and derealization, 38–39, 357; and deterritorialization, 44, 103–4, 194; development of, 6, 8, 33, 52 n.117, 211 n.2; direct, 19, 135 n.20, 156; and ethics, 205; and the event, 30, 159, 161,178, 189, 205, 307, 309–10, 320–21, 322–23 n.9; and fabulation, 201, 206; and history, 20, 51 n.109, 139 n.20, 139 n.74, 155–57, 158–59, 165–67, 171, 215–16, 218; indirect, 19, 134 n.7; and interstice, 44–45, 89, 283, 299, 301 n.12, 302 n.38, 321–22, 341, 361 n.33; and masculinity, 180; and memory, 32, 161, 194, 210, 284, 341; and mutation, 28; and narrative transformation, 53 n.129, 160–162, 165–66; and nomadism, 217–18; and the outside, 20, 43, 173, 211, 282, 299, 344; precursors of, 28; and relations, 42, 373–74; in Resnais, 42, 168, 373–74; and signs, 132, 210, 339–40; and sound, 177–78, 190; and truth, 33, 173, 201, 206; and the virtual, 19, 30, 43, 161, 182, 195, 206, 219, 295, 298–99, 322–23 n.9, 341–42, 361 n.35; and Welles, 52 n.115, 168. *See also* crystalline régime

totalization: in classical cinema, 328, 331; in classical philosophy, 11, 338; and classification, 24; and conspiracy, 37, 54 n.153; creation of, 359 n.15; as desire of the state, 268; dissolution of, 20, 173, 188, 189, 190 n.11; in film theory, 9, 49 n.37; in Hegel, 155; impossibility in image-universe, 92, 338; and morality, 355. *See also* unity

Toufic, Jalal, 199, 201, 202, 205, 207, 208

Touki-Bouki, 240

transcendental empiricism, 53–54 n.143, 342

transcendental idealism, 53–54 n.143, 102

Trio du fantôme, 310, 311

truth: as assurance of sensory-motor schema, 5, 41, 328; authentication of, 205; as creation, 3, 25, 26, 173, 202, 333, 335, 348; in crisis, 4, 26, 33, 47, 173, 185; in documentary, 201, 207; examination of, 165; and ideology, 275; in Kant, 25; and language, 332–33, 335; pluralization of, 207, 236; and representation, 347; as system of judgment, 36–37, 333, 335, 352; will to, 298

Un amour de Swann, 307

unconsciousness, 138 n.51, 266, 268, 278–79, 319, 325 n.28, 330, 339, 344, 361 n.43, 362 n.45

unity: of apperception, 12, 43; of an artwork, 263–264; of the brain, 261, 282, 368; of color, 77–78; and concepts, 7, 20, 154; in Eisenstein, 256, 265–66, 269; of narrative, 203, 207; of the nation, 202; of nature and thought, 83, 267; of a people, 34–35, 266; sensory-motor, 118, 262, 264, 282; of the subject, 43, 313, 324 n.27; of the whole, 262, 266; of the world, 315. *See also* totalization

universal variation, 92, 112

unthought, 41, 189, 195, 211, 275, 279, 300, 338, 339, 354. *See also* impower; outside; problem of thought

values: in African cinema, 229, 234, 247–48 n.42; and classical cinema, 20, 164; critique or revaluation of, 4, 36, 53–54 n.143, 89, 207, 348, 351–54; in democracy, 342; and education, 107 n.39; genetic, 299; and health, 248 n.47;

of images, 222; and judgment, 37; and perversion, 361–62 n.43; in Vertov, 147
van Gogh, 14, 74–83
Velázquez, Diego, 74
Verfremdungseffekt. See defamiliarization
Vertov, Dziga, 96, 142, 143, 148, 149; and cine-eye (*kinoglaz*), 146
vibration, 13, 19, 76, 92, 94, 259, 261, 294, 301 n.12, 306, 313, 352, 374. *See also* affect; sensation; shock
Virilio, Paul, 277, 323 n.9
virtual: and affect, 43, 295, 298, 342; archive, 194; and becoming, 19, 342; and chance, 339; and the concept, 296; and the crystalline régime, 161, 163, 195, 207, 219, 298; doubling, 176, 182, 188, 207–8, 299; and the event, 30, 207, 345, 353, 357; and firstness, 196; and image of thought, 72–73; and life, 343; and memory, 32, 66, 68, 69–70, 161, 195, 340; and monad, 71–72; and montage, 19; and multiplicity, 71; and narrative, 33; and the New Wave, 321–22; and opsign, 202; and the outside, 195, 299, 341; and perception, 21, 118, 145, 340; and perspective, 65, 67, 71; and plane of immanence, 7, 30, 31, 342; and possibility, 341, 345; and powers of the false, 207, 284, 285, 357; and the real, 65, 67, 194, 195; and representation, 260; thinking, 299; and the whole, 176, 261. *See also* actual virtual
Visconti, Luchino, 373
vis elastica. See movement; sensation
visible, 25–26, 38–39, 49 n.37, 73, 75, 105 n.8, 144, 145–46, 173, 188, 200, 204, 205, 211, 255, 257, 261, 299, 316, 317, 318, 319, 325 n.28, 358 n.1, 373. *See also* sayable and seeable
Visit, The, 240
voice events, 178, 189

Waati, 231, 234
war machine, 36, 219, 220, 351, 354
Wavelength, 311
Welles, Orson, 2, 48 n. 11, 52 n.115, 55 n.171, 167–68, 219, 336, 370, 373
Wenders, Wim, 2, 160, 163
Wend Kuuni, 233–34, 241
What is Philosophy?, 10, 62, 261, 286, 287, 290 n.21, 292 n.47, 360 n.26
Where the Green Ants Dream, 224
Whitehead, Lord Alfred North, 2, 16, 93, 269, 287, 290 n.28, 292 n.48, 330 n.4, 312, 313, 314, 316, 321, 341
whole: and capital, 271; and classical narrative, 28, 176; disruption of, 204, 275–76, 279, 298, 299–300; and duration, 18, 155, 294; and history, 155–56, 156–57, 159; and the interval, 44, 261, 263; of memory, 68; and morality, 343; as open, 20, 142, 265, 266, 344; and the outside, 199, 282, 344; and perspective, 64; and realization, 40–41, 54 n.153, 254, 265–66, 273, 289–90 n.19, 355; of relations, 19–20, 131, 135 n.10, 143, 176, 277, 356; and sensation, 260, 264; as subject, 40, 259, 261, 262, 263, 264, 266, 268, 274, 277, 278, 281; and the sublime, 40, 261–62, 263, 281. *See also* subject as Whole
will to power. *See* power
Winchester 73, 317–19
Wöfflin, Heinrich, 27, 158
Woman under the Influence, A, 46
Wordsworth, William, 37
World-image, 32, 93, 337, 338, 360 n.20
World War II, 5, 25, 171, 215, 216, 218, 219
Worringer, Wilhem, 26, 27, 157–58

Xala, 231
Xeno, 4, 18, 90, 98, 296

Yaounde, 243
Yeats, William Butler, 225, 348
Yeelen, 230, 231, 232, 233, 239, 242, 243

Žižek, Slavoj, 179, 182
zones of indetermination, 9, 339, 337, 345
zoom, 68, 311
Zorn, John, 206
Zourabichvilli, François, 22–23, 141–49